P9-DCJ-819

DISCARD

332.4509 D735b
Dormael, Armand van, 1916-
Bretton Woods

T.W. PHILLIPS LIBRARY
BETHANY COLLEGE
BETHANY, WV 26032

BRETTON WOODS

BRETTON WOODS

Birth of a Monetary System

Armand Van Dormael

HOLMES AND MEIER PUBLISHERS, INC.
New York

First published in the United States of America 1978 by
Holmes & Meier Publishers, Inc.
30 Irving Place,
New York, NY 10003

Reprinted 1979

Macmillan Press Ltd
London and Basingstoke

© 1978 Armand Van Dormael

ALL RIGHTS RESERVED

Library of Congress Cataloging in Publication Data

Dormael, Armand van, 1916-
  Bretton Woods.
  Includes index.
  1. United Nations Monetary and Financial Conference,
Bretton Woods, N.H., 1944—History. 2. International
finance—History. I. Title.
HG205 1944.D67   332.4'5'09   77-10651

ISBN 0-8419-0326-6

Printed in Great Britain by
Redwood Burn Ltd
Trowbridge & Esher

For Suzanne

Contents

Preface

The Bretton Woods agreements were the first successful attempt consciously undertaken by a large group of nations to shape and control their economic relations. The stated objective of Bretton Woods was 'the expansion and balanced growth of international trade'. The principal method used to achieve this end was the restoration of orderly exchanges between member countries: 'stability without rigidity and elasticity without looseness'. This, it was hoped, would prevent another worldwide depression. More than twenty years of painful experience had convinced the founding fathers of Bretton Woods that world trade could not be prosperous and that a high level of production could not persist in the face of currency disturbances and their paralysing sequels. During a quarter of a century the rules established at Bretton Woods were gradually and increasingly accepted by member nations. This period coincided with the most remarkable surge of sustained economic growth in history. World trade increased to undreamed-of proportions. Prosperity, growing year after year, soon came to be taken for granted. If economic growth and monetary stability were correlated, Bretton Woods was successful beyond all expectations.

The collapse of the system in the early 1970s was followed by a boom. Soon, however, the delicate machine balancing production, consumption, investment and employment was stalled, causing the worst recession since the Great Depression. Coincidence? Causal relationship? With the answer to these questions this book is not concerned. Nor does it draw any theoretical or ideological conclusions. This is a story. History is a great simplifier. It tells what happened, how and why. If it does not provide solutions to current problems, it often holds salutary lessons.

Bretton Woods brought together a group of extraordinary people. Never before had so many economists and government officials carried the

ix

search for a practical world monetary order so deep and so far. While there was general agreement about the objectives, there were sharp disagreements over matters involving the national interest, or personal pride and prejudice.

Since the breakdown of the arrangements established at Bretton Woods, governments all over the world are once more groping for a mechanism that will set the process of balanced growth in motion again. People engaged in the controversies over the desirable features of a new international monetary order avowedly use arguments based on the interpretation of history. As a guidepost for those responsible for the creation of such a monetary order, this book may prove to have some value.

Acknowledgements

First and foremost, I want to express my gratitude to Professor D. E. Moggridge for his guidance. As editor of the Keynes Papers he had taken the trail I was trying to follow.

I am grateful to Mr Paul Bareau, Dr Edward M. Bernstein, Mr Redvers Opie, Professor E. F. Penrose, Mr Louis Rasminsky and Mr L. P. Thompson-McCausland. Having been witness to the events I describe in this book, or having played an important role in them, they provided me with reminiscences and written material.

The International Monetary Fund and the Senate Committee on the Judiciary supplied me with copies of very useful publications. For permission to cite documents, I should like to thank the Board of Governors of the Federal Reserve System, the Department of the Treasury, the Princeton University Library, the Franklin D. Roosevelt Library, the National Archives, the Controller of Her Majesty's Stationery Office (Public Record Office and Crown Copyright materials) and the Library of Congress. Most of the newspaper articles quoted in this book were made available by the Royal Institute of International Affairs. To each of the members of these institutions who made my research more productive and enjoyable I owe a debt of gratitude.

Waterloo, May 1977   A.V.D.

Prologue

In his message welcoming the delegates of the United Nations to the Bretton Woods Conference in July 1944 President Roosevelt said,

> The program you are to discuss constitutes, of course, only one phase of the arrangements which must be made between nations to ensure an orderly, harmonious world. But it is a vital phase, affecting ordinary men and women everywhere. For it concerns the basis upon which they will be able to exchange with one another the natural riches of the earth and the products of their own industry and ingenuity.[1]

Secretary of the Treasury Morgenthau, in his opening address, stated,

> All of us have seen the great economic tragedy of our time. We saw the worldwide depression of the 1930's. We saw currency disorders develop and spread from land to land, destroying the basis for international trade and international investment and even international faith. In their wake, we saw unemployment and wretchedness — idle tools, wasted wealth. We saw their victims fall prey, in places, to demagogues and dictators. We saw bewilderment and bitterness become the breeders of fascism, and, finally, of war.[2]

The Brazilian delegate expressed the same thoughts:

> There are still in the memory of us all the drama of monetary chaos, of restrictions of all sorts of international trade, of blocked currencies, of economic isolationism, of competition instead of cooperation among central banks, and of general unemployment. The civilized world must not permit a repetition of this tragic situation.[3]

1

The representative of Czechoslovakia dealt with the purposes of the Conference:

> We are gathered here to establish two institutions which will, in my opinion, greatly enhance the peaceful co-existence of all nations and serve as a highway to the security and prosperity for which mankind has striven so long and for which it is even now paying so dearly.[4]

Each in his own words expressed the common determination to break with the legacy of the past, and to help avoid a repetition of the mistakes made after the First World War. Translating aspirations and hopes into agreements and understandings would not be an easy task. But the conference had been well prepared, and was directed with skill and determination. When, after three weeks of arduous negotiations, the chairmen of the delegations signed the Bretton Woods agreements, they shared the conviction that the event would mark the beginning of a new era.[5]

At the closing plenary session, Secretary Morgenthau expressed his satisfaction with the work accomplished:

> I am gratified to announce that the Conference at Bretton Woods has successfully completed the task before it. It was, as we knew when we began, a difficult task, involving complicated technical problems. We came here to work out methods which would do away with the economic evils – the competitive currency devaluation and destructive impediments to trade – which preceded the present war. We have succeeded in that effort.[6]

Lord Keynes, chairman of the British delegation, formulated the general feeling of gratification and confidence in the future:

> we have perhaps accomplished here in Bretton Woods something more significant than what is embodied in this Final Act. We have shown that a concourse of 44 nations are actually able to work together at a constructive task in amity and unbroken concord. Few believed it possible. If we can continue in a larger task as we have begun in this limited task, there is hope for the world. At any rate we shall now disperse to our several homes with new friendships sealed and new intimacies formed. We have been learning to work together. If we can so continue, this nightmare, in which most of us here present have spent too much of our lives, will be over. The brotherhood of man will have become more than a phrase.[7]

Among those who participated in the conference, there was a deep belief that Bretton Woods would remain a landmark in history. For the first time a vast number of countries agreed to set up permanent international institutions with considerable powers and resources, to deal with their mutual monetary and economic problems. They subscribed to a basic set of rules and principles of international conduct. They agreed to submit to a certain degree of international economic discipline and to delegate certain prerogatives of national sovereignty to a new supranational institution, the International Monetary Fund. The specific function of the Fund would be to assure stability of exchange rates, and orderly adjustment when this became necessary. This, it was hoped, would promote co-operation and consultation in areas where every country had, in the past, made arbitrary and often damaging decisions, regardless of the consequences to other nations. By setting up a system of exchange rates that combined the short-term advantages of predictability and fixity with the long-term advantages of flexibility, they hoped to achieve economic stability conducive to full employment. This would eliminate the monetary crises they had lived through, and which had been a major cause of distrust and enmity between nations. It was also projected to set up an International Bank for Reconstruction and Development, to provide long-term credit to war-torn nations in order to permit them to rebuild their economies, thus fostering peaceful coexistence.

After the First World War there had been no such co-operation. Each country had pursued what it considered its own interest. Reparations by the vanquished had perpetuated and exasperated the hatreds unleashed by four years of armed conflict; war debts had been a source of continuous tension between the former allied and associated nations. The inflation of 1923 shook the German people to the depths of despair. The Dawes plan and later the Young plan provided temporary but artificial relief, and the crash of 1929 brought to an end a period of relative prosperity. Millions of people lost their jobs, their savings, their hope. Faced with massive unemployment, governments resorted to import restrictions, currency devaluations and other measures of economic warfare. Each successive disturbance accelerated the drift to self-sufficiency, isolation and impoverishment, until finally the 'have-nots' resorted to armed aggression on the plea of economic self-defence.

In October 1939, after conquering Poland, Hitler offered peace to France and Britain, on three conditions: one of them was the settlement of the international currency problem. But the governments of France and Britain had reached a point of no return. After a long period which had been neither peace nor war, the only way out was war.

1
Keynes and the 'New Order'

It is not surprising that the first practical plans for a postwar monetary and economic order should have originated in Germany. In the spring of 1940 the Axis powers had firmly established their political and economic domination over most of Europe. Britain's energies and attention were totally absorbed by the threat of invasion and the struggle for survival. To many people around the world, even in the United States, it seemed that the war was finished, and a German victory inevitable.

After a brief visit to Paris, Hitler had returned to Berlin, acclaimed as the greatest general of all times. There seemed no limit to the power of Germany and the ability of its people. For years the German government and press had proclaimed that the economic and monetary policies instituted under Hitler were not only the most modern but also the most effective in the world. During the years preceding the war, while other countries were struggling with the effects of the Depression, Germany had solved its unemployment problem and had kept its balance of payments in equilibrium, while importing the goods it needed. Now the time had come for Germany to apply these successful policies and methods to the rest of the European continent.

On 25 July 1940, Walther Funk, Minister for Economic Affairs and President of the Reichsbank, outlined during a press conference in Berlin a plan for the reconstruction and reorganisation of the German and European economy after the war, and for strengthening its position in world trade. He wanted to put an end, he said, to the confusion caused by 'the fancy ideas and plans' published in the press. The 'New Order' would be based on a very close co-operation with Italy, and the German and Italian productive power would be co-ordinated for the reconstruction of Europe. 'We will use the same methods of economic policy that have given such remarkable results, both before and during the war, and we will not allow the unregulated play of economic power, which caused such grave difficulties to the German economy, to become active again.' He then described the principles and methods to be used:

> Money is of secondary importance; the management of the economy comes first. When the economy is not healthy, the currency cannot be healthy. In the framework of a healthy European economy and of an intelligent division of labour between the various European countries, the monetary problem will solve itself, simply by using the right monetary technique. Obviously, the Reichsmark will have a dominating position. The formidable increase of the power of the German Reich will naturally result in the strengthening of its currency.

The existing method of bilateral economic relations would be developed into a system of multilateral trade. Balances would be settled through an exchange clearing. Such a clearing system required fixed parities and stable exchange rates. Each government would manage its balance of payments, so that the problem of debits and credits would gradually disappear.

Funk expected that, after the war, currency restrictions would gradually be removed, except from on capital transactions. In order to maintain the highest standard of living, Europe would continue to import raw materials, food, and other goods from all over the world, in exchange for the high-grade products of its industry. But it must be able, in case of emergency, to reduce consumption, and make itself economically self-sufficient.

Trade with the United States would depend on whether the American government would continue to discriminate against German goods. The United States wanted to be the largest creditor country, and, at the same time, the largest exporter. This was impossible. 'We do not know what the Americans will do with their gold. The gold problem is in the first instance a problem for the United States. In relation to European currencies, gold will not have any importance at all, because the value of a currency does not result from its gold cover, but from a decision of the government.'

The clearing system would make gold superfluous for currency and payment purposes within the clearing. Even outside the clearing, Germany would never adhere to any system based on a means of payment of which it could not determine the value itself. Production would be determined by the available labour, materials and industrial capacity, and not, as under the gold standard, by the amount of gold held at the central bank.

European currencies would be stabilised in relation to the Reichsmark. European countries would be able to trade freely with each other, any balances being offset by the central clearing office in Berlin. Trade with other continents would be regulated by barter agreements, and Berlin would gradually replace London as the world's financial centre.[1]

The German propaganda machine was soon busy proclaiming that the

'New Order' would bring unprecedented prosperity to Europe, and would put an end to the chaotic conditions experienced during the interwar period. For several months, the German-dominated radio and press had a practical monopoly over postwar monetary and economic planning. Neither British radio nor — with very few exceptions — the British press had shown any interest or concern.[2]

In November 1940 the Ministry of Information submitted to Keynes some notes intended to be used as a basis for a broadcast to discredit the German propaganda. The disadvantages of clearings and barter were contrasted with the benefits to be expected from free trade and the gold standard as it had traditionally worked. Keynes immediately sensed that a broadcast along these lines would have little propaganda value, and would most likely have a negative effect on public opinion. Aware of the disastrous consequences of Britain's return to the gold standard, and of the chaotic conditions under the *laissez-faire* policies adopted after World War I, the public might wonder whether something like the 'New Order' should not be given a try.

German propaganda, Keynes wrote, was intended to 'appeal to the wide circles and powerful interests in each country which are inclined in present circumstances to value social security higher than political independence'. It purported to 'offer a stable currency system adapted to the commerce of countries which have no gold, and above all a system of economic order and organisation'. Counter-propaganda on a negative basis would not be very convincing. 'If we have nothing positive to say, we had better be silent.' His position was that Great Britain would offer 'the same as what Dr. Funk offers, except that we shall do it better and more honestly. This is important. For a proposal to return to the blessings of 1920–1933 will not have much propaganda value.'

The merit of the 'New Order' was that it avoided some of the abuses of the old *laissez-faire* currency arrangements, whereby a country could be bankrupted 'not because it lacked exportable goods, but merely because it lacked gold'. After the war, Britain would have no gold, and would owe substantial quantities of sterling to many countries. Common-sense indicated that a return to the currency arrangements that had prevailed under the gold standard was impossible. This did not mean that gold would cease to play its part as a reserve of purchasing power and as a means of settling international indebtedness. Keynes assumed that the British government would continue the existing exchange controls after the war. He also assumed that Britain would put at the disposal of the European countries the surplus commodities that would be available in the British Empire; that Germany would be allowed to resume some *economic* leadership in Central Europe. 'This conclusion is inescapable, unless it is our intention to hand the job over to Russia.' The liberated European countries would require an initial pool of resources to carry them through the transitional period. He therefore contemplated a European Reconstruction Fund, out of which each country would be supplied with the amount of credit required to purchase food and raw materials from outside.

The British government was determined not to repeat the mistakes of Versailles, where, because the participants were too preoccupied with political frontiers and safeguards, the problem of economic reconstruction had been neglected.

> We must make it our business, above most other purposes to prevent the starvation of the post-armistice period, the currency disorders throughout Europe and the wild fluctuations of employment, markets and prices which were the cause of so much misery in the twenty years between the two wars; and we shall see to it that this shall be compatible with the proper liberty of each country over its own economic fortunes.

Britain alone, with the help of the United States, would be able to carry out such a policy. Germany could not hope to end the war with control over the raw materials of the other continents. German propagandists were 'attempting to cover up the emptiness of their hands and the bleakness of the prospect by much vague talk about "the New Order". Mostly words, no doubt.'[3]

Keynes's draft statement to counter the German propaganda was circulated in various ministries. Counter-memoranda were submitted, and meetings held; in the process, Keynes exposed his concept of a postwar currency system and inevitably was asked to explain and clarify his ideas. In a letter dated 25 April 1941 he stated,

> My words meant that international capital movements would be restricted so that they would only be allowed in the event of the country from which capital was moving having a favourable balance with the country to which they were being remitted. In other words they would only be allowed when they were feasible without upsetting the existing equilibrium. ... Whatever one might wish, something of this sort seems to me inevitable, since we shall no longer have a cushion of gold or of other liquid assets, by means of which the immediate effects of unbalanced capital movements can be handled.
>
> My proposals certainly imply a continuation of Payments Agreements or something of the same kind. But I should hope that with experience large elements of a multilateral system could be introduced. That is to say, the aim would be to interfere as little as possible, provided that a balance is maintained with the outside world as a whole. But unquestionably it would involve a discrimination against the United States if she persisted in maintaining an unbalanced creditor position. Again, whether we like it or not, this will be forced on us. We shall have no means after the war out of which we can pay for

purchases in the United States except the equivalent of what they buy from us.

No doubt our hands would be free to fix the exchange parities of sterling. We should no doubt be most reluctant to do this except by agreement. But this would not be the object, which would be almost the opposite. For, with a proper system of Payments Agreements which would prevent an unbalanced situation from developing, there would be no longer much object in depreciating the exchange. The method of depreciation is a bad method which one is driven to adopt failing something better. The currency system I have in view would be that something better. If U.S.A. inflates more than we do, we might even *appreciate* sterling.

This currency system, he hoped, would cover the widest area possible. This meant 'trading goods against goods'. It did not mean direct *barter*; but one trading transaction must necessarily find its counterpart in another trading transaction sooner or later. 'The foreign owner of sterling can, of course, just leave the balance in London, but there is nothing else he can do with it except to purchase goods.' Under such a system, Britain, as an importing country, became automatically an attractive country to buy from, and the system, which was inevitable anyway, might prove a great boon.

The necessity of some such plan as the above arises essentially from the unbalanced creditor position of the United States. It is a necessary condition of a return to free exchanges that the United States should find some permanent remedy for this unbalanced position. Sooner or later one can suppose that she will have to do so. But it would be very optimistic to believe that she will find the solution in the immediate post-war period, even if she tries to mitigate her task by making large presents for the reconstruction of Europe.[4]

By the end of April, Keynes's draft had been considerably refined and had become government policy. Somewhat later, Mr Anthony Eden, in an important speech on British war aims, would use it as a basis for British postwar economic policies. Some references to the 'Funk-mark' and to the advantages of the German clearing system were mentioned, but Keynes once more proved himself an unequalled pamphleteer: 'Hitler has recently found it necessary to give some decent covering to the naked policy of rapine and confiscation on which he has embarked in Europe. He has for this purpose invented what he calls "The New Order".' The reality behind Hitler's high-sounding pronouncements was a plan by which satellite and tributary states would be compelled to the kind of production that suited German convenience, chiefly agriculture. Foreign commerce would become a German monopoly.

It would be a surprising triumph for propaganda to make an up-to-date version of imperialist exploitation verging on slavery seem attractive to the victims. ... The Germans, as the master race, will constitute the new aristocracy in the territories under their domination, while the unfortunate inhabitants of non-German origin will become the mere slaves of their German overlords.

Instead Britain, after the war, would be able to offer to the European countries part of the enormous overseas stocks of food and raw materials being accumulated, and would not interfere with the liberty of the individual nations.

Let no-one suppose, however, that we for our part intend to return to the chaos of the old world. To do so would bankrupt us no less than others. ... We intend to develop a system of international exchange in which the trading of goods and services will be the central feature. Financial and capital transactions will play their proper auxiliary role of facilitating trade. Gold will retain its appropriate place as the central reserve and the means of international settlements.[5]

The British government had come to share Keynes's ideas. For more than a century, Britain had been the herald of free trade and the bastion of the gold standard. This had been the foundation of its wealth and power. During the 1930s the government had been forced to adopt a protectionist policy, and it seemed now that it would be compelled by overwhelming circumstances to continue in this direction. Prime Minister Churchill, a free-trader by inclination and tradition, wrote to Ambassador Halifax,

America's large holding of gold will prompt her to favour one method of conducting international trade, while our lack of gold will probably incline us to something quite different. It must be borne in mind that Great Britain will emerge from the war an impoverished Power. ... Placed as we shall be, I anticipate that we shall not only be forced to maintain for some considerable time the exchange regulations and controls imposed during the war, but that we shall be forced to protect our interests by the bilateral barter-payments agreements advocated by Mr. Keynes, which, however, are highly distasteful to Mr. Hull.[6]

The 'New Order' had constituted the first challenge to Keynes to think about postwar economic reconstruction. The currency system he contemplated was consistent with the policies he had been advocating for Britain for some time. The sterling area would be at the centre of the system, and gradually other countries would join. But the United States, because of its status as a creditor country, refusing to import goods in exchange of its exports, would not be an important part of it.

It would not be long before another impulse, of an entirely different nature, would come from across the Atlantic.

2
Britain and the Dollar Problem

During the summer of 1940 Britain stood alone, facing an implacable enemy with the most formidable army and the strongest air force in the world. German soldiers guarded the Atlantic coast, braced for the invasion of the British Isles, while German submarines roved the seas in search of British ships. Bomber squadrons subjected London and other cities to destructive air raids, in an effort to bomb the population into submission, or at least, negotiation. The future of Britain as a sovereign nation hung in the balance.

On 10 May, the day when the German troops attacked France, Churchill had formed a coalition Cabinet. But neither his fighting instinct nor the indomitable spirit of the British people could prevent the country from falling to the Nazi conquerors. Britain needed ships, airplanes, tanks, guns and ammunition to pursue the battle, and food to keep alive. Its only hope was that the United States would supply the goods required for survival. As soon as he had become Prime Minister, Churchill had decided to wage the war on the basis of unlimited liability, regardless of financial consequences. Huge orders for war material were placed with American manufacturers, although Britain could not pay. Some time in the first half of 1941 Britain would run out of resources, and would need massive credits from the United States government in order to be able to continue the armament purchases.

President Roosevelt had encouraged the British government to place all the contracts necessary, without consideration of the financial implications. He was determined to give Britain all the help he possibly could. From the beginning, the Treasury, headed by Secretary Morgenthau, was the main channel of communication between the various British purchasing missions and the US government. With the President's approval, Morgenthau had gone to the limits of what could be done to help Britain

12

continue the war.

The conduct of American foreign policy, including economic policy, was clearly the responsibility of the Department of State, which served as the principal operating arm of the President in international affairs. It had not escaped the President, however, that the Treasury was one of the few departments in his Administration that had operated on an emergency basis since the outbreak of the war in Europe. In addition, Roosevelt was on closer terms with Morgenthau than with anyone else in the government. The President's announcement of Lend–Lease in December 1940 had been received in London with immense relief and gratitude. Two days after Roosevelt told a press conference of his intention to submit the Lend–Lease bill to Congress, London sent an anxious cable to Sir Frederick Phillips, who had just been appointed permanent Treasury representative in Washington. British gold and dollars were rapidly approaching exhaustion: 'At the present rate of loss they will only last till about Tuesday next.' The practical question was what the US Administration and the British government should do between then and the time when Congress approved the bill.[1]

That was a thorny problem. On 18 December, Morgenthau told Phillips that the President had given him a message authorising the British to go ahead and immediately place more contracts.

> I referred to the question of finance in the intermediate period and reminded him that we had already asked whether arrangements would be retrospective. . . . Morgenthau in reply said that the President had said that it was all right to place orders now. I asked if that definitely meant that all obstacles had been removed. . . . Morgenthau said that the President was the boss and that all the Cabinet were simply his hired men.[2]

President Roosevelt and Morgenthau felt that, if public opinion and Congress were convinced that Britain was 'scraping the bottom of the barrel', this would neutralise opposition and would make it easier to obtain Congressional approval of Lend–Lease. As early as April 1940, before the question of financial help had even come up, Morgenthau had requested that the British government announce publicly the sale of some private investments in the United States. This was not agreed to at the time. During the following months Morgenthau kept repeating his request. The British objected that this would make little difference to the overall financial problem that Britain would face, but Morgenthau insisted on the psychological importance and emphasised that the President felt strongly about it. Compared with the thousands of millions of dollars the United States gave Britain during the war and afterwards, the sums involved were insignificant and their effect on the conduct of the war negligible. It was the forced sale of these investments, however, during the early stages of the war, that put the heaviest strain on the relationship between the two governments, leading to suspicion and misunderstandings, and to occasional outbursts of mutual exasperation.

London had been led to suppose that, once Lend–Lease became law, the President would give all the financial help that was legally possible, including, as regards existing commitments where the goods had not yet been delivered, the reimbursement of advance payments already made. When Phillips cabled that this was a complete delusion, there was disappointment and anxiety. Keynes noted,

> Morgenthau has repeatedly led us to hope (though without full confidence) more than he has performed. Instead of taking a more discouraging line before the necessary legal powers have been obtained and then using them generously when obtained, he has pursued precisely the opposite policy to the extent of actual dishonesty, namely, to encourage us before he had the powers and then to refuse to use them when he has got them.[3]

Morgenthau's fantastic pledges 'that we should be bled white and stripped to the bone', should not be accepted without a protest. Keynes questioned whether President Roosevelt really intended to put Britain to such straits, and suggested 'that it might be as well to call attention to the consequences of what is proposed in plain language and not submit to it in humble silence'. Otherwise, 'it will be open to Mr. Morgenthau day by day to allow us just so much relief as is necessary to keep us on the mat but still breathing. ... If he adopts this procedure he will retain power in his hands to bend us to his will both on the sale of direct investments and on any matter of detail where he has a fancy to do so.'[4]

An answer to the long-term problems would have to be sought at some future time, but there were a number of matters that required immediate and close attention. Despite the numerous telegrams, letters and memoranda pouring in from Washington, it was difficult to ascertain what the US Administration really wanted, and even to determine how far the British officials in Washington intended to go. On 7 April 1941 Keynes noted,

> 'I am not clear what Sir F. Phillips's own policy is in the situation which has now developed. Is it in fact proposed to sell by hook or by crook every direct investment which can conceivably find even a bad market in the course of the next six months or so? ... Surely we cannot contemplate that without a struggle. If, on the other hand, he contemplates only going on with selected direct investments at the rate of disposal which circumstances render practicable, not in fact likely to be very rapid, we shall be seriously short of funds. How short depends on Mr. Morgenthau's decision, which has not yet been communicated to us. ...'[5]

These, and many other questions, clearly needed urgent answers.

The British government was represented in Washington by a group of very able and devoted men, headed by Ambassador Halifax. Once the Lend–Lease bill had been passed, their main problem was to obtain war material quickly enough to build up the military power of the British Isles and the Empire. The pressure of events and the overlapping responsibilities within the Administration made it constantly necessary to improvise. But above all their task was severely frustrated by Morgenthau's demands for the sale of direct investments and for detailed and up-to-date information on the British financial position. It was important, particularly for London, not to let misunderstandings and lack of information about intentions and policies strain the relationship between the two governments. As Sir Roy Harrod states,

> Phillips had not been able to supply quite all that was needed. He had the traditional British reserve. He was temperamentally averse from expiating beyond his terms of reference and what was obviously relevant to the particular point at issue. He had a civil servant's proper caution, and he was not inclined to trust or to impart figures which had not been precisely verified. Thus equipped, he had success up to a point. But the Americans needed something more.[6]

On 18 April the Chancellor of the Exchequer cabled Lord Halifax that he had come to the conclusion that it would be useful to send somebody to Washington 'both to convey my current views of the situation and on his return give me his impressions on possible future developments in the light of any conversations which, with your help, he may be able to have with the President and with Morgenthau'. The Chancellor thought Keynes would be a welcome visitor, and proposed to ask him to pay a brief visit. Both Halifax and Morgenthau immediately agreed.[7] Early in May Keynes flew to Lisbon, and from there to New York. Mrs Keynes and Mr Thompson-McCausland accompanied him. On 10 May they were in Washington, and Keynes asked Morgenthau for an appointment.

On 13 May they met in Morgenthau's office. Keynes had come over, he said, as a 'minister or messenger' of the Chancellor of the Exchequer. Sir Frederick Phillips had not been in London for several months, and this was an opportunity for the British Treasury to make fresh contact with the American Treasury. The British government had been immensely gratified at the conception and drafting of Lend–Lease, and at the expeditious way it had become operative. When Keynes said that he presumed that credit was owing to the American Treasury, Morgenthau attributed the idea to the President. Keynes also expressed gratitude for the arrangements which had permitted Britain to continue its purchases while Lend–Lease was being legislated. Morgenthau admitted that during this period he had personally, without Congressional authorisation, approved British

purchases amounting to $35 million a week. This put him in a difficult
position, and he was reluctant to appear before the Congressional committees, where he might have to answer embarrassing questions. The failure by
Britain to sell any of its direct American investments while the Lend–
Lease bill was being considered added to his embarrassment. The Viscose
sale had now been completed, and it seemed that the British Treasury had
lost no more than $5 million by hastening the transaction. Morgenthau
felt, however, that he had made up for this loss by having Mr Jesse Jones,
Secretary of Commerce, loan Britain $5 million more than originally
anticipated. The bankers who handled the sale had agreed to present the
whole picture to him, before establishing the commission they would
charge.

Keynes said there was no change in the policy of the British government to sell its gold, dollar securities and direct investments. Certain new
developments since the enactment of Lend–Lease, however, gave rise to
questions which should be considered again. The British Treasury was
becoming concerned about the fact that, since Lend–Lease, almost all
purchases, including those made by British importers, who would normally
pay from their own funds, were now handled through government
agencies. This required an immense amount of routine work by both the
British and the US Treasury, and there simply were not the personnel to
cope. Keynes thought that Lend–Lease should be limited to purchases of
armaments and agricultural products. Morgenthau replied he was no longer
responsible for the details of Lend–Lease, and that this should be
discussed with Harry Hopkins, who had been put in charge by the
President. Moreover, Morgenthau felt that a generous interpretation of
Lend–Lease had been in the best interests of Britain, and said that, despite
the warnings he had received, it seemed not to be true that the British gold
and dollar reserves were running out.

Keynes referred to the need for building up British reserves of gold and
exchange to meet unforeseen situations; the next nine months would be a
particularly crucial period, from both a military and a financial standpoint.
He hoped that some arrangements guaranteeing that British needs would
be taken care of during this period could be made with the US Treasury.
Keynes remarked that he was working closely with Sir Frederick Phillips,
and Morgenthau suggested that Phillips attend the next meeting. He also
asked for a written memorandum on the British proposals.[8]

The following day, Keynes saw Morgenthau again, together with
Phillips. Sir Frederick reminded the Secretary of his promise that, when
Lend–Lease was passed, he would take care of the existing contracts.
Now all sorts of unforeseen administrative and political difficulties were
arising, both in London and in Washington. Britain had a common purse
with India and the Dominions, and, if the United States refused to extend
Lend–Lease to India, it would in fact be a refusal to the United Kingdom.
Another problem was being created by the complicated procedure re-

quired by Lend-Lease. The Lend-Lease Act applied only to goods supplied by the US government to the British government. When a private British importer placed an order with an American exporter, the US government had to purchase the goods from the exporter, pass it to the British government, which then in turn had to sell it to the importer. Phillips also mentioned the unsuccessful negotiations with Mr Jesse Jones and with the War Department to take over existing facilities and existing contracts. The deadlock would have to be removed by some method or other, so that Britain would again have some funds available for a working balance. These were complex but urgent problems.[9]

Shortly afterwards Keynes met with Harry Hopkins, as Morgenthau had suggested. When he brought up the question of the old contracts, Hopkins insisted that it had not been anticipated that these would be brought under the Lend—Lease Act, and that the director of the budget had given testimony to Congress that they would not be included.[10]

While Keynes moved from one office to the other, trying to settle some of the problems and also to establish a clearer financial relationship between the two countries, Morgenthau became suspicious and worried. On 18 May he cabled Winant, asking for a 'report of circumstances and underlying purpose of visit of J. M. Keynes to this country'.[11] Winant answered that because of the complicated nature of the Lend—Lease arrangements, the Prime Minister and the Chancellor of the Exchequer had decided it was advisable to send someone to Washington, and that they had personally selected Keynes, because he had a broad view of the situation. Winant thought it was a good choice, and said it was his sincere hope 'that the visit of Keynes is not proving to be unhelpful to you'.[12]

Keynes himself, while he felt that Morgenthau was 'somewhat inscrutable' during the first meeting, thought that the following day 'his attitude proved sympathetic from the start and he was ready to consider details and ways and means of doing what we wanted'.[13]

On 17 June Keynes wrote Hopkins a letter, with copy to Morgenthau:

> In the five weeks which have passed since I gave Mr Morgenthau a memorandum outlining what the Chancellor of the Exchequer had sent me to say, no positive progress has been made. But the possibilities of the situation have been very carefully explored by Sir F. Phillips and myself with the officials of the Treasury Department and with Mr Cox, who have been most kind and sympathetic and helpful but have been up against difficulties which were none of their making.

He repeated once more what he had told Morgenthau five weeks earlier: if what he asked could be granted, 'we should be — relatively speaking — in an extremely satisfactory position'.

> Otherwise, it is a case of spoiling the ship for the sake of a coat of

paint. We have this magnificent conception of Lend/Lease; 'consideration' is being discussed on lines more magnanimous than any hitherto recorded transactions between great nations; and yet, on account of our resources having been so completely exhausted before Lend/Lease came into operation, we suffer anxiety and possible embarrassment through being unable to accumulate the minimum reserves which are necessary to carry the vast financial responsibilities of London. At the present moment the total gold reserves of the Bank of England are less than $50,000,000, and the cash reserves of the British Treasury less than $100,000,000 — which would be laughable if it were not so embarrassing. To build these up, except very slowly, out of our accruing resources is impossible while we are facing the double task of paying off old commitments and financing current expenditure of the sterling using parts of the Empire in the U.S. outside Lend/Lease. Yet it needs only a trifling addition to the assistance we are already receiving to give us the necessary comfort of mind and freedom from daily cares — a gain to our Administration in all the circumstances of the present hour altogether out of proportion to the sums involved.[14]

On 19 June, Morgenthau called Hopkins, who said he had just received a long-winded letter from Keynes and did not like it: 'I don't like his style and approach. My own private opinion is that except from the point of view of the British Treasury, he'd just be well off at home.'

'You and me, both', said Morgenthau.

'Well, now — God damn it, if he's here for the Treasury, the British Treasury, his business is to be writing you letters and sending me copies. You see what he's going to do, he's going to move on any front he thinks he can move on.' After all, maybe he was overemphasising the importance of it.

'No,' said Morgenthau, 'I don't think you are because when I got it, I just said: God damn it.' That was the way Hopkins felt about it too. If he had received a two-line note from Phillips, saying 'we're in quite a jam and wish you could help us — personally I undoubtedly would stir my stumps far more than getting a six-page letter from Keynes, you see? . . . We don't have to be motivated that way. He sort of assumes that we don't give a damn, and it just — it irritates me and it must irritate you more . . . he's just one of those fellows that just knows all the answers, you see?'[15]

Morgenthau had an idea: there would be a meeting every day in his office, with the British representatives and someone representing Hopkins, to determine the British requirements and their dollar reserves for that day. If it could go through Lend–Lease, that is how it would be handled, 'but we want to know the net position of what your dollar has accounted every night and not be told two weeks from now or 30 days from now that you're busted'.

Hopkins thought it was a 'damn good idea', and he agreed that Oscar

Cox would represent him and decide for him.[16]

Keynes's letter had upset Morgenthau, but it also stirred him into action. He asked Keynes, Phillips and Arthur Purvis (Chairman of the British supply council in North America) to attend a meeting at his office. The Secretary suggested that from then on 'we follow a little different procedure than we have in the past. ... We don't know just what the dollar position of the British Treasury is each week. We don't know who the person is who is the Comptroller of Exchange. We don't have all the information of what you spend your dollars for in this country.' Thenceforward there would be a meeting every day and they would decide on the spot about the orders to be placed and how to pay for them. Morgenthau, however, wanted to know 'down to the last sou what the British Treasury position is'. The British thought that some of the information that Morgenthau wanted might be difficult to obtain, but they decided that the scheme was worth trying.[17]

From then till the end of July, Keynes and the other British representatives met almost daily with Morgenthau or with his staff. These meetings, often long and confused, covered a vast field of often complex questions.' They tried to establish procedures and general concepts as to what should come under Lend—Lease; they covered many products, such as steel, cocoa, tin-plate, machine tools, sisal, Australian wool, and film. Often they had to work with incomplete or inaccurate data (much of the information they would have needed was not available), and the sums involved were often extremely small. As the weeks passed, some problems were solved, others remained open. The US Army agreed to take over some of the British contracts. In all these negotiations Harry White proved to be one of the staunchest supporters of the British cause.

In a memorandum he wrote at that time, White criticised the State Department for its 'half-measures, miscalculations, timidity, machinations or incompetence'. The efforts of American diplomatic manoeuvring, he said, had been pathetic.

It has consisted of a 19th century pattern of petty bargaining with its dependence upon subtle half promises, irritating pinpricks, excursions into double dealing, and copious pronunciamentos of good will alternating with vague threats — and all of it veiled in an atmosphere of high secrecy designed or at least serving chiefly to hide the essential barrenness of achievement. ... Where modern diplomacy calls for swift and bold action, we engage in long drawn-out cautious negotiation; where we should talk in terms of billions of dollars, we think in terms of millions; where we should measure success by the generosity of the government that can best afford it, we measure it by the sharpness of the bargain driven; where we should be dealing with all-embracing economic, political and social problems, we discuss minor trade objectives, or small national advantages; ... we must substitute, before it is

too late, imagination for tradition; generosity for shrewdness; understanding for bargaining; toughness for caution, and wisdom for prejudice. We are rich — we should use more of our wealth in the interest of
peace and victory.[18]

Whatever caused White's blast at the State Department, Secretary Hull and
his staff had hardly been involved in the financial negotiations with
Britain.

During the two and a half months Keynes spent in Washington, he had
been almost exclusively concerned with Britain's most urgent needs. This
had been the purpose of his visit. On several occasions, however, and
particularly at the end of his stay, he came briefly into contact with the
State Department, on an entirely different matter: the postwar economic
relations between the two countries, and the reconstruction of the world
economy.

3
The 'Consideration' and Article VII

Whatever he may have had in mind, it was President Roosevelt who prompted the State Department to initiate negotiations with the British on postwar economic policy. On 16 May 1941 he wrote to Secretary Hull,

> I wish you would work out the over-all arrangement between the United States and the British Government relative to the consideration or considerations to be given us by the British in return for the material provided under the Lend—Lease Act. ... Although I presume the agreement will not provide primarily for a return to us of cash, I think, nevertheless, you should consult with Secretary Morgenthau in regard to the broad provisions of the agreement.

It was important, the President stated, 'that we reach an agreement with the British at an early date'.[1]

Shortly afterwards, when Lord Halifax and Keynes submitted to him the 'New Order' draft, the President 'expressed the opinion that it was a fine statement, but showed no enthusiasm for such matters being discussed in detail at the present time'. While he thought it might be advisable to begin discussing postwar problems behind the scenes, he was adverse 'to any public statement at the present time which enters into any detail about post-war arrangements'. The President also felt the initiative and attitude too purely British, and the terms of reference too exclusively European. He wanted South American countries to be remembered in any world statement.[2]

Secretary Hull had immediately asked Under-Secretary Dean Acheson to prepare a draft along the lines requested by the President. Several groups in the State Department produced a number of ideas, and, since Keynes was in Washington, it seemed advisable to discuss them with him.

Keynes thought the draft satisfactory. The

> phraseology of the clause concerning post-war economic relations is
> widely drawn and there is nothing which would seem to require formal
> consultation with the Dominions. I understand that Mr. Hull is
> doubtful whether it is advisable to include reference to post-war
> economic relations. And judging from yesterday's conversation [the]
> President might take a similar line. ... Thus this clause might be
> omitted. The authors of the draft would regret this, since they feel that
> without it [the] document would have insufficient content. But I am
> not clear that this would really be so. It seems unlikely that any
> document materially differing from the above will be presented to us in
> the near future. Either something on these lines will reach us next
> week, or [the] President will decide to put off the whole question for
> the time being.[3]

Keynes had prepared a draft himself, which as Acheson recalled, provided
'merely that lend–lease should be extended; that the British should return
what was practicable for them to return; that no obligation should be
created; and that they would be glad to talk about other matters'. This,
Acheson thought, was 'wholly impossible'.[4]

For several weeks, the State Department continued to rephrase its own
draft, and by the end of July it was ready. On 28 July, Acheson handed
Keynes a 'Draft Proposal for a Temporary Lend–Lease Agreement',
suggesting that he take it back with him to London. As he read the draft,
Keynes asked for clarification of some of the articles, and appeared
satisfied. He then came to Article VII, which read,

> The terms and conditions upon which the United Kingdom receives
> defense aid from the United States of America and the benefits to be
> received by the United States of America in return therefor, as finally
> determined, shall be such as not to burden commerce between the two
> countries but to promote mutually advantageous economic relations
> between them and the betterment of world-wide economic relations;
> they shall provide against discrimination in either the United States of
> America or the United Kingdom against the importation of any product
> originating in the other country; and they shall provide for the
> formulation of measures for the achievement of these ends.

When Keynes read this, he asked Acheson whether the article referred to
imperial preferences, and to exchange and trade controls. Acheson

> said it did, upon which [Keynes] burst into a speech such as only he
> could make. The British could not 'make such a commitment in good
> faith'; 'it would require an imperial conference'; 'it saddled upon the

future an ironclad formula from the Nineteenth Century'; 'it contemplated the ... hopeless task of returning to a gold standard'; and so on.

I pointed out the paragraph did not ask for unilateral promises
from the British, nor did it by any word or phrase seek to impose rigid
or unworkable formulas upon the future. No man was less likely than
the President to want this. Keynes's statements seemed to me 'extreme
and unjustified'. Then, as coldly as I could – which I have been told is
fairly cold – I added that 'the purpose of Article VII was to provide a
commitment, which it should not be hard for the British to give, that,
after the emergency was over and after they had received vast aid from
this country, they would not regard themselves free to take any
measures they chose against the trade of this country but would work
out in cooperation with this country measures which would eliminate
discrimination and would provide for mutually fair and advantageous
relations'.

At this he cooled off and spoke wisely about a postwar problem that
he foresaw far more clearly than I did – our great capacity to export,
the world's need for our goods, and the problems of payment. He
mentioned the division of opinion in England about postwar trade
between the free traders, the advocates of a managed economy, and a
group who leaned toward imperial policies. At the end he thought us
agreed on broad policies but in need of more clarification.

Acheson considered Keynes 'not only one of the most delightful and
engaging men I have ever known but also, in a true sense of the word, one
of the most brilliant. His many-faceted and highly polished mind sparkled
and danced with light. But not all felt his charm; to some he appeared
arrogant.'[5]

Among those who were shocked by Keynes's reaction to Article VII
was Harry Hawkins, Chief of the Division of Commercial Treaties and
Agreements. Hawkins was disturbed by the position Keynes had taken on
'basic questions of economic policy ... which will ... have a vital
relationship to efforts to reconstruct the world on a peaceful basis'.

Keynes had stated that the most-favoured-nation principle, so fundamental and dear to Hull and Hawkins, did not result in non-discriminatory
treatment; it often happened that a country, despite its most-favoured-
nation obligations, applied a generally higher level of duties to the
characteristic products of a particular country; hence it discriminated
against the former without calling it discrimination. Hawkins admitted
that the most-favoured-nation clause did not pretend to insure that a
country's policy would be wholly non-discriminatory or even equitable. It
had a much more modest and attainable objective, which was simply that
any given product of a particular foreign country would not be placed at a
competitive disadvantage as compared with *the like product* from any
other country.

Keynes had also said that

the only hope of the future was to maintain economies in balance
without great excesses of either exports or imports, and that this could
be only through exchange controls, which Article VII seemed to ban.
He went on to say that the language used in Article VII had a long
history; that it permitted all sorts of cunningly devised tariffs, which
were in fact discriminatory and prohibited sound economic monetary
controls.[6]

Hawkins noted that

what Mr. Keynes has completely failed to see and understand is that the
idea of non-discrimination . . . is not a philosophical concept but rather
a matter involving considerations of practical politics and economics.
The imposition of high, though nondiscriminatory, trade barriers for
the protection by a country of its own producers does and has aroused
resentment, but this resentment is mitigated by the fact that a certain
degree of preference by a government for its nationals is understandable
and tolerable. But discrimination in favor of other foreigners is not so
regarded. And above all, he fails wholly to see that after the sacrifices
the American people are called upon to make to help Great Britain in
the present emergency (even though we are thereby helping ourselves),
our public opinion simply would not tolerate discrimination against our
products in Great Britain and, at Great Britain's instance, in other
countries.[7]

Keynes's views were highly disturbing. They ran foul of the policy the
United States had always pursued. Secretary Hull, and the officials in the
State Department, believed in this policy with emotion and conviction,
and anything akin to the bilateral arrangements of the totalitarian
countries was perceived as economic heresy and perverseness.

Non-discrimination was part of the American heritage. As every
schoolboy had read, the American colonies had been forced to grant
special privileges to British trading companies; even after the United States
became independent, the British had tried to monopolise commerce. In his
Farewell Address, President Washington had recommended that, in its
trade with other nations, the United States 'hold an equal and impartial
hand, neither seeking nor granting exclusive favors or preferences'. Ever
since, non-discrimination had been a doctrine upheld by US governments
and generally accepted by the public.[8] It provided the conditions in which
the American economic way of life could unfold, a setting in which
competition could do its salutary and invigorating work. It was consistent
with the widespread opposition to government interference in the free-
market mechanism.

The exponents of non-discrimination generally made a distinction between protective tariffs and preferences. Protection of the home market for the benefit of its producers was an expression of nationalism. It permitted the diversification of a country's economic life, and gave its people an opportunity to develop their resources and talents. It did not infringe upon the rights of other nations, and as such was not aggressive. Preference, on the other hand, was an expression of modern imperialism. In contrast with the policy of protection, it was aggressive. It gave nations who had the political power to impose preferential trade arrangements the economic power to deny competitors equal access to raw materials, markets and investment. Excluded countries would resent such discrimination, and would try to obtain by force what was denied to them through peaceful trade. Thus, preferential treatment bred aggression.

Secretary Hull, in his long devotion as a Congressman and a Senator to a liberal system of free trade, did not approve of high tariffs, however. He had long fought a lone battle against the prohibitive duty rates imposed by Republican Congresses, and even within his party he had been at the spearhead of the fight to reduce tariffs. When he agreed to become Roosevelt's Secretary of State, one of his highest hopes was to embark the United States upon a programme of trade liberalisation, which might set an example to the world. The Ottawa Agreements, inaugurating a comprehensive system of mutual preferences between the United Kingdom and the Empire, had recently been signed. American producers were desperately looking for export markets, and complained bitterly about the unfair discriminatory preferences directed against them. This was in the midst of the Depression. Hull branded the Ottawa Agreements as 'the greatest injury, in a commercial way, that has been inflicted on this country since I have been in public life'.[9]

He took the lead, against strong opposition, sometimes even from the President himself, in a programme of trade liberalisation, using the powers given by the Reciprocal Trade Agreements Act of 1934. The procedure to be used was slow, cumbersome, requiring months of painstaking and expert study. An agreement could be made only with one country at a time. The great advantage, however, was that, once it had been signed, no ratification by Congress was needed. Over the years, Hull and Harry Hawkins, who carried out the details of the negotiations, had developed a considerable pride in their achievements, which they regarded as a great contribution to the maintenance of peace.

In a long memorandum to Hull Hawkins wrote,

Mr. Keynes contemplates the adoption after the war, as a deliberate policy of the United Kingdom, of bilateral and commercial economic arrangements with foreign countries. Although Mr. Keynes presumably is not presenting the views of the British Government on questions of basic economic policy, his standing and influence are such that any views he may have are bound to receive consideration in the United

Kingdom and hence are of real concern to us here.

Keynes had stated that, after the war, the United Kingdom would find itself in need of large quantities of imported goods: food, machinery, raw materials. The means of paying for them would be considerably reduced, and Britain's income from such traditionally important sources as foreign investment, shipping and so on drastically cut. A close control of British international trade would be necessary to make the fullest use of its shrunken resources, and to keep its purchases within its means, while facilitating exports to a maximum. This could be achieved only through bilateral agreements. If, for instance, Britain exported more to Brazil than it imported, and accumulated Brazilian currency that was not convertible into dollars, it would have to use this currency to buy Brazilian cotton rather than American. If Argentina sold more to Britain than it bought, Britain would have to make the sterling balances inconvertible, and induce Argentina to buy British goods, rather than to leave the balances idle.

Keynes felt that the United States should not object to this plan, because, anyway, Britain would be under the *necessity* of adopting it, and it would not be of great consequence to the United States; in addition, as a creditor nation with a large export surplus, refusing to take full payment in goods, and instead, accumulating gold, the United States had 'made any general international system unworkable'. 'When it was pointed out to him that there would be discrimination against American trade, he argued at some length that this term is a vague, ambiguous and largely meaningless one, handed down to us from a dead past, and implied that we should set up new standards of international conduct in the trade field.' Keynes apparently assumed that the United States would not correct its policy, and therefore should not complain if Britain and other countries took matters into their own hands, 'thereby facilitating the creation of conditions which will make possible the kind of international system we seem to want'.

This was radically opposed to the 'non-discrimination' policy of the State Department. 'Mr. Keynes apparently does not realize that there is grave danger that the adoption by Great Britain of export-forcing devices essentially similar to those employed by the Germans will necessitate the adoption of similar devices by ourselves, with the result that a virtual state of trade warfare would exist.'

Given the largely expanded productive capacity of the United States during the war, and the fact that at 'some stage in the immediate post-war period we are likely to find ourselves in another acute economic depression', Hawkins expected that large unmarketable surpluses would accumulate, and that export markets would be needed to relieve this situation. Otherwise, pressures from American producers would compel the government to adopt the same policies as Britain. 'However, the British would be able to employ this particular device in many more instances than could we because we have an import balance in our trade with relatively few countries.' The United States might have to resort, rightly or wrongly, unsoundly or not, to other devices, 'such as the granting of loans and blocking of dollar proceeds, export subsidies or other devices for carrying on trade warfare'.

> But no person in his right mind could contemplate the development of such a situation with equanimity. . . . Unless some means can be found whereby currencies can be made convertible into one another, the British may in fact find it necessary to give preferential treatment to our competitors in order to utilize their foreign funds for much-needed imports. It may also be true that, in the longer run, unless we can bring our import policy into line with our creditor position, no system for multilateral settling of international accounts can be worked out . . . all the talent and resources of this Government should be devoted to the finding of solutions to these problems. . . . This work should go forward immediately. . . . The appropriate instrument for crystallizing and, if possible, settling the issue presented is the lend—lease agreement now under discussion with the British. Article VII of the draft agreement which has been approved by this Department and by the President and submitted to the British, provides in effect that the two countries should collaborate in solving post-war economic problems on a sound basis; but specifies, as part of that basis, that neither should discriminate against the other.

Given the fact that the British government included such professed advocates of imperial preference as Mr Amery and Lord Beaverbrook, 'it might easily happen that British policy, under the influence of Mr. Keynes and others, will be permitted to drift in a direction wholly opposed to ours unless we take pains to make our position clear on every suitable occasion'.[10] Secretary Hull thought the matter important, and sent the memorandum to the President.

Keynes took the draft with him to London. On the way back, he wrote Acheson a letter from New York.

My Dear Acheson:

> I should not like it to be thought because of my cavilling at the word 'discrimination' that the excellence and magnanimity of the first part of that Article VII and of the document as a whole had gone overlooked.

> I will do what I can to interpret the mind of the President and of the State Department to people at home and feel some confidence that a right conclusion will be reached.

> The Ambassador comes on leave in about a fortnight and I dare say that the main discussions will await his return. So do not expect a reply

in the very near future.

My so strong reaction against the word 'discrimination' is the result of my feeling so passionately that our hands must be free to make something new and better of the postwar world; not that I want to discriminate in the old bad sense of that word — on the contrary, quite the opposite.

But the word calls up, and must call up — for that is what it means strictly interpreted — all the old lumber, most-favoured-nation clause and the rest which was a notorious failure and made such a hash of the old world. We know also that won't work. It is the clutch of the dead, or at least the moribund, hand. If it was accepted it would be cover behind which all the unconstructive and truly reactionary people of both our countries would shelter. We must be free to work out new and better arrangements which will win in substance and not in shadow what the President and you and others really want. As I know you won't dispute this, we shall be able to work something out. Meanwhile forgive my vehemence which has deep causes in my hopes for the future. This is my subject. I know, or partly know, what I want. I know, and clearly know, what I fear.

Sincerely yours,
J. M. Keynes.[11]

4
The Clearing Union

As he flew back to England, aboard the Clipper, Keynes had time to reflect on his conversation with Acheson and Hawkins. Between the demands for non-discrimination and convertibility of currencies, as expressed by the State Department, and the system of bilateral trade agreements he himself had been advocating there was no common denominator. The one practically excluded the other. The State Department had made it unmistakably clear that, if Britain followed after the war a policy of extension of the existing bilateral agreements, this would mean a 'trade war' with the United States. These warnings could not be ignored. Nor could the inescapable fact that Britain would emerge from the war as a heavy debtor to many countries; that reconversion from war production would take a long time; that the need for imports would be immediate; and that the chronic shortage of dollars would last several years after the end of hostilities. Having lost its overseas investments, its gold and dollar reserves, Britain would be able to pay for its imports only by its exports. Keynes's visit to Washington had not altered his conviction that the United States would not correct its unbalanced creditor position after the war. How then could Britain open its doors to American exports, and buy at the same time food and raw materials overseas? That was the dilemma.

It seemed futile to make an attempt at reconciling or combining the two policies, and any plan would have to take into account the relationship between the two countries. For the duration of the war, and for some while afterward, Britain was beholden to the United States as one sovereign nation had seldom been to another. Without the constructive co-operation of the American government, no scheme could be expected to work or even come into being. The State Department had made it clear that it intended to pursue Secretary Hull's policy, and to remove gradually the obstacles to international trade. It also intended to do away with exchange and trade controls, and Britain and the other democracies were expected to follow the same policies. Thus a system of bilateral agreements intended to balance international trade, and from which the United States, because of its overwhelming creditor position, would largely be excluded, would be regarded as unacceptable. A currency system that 'would cover the whole of the existing sterling area and possibly other countries', but of which the United States would not be an integral part, would be anathema to Mr Hull.

Keynes had been asked to take back to London the 'lunatic proposals of Mr Hull',[1] as he called them. Now he faced the challenge of devising a formula that would satisfy the doctrinaire demands of the State Department, and the exigencies of the unavoidable debtor position of the British balance of payments after the war; a formula that would be constructive, that could not be interpreted by the Americans as 'discrimination', and that would at the same time solve the virtually insoluble problem of providing debtor nations with sufficient foreign exchange to pay for the imports they needed. This required thinking out anew some fundamental principles, and called for new ideas and new concepts. The problem, which presented seemingly unsurmountable constraints, had to be approached in an unconventional manner. It was here that Keynes was the supreme master. The peerless economic and encyclopaedic knowledge, combined with broad vision and leaps of intuition; the lucid intelligence, capable of rational analysis of the most complex and perplexing problems; the faculty to anticipate future developments – he would need all this for the task that he decided to take on.

Aware of the checks and balances which impeded government action, both in the United States and in Britain, it was important that he adopt the right strategy and the appropriate tactics. During the interwar period, tariffs had considerably reduced the flow of trade and had contributed to unemployment. But it would have been naïve to expect that the powerful groups in Congress, who had a decisive influence over American economic foreign policy, would abolish the protective tariff wall. Britain and other countries faced with a deficit on their balance of payments would have to keep imports down to a tolerable level, and tariffs were one of the methods they would use.

The violent fluctuations in the price levels of raw materials and foodstuffs, aggravated by speculative buying and selling, would require attention in due course. The obstacles to price stability and the balanced growth of international trade had taken various forms during the twenty years between the two wars, and much had to be done to eliminate them. These were complex problems. But a starting point had to be made, and Keynes chose to deal with the monetary problems first. This meant that he would have to face squarely Britain's international financial position after the war. As he explained later, there was a logical reason for dealing with the monetary proposals first. It is extraordinarily difficult to frame any proposals about tariffs if countries are free to alter the value of their currencies without agreement and at short notice. Tariffs and currency depreciations are in many cases alternatives. Without currency agreements you have no firm ground on which to discuss tariffs. In the same way plans for diminishing the fluctuation of international prices have no domestic meaning to the countries concerned until we have some firm ground in the value of money. ... It is very difficult while you have monetary chaos to have order of any kind in other directions ... if we have a firm ground on this particular issue it will be a great deal easier to reach a satisfactory answer on other questions. It is perhaps an accident that the monetary proposals got started first ... but I am not sure that it was not a fortunate accident. ...[2]

But, even limited to proposed agreements on currency, the problem of bridging the gulf between American and British interests and generally accepted ideas was of extraordinary difficulty. Whereas in Britain the 'gold standard' had become a scarecrow, and something to which the country would never return, the Americans had accumulated about two-thirds of the world's monetary gold and were obviously determined that it should keep its value. Any proposal of a currency agreement that would not be based on gold would be unacceptable to the United States.

Over the years, Keynes's ideas about an international monetary system had evolved, but he had never formulated a comprehensive, detailed and integrated plan. In his first book, *Indian Currency and Finance*, published in 1913, analysing the gold-exchange standard as it then prevailed, he stated, 'Speaking as a theorist, I believe that it contains one essential element – the use of a cheap local currency artificially maintained at par with the international currency or standard of value (whatever that may ultimately turn out to be) – in the ideal currency of the future.'[3]

In *A Tract on Monetary Reform*, he addressed himself to the 'evil consequences of instability in the standard of value', and later, in *A Treatise on Money*, he envisaged the possibility of gradually linking up the national currencies into a managed international system, taking the gold standard as a starting point. But it was in the German preface to this book, published a year later, that he outlined the idea he was now going fully to develop:

I now envisage as a possibility of the near future the separation of the countries of the world into two groups, one of which will continue to adhere for a time to a rigid gold standard and the other of which will aim at some form of price stability whilst maintaining a definite but non-rigid relationship with gold. For example, I allow my mind to play with the idea of a currency union which might embrace the British

Empire, Japan, South America, Central Europe and Scandinavia with a common currency unit, the value of which would be kept stable within (say) 5 per cent of the norm more or less (i.e. within a total range of 10 per cent) in terms of a composite commodity made up of the principal articles of international trade in which the adherents to the new currency unit were chiefly interested. . . . Furthermore, there would at all times be a defined, but not invariable, relationship between the new unit and gold.

If countries such as the United States, continuing to adhere to a rigid gold standard, were disposed 'to join an international scheme of management, drawn up scientifically and without reference to obsolete prejudices, . . . I would warmly welcome and explore the possibilities which it would offer.'[4]

In 1933, he had suggested that the London Economic Conference consider setting up an 'international authority for the issue of gold-notes', which would be responsible for the stabilisation of currencies and prices.[5] Now that he had returned to the Treasury, not as a civil servant, but as the most influential economist advising the government, he was able to draw on his vast reservoir of economic expertise, and develop practical plans to be discussed in government offices. Back in London, tired from his visit to Washington, he reviewed with a number of other economists and officials the implications of Article VII, and, after listening for a while to comments and arguments, retired for a few weeks to the country. When he returned, he brought with him 'Proposals for an International Currency Union', a fully detailed plan for postwar international currency policy.

Analysing the 'secular international problem' of maintaining equilibrium in the balance of payments between countries – a problem which had 'never been solved, since methods of barter gave way to the use of money and bills of exchange', except for at two periods, when 'the system of international investment pivoting on London transferred the *onus* of adjustment from the debtor to the creditor position' – he warned that there was no hope of achieving such equilibrium after the war, except by a refinement and improvement of the Schachtian device: 'To suppose that there exists some smoothly functioning automatic mechanism of adjustment which preserves equilibrium if only we trust to methods of *laissez-faire* is a doctrinaire delusion which disregards the lessons of historical experience without having behind it the support of sound theory.' Instead of achieving its avowed goal of promoting the international division of labour, *laissez-faire* had broken down before the war, and had been a 'source of all those clumsy hindrances to trade which suffering communities have devised in their perplexity as being better than nothing in protecting them from the intolerable burdens flowing from currency disorders'.

Moreover in the interval between the Wars the world explored in rapid succession almost, as it were, in an intensive laboratory experiment all the alternative false approaches to the solution —

(i) the idea that a freely fluctuating exchange would discover for itself a position of equilibrium;

(ii) liberal credit and loan arrangements between the creditor and the debtor countries flowing from the mere fact of an unbalanced creditor—debtor position, on the false analogy of superficially similar nineteenth century transactions between old-established and newly-developing countries where the loans were self-liquidating because they themselves created new sources of payment;

(iii) the theory that the unlimited free flow of gold would automatically bring about adjustments of price-levels and activity in the recipient country which would reverse the pressure;

(iv) the use of deflation, and still worse of *competitive* deflations, to force an adjustment of wage- and price-levels which would force or attract trade into new channels;

(v) the use of deliberate exchange depreciation, and still worse of *competitive* exchange depreciations, to attain the same object;

(vi) the erection of tariffs, preferences, subsidies, *et hoc genus omne* to restore the balance of international commerce by restriction and discrimination.

It was only in the last years, almost the last months, before the crash, that after the above trials and errors Dr. Schacht stumbled in desperation on something new which had in it the germs of a good technical idea. This idea was to cut the knot by discarding the use of a currency having international validity and substitute for it what amounted to barter, not indeed between individuals, but between different economic units. In this way he was able to return to the essential character and original purpose of trade whilst discarding the apparatus which had been supposed to facilitate, but was in fact strangling it.

The task of devising a postwar system was made considerably more difficult by the fact that Britain would start out from an existing state of extreme disequilibrium. As he saw it, there were three alternatives.

The first was for the United States to provide liberal relief to Europe during the reconstruction period. This would be helpful, but would provide no lasting solution. The United States could also reduce its tariffs and voluntarily cut its agricultural exports; but there was little prospect that the vested interests would allow this to be done on an adequate scale. A general stimulus of demand, as a result of adopting various New Deal expedients, might bring relief. All this, however, was very uncertain.

A more practical answer would be the second alternative: to develop the system of payments and clearing agreements already in operation, and to continue importing foodstuffs and raw materials through official bodies, giving preference to countries prepared to reciprocate by buying British products. While such a system might succeed in stabilising and balancing trade at a high level, he knew the Americans would not be part of it.

He then set out to sketch the third alternative: 'an ideal scheme which would preserve the advantages of an international means of payment universally acceptable, whilst avoiding those features of the old system which did the damage'. He doubted that this plan would prove as helpful to British interests as the second alternative, at least during the transitional period, but in the long run it might prove a better scheme.

> It is also open to the objection, that . . . it is complicated and novel and perhaps Utopian in the sense, not that it is impracticable, but that it assumes a higher degree of understanding, of the spirit of bold innovation, and of international cooperation and trust than it is safe or reasonable to assume. Nevertheless, it is with this scheme that I should approach the United States. . . . If not this, we can ask, what then? Now that you are fully seized of the essential elements of the problem, what alternative solution do you offer us?[6]

In the Currency Union proposals he amplified the basic ideas he had sketched ten years earlier, when he had considered the linking of national currencies into a managed international system. There were, however, many innovations.

All foreign exchange would be centralised in the hands of central banks, dealing with the public through the usual banking system. International transactions would be cleared between central banks, operating their accounts with an international clearing bank. Central banks would have control over the purchase of foreign exchange by nationals, but must be prepared to sell their own currency to another central bank against a credit on their clearing account.

Currencies would have a fixed value, determined in terms of the bank money of the clearing bank, which would itself be expressed in terms of a unit of gold.

A central bank whose account was in debit by a certain amount, and for a given time, would be allowed to depreciate its currency by an amount not exceeding 5 per cent within a year. It would also be allowed to borrow. If, however, the debit exceeded half its quota, the governors of the clearing bank were allowed to *require* a depreciation, or that the central bank hand over the gold in its possession, prohibit outward capital transactions, or even withdraw from the system. In the event of withdrawal the debit balance would be transferred to the reserve fund of the clearing bank.

Conversely, a central bank whose account had been in credit might be required to appreciate its currency; it could also grant loans to deficit banks. At the end of each year, the credit balance of any member, in excess of its quota, would be transferred to the reserve fund. Such a member could withdraw from the system at a year's notice, but would have to surrender its balance to the reserve fund of the clearing bank.

No interest would be charged on credit balances, but a progressive interest would be charged on debit balances.

The clearing bank would set up an account in favour of a supranational policing body, charged with the duty of preserving peace. An account would also be set up in favour of an international organisation charged with postwar relief and reconstruction.

By this means all risk is avoided of any country being required to assume a burdensome commitment for relief and reconstruction, since the resources will be provided in the first instance by those countries having credit balances on their Clearing Accounts for which they have no immediate use and are voluntarily leaving idle, and in the long run by those countries which have a chronic international surplus for which they have no beneficial employment.

Accounts would also be opened in favour of international bodies charged with the management of commodity control, and to finance stocks of commodities.

The plan was circulated in the Treasury early in September 1941. According to Lord Robbins,

It would be difficult to exaggerate the electrifying effect on thought throughout the whole relevant apparatus of government of the production of this document ... nothing so imaginative and ambitious had ever before been discussed as a possibility of responsible government policy ... it became as it were a banner of hope, an inspiration to the daily grind of war-time duties.[7]

There was some criticism: it was too grandiose, almost utopian, something for which the world was not yet ready. Keynes continued to redraft and refine it, as it went through the scrutiny of several interdepartmental committees. Gradually, the elegance and clarity of style added to the originality of thought and the breadth of vision took hold of those who read it: 'the excitement of something really great and novel began to filter through in the minds of the various officials, however staid; there was something irresistible about it'. Soon it acquired the status of a Treasury plan. Its aims were much broader and more comprehensive than those finally embodied in the Bretton Woods agreements.[8]

On 11 February 1942 a fourth draft was given to ministers. The

Union was now called 'International Currency (or Clearing) Union'. It
was to be based on international bank-money, called 'bancor', and
fixed — but not unalterably — in terms of gold, and accepted as the
equivalent of gold by all members of the Union for the purpose of settling
international balances. Keynes assumed that through adequate measures it
would be possible 'to prevent the piling up of credit and debit balances
without limit, and the system would have failed in the long run if it did
not possess sufficient capacity for self-equilibrium to prevent this'.

The idea of a reserve fund replenished by the balances of the surplus
countries had been dropped, and equilibrium would be maintained or
restored through exchange appreciation or depreciation and through other
measures.

The basic concept underlying the Clearing Union was simple: to apply
between countries the essential principle of banking as it existed within
each country. 'This principle is the necessary equality of credits and
debits, of assets and liabilities.' The plan aimed at substituting an
expansionist for a contractionist pressure on world trade. Each member
country would be allowed overdraft facilities (as they existed in the British
banking system) proportionate to the importance of its foreign trade and
subject to certain regulatory provisions. Since credit balances were resources which a country voluntarily chose to leave idle, and represented a
potential purchasing power it was entitled to use at any time, it would not
be harmed if those balances were put at the disposal of other countries,
instead of being withdrawn from circulation and thus 'exerting a deflation-
ary and contractionist pressure on the whole world including the creditor
country itself'.

> No depositor in a local bank suffers because the balances, which he
> leaves idle, are employed to finance the business of someone else. Just
> as the development of national banking systems served to offset a
> deflationary pressure which would have prevented otherwise the devel-
> opment of modern industry, so by extending the same principle into
> the international field we may hope to offset the contractionist
> pressure which might otherwise overwhelm in social disorder and
> disappointment the good hopes of our modern world.

The overdraft facilities would allow time for necessary adjustments. They
did not, obviously, provide any long-term solution against a continuing
disequilibrium, 'for in due course the more improvident and the more
impecunious, left to themselves, would have run through their resources'.
Therefore, rules and a machinery were to be set up to provide that
equilibrium was restored. The most difficult question here was whether
the individual countries should assume responsibility and power to decide
what measures to take, or whether this authority should be given to the
management of the Union.

The United States and the United Kingdom would be founder-states, and given a special position. They would agree between themselves the initial values of their own currencies in terms of bancor, and the value of bancor in terms of gold; the initial values of the currencies of the other members would be fixed when they joined the system, and in agreement with them. From there on, a member country was not allowed to alter the value of its currency in terms of bancor without the permission of the governing board of the Clearing Union, except under predetermined conditions; during the first five years after the inception of the system, however, the board would give special consideration to appeals for adjustment on the ground of unforeseen circumstances. Members would have to pay a charge on their balances existing with the Union, *whether credit or debit*, and these charges would be progressively higher. Thus, in order to avoid any charges, members should try to keep their balances as close to equilibrium as possible. The methods envisaged to correct a disequilibrium were very similar to those described in Keynes's first draft.

The great advantage of the proposed Clearing Union, as Keynes saw it, was that it restored unfettered multilateral clearing among its members, and that action was necessary only when a country was out of balance with the system as a whole: 'Compare this with the difficulties and complications of a large number of bilateral agreements.' Obviously, he had now abandoned the bilateral approach and adopted a multilateral system, at least as far as monetary arrangements were concerned.

Gold, since it still possessed great psychological value, would have a substantially unchanged position. Bancor would be defined in terms of gold, and member countries would be entitled to obtain bancor credit by paying gold to the credit of their account, 'thus securing a steady and ascertained purchaser for the output of the gold-producing countries and for countries holding large reserves of gold'. Members, however, could not demand gold against their bancor credits. Thus the convertibility between bancor and gold was one-way. If the Clearing Union found itself in possession of a stock of gold, it could decide to distribute the surplus to member countries possessing credit balances, proportionately to such balances.

As far as capital movements were concerned, 'It is widely held that control of capital movements, both inward and outward, should be a permanent feature of the post-war system – at least so far as we are concerned. If control is to be effective, it probably involves the *machinery* of exchange control for *all* transactions, even though a general open licence is given to all remittances in respect of current trade.'

Keynes saw the plan as a measure of financial disarmament, inviting members 'to abandon that licence to promote indiscipline, disorder and bad-neighbourliness which, to the general disadvantage, they have been free to exercise hitherto'. No greater surrender of sovereignty was required than in any commercial treaty: the obligations would be entered into

voluntarily and could be terminated on certain conditions by giving notice.
The United Kingdom and the United States would bring the Clearing
Union into existence as joint founder-states. Other members would be
brought in as soon as they had established an internal organisation capable
of sustaining the obligations of membership. This approach had the
advantage that both countries 'could settle the charter and the main details
of the new body without being subjected to the delays and confused
counsels of an international conference'. Moreover, membership would be
established as a privilege, 'open only to those who conformed to certain
general principles and standards of international economic conduct'.
Keynes thought of his plan as capable of arousing enthusiasm, because it
made a beginning at the future economic ordering of the world, and might
help to create the conditions and the atmosphere in which much else
would be made easier. It would, however, not solve all problems: 'If,
indeed, we lack the productive capacity to maintain our standard of life,
then a reduction in this standard is not avoidable.'[9]

Over a period of twelve months Keynes had revised and refined his
proposals, often in response to suggestions or criticism. Several of Britain's
most able economists had been called into government service; they were
the first to see the plan. Among them were Professor (later Lord) Lionel
Robbins, Professor Dennis Robertson, Mr James Meade, Mr Roy Harrod
and Sir Hubert Henderson. Lord Catto, Sir David Waley and other
Treasury officials had submitted observations and comments. When
Keynes circulated his initial proposals, Waley did not share the optimism
'in the belief that Barter is the best method of international trade and that
we shall find our salvation if we adopt this method which, having been in
abeyance from the Stone Age till 1939, was then re-discovered by Dr.
Schacht'.[10]

Mr Thompson-McCausland thought that the International Clearing
Bank suggested by Keynes was only a means to an end, and that it would
be a waste of time to develop a detailed criticism of the Bank as such. The
criticism should be directed at the agents of adjustment Keynes suggested:
(a) the appreciation or depreciation of currency was a clumsy and often
ineffective instrument for correcting any serious maladjustment; (b) the
automatic surrender of surpluses was a mirage based on the assumption
that surplus countries would be content to go on forever subsidising deficit
countries and submit themselves to an automatic international charity
levied by the board of an international organisation.[11] As a result of such
criticism, Keynes gradually modified his original concept and came to
accept currency multilateralism. Until the end, however, he maintained
that currency multilateralism did not necessarily imply commercial multilateralism.

On 4 August 1942, Keynes circulated within the Treasury a redraft of
his 'Proposals for an International Clearing Union'. He felt it was now in 'a
shape suitable to be passed on to the Americans, the Dominions and (in

due course) others outside Whitehall'.[12] This was the plan the British Treasury now wanted to submit to the US government. To begin with, Keynes had intended that, before developing his ideas into an integrated proposal, he should submit his views to a group of American experts and listen to what they might have to say. This would have avoided the crystallisation of ideas that were not acceptable to both. However, though for several months, beginning early in February 1942, he sought through the American embassy in London and the British embassy in Washington to establish contact with the American government and to start discussions on postwar planning, his approaches had been in vain. Initially they had been ignored, and later the State Department had turned down the requests under the pretext that the US government was not yet ready for such discussions.[13] At the US Treasury, meanwhile, a small group of people had been working feverishly on their own plan, which, although it differed from the Keynes plan in many ways, covered the same ground, had the same basic purposes, and presented some striking similarities to it.

5
The Stabilisation Fund

Whatever may have prompted him to do so, on the morning of Sunday 14 December 1941 Secretary Morgenthau called Harry White and asked him 'to think about and prepare a memorandum and plan for setting up an Inter-Allied Stabilization Fund'. He had in mind 'a Fund to be used during the war to give monetary aid to actual and potential allies and to hamper the enemy; to provide the basis for post-war international monetary stabilization arrangements; and to provide a post-war "international currency" '.[1]

By his own admission, Morgenthau lacked theoretical expertise in international finance. As Secretary of the Treasury, however, he had accumulated considerable practical experience, and had generally relied heavily on the advice of Harry White and other economists in the Department. Where he picked up the idea of an 'international currency' does not seem to be recorded in the official files.

A week before giving White the assignment to think about postwar monetary stabilisation, Morgenthau had announced to his staff that he wanted to give him the status of Assistant Secretary, although he could not give him the title. The Japanese attack at Pearl Harbor had drawn the United States into the war. 'He will be in charge of all foreign affairs for me. ... I want it in one brain and I want it in Harry White's brain', the Secretary commented.[2]

Immediately after announcing his decision, Morgenthau called Secretary Hull and told him that he was rearranging his organisation at the Treasury and had designated Harry White to be in charge of foreign affairs and relations with the State Department. 'Well,' said Hull, 'he's a mighty suitable man. ... He's a very high-class fellow. ... Capable.'[3] He was indeed, and remarkably well qualified for the task his chief had given him.

Born in Boston, Massachusetts, in 1892, to Russian immigrants, Harry had finished high school in his native city and worked for two years in the family hardware stores. He then decided to become a farmer, but soon returned to the hardware business. After serving in France as a lieutenant, he ran a government institution for war orphans, and later took an interest in a boys' camp. In 1922, at that time a married veteran and nearly thirty years old, he decided on an academic career, determined to make up for lost time. He intended to concentrate on the study of government, but, realising 'that most governmental problems are economic', he switched to economics. A brilliant student, he obtained a master of arts degree in economics in 1925, and was awarded his doctorate for a thesis entitled 'The French International Accounts 1880–1913'. His doctorate, however, did not bring him any advancement, and he soon realised that he would not be able to find a place on the Harvard faculty.

He left Boston to become assistant professor at a small college in the Midwest. A year later he was promoted to professor of economics. The year was 1933, and White was then forty. He was a good teacher, but he did not like the job, feeling that the work and the position were beneath his capabilities.[4]

The country was going through the depth of the Depression, and President Roosevelt had started his first term with a series of revolutionary 'New Deal' measures. International trade had disintegrated and all over the world protective barriers were set up by countries trying to insulate themselves from the consequences of the general distress.

White's interest had 'been aroused by the growing claims that our domestic economy must be insulated against critical disturbances' by restricting imports. He wondered whether it would not be possible to render the domestic economy less sensitive to disturbances without sacrificing the stabilising influences of international economic relations or the gains from foreign trade.

> The path, I suspect, may lie in the direction of centralized control over foreign exchanges and trade. I have been spending the spring and summer reading and thinking about the problem but my opinion as yet is unsettled. I am also learning Russian in the hope that I may get a fellowship which will enable me to spend a year chiefly in Russia. There I should like to study intensively the technique of planning at the Institute of Economic Investigation of Gosplan.[5]

Instead of going to Russia, he went to Washington. On 7 June 1934, Professor Jacob Viner, who had been asked by Secretary Morgenthau to make a comprehensive study of American monetary and banking legislation, wrote to White that he was 'very anxious to have your assistance in the conduct of this study, and I hope that you will be able and willing to come to Washington for this purpose'.[6] White immediately accepted, and within a few days started work at the Treasury.

Three months later he submitted to Professor Viner a 450-page report entitled 'Selection of a Monetary Standard for the United States'. It is evident from this report that White's basic ideas on the monetary standard that was 'best suited to American needs' had already crystallised. He stressed the need for fixed exchange rates, international co-operation, and the use of gold for the ultimate settlement of international transactions.

White immediately established himself as an indefatigable worker, a resourceful brain, and an efficient organiser with a remarkable ability for translating economic theory into practical administrative policy. Like Morgenthau, he was an ardent New Dealer. In 1936 he was promoted to Assistant Director of Research and Statistics, and in 1938 Morgenthau appointed him Director of Monetary Research, a position expressly created for him. His functions included the 'preparation of analyses and recommendations to aid the Secretary of the Treasury in the formulation and execution of monetary policies of the Treasury Department in connection with the Stabilization Fund and other operations ... and economic analyses relating to the customs activities of the Treasury'. By any standards, White's career was meteoric. He soon developed a considerable intellectual ascendancy over the Secretary, who came to rely on him more than on anybody else in monetary and financial matters. In August 1941 White was given the additional title and duties of Assistant to the Secretary.

As principal analyst in the division of monetary research and statistics, and later as director of monetary research at the Treasury, White's main concern, for several years, had been with monetary problems. He had been involved in the management and operation of the stabilisation fund. International co-operation, stable exchange rates, and a monetary system based on gold were the things uppermost in his mind when he started working on postwar monetary planning. The instrument to avoid unwanted repercussions of economic disturbances, in a world in constant state of flux, would be an international stabilisation fund.

Two weeks after Morgenthau gave him the assignment to think about postwar international monetary stabilisation arrangements, Harry White had ready a twelve-page memorandum: 'A Suggested Program for Inter-Allied Monetary and Banking Action'. According to White there were two major tasks that needed to be undertaken in the international monetary and banking field:

(1) provision of the means, the instrument and the procedure to stabilise foreign exchange rates; and
(2) the establishment of an agency with adequate means and powers to provide the capital needed by Allied countries for economic reconstruction, and to supply the short-term capital necessary to increase the volume of foreign trade, where such capital was not available at reasonable rates from private sources.

The two parts of the programme were to be kept distinct. Though in some of their facets and in many of their consequences there was a considerable degree of interdependence and interaction, 'they are sufficiently different in character to call for an entirely different set of resources, of responsibilities, of procedures and criteria for functioning'.

White recommended that two separate institutions be established: an Inter-Allied Bank, and an Inter-Allied Stabilisation Fund. Though the creation of both would aid considerably in the functioning of each, either agency could function without the other. White also suggested that both agencies be established before the end of the war: it would take many months to set up such agencies, and 'it would be ill-advised if not dangerous to find ourselves at the end of the war unprepared for the stupendous task of world-wide economic reconstruction'.

The specific objectives of the Fund would be: the stabilisation of exchange rates; the establishment of a 'costless' clearing-house for foreign exchange; stability of price levels; reduction of foreign-exchange controls; and elimination of multiple currency and bilateral clearing arrangements.

The Fund would deal only with the treasuries and, as the treasuries' fiscal agents, the central banks of the participating countries. The Fund would consist of $10,000 million in gold, currency, and government securities. Each participating country would turn over to (or invest in) the Fund a certain amount, 'based upon pertinent considerations including national income, gold holdings, population, foreign debt'. Control of the Fund would be vested in the representatives appointed by the participating governments. Each representative would have a number of votes somewhat reflecting the value of his country's investment and contribution; but, 'In view of both the size and quality of the U.S. contribution (there being no question about a possible inability to exchange dollars for gold for purposes of settling international balances) the U.S. should have enough votes to block any decision, i.e. more than 20 per cent.' The treasury of each participating country would have the privilege of offering to the Fund its local currency in return for any other currency, except dollars, at rates determined by the Fund. If a member country wished to purchase dollars from the Fund, 'paying for it with local currency, the Fund will consider under the then prevailing circumstances how much of the particular country's local currency it is willing to hold and will further sell that country dollars or gold only if it is to use it to settle payments among member countries'.

In order to be eligible for membership, the participating countries would have to fulfil the following conditions:

(1) agree to alter their exchange rate only with the consent of the Fund, and only to the extent and in the direction approved by the Fund;
(2) agree (after a certain period of adjustment) to operate without foreign-exchange controls, excepting possibly exchange to be used for

short-term capital movements;

(3) agree not to enter upon any bilateral clearing arrangements;
(4) agree not to permit gold to circulate as a medium of exchange within the country, and to concentrate all monetary gold in the central bank or in the treasury;
(5) agree not to adopt any monetary banking measures promoting either serious inflation or serious deflation without the consent of a majority of the member votes of the Fund;
(6) agree to embark upon a programme of gradual reduction of existing tariff schedules without any increase in schedules except with the approval of the Fund; and
(7) agree not to permit any defaults on foreign obligations of the government, central bank, or any other government agency, without the approval of the Fund.

The plan also described the conditions under which the Fund would operate: currencies would be bought and sold by the Fund only with the approval of four-fifths of the member votes, and a service charge of $\frac{1}{32}$ per cent would be imposed on each transaction. Rates would be subject to change only with the consent of fourth-fifths of the member votes. The dollar would have a special position:

> No dollars shall be sold (a) unless the purchases by a participating country of dollars from the Fund will not directly add to the gold and dollar exchange holdings of the purchasing country, and (b) provided further, that the participating country's gold and dollar exchange holdings are not rising above a pre-determined level. . . . The purpose of the first of these two requirements is to make certain that the acquisition of dollars from the Fund paid for with local currency shall be used exclusively in the settlement of international balances. The second requirement is to prohibit the use of the Fund for acquisition of dollars to settle balances of payments while permitting the acquisition of dollars from outside the Fund for the purpose of building up dollar reserves.

White conceived that the Fund's currency transactions would take place on a day-to-day basis. The rules and regulations governing these transactions would be promulgated by the board, by unanimous approval. Instead of each country operating its own stabilisation fund, under rules similar to those of the Tripartite Agreement, there would be just the International Stabilisation Fund.[7]

On 6 January 1942, White sent Sumner Welles, then Under-Secretary at the State Department, a memorandum outlining his ideas for an international stabilisation fund. Welles was preparing to go to Rio de Janeiro for a conference with the Latin American countries, and White suggested that he bring up the subject there. The conference passed a resolution recommending that 'the Governments of the American Republics partici-pate in a special conference of Ministers of Finance or their representatives to be called for the purpose of considering the establishment of an international stabilization fund'.[8]

From January to April 1942, White and his assistants at the Treasury continued to refine and elaborate the proposals. The successive drafts have been preserved. In the White Papers at Princeton University there is a draft typed on copying paper and dated 27, 28, 29 and 30 April 1942. Some of the pages are missing. This was obviously a working draft; it contains typing errors, corrections, handwritten remarks and questions, and blanks. Also in the White Papers, there is a beautifully typed draft in a black cover, dated April 1942. It is basically the same as the draft mentioned above, but the blanks have been filled and the errors corrected. The mimeographed draft that Harry White gave Morgenthau on 8 May is almost identical to the April draft, but is dated March 1942 and obviously antedated. It is a long document, basically an amplification of the December draft, with many details of a highly technical nature. It establishes White as a determined internationalist, convinced that stability of currencies could be achieved only through co-operation between countries. He considered his proposals and comments 'solely for the purpose of providing a starting point for intelligent discussion, and in order to call attention to many of the difficulties which would have to be satisfactorily met before a workable and acceptable plan may emerge'.

It is virtually certain that some of the powers and requirements included in the outline of the Fund and the Bank will not survive discussion, compromise, prejudice and fear of departure from the usual. Some may not stand the test of political reality, and some may be unacceptable on technical grounds, while others may be generally regarded as going too far toward 'internationalism'. ... There is a desperate need for instruments which will pave the way and make easy a high degree of cooperation and collaboration among the United Nations in economic fields hitherto held too sacrosanct for inter-national action or multilateral sovereignty. A breach must be made and widened in the outmoded and disastrous economic policy of each-country-for-itself-and-the-devil-take-the-weakest. Just as the failure to develop an effective League of Nations has made possible two deva-stating wars within one generation, so the absence of a high degree of economic collaboration among the leading nations will, during the coming decade, inevitably result in economic warfare that will be but the prelude and instigator of military warfare on an even vaster scale.[9]

Morgenthau had suggested that White provide, in his plan, for an 'international currency'. When White comes to this subject, in the draft on the Bank, dated 28 April 1942, his tone grows polemical. Except for 'one advantage, though of minor importance', he saw no need for an international currency. The only advantage might be that a 'universally recognized international monetary unit of account would be helpful in the presentation of those statistical series which are pertinent to international comparisons of quantitative data measured in money terms'. To the question, however, of whether there is a case for the use of a new international unit as a *supplement* to local currencies, in order to facilitate international trade and finance, 'The answer is an unqualified "No".'

A 'trade dollar' or 'Demos' or 'Victor' or 'what-have-you' unit of currency supplementing the United States dollar, whether of the same or different value, would no more help foreign trade than would the adoption of a new flag. . . . An importer, exporter, bank, or a tourist has simply to make conversions from one currency into another in his transactions. Were it possible to eliminate by use of an international currency the arithmetical labors involved in the conversions, it would indeed, be a convenient device, though by no means a very important one. . . .

For many decades the British pound sterling was regarded virtually as an international currency unit. But its utility as an international unit of account and also as a common medium of exchange in many international financial and trade transactions rested on the fact that sterling was for a long time most stable in terms of gold value. . . . But when sterling lost its stability in terms of gold, its use as a unit of account rapidly diminished. Only the United States dollar has any chance of serving in that capacity now. However, if an attempt were made to recommend the use of the dollar as the international unit of account, there would unquestionably be some opposition on the part of those countries who, out of reasons of national prestige or anticipated monetary loss, would prefer not to promote a broader use in international use of a currency unit of some other country. . . . There are deemed to be some national prestige values and possibly slight economic gains in trade and financial transactions that accrue to a country having a currency that is widely used as an international unit of account. For that reason a new unit belonging to no country would be more welcome to most countries than the unit of any selected country. . . .

Obviously, a new unit of currency would have to be defined. . . . To set the value of the new currency unit in terms of some existing currency has the disadvantage of subjecting the new unit to the variations of the currency to which it is tied and also to raise question of 'favoritism'. A unit of account does not have to be set in terms of gold. It could, of course, be set in terms of some commodity other than

gold — tin, platinum or any material. It could even be set in terms of an
average basket of goods or an aggregate of goods. But examination of
the various possibilities will reveal that the only practical solution is to
set the new currency unit in terms of a given physical volume of gold.

Thus, in contrast to 'some persons who seem to think that all foreign
exchange problems would be solved if only all countries adopted the same
international unit for use in international transactions', White set out to
'demonstrate how absurd that belief is'. Moreover, 'the specific nature of
the new currency is never described, nor are the gains that are presumed to
result from such a currency ever stated in meaningful language'.[10]

The reader may conclude, as does the author, that, through some gossip
or indiscretion, Morgenthau and White had vaguely heard about Keynes's
'bancor', without really understanding its purpose or meaning, that they
also knew that Keynes was working on a postwar currency plan, and that
they took the view that something had to be done to counter it. This,
however, is mere conjecture.

Secretary Morgenthau's concept of a future international monetary
order was based largely on White's ideas. On 13 June 1941 he had stated
before the Banking and Currency Committee of the Senate,

> I venture to predict that the experience in international monetary
> cooperation gained through the Tripartite Accord will prove of perma-
> nent value. I believe that the machinery, which functioned in a spirit of
> cooperation and equality, promises more for future international
> economic organization than any of the aggressive monetary devices
> which now hold sway. . . .
>
> The Stabilization Fund has proved its value during years of un-
> paralleled crises in international trade and finance. Long ago we made
> the dollar the strongest currency in the world. Foreign nations and
> foreign individuals have preferred the dollar to all other currencies. . . .
> Nobody can say what kind of international economy will emerge from
> this war. But it would surely be unwise if we chose this time to let
> private speculators and foreign governments determine the exchange
> value of the dollar.[11]

6
Harry White Catches Up...

Early in February 1942 Keynes finished the fourth revised draft of his proposals for an International Clearing Union. The document had been discussed, first in the Treasury and later in interdepartmental committees. The excitement it had created when it was first circulated had not prevented a detailed scrutiny and critical examination. The Bank of England objected to it. Some economists, particularly Sir Hubert Henderson, strongly opposed it. 'But in the course of discussion, comment and redrafting, gradually, over a period of many months, by an imperceptible process, it came to be regarded as the main Treasury plan.'[1] Considerably modified and expanded, it had the elegance of style and the unusual breadth of vision characteristic of Keynes's writings. On 11 February it was submitted to the ministers.

Through various channels the news was reaching London that the United States government was also busy with postwar currency planning. A memorandum dated 6 February 1942 stated that the Americans 'are certainly turning over in their minds sweeping currency ideas. This follows from the memo by M. Pasvolsky that we have seen.' A government official close to Harry White had stated at a meeting in Washington that after the war 'there will be an international currency arrangement of some sort'. Another indication was a report of a plan that included 'the creation of a free international currency'. The conclusion to be drawn

> is that if we delay too long we may be faced with an American currency plan. . . . This will have the following disadvantages:
>
> (1) The American currency plan . . . may well be so rigid that we will be bound to oppose it (probably on the usual balance of payments line) and open ourselves once more to the charge of obstructionism.

(2) If we put forward Mr. Keynes's ideas, we may reasonably hope that our action will go some way towards removing the impression that we have no intention of co-operating with the United States Government in their more radical plans for economic reconstruction after the war. If the Americans get in first this opportunity will be lost.[2].

Keynes himself was impatient to start discussions as soon as possible. A few days before his Clearing Union proposals were submitted to the ministers, he had a conversation with the US ambassador in London, J. G. Winant, and his economic adviser, E. F. Penrose. He asked them what procedure was contemplated for the conversations foreshadowed in Article VII, on the assumption of course that the Lend–Lease agreement would be signed. Winant, who was shortly leaving for Washington, proposed to discuss the question with the State Department. His suggestion was that he would bring back with him, when he returned, a small team of 'expert and influential government officials and advisers', who would privately, informally, and without commitment review with a group of economists in Whitehall tentative plans embodying what seemed desirable on economic grounds. If these conversations showed signs of reaching useful conclusions, they might serve as a basis for more formal negotiations.

> We then had some talk about the appropriate composition of the small delegation. . . . Mr. Acheson . . . is certainly the man one wants to get from the State Department and would form the most suitable leader of the party. Dr. White is the Director of Financial Research, but exercises a wide influence over policy generally. He carries great weight with Mr. Morgenthau. . . . All these men are of great ability and intelligence and would be easy to work with, though exceedingly tough customers. Certainly anything acceptable to them as a body would carry great weight in U.S. administrative circles.[3]

When Ambassador Winant made the suggestion at the State Department, he was told it was too soon to start such conversations. And, when the British embassy enquired about the reasons for the delay, Acheson expressed the view 'that something like two months from now might be a convenient date. He seemed to assume that he would be in charge of negotiations on the American side.'[4]

Lord Halifax thought the British team should include Keynes, Phillips and Opie: 'I attach great importance to Opie being [included] as he is a very sound economist, good negotiator and persona grata to Americans. I also think it would be desirable to have Keynes in on the discussions rather than in the position of critic at (a) later stage.'[5]

On 23 February 1942 after almost seven months of negotiations, the Lend–Lease agreement was signed in Washington. It was expected in

London that the proposed conversations to be held 'at an early convenient date' would soon start. But, to the dismay of Ambassador Winant and his advisers, Washington did not react to the telegrams urging fulfilment of the commitments of Article VII. For months the State Department, the Treasury and the White House had pressed for the acceptance of Article VII, but now that it had been agreed to they seemed to have lost all interest.[6] Phillips inquired a number of times at the State Department about the reasons for the delay. He was told that 'they were by no means so well advanced in their preliminary studies as, he understood from Winant, we were'. It would take some time before they could start the conversations.

With each passing week, uneasiness and apprehension grew in London. At the Foreign Office, Nigel Ronald came to feel that 'the State Department half suspected that we intended to put a number of fast ones across them unless they come to the conversations with their case very elaborately prepared. It may also be inferred that the frequency with which Mr. Winant has had to use the name "Keynes" may have touched up some wounds which we had hoped had now healed over.' He thought that 'we should draft a telegram to Washington as a chaser . . . to preclude the possibility of the Americans over-preparing their case and simultaneously so far deferring the conversations that we here should be led insensibly to become overmuch wedded to our proposals.' The longer the delay before conversations actually started, the greater was the danger that 'what had been evolved as a constructive suggestion to serve as a basis of discussion gradually became transformed into an article of faith to be fought for tooth and nail'.[7]

Ambassador Winant also became increasingly concerned, and sent cable after cable to the State Department, asking for an early beginning to the informal conversations. Through conversations between Keynes and Penrose, Ambassador Winant gradually became aware of the general character of the British plan, and he approved of it. He cabled Washington,

> Both Ronald and Keynes stressed the balance of payments question and it seems likely that instead of directly attacking the problem of tariffs the British will stress the need for making financial arrangements that will ensure an adequate supply of foreign exchange for the purchase of essential imports, since their principal apprehension is that, particularly in the first two years after the war, they will not be able to obtain the imports necessary to get back reasonably near their pre-war standard of living and to undertake essential physical reconstruction.[8]

It was also learned that 'Keynes has abandoned support of bilateral discriminatory arrangements to meet balance of payments difficulties and has energetically worked on other solutions. James Meade, who has become increasingly influential and who powerfully influenced Keynes to abandon bilateralism, says confidentially that Keynes' attitude is now all that can be desired on the matter.'[9]

On 10 April a memorandum was submitted to the War Cabinet with the recommendation that authority should be given to begin 'as soon as possible informal, non-commital and exploratory talks with American representatives in the course of which the United Kingdom representatives should compare notes with the Americans on a number of constructive ideas, some of which have been formulated in the Treasury Memorandum.' It also suggested that Russia be brought into consultation at an early stage.[10]

The general declarations of Article VII were no more than aspirations until they had been clothed in policies calculated to realise them. It was felt that, if Britain started by accepting the desirability of restoring multilateral exchange, while explaining the very serious practical difficulties which would confront both it and other countries before these objectives could be realised, the United States Administration might be 'prepared to give full consideration both to the difficulties and to any solutions which we may have to propound'.

The War Cabinet decided that the project should be pursued, and that preliminary informal, exploratory and non-committal talks should be begun as soon as possible. The experts engaged should have the fullest discretion to discuss all possible lines of action. The purpose of the talks would be to thrash out, on broad lines, 'measures designed to deal with the outstanding problems of post-war economic reconstruction'. Ambassador Halifax was asked to inform the government in Washington of the decision.[11]

Meanwhile, Harry White had worked intensively to complete the assignment Secretary Morgenthau had given him. On 8 May 1942 he gave Morgenthau a voluminous 'preliminary draft': 'United Nations Stabilization Fund and a Bank for Reconstruction of the United and Associated Nations'. It was a substantial piece of work. A separate folder, labelled 'Conference of Finance Ministers of the United and Associated Nations', included a draft of an invitation that it was suggested that President Roosevelt send to the governments of the United and Associated Nations, and a detailed agenda for the conference to be held. In his letter to Morgenthau White stated,

The important decision to be made at this time is not the merits of a particular plan, but rather, the question as to, first, whether a conference should be held, and if so, who shall call the conference and when it shall be called. There is at least a couple of months of preliminary work necessary between the calling of a conference and the first meeting of the Ministers. It is not assumed that we would present to the conference any specific plan, though a general outline might be made available informally.

If you believe we should go ahead, a decision will have to be made whether you should approach the President directly, or whether to submit the idea to the State Department or Board of Economic Warfare first. There are a number of other points of preliminary 'tactics' that would need to be determined before anything is done. I believe the whole business, if handled correctly, can be extremely important.

This is not a matter that can be postponed indefinitely, inasmuch as we are committed by a resolution of the Rio conference. . . . Furthermore, if the Treasury doesn't initiate a conference on the subject it almost certainly will be initiated elsewhere, and it should be pre-eminently Treasury responsibility.[12]

At his staff meeting of 12 May, Morgenthau congratulated Harry White. 'It is a masterly job', he said. 'I want to compliment you and your organization on international stabilization.' The next step, Morgenthau thought, was to approach Secretary Hull, 'because without his support this thing would be torpedoed'. If he went straight to the President, the answer would be, 'Well, what does Hull think? I will send it over to Hull.' The diplomatic thing was to see Hull first.

White agreed that 'it is quite true that Hull is the top dog on this question ... during the war'. This plan, however, involved postwar monetary policy.

But Morgenthau was in a cautious mood: 'If I go to the President the first thing he will say is, "Well, this is foreign affairs." ' Then Hull and others might jump on him, and 'the President would say, "This is an example; I will make this as an example." '

'Think about it', he told White, 'I will give you twenty-four hours.' White thought about it, and suggested 'to hit them both at the same time'.[13]

Three days later, Morgenthau sent President Roosevelt a copy of the plan White had prepared. In the accompanying letter he stated,

I am convinced that the launching of such a plan at this time has tremendous strategic as well as economic bearing. It seems to me that the time is ripe to dramatize our international economic objectives in terms of action which people everywhere will recognize as practical, powerful and inspiring. In the flush of success our enemies always dwelt upon their 'New Orders' for Europe and for Asia. There could be no more solid demonstration of our confidence that the tide is turning than the announcement of the formulation in concrete terms, and the preparation of specific instrumentalities for what really would be a New Deal in international economics.

If the President thought the idea was worth pursuing, Morgenthau would ask the Board of Economic Warfare (BEW), the State Department and the

Federal Reserve Board 'to work with the Treasury on these plans with a view to your calling a conference to be held in Washington of Finance Ministers of the United and Associated Nations'.[14]

President Roosevelt suggested that 'the studies now in progress should be continued with the State Department and the B.E.W. and the Export–Import Bank. You might speak to me about this again after you have done this and after you have got the opinions of the Secretary of State and the Under Secretary of State.'[15]

On 20 May Morgenthau sent a copy of the White plan to Secretary Hull, telling him about his correspondence with the President, and suggesting that Hull designate someone to represent the State Department at a meeting to be held shortly. Hull wrote back that he would 'be happy to have the Department of State take an active part in a study of your interesting proposal' and 'to have a continuing contact established between this work and the work of the now functioning Advisory Committee on Post-War Foreign Policy'. He designated Leo Pasvolsky and Herbert Feis to represent the Department.[16]

At a meeting of 25 May, called by Morgenthau, and at two meetings thereafter of an interdepartmental committee, White outlined his plan for a Fund and a Bank. There was unanimous feeling that the study should be pursued. The State Department recognised the primacy of the Treasury in monetary affairs, even though the plan encroached upon the field of foreign relations. The objectives and the purposes of the Fund and the Bank were desirable, but there was disagreement about the procedure to be followed.

Morgenthau's interest in the Stabilisation Fund had grown rapidly: 'In the first place it happens to be my own little pet theory . . . and in the second place, if it goes through, it will be the first post-war legislation.' The State Department's objections about procedure, he thought, were simply a pretext to prevent the Treasury from moving ahead. He decided to call another meeting to clear the air, and invited a number of people from different agencies who were close friends of Harry White and who, in the case of disagreement with the State Department, would be on the side of the Treasury.

One of these was Lauchlin Currie, administrative assistant to the President. 'Want to get in on a fight?' Morgenthau asked him. 'There's dirty work at the crossroads.'

'Really? Oh, really? Well, I'm always prepared to gang up with the Treasury against State.'

Both laughed. 'What a good nose you have', said Morgenthau. 'Harry and I need you , . . the idea is to kill it you see. Because we've got an idea and State hasn't, and they don't want anybody else to have any ideas.'[17]

White was now ready to move forward and to start discussions with representatives of other countries. He did not want, at this stage, to be confronted with Keynes. In order to strengthen his position, he first wanted to have 'a clear indication of the degree of agreement existing among the technical advisers of the various governments'. This would 'give important guidance to our own plans for the post-war period in the field of international financial and monetary problems'.[18]

Secretary Morgenthau felt that the time had come to invite the finance ministers of the Allied countries to send financial experts to Washington in order to discuss the proposals, and to prepare an agenda for a possible international conference. International financial relations, however, were the responsibility of the State Department, and he could not take any initiative without Secretary Hull's agreement.

On 2 July Secretary of Commerce Jones, Eccles and Goldenweiser of the Federal Reserve, and Acheson, Pasvolsky and Feis, representing the State Department, met in Morgenthau's office. White had also invited some of his close associates, whose role it was to confirm his interpretation and position in any disagreement with the State Department.

White started out the meeting by stating that the interdepartmental committee 'seemed to be in general agreement that the objectives were desirable'. With the exception of the representatives of the State Department, there also seemed to be agreement on the procedure. White proposed that the finance ministers of all friendly countries be invited to send technical experts to an informal meeting in Washington, which would consider any proposals for the establishment of an International Stabilisation Fund and a World Bank. No formal plan would be presented. Each expert could come to these meetings, make his own suggestions and explore whatever idea he wished. These meetings would be among technicians only. 'You and I couldn't attend', Morgenthau told Secretary Jones.

The State Department wanted to follow a different procedure, Acheson said. It had been in contact with the British and the Russians, and the feeling on all sides was that, before convening a large meeting, there should be bilateral discussions with representatives of the major powers. The British were becoming very nervous; they feared that a plan would be put before a large group of people, and that the plan would crystallise before they had an opportunity to discuss it privately and frankly.

For Morgenthau the main question to be resolved was, 'what has Mr. Hull got in mind? Does he want us to go ahead with this thing? Does he want us to kind of let the thing peter out, or just what has he got in mind? I mean, that is what I would like to know.' Secretary Hull would like the discussions to begin with Britain and the other principal powers, 'instead of getting everybody together at the same time', Acheson said.

And who would have to represent the United States in the talks with the British, Morgenthau wanted to know. Acheson thought he 'would like a committee of experts', but he did not know who should be on the committee.

It was decided that Acheson would find out whether Secretary Hull agreed to let the committee of which White was chairman start the talks with the British, the Russians, the Chinese, and so on. Despite an objection from one of White's assistants, who felt that 'We don't see why there must be an advance clearance with the British when we haven't even got a clear-cut proposal', Morgenthau decided that this was the procedure to follow:

> if those are Mr. Hull's wishes, I haven't got energy enough . . . to get into an interdepartmental fight. . . . This comes in the realm of foreign affairs. If after considering it and discussing it with his people that is the way he wants to do it, . . . why then I want to go along that way. But I just haven't got energy enough to raise four and a half billion dollars a month and to fight other departments at the same time.[19]

Secretary Hull agreed to the procedure as it had been outlined by Acheson: for the time being, the calling of a conference would be held in abeyance; informal consultations should be arranged with the British, the Russians, the Chinese, and some other of the more important nations; and the subject of the discussions should be broadened to include financial and monetary problems and institutions in general. It was also 'felt to be highly desirable to submit no American plan for consideration at the meeting, but rather to explore the possibilities of developing a plan within the technical meeting, which would then prepare an agenda for an international conference'.[20] At a meeting held with State Department officials on 11 July and under his chairmanship, White agreed to this procedure. He could now move ahead.

After six months of vain attempts to establish contact with the Americans and to obtain their agreement to discuss postwar planning, it now seemed that progress was finally being made. However, when Sir Ronald Campbell of the British embassy in Washington called on Secretary Hull on 14 August, he was told that

> this was not the time for formal conferences between any of our governments relating to post-war programs and policies, that there is bitter feeling against what is called neglect in prosecuting the war, when we are losing the war every day for the sake of sitting down and engaging in long-winded conversations and formal conferences about post-war policies and programs, which it is possible could and would never eventuate.

The Secretary said he would be glad to have 'any appropriate official in an entirely informal and unofficial manner sit down and talk with any economist, who may come here from Great Britain or any of the twenty-eight United Nations', but that 'there would be no decisions and merely the groundwork laid for conference and decision at a suitable time'. But he added that 'this Government is in the meantime desirous of any progress that can be made under the foregoing plan'.[21]

Phillips's comment was that 'Mr. Hull's statement to Sir R. Campbell' should not be 'taken as precluding informal discussions on financial matters with the United States Treasury, at any rate unless and until United States Treasury themselves take that view'.[22]

Dean Acheson also seemed to have lost interest. When Phillips told him that he had been instructed to take up with him some 'ideas regarding a stabilization fund which were being developed in London', he was told that 'financial matters were . . . under Assistant Secretary Berle . . . and Sir Frederick should discuss with Mr. Berle the procedure for developing his ideas on this matter'.[23] A few days later

> Acheson agreed that United States showed less eagerness to get on with discussions than was the case in December. . . . He thought that a number of internal questions of procedure will have to be settled before United States will be able to make progress. . . . They would probably set up an interdepartmental committee in which the Treasury and the Federal Reserve Board would be associated with the State Department.[24]

Shortly afterwards Phillips again called on Acheson, who told him that, although he had no precise information on the plans of the State Department, his guess was that the conversations would have to take place in Washington and not in London. The main difficulty in sending representatives to London lay in the choice of two or three people out of several departments who would expect to be represented. Any recommendation the State Department might make would be 'hotly opposed by Departments or individuals who resent having been left out'.

'Unless there is a complete change here,' Phillips cabled,

> which I do not expect, they will not send representatives to London. We have not been told anything concrete about state of their preparations on technical side for proposed discussion. . . . It is not possible to make a guess at the date when Americans will be ready to begin formal discussions, even in Washington, supposing you agreed to that. Obviously, it depends on the outcome of the struggle for power within the Administration. In view of the situation in Washington, I am strongly in favour of giving Morgenthau and Acheson, simultaneously, some advance outline of Clearing Union plan for two reasons: (1) this is our only means of making progress; (2) by so doing, we seize the opportunity to influence Americans before their ideas have passed out of the formative stage.[25]

There was reluctance in London to adopt this procedure, because, if the

Clearing Union plan was presented separately, and not as part of a general discussion, the Americans would criticise and oppose it, since, obviously, the United States, being the creditor country, would be on the giving end, while Britain, as the debtor country, would be only on the receiving end.[26]

Finally this reluctance was overcome, because of the strong desire to make progress. By the middle of July the Chancellor of the Exchequer had authorised Phillips to give the Americans an advance outline of the Clearing Union plan. Phillips indicated the general nature of the plan to Acheson and to Morgenthau. He cabled London, 'Morgenthau was greatly interested and asked me to explain the plan to him at length next week.'

On 4 August Keynes circulated a redraft that he considered 'suitable to be passed on to the Americans, the Dominions and (in due course) others outside Whitehall'. He gave it the subtitle 'Not Utopia, but Eutopia'. There were some small changes of phrasing and some drastic alterations of order, but the substance was not significantly changed.[27]

In London, it seemed that the time had come to send a high-ranking government official to Washington in order to find out what the Americans had in mind, and to discuss with them a variety of questions. Richard Law (later Lord Coleraine), then Parliamentary Under-Secretary of State ˙at the Foreign Office, who had taken considerable interest in postwar economic planning, seemed the most suitable. He would take with him several copies of the latest version of the Clearing Union plan, and discuss it with various departments in Washington. Shortly before he left, he met with Keynes, who told him that he

> thought that it would prove on the whole generally acceptable to Americans, more especially perhaps to New Dealers, but that Mr. Hull might possibly take the view that it was too grandiose. He thought however that the difficulty would be that until they had ended their departmental squabbles it would be extremely difficult for us to get the general agreement of the Administration even in principle to the plan. On the whole the best tactics would be for us 'to play in' with the State Department and the Treasury rather than with the B.E.W.

He did 'not despair of the appointment of Mr. Berle as officially in charge of any financial talks. . . . Though Berle knew nothing about finance he had a very quick brain and might soon pick it up.'

Keynes also emphasised the danger, in negotiating with Americans, of mistaking goodwill for an ability to deliver the goods. As regards the Clearing Union itself, Keynes thought that, if it was going to be a success, it should not be associated in the public mind with charity on an international scale, but should be considered as something which was likely to benefit all countries, including the creditor countries. Therefore, relief and reconstruction should be dealt with separately.[28]

Late in August the Clearing Union plan was handed to the State Department and the Treasury. Morgenthau, and particularly Harry White, had been pressing for a written version since Phillips had given them an outline of the plan. At about the same time, White gave Phillips a copy of the Stabilisation Fund plan, adding that it did not have the same status as the British plan, and that he gave it to him unofficially. Sir Frederick Leith-Ross reports that White gave him a copy of the document before Phillips received his.[29]

7
...And Takes the Lead

A full year had passed since Keynes had first circulated his 'Proposals for an International Currency Union' in the Treasury. A considerably revised version was now available in Washington, and it was agreed that conversations should start immediately. On 10 September 1942, the first discussion of the Keynes plan, now called 'Proposals for an International Clearing Union', took place at the State Department, in Mr Berle's office. Phillips and Opie, Pasvolsky and White were present. Berle said he understood that 'this was an unofficial document, though it had been thoroughly canvassed by the British Government. Sir Frederick Phillips said that this was true. ... It was informal in the sense that formal discussions under Article VII of the Lend—Lease Agreement had not yet commenced. But if they were to commence, this would be one of the formal documents promptly laid upon the table.' Berle then said that, while he understood that the discussions were strictly British—American, 'we had, in similar matters, found it highly desirable to draw in, when appropriate, other pivotal members of the United Nations, notably Russia and China. We felt it unwise to give any impression that the British and American Governments were making up a plan and then requiring everyone else to take it or leave it.' White stated that there were a number of projects circulating, covering more or less the same ground, from a number of quarters, 'and he thought it would be proper for us as a matter of strictly intellectual exploration to examine these ideas'. He emphasised that at this stage the discussions should be among experts, who would reach whatever agreement was possible on technical questions without regard to political difficulties which might come up as soon as the discussions went beyond them. Phillips noted that 'Berle and Pavolsky were in favour of discussing with us the Clearing Union as a basic document rather than discussing the subject matter at large, which seemed to be the inclination of Dr. White.' Turning to the substance of the document, Berle observed that he

> was happy to find that there was a considerable area in which Lord Keynes' memorandum coincided with some of the thinking which had been unofficially done in the Treasury. It was notable that as a point of agreement the Treasury had unofficially indicated the necessity of some central organization or institution to deal in international matters with certain phases of the problems of international finance; this also seemed to be the central idea in Lord Keynes' plan.[1]

At this point, White said that he had unofficially given to Phillips a copy of his memorandum on an international stabilisation fund and an international bank; 'that this document did not have the same standing that was provided by Keynes' memorandum; but that in a considerable measure they did agree in general range'. When Pasvolsky intervened to state that a number of other studies were being made, relating to the British balance of payments, and that they were near completion, White 'expressed his extreme scepticism of such work, which he regarded as love's labour lost', and stated that 'it was impossible to speculate fruitfully on the problem'.

Pasvolsky then said that there were a number of specific questions he would like to ask concerning the Keynes memorandum, and proposed to prepare a list for the next meeting.[2] Phillips sent a memorandum about the discussion to Keynes, who agreed that it 'was in fact not so bad'. He advised Phillips that 'the Allies are extremely interested to get a sight of it and anxious for a discussion. My own feeling is that the sooner we can allow private leakage to a few selected Allies, the better. Do you think there would be any objection to this after November 3? By that time the paper will surely be all over Washington, and the Allies will soon be getting it through American sources.' As for the conversations with the Dominions, they were not going too well. They did not know what the proposed meetings were all about, and appeared 'luke-warm and not much interested'. South Africa had advised that it could send only an observer, and a message had just been received from New Zealand 'that the war will last for years and years and that it is premature to discuss any post-war subjects'.[3] On 6 October, Berle gave Phillips the list of questions. He remarked that certain main points of the Clearing Union proposals were obvious:

> Britain and probably other countries would need goods and were faced with adverse balances. There were only two ways as yet worked out of settling these balances – gold, if gold is acceptable, and otherwise goods. Lord Keynes' proposals really came to giving to the proposed Clearing Union a method of creating money which could be used in settling these balances. In practice this would probably mean that we

would acquire considerable amounts of this new money which could be availed of only by taking goods.

When Phillips objected, saying that the money could be used for foreign investment, Berle said 'we realized this; so that what it really came to was a method by which American, and possibly other goods, could be made available to certain countries, notably Britain, on what was in fact though not in form a credit arrangement, terms of the credit being, of course, the degree of usefulness of this international currency'. This raised 'squarely a problem which the American Government would have to face, and in facing it would have to take account of Congressional opinion and public sentiment'.[4]

The questions themselves were either of a technical nature, or were concerned with aspects of the plan that were of particular interest to the Americans themselves. Would the fixed rates be maintained through a Stabilisation Fund or by an agency that would control the exchange transactions? How could the quantum of international currency be contracted to reduce 'effective world demand', as the plan mentioned? What was the contemplated order of magnitude of the total bancor quotas? What was the maximum amount of US dollars which the United States might be obligated to provide in return for bancors during the first five years of operation? Was it not likely that the countries that were expected to develop large creditor accounts with the Clearing Union would be in a minority, and that the debtor countries would have a voting majority and would control the policies?

Phillips sent the list of questions to London, and commented that the Americans seemed to 'indicate some fear that the Union would have Bank of Issue functions which would have an adverse reaction on the position of the dollar, and that the plan might involve the United States in lending an indefinite amount to the rest of the world, although the fact of lending might be thinly veiled'.[5] This aspect of the plan, which caused suspicion in the United States, did not escape the British officials, who, on the contrary, thought it highly desirable. R. H. Brand, who would later replace Phillips as the British Treasury representative in Washington, commented,

the Governing Board has enormous powers, equivalent to creating as much gold as it likes without any trouble or expense, and it clearly will have to exercise great discretion. It is true that the Union being a closed system, and therefore every debit being represented by a corresponding credit, it will be able always to honour its cheques. Nevertheless if one applies the test of whether the Union was solvent in the sense that if it was liquidated its creditors could be paid off in real wealth of some kind, e.g., gold or other currencies which would be sold at their face value or somewhere near it, its solvency would depend on the care with which its advances had been made. . . . Therefore, much would depend

on the ability of its management. It offers a wonderful possibility of its
board coming to the assistance of weaker countries, so to speak, on the
back of the stronger countries without the latter knowing it, or at any
rate without Congresses and Parliaments knowing what was happen-
ing.[6]

On 13 October 1942, Morgenthau and White left for England, and for
two weeks they travelled around, visiting aircraft and other war-equipment
factories, inspecting military and naval installations, looking at bombed
areas, and meeting with General Eisenhower's staff and with British
officials. One of the purposes of the trip was to prepare the currency
arrangements for the impending landings in North Africa. It was not
intended that the postwar currency plans should be discussed. But
Ambassador Winant, who had met Morgenthau and White on the day of
their arrival in London, felt that this would be an excellent opportunity to
bring White and Keynes together. He obtained Morgenthau's agreement to
a private discussion, and asked Penrose to arrange it. Keynes had an
important meeting in the afternoon, and White had to leave in the evening.
Penrose recalled, 'When I mentioned Keynes's engagement in the afternoon, Dr. White, who was as much of a prima donna in his way as Keynes,
said abruptly, "I don't want to talk with anyone except Keynes." '
Keynes's engagement was cancelled and a private meeting was held at the
embassy. Winant, Penrose and two other officials were also present.

The exchange of views was left almost wholly to Keynes and White. It
was lively and at times somewhat acrimonious but exceedingly fruitful.
There was a substantial area of agreement but there were also sharp
differences. Keynes thought the fund proposed by White would not be
large enough. White considered it would be impossible to get more, if as
much, out of Congress for the U.S. share. This led to some controversy
over the question whether the capital should be subscribed or created as
a new issue, as Keynes proposed. Keynes vigorously attacked the idea
of subscribed capital but White held to it as the only approach that
Congress would accept. He also attacked as politically impossible the
proposal of Keynes to use the Clearing Union to finance relief and
reconstruction or any part of it. Keynes made it clear that the proposal
that a four-fifths majority vote should be required before a change in a
country's exchange rate could be made would not be acceptable to
London. Britain, because of its precarious financial position, must retain
considerable freedom to act unilaterally in such matters if necessary, he
maintained. Differences arose on the voting system and other points.
Finally Keynes argued for direct negotiations between the U.S. and
U.K. alone or possibly with the Dominions and the Soviet Union added,
while White maintained that this would create suspicion of an Anglo-
Saxon financial 'gang-up'. Keynes heatedly argued that, the subject

matter being complicated, it was essential that the U.S. and U.K. should work out a plan themselves, invite the Russians, in order to allay suspicion, and perhaps the Dominions and French, to join, and then set it up and invite the rest of the world to join. ... At the close of the meeting ... both White and Keynes agreed that as a result of the exchange of views they would return to their colleagues with proposals for modifications on a number of points.[7]

Although the meeting had been entirely unofficial, since the State Department had not given permission to start conversations on postwar economic planning, both White and Keynes had been given an opportunity to state their position. A few days after this meeting, on 13 November, the State Department advised the British that it was now ready to embark on exploratory and informal discussions. The three main questions to be discussed would be monetary arrangements, commercial policy and international long-term investment.[8]

After the meeting with Keynes in London, Harry White disappeared from the scene for several months, and the conversations were carried on in the State Department. Whereas White had approached the postwar problem from a monetary viewpoint, the view held by a strong group in the State Department was that the problems were fundamentally 'those of trade relations (except perhaps in the immediate post-war period) and that monetary arrangements will be of no avail unless the problems on the trade side are solved. This is not to under-estimate the importance of the monetary arrangements.'[9]

On 25 November, Phillips sent Berle a revised version of the Clearing Union plan, and Keynes's answers to the questions asked by the State Department. On the method to be used to maintain fixed exchange rates, he stated that it was 'certainly intended that member Governments should be required to take active steps to keep quoted rates of exchange within gold points or their equivalent', but he did not indicate what steps he had in mind. He agreed that 'it may be the case that the scheme should be amended so as to provide the Governing Board with powers to check an undesired inflationary tendency in effective world demand'. In order to allay the fears expressed by the State Department that creditor countries would be exposed to an unlimited liability, Keynes explained in his revised version that it was only at first sight that this seemed to be the case. 'The liability of an individual member is determined, not by the quotas of the other members, but by its own policy in controlling its favourable balance of payments.' All that was being asked of it was that it maintain, for just so long as it chose, a bancor credit for as much of the surplus of its balance of payments as it did not choose to employ in any other way. To meet the objection that it would be the debtor countries who would control the policies of the Clearing Union, Keynes proposed that in certain cases the voting rights of the debtor members should be reduced and those of the creditor members increased. On the other hand he stated, 'It is quite impossible to forecast which countries are likely to develop creditor accounts.'[10] Sir Frederick Phillips reviewed these answers with Mr Berle, Mr Pasvolsky and Mr Feis, who felt that, while some of them were satisfactory, others had to be left for subsequent discussion. The US representatives also needed more time to study the Clearing Union proposals. When Keynes received the report on this meeting, he became suspicious. The discussion 'suggests a very harmless, indeed, almost too harmless an atmosphere. Nothing difficult or dangerous seems to arise there. . . . This report gives me the impression that Feis is an advocate on our side, that Pasvolsky understands it all only to a limited extent, and that Berle, though friendly, is extremely on the cautious side.' The State Department had promised counter-suggestions on certain points. Keynes was not very hopeful that this would clarify the position: 'Unless these counter-suggestions contain a surprise, either favourable or unfavourable, the question arises "what next?".' Keynes was well aware of the fact that the State Department did not consider the Clearing Union or White's Stabilisation Fund as a cure-all. He had been working on a plan for the international regulation of primary products. He sent a copy of it to Phillips, advising him that it had not been given official status, but that he did 'not see any reason to suppose that Ministers will withhold that mild degree of blessing with which they are accustomed to allow us to take the next step — in this case of showing it to the Americans'.

In the same letter, he advised Phillips that Whitehall was working on a plan for commercial policy, although he himself was not in close touch with it. He expected that on this document there would be much controversy and delay on the part of ministers. It might well be that Whitehall would decide 'that it is not advisable for us to take the initiative'.

> Whether the official document, when we get it, will be in the most advisable form for submission to the Americans I personally am far from sure. On the positive side I am in considerable sympathy with Hubert Henderson that the technique of import restriction has many advantages over tariffs, particularly for this country, and that we should not willingly relinquish it. On the other hand, it is not easy to devise a method or formula which is entirely clear of the charge of lending itself to discriminatory methods. Efforts are being made now to produce a non-discriminatory technique. At any rate it would, I hope, be made clear that, if we ask for the continuance of import restrictions, we shall put it forward as merely an alternative way of attaining the same result as tariffs and will promise to provide that import restrictions will be used only on occasions when it is possible to apply them in an entirely non-discriminatory manner. On the question of preferences it would be interesting to know what you think of the politics of the

matter.

He was also thinking about international investment:

> Is Harry White giving any sign of life here? I still remain of the opinion
> that, in this matter at any rate, it is better for the Americans to take the
> initiative. I am wondering, however, whether it would be helpful to
> take that half of Harry White's draft which relates to international
> investment and try to lick it into shape. Would Harry resent this, or
> would he appreciate it?

The question now was how to proceed in order to prevent 'the post-war
economic discussions being hopelessly bogged'. One alternative was 'to jog
along by the same sort of very informal procedure . . . handing over any
document as soon as it is ready; proceeding piece-meal by very tentative
measures and gingerly steps'. This would be rather hopeless. 'Moreover, at
the end of it all, we should only have dealt with a few young gentlemen at
the State Department and will have failed to reach any sort of definitive
conclusions.' A second alternative was that a small British deputation
should join Phillips in Washington 'with the object of having a continuous,
more or less formal conference with some corresponding American body,
occupying at least a month. On our side, that would not present any
particular difficulty. But is there a sufficient prospect of the Americans
setting up a similar body for us to deal with?' This procedure required that
two essential conditions be met. 'The State Department should be
prepared to discuss . . . on an authoritative basis, with the intention that
any results which are reached would be submitted to the two Governments
in a perfectly formal manner.' The second condition was that

> the body in question should be really representative of the Administra-
> tion as a whole, and not merely a private tea-party of the State
> Department. If the President deliberately hands over the whole post-
> war matters to the State Department, perhaps with some assessors from
> the Treasury and elsewhere, well and good. But it should be clear that
> we are dealing with the Administration as a whole and are not open to
> subsequent attack by some other Department in Washington which was
> not represented and thinks it ought to have been.

A third, and perhaps better, alternative, would be to revive an idea which
had previously been turned down. The two governments would appoint a
joint Anglo-American Commission of small numbers to prepare some ideas
for consideration in Washington and London.

> The Governments would, of course, be in no way committed to the
> Commission. The fact of the Commission's appointment would be

public. They would treat the job as a whole-time one carried out partly in Washington and partly in London, occupying them from three to six months. . . . When the Commission had reported, then its conclusions would, if the two Governments so decided, be put before a wider body of Powers for their consideration. . . . Progress could be made to a fairly high degree of finality without the Governments having to take premature responsibility. Yet the existence of the body would provide them with a good explanation to the public, if they were charged with not getting anything done. This procedure would perhaps lift the whole matter out of the rut, prevent it from getting bogged down and give it a more authoritative position.

It was important, Keynes felt, that the public should know about the plans:

We have to bear it constantly in mind that, in the long run, large economic projects cannot possibly come into existence except with the aid of an instructed and educated public opinion. . . . The public will not, of course, be able to pass judgment on any of the details. But they will be influenced by the general atmosphere. The preparation of the right atmosphere must not be overlooked; and we must not think that we can get very far merely by drafting very sensible details.[11]

While Keynes was thus trying to make progress with the Americans, he had to cope with criticism of the Clearing Union in London. Sir Hubert Henderson kept stating that it was necessary to have equilibrium in the balance of payments, and that the Clearing Union by itself did not provide the solution.[12] He also opposed the 'Project of a Commercial Union' prepared by the Board of Trade. He felt that 'large schemes of international co-operation have already been formulated on the British side for the problems of monetary policy and the regulation of primary commodities. I believe . . . we should allow the Americans to put forward any proposals that they may be able to make in the field of commercial policy.'

Representatives of the Dominions and India were equally critical of some aspects of the Clearing Union plan. At meetings held at the end of December 1942, they criticised the role and privileges of the 'founder states'. They also objected to the fact that countries other than the United States and Britain would be presented with a plan they practically had to take or leave. It was doubted that the Clearing Union would be of much use during the immediate postwar period, when many countries would require relief. It was also suggested that economic blocs such as the sterling area should be discouraged, as militating against the spirit of the Clearing Union, and that it should be explicitly stated that the world would be on a bancor and not on a gold standard. Some of these objections had to be taken into serious consideration.[13]

On 9 January 1943, Phillips advised London that none of the alternatives suggested by Keynes would be acceptable to the State Department. Instead of negotiating with the British first, on the basis of the plans that had been exchanged, they wanted to start discussions with experts from Russia, China and other countries, in the expectation that a plan would emerge. If London wished to submit the Clearing Union plan to the Russians and the Chinese, there would be no objection.[14] This, Keynes noted,

> is far from fragrant in my nostrils. Once again, apparently, the Americans are running away from taking up any line and would propose rather to put up the Harry White plan, which carries no authority with it and to which they are in no way committed. In this way they can hope to exhaust our energies boxing with a man of straw. . . . Finally . . . the meeting, when it takes place, will not be purely Anglo-American, which is what we have been aiming at hitherto, but polyglot. This is a bad plan if we want to get anything workable. But, if we have successfully canvassed the Allied Governments, and if there is a Canadian representative, it might not be too bad. The suggestion makes it all the more advisable to get hold of the Allies as soon as possible. On the other hand, to bring in Russian and Chinese representatives at this early stage, before the British and the Americans have cleared their own ideas between themselves, seems a stupid, futile notion.[15]

Keynes's conclusion was that the next step should be a conference with the Allies occupying the latter half of February. Sir David Waley felt, however, that, before taking this step, it would be advisable to find out through the embassy in Washington 'whether the U.S. are prepared to go forward in a business-like way with post-war economic talks or whether they think it is wiser to put off any real discussion for a while. A frank talk would clear the air.'[16]

On 30 January the Treasury cabled Phillips, advising him that it was intended to give a copy of the Clearing Union plan to the Russian and Chinese governments, and to discuss it with the European Allies. It was hoped there would be no objection in Washington.[17] On 1 February the State Department sent a copy of the Stabilisation Fund plan to the British embassy with the comment that 'These documents were prepared by the technical staff of the United States Treasury in consultation with the technical experts of other departments of this Government. They are intended to serve as a basis for discussion rather than represent, at this stage, an expression of the official views of this Government. Like copies are being sent to the Russian Ambassador, to the Chinese Ambassador . . . .' The plan would also be sent to other nations, with the suggestion that they send their technical experts to Washington and 'discuss with our technical experts the feasibility of international monetary cooperation along the lines suggested in these documents or along any other lines they may wish to suggest'.[18]

The news of the action taken by the State Department caused frustration in London. It would now become impossible to avoid 'the position in which two competing proposals will have to come under common review'. Phillips was asked to advise the State Department that London considered it essential to delay the communication of the United States document to any country other than Russia and China, until 'agreed plans for future procedure have been formulated. ... The American Memorandum and the Clearing Union Plan have a great deal in common and are not so far apart as to preclude the usefulness of trying to conflate them. This is the course which we should much prefer.'[19]

When Phillips put this suggestion before the State Department, he was told that the United States intended to proceed with the meetings as contemplated. The conversations would be limited to monetary arrangements. In London, this was considered highly unsatisfactory. Neither the Russians nor the Chinese had sufficient technical competence to help reconcile the two plans. This made it even more important to put the Clearing Union plan as quickly as possible into the hands of the Allied finance ministers in London.[20] As Keynes saw it,

> The next step is for us to decide in our own minds what attitude we are going to take to the White draft. The alternatives are: that we make yet one more attempt to get an agreed Anglo-American version covering the objects of both proposals; or we can agree to allow the discussion to proceed on the basis of the White draft; or we can press for the Clearing Union to be taken as a basis for discussion; or we can have a set-to fight between the two approaches at the meeting of experts.

Before taking a decision it was necessary to make an analysis of the White draft, and this was 'a fairly heavy job, which one cannot do satisfactorily unless one can get some uninterrupted time at it'. It would also be useful to find out which of the two drafts was likely to appeal most to the Europeans. 'But before committing ourselves definitely to a major monkey-house, I should like to get the preliminary reactions of those monkeys who will be optional guests.'[21]

On 17 February the Treasury cabled Phillips, asking him to inform Berle that 'we are communicating Clearing Union draft to Russian and Chinese Governments and intend shortly to communicate it informally to Allied financial experts in London. We will not do so however until we hear the result of your meeting . . . .' The same day, Phillips cabled from Washington that the White plan would be circulated to the Latin American and European Allies as well as to the Dominions. The Chinese had already agreed to send experts. The Russians had merely asked for more copies.

There was no objection to communicating the Clearing Union also to the Allies. Phillips had 'put it to Berle strongly that we had been left in ignorance of their views on Clearing Union since giving them our answers to their questions at the end of November. The promised further discussion had not taken place and United States had gone off at a tangent from procedure that had been developing since May'. Berle agreed that it might be useful to discuss between them the differences and similarities between the two plans, and it was decided to meet again the following week.[22] Although the procedure envisaged by the Americans seemed odd, it was felt in London that there was no choice but to go ahead in a similar manner.

Keynes, meanwhile, had found time to study the White plan. In a memorandum dated 18 February 1943 and entitled 'The Berle Plan', he stated that he could not make up his mind about the Berle Memorandum from a technical point of view unless there were further elucidation of it. He understood it to be a combination of Tripartite Agreement with American Stabilisation Fund principles.

> If that is correct it would appear to be incompatible with Exchange Control on the British or continental model, where there is only one eventual holder and source of exchange and consequently no exchange market in which a Stabilisation Fund can intervene. The only innovations, as compared with the pre-war period, appear to be the provisions for controlling capital movements, apparently by 'freezing' machinery, and for liquidating 'blocked balances'.

The basic idea of the Stabilisation Fund was a 'limited liability' subscription, while his own plan aimed at an International Clearing Union 'with a wide use of credit'. As Keynes saw it, some of the major differences were as follows.

Stabilisation Fund – Unitas	*Clearing Union – Bancor*
1. Initial quotas levied by way of a general subscription of capital.	1. Initial quotas provided by a creation of international credit.
2. Quotas represent a right to purchase the deposits of other members.	2. Quotas represent a claim to overdraw on international account.
3. Presumption that individuals remain free to deal in exchange with one another for 'current account' purposes.	3. Requirement that exchange transactions be centralised with the Clearing Bank through national controls.
4. Control over capital movements in principle, but in practice by *ex post facto* use of	4. Control over capital movements implying prior scrutiny of all transactions and preventive

correctives.

5. Sanctions provided against the weaker party.

6. General intention to share existing foreign resources, but to stop short of expansion, whether general or particular.

7. Countries ruined by war get nothing but the mobilisation of blocked balances.

action.

5. Correctives deliberately applied (at least equally) to the stronger party.

6. General intention to be 'expansionist'.

7. Special attention paid to smaller and poorer countries.

Keynes also attached a list of questions to be submitted to Washington.

Sir Wilfrid Eady thought it would be dangerous, now that it was established that the two plans were radically different in approach, to attempt a compromise statement: 'any premature suggestion that we think a compromise is possible would merely mean slight modifications of the Harry White paper'.[23]

In a memorandum to the Chancellor of the Exchequer, Sir David Waley expressed his dissatisfaction with 'the preposterous procedure of the Americans'. The White proposal was difficult, obscure and technical, but the Americans intended to see experts of each country, as they came to Washington, and then, in the light of those discussions, decide whether or not to hold a conference. It was necessary that the representatives of the United Nations would also have an opportunity to discuss the Clearing Union. 'It will, of course, be very unfortunate, if the impression is created that the rival plans are being put up for auction, but there again we cannot help ourselves.'[24]

Thus, while in Washington Phillips and Opie would continue to analyse with the State Department the similarities and differences between the two plans, the experts of various countries would be invited to discuss the main points of the two drafts with the Treasury. This would reveal whether they had any preference for one or the other. On 23 February, Phillips advised London that there would be no objection from the State Department to an early circulation of the Clearing Union plan, but that it should be presented 'not as a Government pronouncement but as being on expert level. Berle agreed that conversations between the British and the American experts might take place, although this must be done without appearing to present other nations with a fait accompli.'[25]

A few days later, copies of the Clearing Union plan were sent to the Allies. When Keynes met Ambassador Maisky at a party given in London by the Russians, he mentioned that a paper was being handed to Molotov, and 'begged that they would send us one or two people from Moscow with whom we could really get into conversation. Maisky, as usual, grinned and said that all would be much easier if a second front was going on'.[26]

Keynes himself felt that, since Russia had a policy of state trading, and exercised complete control over imports and exports, she could maintain her bancor position depending on the policy she deliberately adopted. The proposals involved no interference with the internal policy of the country. 'Since Russia is the second largest gold producer in the world and possesses large stocks of gold, the provision which ensures her a market for it is particularly valuable: Failing this, Russia can have no assurance that at some time her gold reserves and her gold producing capacity will become useless to her.' It was not essential that Russia become a member. However, 'it would be extremely unfortunate if she were to stay out since this is an experiment in international government, in which it would be valuable for the whole world that she would play her part, particularly as the Clearing Union looks like being the pivot round which other international organisations on the economic side are likely to move.'[27]

Early in 1943, although Keynes had been working on the Clearing Union for almost a year and a half, and White on his Stabilisation Fund for more than a full year, nothing of these activities had become known outside the two governments. It was Harry White who first outlined before a broader audience his concept of a postwar monetary order. The occasion was the annual meeting of the American Economic Association.

Addressing a group of economists, he stressed the need for international co-operation in order to achieve currency stability. This could best be achieved through 'an international agency organized by the governments of the world' to provide capital for relief and reconstruction; an international organisation to provide the means of maintaining stability; and a mechanism 'whereby such changes in exchange rates as may from time to time become necessary can be made in an orderly manner by multilateral agreement'.

When a country's balance of payments is in severe disequilibrium for causes that do not appear to be temporary, then altering the value of that currency in terms of other currencies is one of the numerous ways in which the disequilibrium might be corrected. Which of the several methods available to a country is best suited to accomplish the desired objective depends on the cause of the disequilibrium, the circumstances, the country, the time, and the situation in certain other countries.

He expressed the belief that new agencies 'with powers and resources adequate to handle the complex and grave problems with which we shall be confronted' were called for: 'I believe the United Nations should establish an international stabilization fund and an international bank.'

The success of international monetary co-operation would depend primarily on the participation and leadership of the United States.

The dollar is the one great currency in whose strength there is universal confidence. It will probably become the cornerstone of the postwar structure of stable currencies. The United States holds the greater part of the world's resources of gold and foreign exchange. These resources must be available to give assurance of universal strength and confidence in the stability of currencies.

Stabilisation of currencies was not an end in itself, but only a means to full employment and a rising standard of living. 'Nevertheless, stable currencies are an important element in the healthy environment which is indispensable to the attainment of that full employment and rising standard of living everywhere.'[28]

In London on 2 February, the Chancellor of the Exchequer, Sir Kingsley Wood, in a speech delivered in the House of Commons, gave in vague outline the currency system the Treasury wished to see established after the war. He declared himself opposed to bilateralism and blocked accounts, but also to speculation in foreign exchanges and international short-term movements of funds. Not once was the word 'gold' mentioned. He visualised the creation of an international monetary authority which would provide orderly and agreed methods of determining the value of the various currencies and would eliminate the danger that countries would seek by unilateral action to restore their competitive position through exchange depreciation. Rules would be set up to 'free the international monetary system from those arbitrary, unpredictable and undesirable influences that operated in the past as the result of large-scale, uncoordinated speculative movements of short-term capital'.[29]

The speech caused a good deal of comment, and the financial writers in the press tried to read into it more than the Chancellor had said. *The Economist* commented, 'The mechanism thus envisaged is obviously of the multilateral clearing type, operated by central authorities in each participating country, and subject to the control of an international authority whose decisions would clearly have to be backed by sanctions of some form if they were to be effective.'[30] In the *News Chronicle* the City editor stated, 'The only alternative left is bilateral clearing agreements between pairs of countries. No doubt many of these now existing will survive, and many more will be created. But a multitude of bilateral arrangements will soon become unworkable, and will almost inevitably coalesce in one or more 'multilateral' associations . . . .'[31]

On 4 March the Treasury announced in London that conferences were being held with Allied finance ministers to discuss currency arrangements in Europe after the war, and other postwar financial questions of common interest. Representatives of Russia, China and of the Dominions had attended. On the same day, Secretary Morgenthau sent copies of the Stabilisation Fund proposal to the finance ministers of thirty-seven countries. He invited them to send 'one or more of your technical experts to Washington . . . to discuss with our technical experts the feasibility of international monetary cooperation along the lines suggested therein, or along any other lines you may wish to suggest'.[32]

Muffled echoes soon escaped from the shuttered rooms in which the discussions were held, and it soon leaked out that a 'Keynes plan' had been distributed to the European Allies. Rumours about an American plan on the same subject caused speculation and curiosity. Since few details were known, the comments in the press were inevitably inaccurate. Following these leaks, a Member of Parliament put down a question on the postwar proposals, which the Chancellor of the Exchequer would have to outline in so far as they were not by nature confidential. He could refuse to answer, or dodge the question, but a responsible minister could not go on declining information indefinitely. The Chancellor wished to tell the House of Commons that tentative plans for monetary stabilisation had been worked out, but before doing so he wanted to obtain the agreement of the State Department. When, on 15 March, Phillips and Opie put the question before Berle and Pasvolsky, they were told that 'I did not see that we could ask them not to publish their own Plan if they so desired.' Phillips inquired whether the Americans would not publish their plan also, but White, who was present, stated that the matter had not been cleared with President Roosevelt, and that he would take it up with Secretary Morgenthau.[33] Two days later, Morgenthau sent a memorandum to the President, suggesting that 'To avoid unnecessary and troublesome rumors, I believe it would be desirable to inform· the Congressional leaders of our studies.' Following the publication of a number of articles in the American press, several Congressmen had asked Morgenthau questions about the postwar plans, of which they had not been informed. Morgenthau also suggested to the President that a press release be issued, but Roosevelt disagreed.[34]

When, on 24 March, Phillips went again to the State Department, Berle told him 'that they had definitely decided not to publish their plan'. Phillips had also asked, at Keynes's suggestion, whether Keynes could discuss the Stabilisation Fund in London with the finance ministers from the Allied countries. This was not acceptable, because 'although indeed an observer from [the] United States Embassy was present, there was no-one who could explain or defend [the] point of view of United States experts'. This was confirmed by White, who suggested 'that any discussion of the Stabilization Fund proposal by the Allied Finance Ministers in London should be postponed until after we have had an opportunity to carry on explanatory discussions here in Washington. Needless to say, we will avoid consideration of the Clearing Union in our discussions until you have had an ample opportunity to conduct your explanatory discussions.'[35]

On 24 March, Phillips called on Morgenthau, to discuss, among other subjects, the publication of the British plan. Morgenthau 'did not seem well acquainted with the course of events'. He indicated, however, that he was not in agreement with the decisions already made, and urged Phillips to cable the Chancellor 'to consider whether [a] wiser course would not be to postpone publishing until experts have met in Washington'. He feared that, if the British and American plans were published separately, opinion might harden and agreement be made more difficult. 'If things are not handled with the greatest care, the goose may never lay the .egg.' Phillips thought it might be difficult to meet Secretary Morgenthau's request, given the fact that the Chancellor had in the meantime made a promise that the plan would be published, and that Prime Minister Churchill had referred to it in a broadcast. The procedure suggested by Morgenthau would result in indefinite postponement of the publication, since discussions were to be carried out separately in London and in Washington. There had already been leaks as regards the British plan and further leaks about both plans were not impossible. He would, however, communicate the message to the Chancellor.[36]

The Chancellor 'considered most carefully whether it would be possible to postpone publication', but feared

> that it would be quite impossible to postpone . . . for more than a week or ten days. This would only lead to a series of daily questions in Parliament with requests for reasons why publication is delayed despite statements made by Prime Minister and Chancellor. Also there are statements almost every day in the press purporting to describe Clearing Union Plan and attitude taken up by various parties in regard to it.

He would emphasise clearly that the British plan was put forward as a basis for discussion, along with any other plans.[37]

Morgenthau asked to postpone publication at least until 8 April. He was consulting with the President, and also had to consult a Senate committee on the desirability of the publication of the American plan. On 1 April the President definitely decided against publication of the Stabilisation Fund plan. Morgenthau had strongly recommended publication, but after meeting with Roosevelt he had to tell White,

> Now on stabilization, Harry, I told the President about going up before the Senate, and the President is very emphatic — no publication of the American plan. He said: 'These things are too early. We haven't begun to win the war.' He said, 'All these plans — it is all right to talk about them. What the English want to publish is all right.' . . . I talked quite a lot about it to the press . . . I told them I was going up before the Senate; about the technicians coming here; that everything is very tentative; that we are going ahead, exploratory, so forth and so on.[38]

Indeed, at his press conference earlier that day, Morgenthau had announced that a United Nations Monetary Conference would be held in

Washington, and that tentative proposals for the stabilisation of currencies had already been presented to a number of countries. He also disclosed that the State Department and the Treasury had held currency discussions with thirty-eight nations.

Because of the President's decision, Morgenthau now reluctantly had to agree that the British plan would be published alone. In London, the necessary arrangements were made to publish the Clearing Union plan on 8 April. 'Necessary steps will be taken to see that no summaries of it appear before.' With precaution and careful timing, the government would see to it that publication took place according to plan.

Keynes had closely followed the reaction of the British and American press. He was convinced that publication of the plans was essential, and he seems to have appraised in a realistic way the chances of his own plan:

On the tactics of the matter I do not feel dissatisfied. The sooner steam is blown off, the better. No harm that some of the early comment should be based on misconception. But the main point is probably this. Looked at from the worst point of view, so far as the Clearing Union aspect is concerned, I think all this enormously increases Harry White's chances. The real risk has always been that the U.S.A. would do nothing. At the present stage the main point is to create an atmosphere in which that becomes extremely difficult. It is very difficult to predict at the present stage how the two schemes will be thought to compare by the time that the American experts and responsible commentators have really got down to them. But, in any case, the Harry White scheme represents a big advance, and if it turns out that that is the sort of set-up which appeals to people, it will not be too difficult to make something of it. But it is a long time too soon even to breathe a suggestion of compromise. When public opinion has fully disclosed itself, one can then think again. The main point at the present stage is that America should get itself committed to *some* scheme.[39]

8
The Plans are Published

On 5 April 1943, a few days after President Roosevelt decided against any publication, the London *Financial News* carried on its front page full details of the American plan. In addition to a very compact and accurate summary, there were many authentic provisions of the White plan. The text was immediately cabled back to the United States by press correspondents.

In Whitehall there was considerable embarrassment. It could not be established where Paul Einzig had obtained the information, but certain details seemed to indicate it had been taken from the draft sent by the US Treasury early in March to the finance ministers of thirty-seven countries. When Phillips saw Morgenthau that day, he was visibly on the defensive, although Morgenthau assured him that he 'wasn't for a moment thinking that the British Treasury would' have been part of this. 'There are repeated rumors that the leak was from an alleged embassy in London', said Phillips. 'Would you write it on a piece of paper for me?' Morgenthau asked. Phillips wrote down the name. 'This thing ought to be a lesson for us', said Morgenthau, 'that anything that we want to do that is really important, we just can't take all these countries into our confidence.' 'I am afraid so', said Phillips.[1]

In London, the government investigated for quite some time the leak to the *Financial News*, but could not identify the source. There was no press censorship, and newspapers were entitled to take their own view of matters which should be made public. Paul Einzig had often criticised the secrecy in which the financial discussions had been conducted, and he might plead that he and his paper were serving the public interest in bringing matters out into the open. 'The whole matter is rather a pity because Einzig . . . is an acute critic and says some very useful things in the *Financial News*. . . . But because of his unreliability we cannot make any

76

use of him.'[2]

At his press conference, on the day of the publication in London, reporters tackled Morgenthau about the leakage. 'Someone has broken faith', he said. 'I have good reason to know it is not the British, but you must remember there are ten Governments in exile over there. It was most embarrassing for me to hear the broadcast of my proposals before I met the Senate Committee and to realize that I had been scooped myself.'[3] That afternoon Morgenthau outlined before the Senate committees his tentative postwar currency-stabilisation plan.

On 7 April 1943, the American plan was released in Washington and the British plan in London. Neither acknowledged the existence of, or made any reference to, the other. The financial writers, and the press in general, devoted a good deal of space to analysis and comment. The conditions in which the plans had been made public inevitably resulted in an appearance of Anglo-American rivalry, despite sincere denials by both governments. As a result, much of the press comment concentrated on the level of power politics and competition. The American press generally noted that each plan was inclined to serve the dominant interest of the country where it originated, the British proposals emphasising trade power, and the American plan emphasising gold power. The more influential papers, mostly conservative and Republican, criticised both plans, more on the ground of Keynes's reputation as 'father of New Deal financing' than from examination of the proposals themselves.

Whether expert and balanced, or clamorous and superficial, press comments in both countries tended to take a stand on patriotic ground rather than on the intrinsic merit of each plan. It was generally noted that the international accounts of both countries would be very different after the war, the United States being a creditor country with a tremendous export potential, while Britain would be a debtor, unable for a number of years to export sufficiently to pay for its imports, while at the same time having to liquidate outstanding debts.

Both plans, it was noted, assumed that equilibrium of the balances of payments was possible. Their central aim was to provide temporary credit facilities for countries faced with a deficit. Both plans contemplated that this assistance would be limited, and that the deficit countries would make the necessary adjustments to bring their balance of payments back to equilibrium before their credit line was exhausted. In the long run, they would work only if the nations' balances could be brought into equilibrium by the methods contemplated, and if these methods worked quickly enough to keep the borrowing within the predetermined limits.

In Whitehall, not all were convinced. A memo written by a member of the Committee on Reconstruction Policy, and dated 7 April, reveals much scepticism. The author admitted that an 'international clearing bank will undoubtedly be valuable in strengthening international banking co-operation and in teaching the habit of internationalism in monetary control.

. . . There does, however, seem to me to be a danger that the theoretical beauty of the plan will cause its practical merits to be exaggerated and thus lead not only to disappointments but also to errors in practice.' He also detected an incompatibility between the monetary policy and the commercial policy the government was planning: 'an international monetary system, with the abandonment of central banking sovereignty, is consistent only with an international system of trade control, with abandonment of commercial sovereignty; and this is certainly not in prospect'.[4]

Keynes himself was very pleased with the developments. He noted that the European Allies, without exception, 'not only prefer the Clearing Union, but prefer it very strongly, for what I, at any rate, would regard as sound fundamental reasons'. The Allies were perplexed on how to tackle the Americans about it, and several of them had asked Keynes's advice. He told them that, while they could let the American Treasury know how much they preferred the Clearing Union, they

> should avoid controversy or advocacy at this stage, should probe the White plan with questions rather than objections, and should urge that it ought not be too difficult to find a means of harmonising the plans if a general conference of experts could be called together for the purpose. . . . If we only could persuade the Americans that London is a better climate than Washington in summer. But I suppose that is hopeless.

Keynes still felt that 'After all, the Harry White plan is not a firm offer.' The real danger was that there would be no plan at all, or that Congress would run away from the American plan itself.

> No harm, therefore, at least so it seems to me, if the Americans work up a certain amount of patriotic fervour for their own version. Much can be done in detail hereafter to improve it. . . . Isn't it a very good thing, for the same kind of reason that we have got to the point of publishing the two plans? If in fact we had managed to reach a compromise behind the scenes, isn't it about ten to one that Congress would have turned it down? The present tactics allow steam to be blown off at an early stage without injury to anyone. We must get over our teething troubles in public. We must know the worst, if there is a worst, about Congress at an early stage. . . . So, in spite of grumbling, I do not really feel at all discontented at the general course things have been taking.[5]

On 12 May the Chancellor of the Exchequer, Sir Kingsley Wood, explained to Parliament the major features of both plans. He was clearly anxious to avoid any invidious comparisons; what counted was not so much the merits of the Keynes plan as the possibility of a working compromise which would embody the best features of both plans. The authors of the two plans had genuinely attempted to see an international problem from an international point of view, and tried to develop an international solution. During the debate that followed, inevitably only the surface of the problem was touched. This was a highly technical subject, and members preferred to state enlightened generalities, rather than venture into the deeper waters of economic analysis. Members generally made it clear that they preferred the British plan, because it was more flexible, simpler, less tied to gold. Although there was no dissent from the Chancellor's view that gold should have some place in the new system, several members criticised the American plan as representing a return to the gold standard. It also interfered too much with national sovereignty; each country should be allowed to regulate its own affairs, including exchange control, and not be subject to the dictates of an international organisation. Other members felt that monetary plans were premature, and should follow instead of precede trade and investment plans.[6]

On 18 May, Keynes, lately ennobled as Baron Keynes of Tilton, made his maiden speech at the House of Lords. With his extraordinary gift for describing financial processes in ordinary words, 'He . . . made the obscure clear, and what might have been dreary, bright.' The Clearing Union plan, he said, was the embodiment of the collective wisdom of Whitehall and of experts and officials throughout the Commonwealth. It was, he hoped, the first of several plans, for it attempted to deal with one aspect only of the economic problem, and it could not stand by itself. 'The principal object can be explained in a single sentence: to provide that money earned by selling goods to one country can be spent on purchasing the products of any other country. In jargon, a system of multilateral clearing. In English, a universal currency valid for trade transactions in all the world. Everything else in the plan is ancillary to that.' It was not necessary to dispossess gold from its traditional use. The bancor would supplement gold, and the total supply of both would be regulated. 'The new money must not be freely convertible into gold, for that would require that gold reserves should be held against it, and we should be back where we were, but there is no reason why the new money should not be purchasable for gold.' He did not like the names bancor nor unitas, and he hoped 'some noble Lord will have a better inspiration'. The initial reserve provided by the Clearing Union was not intended as a means by which a country could regularly live beyond its income; it should be regarded as a reserve with which to meet temporary emergencies and allow a breathing space. Keynes then outlined the main features of the British and of the American plan, stressing the fact that the 'Treasuries of our two great nations have come before the world in these two Papers with a common purpose and with high hopes of a common plan'.

But at this point I draw your Lordships' attention to a striking feature of the proposals. Under the former gold standard, gold absorbed by a creditor country was wholly withdrawn from circulation. The present proposals avoid this by profiting from the experience of domestic banking. If an individual hoards his income, not in the shape of gold coins in his pockets or in his safe, but by keeping a bank deposit, this bank deposit is not withdrawn from circulation but provides his banker with the means of making loans to those who need them. Thus every act of hoarding, if it takes this form, itself provides the offsetting facilities for some other party, so that production and trade can continue.

The British proposals nowhere envisaged exchange rigidity. But exchange rates affect other countries also. Therefore, alterations of exchange rates should not be made by unilateral action.

We do indeed commit ourselves to the assumption that the Governing Board of the Union will act reasonably in the general interest, and will adopt those courses which best preserve and restore the equilibrium of each country with the rest of the world. ... But if, in the event our trust should prove to be misplaced and our hopes mistaken, we can nevertheless, escape from all obligations and recover our full freedom within a year's notice.

Most critics had overstated the difference between the two plans, which were born of the same climate of opinion and were identical in purpose.

I have not the slightest doubt in my own mind that a synthesis of the two schemes should be possible; but it does not seem advisable to attempt it until there has been time and opportunity to discover what the expert opinion of other nations and of all the world finds difficult or unacceptable in either scheme, and what it finds sensible and good. In the light of that opinion, the synthesis in due course should and must be attempted. I trust that your Lordships will wish the two Treasuries God-speed in their high enterprise.[7]

Keynes knew that he would have to compromise, but it was very important not to discuss compromises 'until the right time arrives, and ... this decidedly is not yet'. The results of the public discussions and criticisms had made it clearer in his mind what the substantial points were, and where he could give way without serious injury. Voting power was decidedly unimportant. 'Indeed, so little attention was paid to it that we had not even examined how it would work out in practice. Some of the American press comments dealing with this as a branch of power politics is, in its way, an extraordinary exhibition of vulgarity.' The principal question on this point was White's proposal of a four-fifths majority on all the most important matters. If he would yield on that, the question of formula was unimportant.

Personally, he did not understand what White meant with the provision of rationing scarce currencies. 'There are those (e.g. Roy Harrod) who argue that this is a splendid, comprehending gesture by U.S.A. to throw the whole burden on the shoulders of the creditor . . . I find it difficult to take up so buoyant an attitude. It seems to me that at the most Harry White has put a quick one across the State Department and that the real significance of this provision has escaped notice.'

The most fundamental question, and the one 'on which we should be slowest to compromise', was the difference between subscribed capital and the banking principle. 'This is also the view of the Europeans. If we could hold firm on the banking principle, we might compromise freely on everything else.'[8]

In Washington meanwhile, there had been an official announcement that the Treasury, though consulting with others, would be expected to 'carry the ball'. 'The State Department are lying very low', Phillips noted. 'I think, therefore, I shall go to Morgenthau in future, and not to Berle.'[9]

After struggling for a full year to wrest from the State Department the authority and responsibility for international postwar monetary planning, Morgenthau and White had won. Immediately White moved ahead. On 14 April he cabled the US embassy in London, asking the embassy to inquire when the financial experts of the European governments-in-exile would come to Washington, and who would come. It was planned to meet separately with the representatives of each government. A formal conference of finance ministers would be called at a later date, if an adequate area of agreement emerged from the discussions among the experts. White did not invite any British experts, nor did he indicate when an invitation would be forthcoming. The British experts would be given an opportunity for bilateral discussions when this was convenient, but they would not be allowed to attend meetings with the delegates from other countries.

Meanwhile Keynes learned from the US embassy that the discussions with the European Allies would embrace the 'various' proposals which had been submitted, although Morgenthau had asked that the Stabilisation Fund should not be discussed in London, and had of his own motion undertaken not to discuss the Clearing Union in Washington. Keynes protested, 'It does not seem to me wise practice to let pass in silence such flagrant discrepancies of utterance. If such action was on our side, it would certainly not be passed over in silence. It is not at all good for the soul of Mr. M. that he should be treated too much otherwise.'[10]

On 22 April, White started his discussions with the Canadians, who not only held a special position between the British and the Americans, but also had several highly qualified financial experts. White explained to them the purpose of the Fund, as he saw it — namely, a permanent organisation to deal with the problem of monetary instability. This organisation, he felt, and the Canadians agreed, would stand on its own: 'although measures in the field of commercial policy and investment could be applied at the same time as measures in the field of monetary relations, there is no need for simultaneous formulation of plans for such measures'. The Canadians felt that the Fund should be considerably larger than $5000 million. Mr Rasminsky also stated that the Canadians objected to the four-fifths voting requirement, which would in any case be unnecessary, since there would always be several countries that would join the United States in objecting to any important change. White promised that he would reconsider this provision. Mr Mackintosh suggested that countries in a creditor position be given a larger voting power than originally granted to them on the basis of their quotas, and that the voting powers of debtors be correspondingly reduced. White welcomed this idea.

> Asked for any features of the British paper which the Canadians might want included in any final agreement, Mr. Mackintosh expressed concern about the degree to which the American plan permits the Fund to exercise wide banking functions for which there is no authority in the British proposal. He thought also that the British plan had the great advantage of such extreme simplicity that a country's international accounts would be dramatically presented. . . . He then indicated that the overdraft concept in the Clearing Union Plan is no more readily acceptable in Canada than it is in the United States since, in private banking practice, overdrafts are not used in Canada.[11]

When the Canadians reported to Phillips about their discussions with White, they mentioned that they had pressed him to explain what would happen when a currency became scarce. Presumably the country in question would take 'appropriate action' to prevent its currency from appreciating in terms of every other? White's answer was that it was on all the other countries that the onus of taking 'appropriate action' would lie; the proposal would be amended to make this plain. He was not explicit as to what would be included in 'appropriate action', but when the Canadians asked whether countries would be allowed to embody in a commercial treaty a clause releasing it from the obligation not to practice discrimination, this suggestion was 'received with dismay'.[12]

After these discussions, which were to be resumed later, the Canadians decided to produce their own, independent plan.

The Australians were mainly concerned with the fact that their quota should be of an adequate size, which they viewed as being about 5 per cent of the total quota. They also expressed concern over the likelihood that an international organisation might not recognise in all circumstances the propriety of the Australian policy of sustaining full employment. White asked them to draft an appropriate provision.

One after another, delegations from the other governments that had been invited to send experts to Washington arrived. The Europeans, although they had expressed to Keynes their preference for the Clearing Union, apparently had a change of heart. Phillips cabled London,

> Whatever they said in London Dutch and Belgians arrived here with no intention of supporting Clearing Union. Clark told me that Gutt informed him he had full authority from Belgium Government to accept United States plan as it stood apart from liberum veto. Australians, Poles and Norwegians spoke in favour of Clearing Union. Czechs and French while critical of the stabilization fund made no open statement in support of clearing union ... European allies have come to conclusion on political grounds it will be impossible to get Americans accept a scheme without a capital subscription. We nevertheless fully maintained our position on superior merits of Clearing Union principle.[13]

On 27 April, Ambassador Winant had cabled Morgenthau that the Dutch expert Dr Beyen had prepared a commentary on the plans, and that he clearly favoured the principle of the Keynes proposal. It was planned to discuss the merits of both plans, in an 'attempt to secure in advance an agreement among the European delegates to plump for the Keynes plan when they go to Washington'. By the time they arrived in Washington, however, most of the European delegates were ready to support what was politically opportune, rather than what they had thought to be technically superior.

The Chinese government decided to 'treat the forthcoming discussions as essentially diplomatic and political, and not technical in character, and this factor would be taken into consideration when appointing the head of the delegation'. China was mainly concerned by the fact that Russia would be given a role in the new organisation far beyond what her financial and economic strength justified. The Chinese delegates therefore concentrated their efforts on using their political bargaining power, in order to get the same advantageous treatment as the Russians.[14]

On 6 May, Sir Frederick Phillips had handed Morgenthau a message from the Chancellor of the Exchequer, who inquired about the procedure the US Treasury wished to follow. Morgenthau suggested that Phillips discuss this with Harry White. 'Sir Frederick agreed and added that they had not met for some time on discussions of stabilization plans. The last conference he had on the subject was in Mr. Berle's office at the State Department.' Phillips asked whether Morgenthau preferred that he 'come to the Treasury or to Mr. Berle's office. The Secretary replied that these matters were to be discussed in the Treasury; he regarded the stabilization fund discussions as Treasury problems and he wished Sir Frederick to take up such matters with the Treasury directly. The Secretary went on to say that Secretary Hull knew that the Treasury was handling the matter.[15]

During the second half of June, White had several meetings with a group of British experts, which included Phillips and Opie, as well as Professors Robbins and Robertson. The British emphasised that no satisfactory system of multilateral settlements would be possible unless both creditors and debtors accepted responsibility for making it work, by keeping their balances within reasonable limits through their own action. White felt that it would be more difficult for creditors to reduce their balance than for debtors. He was concerned that Congress would object to the British plan mainly on the ground that it provided no limit to the commitments undertaken by the United States. The British stated 'that of course a limit on commitments of creditor countries was quite possible under Clearing Union but in our opinion was undesirable as it would have result of creating from start a doubt whether scheme would succeed'.[16]

The British insisted that in their country an adequate degree of flexibility was an overwhelming political consideration. There was considerable fear of making again the mistake of setting the rate of the pound at too high a level and not being able to do anything about it. Mr Goldenweiser, of the Federal Reserve, proposed that rates be changed by a majority vote for the first five years, with permission for a 10 per cent unilateral change if a country experienced a persistent adverse balance.

> Mr. Robbins expressed the view that there ought to be even greater flexibility than 10 per cent. Sir Frederick said he did not believe any fixed percentage change was of much value because when a change becomes necessary we must get below whatever valuation is considered by market opinion to be the proper one. Mr. White said that in his view the market doesn't know what the proper valuation is. Rather, the market valuation is based on a guess with respect to future rates. Moreover, the market is influenced to a considerable degree by capital movements and if a change were imminent it probably would be necessary to control capital movements.

White indicated that he might be willing to accept a majority vote for changes in exchange rates, and he might also accept a unilateral change of 10 per cent, after consultation, and for a limited period after the Fund's operations began.

Sir Frederick Phillips wanted to know whether a country would have to use all of its gold before it would be allowed to draw from the Fund, and White stated that this would be a decision for the Board to make.

According to White, American acceptance of an international monetary agreement required, at the least, the fulfilment of three basic conditions:

that the Fund should operate on the basis of national contributions; that these contributions should consist in part of gold, and that the contribution of the United States should not exceed $3000 million; and that the exchange rates of the principal currencies should be determined before the Fund was established. The British experts 'expressed a desire to report on these points to their Government and to ask for an indication as to their acceptability, as well as to whether or not the British likewise might want to put forward certain minimum requirements from their point of view'.[17]

Keynes was, of course, kept informed about the conversations as they progressed. He had already accepted the fact that a limit should be imposed upon the obligation of any one country. 'Personally, I have never had as strong an objection to compromising on this point as some other people have had. The difficulty of what happens when the limit is reached is practically the same under either scheme.' He was now also ready to agree to the subscription principle. 'We also accept the U.S. formula for quotas and voting power, and the general shape of the [Stabilisation Fund]. We are prepared to agree, as a condition of the scheme, that the initial exchange rate between pound and dollar shall be £1 = $4.'

His own essential conditions were that the Fund should not deal in a mixed bag of currencies but only in unitas. The gold subscription should be reduced to 12½ per cent of the quota, in order not to give the scheme too pronounced a gold-standard appearance, and not to reduce its expansionist possibilities by draining gold from countries whose reserves were already very limited. The provisions for elasticity and for preserving a member's sovereignty in deciding its exchange rate should be reconsidered. 'The greatest objection to [the Stabilisation Fund] in its revised version is that a creditor country can go on absorbing great quantities of gold as heretofore, before any real pressure is put upon it. . . . Thus, in effect, *all* the proposals of [the Clearing Union] intended to discourage such a development are dropped.' As it stood, some of the features of the new Stabilisation Fund draft were entirely unacceptable: sterling would be rigidly tied to gold, with complete surrender of Parliament's sovereignty. It was also necessary to make the plan 'capable of intelligible exposition to Parliament and the public, . . . unless we are to loose face altogether and appear to capitulate completely to dollar diplomacy'.[18] White, meanwhile, continued to move ahead, and at the end of July Secretary Morgenthau advised the US embassy in London that, as a result of conversations with technical experts of about thirty countries, the draft proposal of the Stabilisation Fund had been considerably revised, and that it would be published about 10 August. The draft itself was dated 10 July.

When Keynes read this new draft, he noted that there were quite a few changes, but nothing of importance. The changes which he had believed White would be willing to make had not been made. Now he was told that this new draft had already been given to the Senate and House Committees. 'Thus, without further consultation, the Americans will have nailed their flag to this new mast, including the large increase in the gold subscription, although they are aware that this provision is not acceptable to anyone.'[19] Now it would become very difficult for Anglo-American conversations to take place on the basis of fundamental principles, and not on the detailed Stabilisation Fund draft. In a cable to the British embassy, London suggested that a way be found to ensure that the new draft be considered 'as an American product revising their previous draft after discussions, but that no inference can be drawn that either we or the other countries agree to the draft.'[20]

In Washington, the State Department resented being eclipsed by the Treasury, and Berle had told White that it was becoming 'desirable to consider the development of the currency stabilization projects as part of the whole post-war program'. The British had indicated their desire to discuss such projects. White mentioned that he had been working on a proposal for international investment, but that it was necessary to keep the two plans separate. While an investment programme might facilitate the acceptance of a currency plan by other countries, it might be difficult to have it accepted by Congress. If he could establish an area of agreement sufficient to justify the convening of a conference within the next few weeks, he would report to the Secretary of the Treasury for instructions, and the Secretary in turn would inform the President, asking him whether he had any suggestions or instructions.

In the meantime, White's staff continued to work on the Stabilisation Fund plan, and by mid-June 1943 they had produced a tentative quota scheme, providing for total quotas of about $10,000 million. The basis of calculation was the national income, gold and dollar reserves, imports, exports, and some other criteria. The British immediately objected to the fact that dollar reserves should be considered equivalent to gold. Halifax cabled, 'It is derogatory to sterling to count dollars only as equivalent to gold. ... I think we should argue for gold only.'[21] London was not dissatisfied with the quota the US Treasury had allotted, but thought it awkward to apply the same formula for contributions and borrowings. 'The possession of large gold reserves properly qualifies for a high contribution but is not a good criterion of what a country may need to borrow.'[22]

During the meetings with the delegates from the other countries, White discussed not only the Stabilisation Fund, but also the Clearing Union. In the process, several of the provisions of the Stabilisation Fund were altered, and came to look more like those of the Clearing Union. Certain alterations were made providing for a somewhat greater elasticity of the exchanges. The principle of capital subscription was maintained, and a suggestion which was judged startling by the British and opposed by them — namely, that the proportion of gold required from each country should be 50 per cent of its quota, or 50 per cent of its gold reserves, whichever was less — was later withdrawn.

Meanwhile, the Canadian experts, after their discussions with Keynes in London, and White in Washington, produced a plan of their own for an 'International Exchange Union'. They noted that

> The main objectives of the American and the British proposals appear to be identical, namely, the establishment of an international monetary mechanism which will aid in the restoration and development of healthy international trade after the war, which will achieve a high degree of exchange stability, and which will not conflict with the desire of countries to carry out such policies as they may think appropriate to achieve, so far as possible, economic stability at a high level of employment and incomes.

They warned that it would 'be dangerous to attach too much importance to monetary organization of and by itself, if this resulted in neglect of other problems which may even be more important and difficult, or in a misguided faith that with a new form of monetary organization the other problems would solve themselves'. A start, however, had to be made somewhere, and the problem of international monetary organisation was a logical and fruitful starting-place.

The Keynes plan and the White plan differed as regards the techniques to be used in extending credit to countries who needed it, and as regards the amounts that might be involved. The objectives of the plans, and the results that might be expected were limited in nature:

> To avoid misunderstanding it should be emphasized that it would be extremely dangerous to use short-term credits as a device to cover up basically unsound positions. This would be no less disastrous in the international than in the domestic field, and any monetary system which made such an attempt on a large scale would inevitably break down. . . . No debtor country can live beyond its resources indefinitely; and no creditor country can persistently refuse to lend its surplus abroad or make other adjustments to its creditor position without ripping the international fabric.

The extension of temporary credit was not a cure-all; it merely provided time for adjustments, and, unless unbalanced positions were brought into equilibrium, any arrangements made would break down.

Member countries would agree to make resources available to the Union, each according to its quota; the aggregate of the quotas would amount to $8000 million. The Union would have an international monetary unit – no name was suggested – equivalent to $137^{1}/_{7}$ grains of fine gold, which was, as in the case of unitas, equivalent to US$10.[23]

In London, the plan was received with considerable reservations. It was noted that the Canadians were much closer to the American concept than to the British. The Canadian plan was promptly dubbed 'off-White'.

It was partly owing to the insistence of the Canadians, however, that the reduction of the aggregate quota to $5000 million was reconsidered and White agreed to increase the quota. The Canadians also objected to the US veto power, and recommended that an exchange depreciation be allowed of up to 10 per cent; they also suggested that permission for exchange depreciation should depend upon examination of a country's entire exchange position rather than just on its balance with the Fund. Mr Rasminsky

> told White that the Canadians could not take part in any international agency yet envisaged on the basis of complete elimination of exchange controls. Rasminsky would expect that Canada could go back to the type of exchange control which existed prior to May, 1940. ... Rasminsky's main criticism of the Keynes approach is that it is not generally considered to be good banking to have the debtors control the bank and this the Keynes plan would provide. On the relation of gold to the two plans, Rasminsky believes that regardless of its merits, gold will continue to play an important role. Facetiously he stated that he believed gold would remain acceptable at least until the final exploitation of the Canadian mines, although he wouldn't be sure about the South African mines.[24]

Some of the smaller countries invited to the monetary conversations had not sent any representatives to Washington. But among the major countries the only one that had not shown any sign of interest was Russia. The Russian embassy in Washington had repeatedly told White 'that they are very interested and that they will send representatives, but so far they have never arrived'. When, on 19 August, Secretary Mongenthau asked Mr Gromyko whether the Russian government intended to participate in the monetary discussions, 'Mr. Gromyko replied that he had communicated with his government ... but he had not yet received any reply.'[25]

On 9 May 1943 the *New York Times* published the greater part of a plan prepared by Messrs Hervé Alphand and André Istel, which came to be known as the French plan. The authors warned that a return to a generalised system of multilateral trade should not be expected until some time after the hostilities had ended. The countries of continental Europe would be faced with the immediate problem of feeding their population and importing essential supplies. It would be impossible to let imports come in freely; the governments would have to control for some time both their volume and their nature.

It was necessary to conceive a practical system that would be applicable as soon as the hostilities were over, both for the countries that would institute foreign exchange and foreign trade control, and for the countries that would maintain a system of free foreign trade and exchange. The authors suggested that the principal nations, as in the case of the Tripartite Agreement, conclude a monetary accord among themselves, to which other nations might be invited to adhere. Official parities of the currencies of the participating countries would be fixed, and would not be changed without preliminary consultation, or, preferably, agreement.

The stability of exchange rates would be assured if the monetary authorities (either exchange equalisation funds or central banks) undertook to buy at the specified rate the currencies of other participating countries offered through *authorised* channels, and to hold them at their own risk, within specified limitations and guarantees. Alphand and Istel also suggested the establishment of a Monetary Stabilisation Office, to keep account of all exchange transactions effected by the monetary authorities of the participating countries. The Office, knowing the balance-of-payments position of each country, would be able to provide valuable information concerning disequilibria, and suggest methods to correct them.

As for an international currency: 'Gold is the international currency of the future.' It had been 'consecrated by a mystic thousands of years old'. Its function as chief economic regulator, however, should not be revived.

It was suggested that this system, which was admittedly not entirely satisfactory, be started on an experimental basis, and improved gradually.[26]

In London, the government had been kept aware of the course of the discussions going on in Washington. However, British officials had been permitted to attend only some of the larger meetings taking place, and for the rest had depended on information passed on by White or representatives of other countries. Forced to accept the fact that the US Treasury had taken the lead in postwar monetary discussions, Whitehall became increasingly concerned that 'the United States will take the initiative in producing, without consultation with us, further proposals which are not in the general interest. This danger can best be met by a comprehensive approach which will give a plausible reason for delay.' The decision was made to send a telegram to Ambassador Halifax:

> His Majesty's Government feel that the moment has come to initiate with the United States Government informal and exploratory talks on the whole field covered by Article VII, and that it is important for these talks to start without delay. ... They see great advantage in handling the essentially inter-related matters covered by Article VII as a coherent whole. In pursuance, therefore ... they intend, if the United States Government see no objection, to send to Washington not later than the first half of September a strong delegation of officials led by a Parliamentary Under-Secretary of State which would be capable of dealing with all these subjects and, in particular, monetary policy, international investment, the regulation of primary products and

commercial policy. ... His Majesty's Government ... continue to
regard as of the greatest importance the attainment of prior agreement
on such matters between the United States and the United Kingdom
Governments before they are discussed in a wide international field.

Secretary Hull, after Halifax submitted this message to him, thanked the
Ambassador, 'and without intimating any attitude said the matter would
be given early and earnest consideration'.[27]

On 12 August the embassy cabled London, 'White agrees that the next
step should be Anglo-American discussions on the basis of fundamental
principles. He is anxious that such discussions should take place not later
than the first half of September.' The Foreign Office cabled back, 'We
note White's wish to have monetary discussions with us not later than first
half of September. Though we shall be ready for that date, it is difficult
for us to decide on this point until we know answer about delegation on
Article 7 as a whole.'[28]

On 18 August the Washington embassy advised that the US government
was in accord with the British suggestion, but that the conversations on
monetary policy would continue in the existing channels – namely, the
two Treasuries – and that these should also deal with the subject of
international investment.[29]

Ten months had passed since Keynes and White had met each other
briefly at the US embassy in London. Sir Frederick Phillips had suddenly
died, and Mr Redvers Opie, economic adviser to Ambassador Halifax, was
now carrying on most of the direct contacts with White. White had written
a 'very friendly' letter to Keynes, welcoming the forthcoming conversations and putting forward the following as the minimum requirements
that an international monetary agreement of the type suggested would
have to fulfil to be acceptable to the US Treasury and be likely to be so to
Congress:

(1) the new international institution should be started off by capital
    subscription, instead of operating on the 'banking' principle proposed
    by the Clearing Union;
(2) there should be a ceiling to the liability of any member country to
    grant credit to the new institution and to those of its members who
    were in debit;
(3) the gold value of the dollar must not be subject to change without the
    approval of Congress; and
(4) the initial exchange rate between the dollar and sterling should be
    $4 = £1.

The British minimum requirements were, at this stage, the following:

(1) unitas should be made a genuine international 'money of account',

and not merely a book-keeping unit equal to $10;

(2) the initial gold subscription should be relatively small;
(3) the size of the Fund must be adequate: instead of the $5000 million being considered by the US Treasury, it should be raised to $10,000 million; and,
(4) since it seemed unlikely that Parliament would agree to a restriction of national sovereignty, member nations should maintain control over the exchange rate of their currencies.[30]

Shortly before his departure for Washington, Keynes told Ambassador Winant that 'he believed that in a weekend of conversations Dr. White and he could reach agreement on most basic points of the currency proposals'. When White was made aware of this conversation, he was much encouraged, since this 'seemed to suggest that the differences are not basically profound'.[31]

Some did not share this quiet confidence. When the British embassy in Washington learned that London now wanted, as a minimum requirement, to maintain its sovereignty over the exchange rate of the pound, it warned that this would

> come as a great shock ... I believe that I should warn you of the reactions which Robertson and I anticipate. I do not know how much detailed consideration you have been able to give to [the provision] ... by which we should undertake not to enter upon any new bilateral clearing arrangements ... can we properly give the undertaking asked for about not entering upon any new bilateral clearing arrangement unless with the permission of the fund? If we cannot, that also would come as a great shock.[32]

9
The Public Debate

On 2 February 1943 the Chancellor of the Exchequer, Sir Kingsley Wood, made a statement in the House of Commons indicating that the government was preparing plans for a postwar monetary order. He wanted 'an orderly and agreed method of determining the value of national currency units, to eliminate unilateral action and the danger which it involves that each nation will seek to restore its competitive position by exchange depreciation'.[1]

Even before Sir Kingsley Wood's statement, there had been press comment on postwar monetary plans, and a number of people had made statements which indicated that they knew more about these plans than they wished to say; but, overall, the secret had been well kept.

Early in March 1943, the British government issued an announcement stating that representatives of the Allied governments were meeting in London to discuss postwar currency problems. The House of Commons submitted the Chancellor to a barrage of questions, but obtained little information, except that Parliament would have an opportunity to discuss the plans in detail before the government entered into any definite commitments with other governments.

On 21 March, Prime Minister Churchill announced that the British government had lately put before the United States and the Dominions 'and our other friends and allies' some tentative suggestions for future management of exchanges and of international currency, which would shortly be published. All this activity in London had not escaped the attention of the US Treasury.

On 29 March a US Treasury spokesman announced that a conference would shortly be held 'in an attempt to effect a meeting of minds on conflicting ideas expressed on the one hand by Lord Keynes . . . and on the other by Harry D. White'. Mr White's report was a closely guarded secret. At his press conference that day, Morgenthau carefully avoided any comment on either plan. He declined to answer half a dozen questions as to when the plan would be made public, how it differed from the Keynes plan, and whether it had been discussed with representatives of other countries. It had been hoped that a single plan could be developed jointly by Americans and British, but with the publication of some details of the British plan a kind of rivalry was developing between the two proposals. Morgenthau added that he would hesitate to call the White proposals 'a plan'.[2]

While the details of the White proposals were still a secret, whatever was known about the Keynes plan was rejected by the papers reflecting the views of the banking world. The *Wall Street Journal* said,

> The preliminary impact of the thing upon the nerves of this newspaper, fairly hardened as they are by its experience of the last few years compels it to say that in proposing this plan Keynes is far in advance of the foremost skirmish line of our post-war planners, for the men who control his proposed bank would possess powers to control human activities the world over beyond anything that our most starry-eyed of young progressives have yet dared to envisage. In point of fact those powers would be all that one would need for World Domination if fully exercised.[3]

Much of the criticism in the American press was aimed at the New Deal, rather than at monetary stabilisation itself. The British proposal was criticised because of Keynes's reputation as 'father of the New Deal financing', rather than from examination of the proposals themselves. The conservative—isolationist papers were obviously the most critical; but even the moderate and internationally-minded papers found little to be enthusiastic about. Both proposals implied the surrender of some measure of sovereignty, which would be hard to accept. The United States would not be treated as different from the debtor nations; America's gold would be rendered increasingly valueless; and Uncle Sam would be made an 'Uncle Sap' for the rest of the world. The *New York Times* started by attacking Keynes as having

> acquired world-wide reputation as an antagonist of stability of foreign exchange rates and as a champion of currency devaluation, and credit expansion. . . The disintegration of the international division of labor and the excesses of economic nationalism were corollaries of some of the teachings of this eminent adviser of the British Government. . . The gold standard was, without any international agreements, the most satisfactory international standard that has ever been devised. It stabilized foreign exchange rates within very narrow margins. It is often said that the gold standard 'failed'. The truth is that governments

sabotaged it deliberately, because it interfered with nationalistic 'plan-ning' that governments preferred to stability of exchange rates. ... It is not necessary to invent elaborate technical devices to secure monetary stability. The nineteenth century developed them through the gold standard.[4]

Other papers, such as the *Christian Science Monitor*, published whatever information became available to them, but in an uncontroversial tone. Most of them preferred not to speculate on such highly technical questions.

After 5 April 1943, when the *Financial News* published details of the American plan, and after the two plans were published separately in Washington and in London, the press (especially the publications con-cerned with economics), the politicians, the bankers, and whoever was interested submitted the plans to scrutiny. Inevitably, because of the circumstances in which the plans had been published, the comments focused on the differences, and took the form of Anglo-American rivalry.

Some commentators thought it unfortunate that officials in the two countries seemed to regard themselves as in a race with each other to get their plans into the hand of other governments. The *Christian Science Monitor* commented,

> Americans will be no less surprised than Britons to learn that the United States plan has already been submitted to thirty-seven nations, with approval by ten indicated. ... These developments reflect not necessarily a fundamental disagreement over objectives and methods; but they do reflect on the part of some authorities a nationalistic zeal quite out of keeping with the purposes of the plans they seek to further.[5]

Other papers outdid the government officials in nationalistic zeal. The *New York World Telegram*, while admitting that 'we do not know quite as much re international monetary stabilization as we think we know about baseball', recalled that

> the kid who owns the ball is usually captain and decides when and where the game will be played and who will be in the team. While international monetary stabilization is not baseball, it is a game. Gold is as necessary to that game as the ball and bat are to baseball. Since the U.S. now owns some twenty-two billions of the world's reported twenty-eight billions of gold, we think Uncle Sam is going to be the captain of the team or there will be no game ... the idea of 'supplanting gold as the governing factor' and apportioning the voting power on the basis of pre-war trade, which would give Britain about fifty per cent more voting power than the U.S., not only is not good

baseball — it is not even cricket.

The New York banking community was not openly critical at first. Winthrop W. Aldrich, chairman of the Chase National Bank, after thorough analysis of the two plans recently issued in Washington and London, offered his alternative solution:

> At the end of the war this country can render its greatest contribution to world recovery by checking domestic inflationary forces, by resuming gold payments, and by removing all foreign exchange controls. If these policies were followed, the dollar would constitute a sure anchorage for the currencies of other nations and would become a generally acceptable international medium of exchange. All international transactions, including those of a bilateral or multilateral character, including the exportation or importation of goods, including short or long-term capital movements, could be cleared on the basis of a dollar freely redeemable in gold and freed of foreign exchange controls. An important step towards the establishment of such a currency has already been taken by Congress in its refusal to prolong the power of the President to devalue the dollar further. ... Through a renewal of the reciprocal trade agreements act we now have an opportunity to give tangible proof to the rest of the world that we are prepared to make further downward revisions in trade barriers. ... If we do all this, neither of the other plans will be necessary.[6]

A spokesman for the Federal Reserve Bank of New York compared the monetary proposals to the work of an architect who designed the roof of a house without bothering about the floors, and the *Guaranty Survey* warned its readers that the United States, as the chief creditor nation, would have to be prepared to confront a combination of debtor nations advocating a course favourable to themselves at the expense of the creditor. It felt that it was 'inconceivable that this country could, under any circumstances, become a party to such an agreement'.[7]

But these public statements were only the first skirmish in a battle that would last for several years.

In Britain, much of the initial reaction of the press to the Keynes plan, following its publication, was favourable. *The Times* called it 'a landmark on the path of progress towards a rational financial and economic system', and the *Daily Herald* proclaimed,

> Enlightened, stimulating and admirable. ... Here at last is something which breaks away from the doctrines of the past ... an entirely new approach to the problem of international monetary arrangements. It will hardly commend itself to the Bank of England. For it departs from the rigid orthodoxy of that institution. The plan puts gold in its right

place ... puts decisive control over vital external operations in the hands of the Government ... aims at setting up an international authority which is responsible to Governments instead of private banking interests. It provides the control through which alone we can avoid the disastrous recurrence of trade slumps and booms.[8]

According to *The Times*, neither plan could be properly understood except against the historical background of the years between the wars. The aim of both was to provide a workable system which would do what the gold standard did well and avoid what the gold standard did badly. The paper did, however, draw attention to the limitations of the plans. Their great advantage was that, instead of being driven into deflation in an effort to reduce the drain on their gold reserves, deficit countries could now borrow from an international institution and continue to plan a normal expansion of their economy. 'But obviously this could not go on indefinitely.' Another limitation was that 'International arrangements to regulate the relations and exchanges of currencies are merely the book-keeping system for international trade. A sound business can be ruined by bad bookkeeping, but the best bookkeeping in the world will be useless without sound trading methods.'[9]

The British press generally preferred the Keynes plan to the White plan. Keynes's plan was couched in simple and clear language, and bore the imprint of his genius. The American plan bothered the British analysts because it put gold back on its former pedestal, or nearly there. Although it was accepted that gold should have some role, a return to the rigid gold standard, after the experience the country had gone through after 1925, was unthinkable.

As the weeks passed and the plans were submitted to more detailed analysis, much of the initial enthusiasm made way for growing scepticism and outright criticism. The June 1943 issue of *The Banker* noted,

> The Government will thus have a hard task in persuading Parliament to accept a system based on the Keynes Plan. It would have an impossible task if it attempted to obtain approval of a system based largely on the White Plan. ... The outlook for a compromise acceptable to both legislatures is none too promising. The idea that agreement must be reached at all costs, and even that an unsatisfactory agreement would be better than no agreement at all must be rejected.

The public statement made by Harry White that the British would be among the last to become involved in the postwar monetary discussions had been received with some misgivings. American insistence on a return to the gold standard, which it was understood in Britain would be dominated by New York, and which had failed during the interwar period, annoyed British opinion. The controversy around the question of whether or not exchange controls should be retained after the war continued to grow in intensity. Concern about the need to safeguard sovereign rights in the determination of the value of the currency became more evident.

With each redraft of the White plan it seemed to become more unacceptable; it now became evident that the United States wanted an absolute veto power on any matter brought before the new international organisation. The proposed gold contribution was suddenly raised to 50 per cent of the quota. As time passed, the gulf between the British and American approaches to the problem widened. The publication of the Canadian plan was another blow to British expectations. After the plan was made known, *The Banker* noted that this strongly suggested 'that the "Clearing Union" principle must now be regarded as dead'.[10]

Harry White, meanwhile, kept moving ahead. On 26 August he stated that experts from the United States, Britain and Canada had been meeting, that the representatives of the three countries were in complete agreement on the objectives, and that the technical differences were of a minor nature.[11]

Within the United States, opposition to the plans came from various quarters. There were those opposed to joining any international organisation at all. Others felt that the United States should provide help to a certain number of countries, but that this should be done at its own discretion and in a direct way, and not through an international organisation in which the debtors would be the majority. Although these groups had some vocal and powerful spokesmen in the press and in Congress, they were a minority.

Far more effective and better organised was the opposition of the financial conservatives who advocated a return to financial orthodoxy, which meant the gold standard. Now that the country had recovered its prosperity, they were convinced that in the coming elections the forces that had brought Roosevelt to power during the depth of the Depression could be defeated. They rejected the New Deal experiments, government intervention in the economy, deficit spending, and the tricky devices that they detected in the Keynes and White plans. This opposition was spearheaded by the New York financial community, which resented the fact that, under Morgenthau, the Treasury had wrested from the Federal Reserve Bank of New York, which they controlled, authority over the international monetary affairs of the United States. Some of their most able spokesmen were economists, college professors, who were or had been advisers to commercial banks or to the Federal Reserve itself. Among them John H. Williams and Benjamin Anderson commanded the most formidable following in Congress. They saw salvation only in a return to the gold standard as it had functioned in the nineteenth century, with the implied assumption that the sterling standard would be replaced by a dollar standard.

Commenting on the position taken by this group *The Banker* noted,

'Outside a very narrow circle, American economic thought seems unfortunately to be as backward as American industry is progressive.'[12] After the publication of the plans, as Harry White and other Treasury spokesmen started making statements and issuing releases to the press, as it became evident that the United States would play the dominating role in the new international organisations, press comments in the United States became more favourable.

In Britain the trend was in the opposite direction. When the Keynes plan was first published, the emphasis was placed almost exclusively on the fifth object of the plan: 'We need an agreed plan for starting off every country after the war with a stock of reserves appropriate to its importance in world commerce, so that without due anxiety it can set its house in order during the transitional period to full peace-time conditions.' Yet, as it became obvious that it was not the Keynes plan, but the basic plan put forward by the US Treasury, that had the best chance of being adopted, criticism grew and opposition stiffened. And when, on 19 August 1943, a revised draft was made public, attributing to gold an even larger importance than before, comment in Britain became utterly hostile. Commenting on the new draft, White said, 'the British formula, so far as we are concerned, is out . . . . I can assure you that we have no intention of selling our own interests down the river, because the moment we did that it would be kicked out by Congress'. However, he thought that the differences between the United States and Great Britain had been reduced to 'one or two'. Keynes was equally optimistic. He was preparing for another visit to Washington, with the expectation that 'he and Dr. White could reach agreement on most basic points of the currency proposals in a weekend of conversations'.[13]

The public at large took only a superficial interest in these plans, of which it understood neither the technicalities nor the implications. Whatever opinion formed itself was based on instinct rather than on reason and understanding.

The official negotiators could express themselves freely at home, behind closed doors. But, as soon as they engaged in their efforts to reach agreement or compromise, their dealings resembled a fencing bout — with feints and subterfuges, a sequence of attack and defence with the object of scoring a touch and winning a point — where positions were taken and abandoned not for their own sake, but for that of some undisclosed ulterior motive.

Both Keynes and White were supreme masters of the art.

10
The Washington Conversations

Early in September 1943, an important delegation of British officials sailed for the United States. Headed by Mr Richard Law (later Lord Coleraine), the group was to meet the Americans for the 'early conversations' called for almost two years before under Article VII. Also in the delegation were Lord Keynes; Sir David Waley and Mr F. G. Lee, of the Treasury; Professor L. (later Lord) Robbins, of the Offices of the War Cabinet; Mr L. P. Thompson-McCausland, representing the Bank of England; Mr Nigel Ronald, of the Foreign Office; and representatives of the Board of Trade, the Colonial Office and the Ministry of Food.

The discussions covered a broad field. In addition to international monetary policy, they were to review commercial policy, international investment, commodity policy, and, in general, all questions relating to measures designed to improve international trade.

A year had passed since the Clearing Union plan and the Stabilisation Fund proposal had been exchanged, and some progress had been made towards a compromise. White had recently indicated what the United States took to be the minimum conditions of agreement:

(1) the new institution must be started off by capital subscription;
(2) the liability of members must be limited;
(3) the gold value of the dollar must not be subject to change without the approval of Congress; and
(4) the initial exchange rate between the dollar and sterling should be $4 = £1.

White had offered two concessions: the aggregate subscriptions would be raised from $5000 million to $10,000 million, and a bare majority would be sufficient to approve changes in exchange rates. The minimum con-

99

ditions put forward by the British government were: unitas should be made an international money of account; the initial gold subscription should be no more than 12½ per cent of the quota; and member countries should retain control over their exchange rates. London also suggested that the decision to modify exchange rates should be based on some objective criterion or test.

Shortly after his arrival in Washington, Keynes had a 'friendly and uncontroversial' conversation with White, who indicated that 'he was keeping an open mind and ready to give careful consideration to anything we might suggest'. He asked Keynes for a written note on the question of making unitas a real currency. He had no fixed preconception on the matter, but thought there may be many practical difficulties. He agreed that the aggregate subscription should be increased to $10,000 million for the world as a whole; his main concern was to keep the initial subscription of the United States down to $3000 million. Keynes noted, 'We were both of us trying to keep snags and difficulties in background, and . . . [the] whole conversation took [the] line of minimising difficulties rather than solving or developing them.'[1]

Shortly afterwards they had another private conversation about making unitas a money of account. White said that this question was one of great difficulty, although it did not raise any political problem. When White stated that he assumed Britain would return to full convertibility of sterling, Keynes 'made it clear that the United Kingdom did not contemplate going on to a gold or dollar standard, but might be prepared to go on to a Unitas standard'.[2] Keynes also immediately sensed White's tactical approach. He cabled London, 'The Americans do not propose to give us their considered reactions until after they have had all our suggestions before them.'[3] This was the first meeting between Keynes and White since their brief confrontation in London in October 1942. White was well aware of Keynes's ability as a debater. But he also knew that he represented the stronger power, and he claimed to know what would be acceptable to Congress; and anything Congress would not accept was obviously out of question. White had decided that first he should ask Keynes to formulate the British position on major questions; then, having sized him up, forcefully state the American point of view. Keynes had been instructed to secure, so far as possible, the essential elements of the Clearing Union.

The discussions between the British and American groups lasted for about three weeks and took place at the Treasury. The American group was generally made up of about a dozen people, representing the Treasury, the State Department, the Federal Reserve, the White House, and other government agencies. Much of the time, Keynes and White monopolised the debate. Sir Roy Harrod described the protagonists:

White was difficult, there was no doubt; Keynes, although not sparing him in verbal debate, exercised tact and forbearance. White's own feelings were more subtle. Only a few years ago, before his star had risen, he had revered Keynes as the greatest living economist. Now he was confronting him as a negotiator on an equal footing – or rather, on an unequal footing, for he himself represented the stronger power . . . .

Their modes of debate were diametrically opposed. White was full of vigour and manful thrust. He could be wrathful and rude. His earnestness carried him forward in a torrent of words, which sometimes outstripped his grammatical powers. Keynes, we know, was different; he was always ready with his beautifully polished sentences; he detected any inconsistency in the opposition, even in the most abstruse matter, with lightning celerity, and pointed it out with seeming gentleness in barbed and sometimes offensive sentences.[4]

Thus, while Keynes was 'sorely tried by White's rasping truculence', White, fearing that he would be unable to stand up to Keynes in a debate attended by a large group of people, tended to over-react, to the point that it affected his health.[5] At home, Keynes had become accustomed to persuade people, often against themselves; but here the magic failed.

Their first meeting took place on 15 September. White asked Keynes to outline the views of the British on the circumstances in which exchange rates might be altered. Keynes emphasised that there was general agreement on the need to establish stable exchange rates; but, at the same time, several ministers in London held strong views on the need to avoid rigidity. In this respect, these ministers were not satisfied with either the Clearing Union or the Stabilisation Fund. Some were opposed to a camouflaged return to the rigidities of the gold standard. The President of the Board of Trade, on the other hand, thought that competitive exchange-depreciation should be avoided, and that there should be more discipline in the exchange markets. This could, perhaps, be brought about by some objective test, so that permission for depreciation could be granted when, for instance, the internal value of a currency rose disproportionately. The task of the British group, Keynes explained, was to synthesise these views, and to put forward suggestions as a basis for discussion.

White answered that he had no desire for rigidity. The Stabilisation Fund provided for a unilateral depreciation of 10 per cent during the transitional postwar period. Later on, however, it would be preferable to rely on the Fund's discretion rather than on objective tests to determine whether a rate of exchange should be altered. Keynes thought that, possibly, after a few years, when the management of the new organisation had gained experience, this might be desirable. But, even then, he felt it would be dangerous for a government to discuss its financial affairs in 'mixed company'. White disagreed: long before any alteration of an exchange rate became necessary, the important members of the Fund would be aware of it, and even the press would discuss it. A public discussion would not be practical, but confidential consultation would merely be to recognise reality. White argued that

> speculation would in practice be held in check by the exchange controls which he recognized must remain in existence throughout most of the world. He distinguished between exchange controls and exchange restrictions. Controls he envisaged as a machinery of scrutiny which would be maintained even by countries in a strong position but would normally be administered with the greatest possible leniency. If, however, a country found itself getting into difficulties, the control machinery would be administered with increasing strictness to enforce the necessary exchange restrictions so long as they might be required.[6]

Keynes started out the second meeting, on 17 September, by objecting to the Stabilisation Fund proposal that a change in the value of unitas could be made only with the approval of 85 per cent of the member votes. He suggested that such a change should be made by decision of a bare majority. White 'said that alteration by a bare majority would be entirely impossible. The choice of the 85% vote was deliberately intended to safeguard the position of the U.S. It would be impossible to submit to Congress a plan giving other countries the power to determine the gold value of the dollar. Nevertheless, it was clear that there should be some safeguards with other countries as well.' Keynes made various alternative suggestions, but White could not agree. They then turned to the size of the quotas. Keynes said the total for the United Nations should be $10,000 million, and an additional $2000 million should be available for nations that would join later. If the Fund was to be successful, it must be large enough to give confidence, especially if the principle of limited liability was accepted. Members must feel secure that the amounts available would be sufficient to maintain the stability of exchange rates. The United Kingdom would not wish to make use of the Fund if it did not meet these requirements. White said that, if members borrowed more than 50 per cent of their quotas, pressures would develop on the scarce currencies, and the Fund might refuse to grant more facilities. The Fund would supervise from the start how members used their quotas, but action would be taken only in cases of too rapid withdrawal or flagrant misuse of the funds obtained.

In the discussion which developed over the disciplinary powers of the Fund, each party stated its position. Keynes saw the Fund as a passive transfer agent, rather than as an active body with discretionary authority. He agreed that the Fund should refuse credit to an irresponsible small country anxious to exploit a new source of borrowing, but said that it should not do so to a developed country managing its affairs prudently. To White, the exercise of discretion based on qualitative judgement was essential.[7]

At a later meeting, Keynes elaborated on the British proposal to turn unitas into an international currency. He said he wanted a system which looked different and was different from the prewar system. The Stabilisation Fund proposal contained a provision that the accounts of the Fund should be kept in unitas, and this contained the germ of agreement on the subject. Adolf Berle remarked that a formula should be found both to free the British people from the fear that they might have to subordinate their internal social policy to external financial policy, and to assure the United States that a share of its production was not claimable by tender of a new, 'trick' currency, and that the economic power represented by the US gold reserves would not be substantially diminished.[8]

Keynes started the meeting of 28 September by saying that the British group would reserve its position on the quotas allocated to some of the smaller countries, and he asked White for a list of these quotas. White answered that quotas were not a limiting factor in the Stabilisation Fund, and that, if the Fund approved, a small country could obtain three or four times more funds than the amount of its quota. His draft appeared to be more flexible than the British proposal. He confirmed once more that he was in favour of increasing the aggregate quotas to $10,000 million, although this had not been officially communicated to the British group. Keynes confirmed that his group accepted the limitation of the US commitments to $3000 million.

Keynes then elaborated on his objection to the fact that the Fund would deal in subscribed securities. As he conceived the system, it was up to central banks to take the initiative in relation to another central bank, and the Fund would merely register the book-keeping transfer. He also felt that countries should have a right to multilateral clearing, and that this conflicted with the Fund, which would accept only currencies 'in good standing'. White wanted to know who benefited most from the arrangements about which Keynes complained. Would it not be those countries who, without the help of the Fund, would be unable to buy goods abroad? It seemed as though the British, unable to secure a redistribution of real gold, proposed to create a substitute out of thin air. It was dangerous to expose the new organisation to outside uninformed criticism using this kind of argument. White emphasised that the American and British plans produced identical results, but that he considered that the latter was more acceptable to public opinion. The Fund would be active only where the US proposals called for policing. Otherwise it would be passive. The Fund enabled the strong to help the weak, as long as the weak behaved. The strength of the Fund came partly from the gold subscription of the stronger members, principally the United States.[9]

On 4 October, Keynes brought up the question of what would happen if a member broke the Fund's rules. He was prepared to consider that, in this case, after a member had used two-thirds of its borrowing power, the Fund would use its discretionary power on the remaining third. White answered that the American group considered the Fund's facilities a privilege, not a right; and that misbehaviour of a member should therefore entail withdrawal of the privilege. Nevertheless, he appreciated the British point of view, and proposed that members should be free to obtain currencies from the Fund, up to their gold subscription; thereafter, the Fund would have the right to refuse additional facilities. Keynes then stated that it would be necessary to define the term 'flagrant abuse' as used in the White plan. The United Kingdom probably would not accept the US proposal that the Fund be allowed to scrutinise its actions, as soon as its withdrawals equalled its quota. No major country would tolerate such inquisition. White said that he could see the difficulty of an international board sitting in judgement on a government, and offered to redraft his proposals on this point.

White was also prepared to agree that a country should be allowed to alter its exchange rate unilaterally up to 10 per cent; and that members wishing to make a further 10 per cent change should have the right to an answer within forty-eight hours. If the application were refused, the member would be entitled to withdraw after six months' notice. Keynes argued that, instead of having to seek approval by the Fund, the member should only consult. But White felt he had already made concessions, perhaps beyond what American public opinion would accept. Keynes suggested that, instead of having to wait six months before it could withdraw, a member should be entitled to withdraw immediately, since its position in the Fund during those six months would be very uncomfortable.[10]

On 6 October White suggested that the time had come to prepare for the drafting committee a directive covering the main points of agreement, and to make sure that both groups clearly understood the implications of these main points. Keynes agreed that the directive should be prepared in the terminology of the Stabilisation Fund, but stressed that London would not be committed to this formulation.

White then returned to the question of immediate withdrawal. This he could not agree should be allowed, since, he argued, a country that had signed a multilateral agreement should not, simply because the agreement was no longer suitable, be free to withdraw by unilateral action. Also, by threatening to withdraw, a country might try to blackmail the Fund into accepting changes of parity when they were inadvisable. Keynes maintained that, in view of the instructions his government had given, he could not agree that withdrawal should be other than immediate. A 'cooling off' period was not practicable while the exchange was under heavy pressure. After some discussion, a consensus developed that there was little advantage in retaining countries in the Fund against their will, and that, if it were decided to include a period of notice in the rules, this should be generalised to all circumstances, and not applicable only to modifications of exchange rates.[11]

At the meeting of 8 October there was further discussion of the procedure for preparing and then dealing with documents setting out the areas of agreement between the two sides.

The following points were agreed:
(1) There should be a document setting forth the agreed definitive proposals of the two groups in the form of a directive in general terms to the Drafting Committee. This document would eventually be published, and would form the basis for discussion in the Parliaments of the United Nations.
(2) A further document of equivalent status, being a record of more detailed points of agreement, should be drawn up for use by the U.S. and U.K. representatives at the Drafting Committee stage.
(3) No action would be taken until agreement had been obtained on both documents. Thereafter, discussion would not be reopened on the points agreed.
(4) The definitive proposals would be published before the drafting committee stage.

It was tentatively agreed that the points of difference should be noted in the record to be attached to the definitive proposals.[12]

The above excerpt from the British minutes shows the painstaking care, the precautions and the safeguards surrounding the conversations. It also seems to indicate Keynes's belief that, by thrashing out one issue after the other, thus reducing the areas of disagreement, and gradually arriving at a meeting of the minds, it would be possible to draft a document embodying proposals acceptable to both parties.

On 9 October, White gave Keynes a draft statement of what was supposed to be the record of their conversations and the principles agreed upon between the two groups. Keynes read the document and threw it on the floor. It was useless to continue the negotiations, he said. At this White replied, 'We will try to produce a document Your Highness can understand.'[13] The draft was withdrawn, and later during the day a new version was produced, one document stating the points of agreement, and one indicating the areas on which there was a difference of view. Keynes emphasised again the desire of the British government to monetise unitas. It was agreed that White and Keynes would initial both documents, that there should be no publication until agreement had been reached on all points, that any of the arrangements could be altered by either side after consultation with the other, and that the arrangements should be recorded in an exchange of letters. It was also agreed that both sides might issue a statement to the press, indicating that the discussions had been cordial and fruitful, and were being continued.[14]

On 15 September, at White's request, Keynes gave White a memorandum on the problem of securing sufficient elasticity for changing the exchange rates, which was one of the most difficult points. Keynes listed three main difficulties:

(1) the uncertainties of the immediate postwar period, and the risk of
    mistakes in fixing the initial rates;
(2) the question of how far nations should surrender their sovereignty
    when establishing a new rate of exchange for their currency; and
(3) the technical difficulty of discussing proposed changes beforehand in
    mixed company.[15]

A few days later, Keynes reported to the British delegation that he had
had another meeting with White, who had been very conciliatory; he had
said, in fact, that he would accept the substance of all the points put
forward by the British, provided Keynes could obtain the approval of the
Federal Reserve on the aggregate quotas and on the gold subscription; on
the monetisation of unitas he would have to obtain the approval of the
private bankers, which White expected to be difficult to get.[16]

The Federal Reserve was accommodating. Dr Goldenweiser and Mr
Gardner indicated they would not press for more than 12½ per cent gold
subscription; they also agreed that the Fund should be a passive agent. So
far, the Federal Reserve had not expressed any view on the Stabilisation
Fund proposal, but it seemed that members were gradually becoming
'mentally committed'.[17]

Keynes spent several days in New York, in discussions with bankers,
but nothing positive seems to have resulted from it.

White's attitude towards Congress was somewhat more ambivalent. He
expected a great deal of opposition.

> He felt sure that every kind of lip service paid to the necessity for
> collaboration and the need for taking measures that would prevent
> disruption of good relationships, would be met with general agreement
> as long as the subjects were confined to generalizations. He was fearful,
> however, that generalizations would, in many cases, be a cloak for an
> attack on particular plans that were proposed. What made the problem
> easier, he said, was that monetary problems were of necessity technical
> and intricate, so that Congressional discussion on the subject might not
> be very relevant, and Congress might be inclined to go along with what
> they would regard as expert opinion.[18]

The conversations on monetary policy were concluded on 9 October.
The main document that emerged from these conversations was a 'Joint
Statement by Experts of United and Associated Nations on the Establishment of an International Stabilization Fund'. The Joint Statement outlined certain principles which both parties were prepared, as technical
experts, to recommend to their respective governments, subject to agreement being reached on the points still in dispute.

The document started out with a reservation made by the British delegation:

> The following draft is intended to set out and illustrate certain principles. It is expressed in terms of a Fund which holds members' currencies. This form of expression has been used to meet the convenience of the U.S. Treasury and in no way commits the British representatives to recommend acceptance of such a form.

On the purposes of the Fund there was complete agreement: exchange stability, orderly exchange arrangements, multilateral payments facilities on current transactions, shortening the periods and lessening the degree of disequilibrium in the balances of payments. All this was 'intended to facilitate the balanced growth of international trade and to contribute in this way to the maintenance of a high level of employment'.

There was wide agreement on the method of operation of the Fund. The par value of currencies would be expressed in terms of gold. The provision regarding the 'scarce currencies' was included. On a number of points, White had come close to Keynes's views: the aggregate sub-scriptions were to amount to $8500 million for the United Nations, and $10,000 million for the world as a whole; members could withdraw from the Fund by giving notice in writing; all decisions would be made by majority vote, except where the question was one of changing a member's quota.

Keynes agreed that parity changes would be made only with the approval of the Fund. The Fund, however, could not withhold approval if the change was essential to the correction of a fundamental disequilibrium; neither would it reject on the ground that it was domestic social or economic policies that had led to the application. For the first change, up to 10 per cent, no permission was needed; and, for a further change of up to 10 per cent, the Fund would have to give its decision within two days. It was not stated whether the Fund or the member country was to decide whether there existed a fundamental disequilibrium, nor was any attempt made to define the concept.[19]

At the conclusion of the negotiations, it was agreed that White and Keynes would exchange initialled documents, and would also determine future procedure. Keynes sent initialled papers; White never did.

Parallel to the monetary conversations, several American and British groups held numerous meetings on a wide variety of economic questions. On both sides an attempt was made to appreciate each other's difficulties, but, while useful information was exchanged, these conversations were not pursued with the same determination as the monetary plans. White showed no interest in these conversations. He 'had expressed the view that in the British statements the inter-connexity of the various topics had been over-emphasised. He saw no necessity to report to Plenary Sessions on the progress of the currency or investment discussions.'[20]

Keynes was of different opinion. He thought it necessary to prepare plans for commercial policy, and other arrangements involving international economic co-operation. A satisfactory international monetary system, however, was a prerequisite for the successful operation of the other facets of international trade. Commenting on the meetings, Richard Law remarked that

> this was probably the first time in history that officials of different countries had met on such a basis. . . . Usually, the politicians decided in the first place what courses of action they thought would commend popular approval in their countries, and then instructed the technicians to work out arrangements to implement these conclusions, but on this occasion the process had been reversed; the technicians were examining the problems together and attempting to reach solutions that appeared to them to be right on merits before submission to Cabinet Ministers.

11
An 'Agreement' on Principles

After several weeks of negotiations in Washington, Keynes had returned to London. He and White had been making speeches at each other, and although they agreed on a number of questions, many areas of disagreement remained. Keynes had refused to sign the draft purporting to be a record of their conversations, and White had not initialled the revised version that was subsequently distributed.

On 19 November, White sent Keynes a letter with a Draft Statement of Principles revised so as to reflect his latest views. He wished a joint statement to be published in the near future and handed to the Allies; and then, without further discussion, to proceed with the conference.

In London, however, the government had to follow established procedure: after agreement had been reached on a technical level, the joint statement would have to be published, and discussed in Parliament. It was only then that the ministers would consider whether they should become committed to the scheme as it stood, or in an amended version. In addition, the Dominions would have to be consulted, and their views would weigh heavily in the ministers' decision.

Keynes answered that he had 'been working through the text with a view to tidying up rough edges and to seeing how far outstanding points of difference, as recorded in the draft I brought home, can be rubbed away'. He had prepared two new versions of the text, as he would prefer it: one in terms of unitas, the other in terms of a mixed bag of currencies. The draft statement that he had brought home from Washington had not yet been considered by the ministers, nor were any Cabinet instructions available as to whether it was acceptable for the next stage of discussion. The document was still strictly on a technical level. He also explained in detail to White the successive steps of the procedure the British government would have to follow. On the substance of the Draft Statement of

Principles, while he agreed to some of the proposals made by White, some other provisions were not acceptable: 'we do not agree that the Fund should be entitled to interfere with the use of a country's own reserves'. The British government was also beginning to give close attention to the arrangements to be made during the immediate postwar period, which it was provisionally estimated would last for about three years. During that period it was intended to maintain the sterling-area arrangements, and to make bilateral payments agreements with countries outside the sterling area. 'Our object in all this would not be to move away from the objective of multilateral clearing in the direction of bilateralism. On the contrary, we should endeavour so to operate the arrangements as to move as far and as rapidly in the direction of multilateral clearing as was compatible with our way meanwhile and maintaining the stability of our international monetary relations.' Prospective members should have as much opportunity as possible to see their way through the transitional period, before undertaking the obligations of membership. This also had the advantage of emphasising that the Fund would not be used for reconstruction and relief. Another point was the name to be given to the future organisation. Instructed opinion in Britain disliked 'Stabilisation Fund' because it seemed to imply the intention to intervene in the market, just as stabilisation funds in the past had operated to support exchanges. Keynes suggested 'International Monetary Union' or some similar alternative.[1]

Sir Frederick Phillips had died suddenly, and it was now Mr Opie who would be the main British representative in Washington to continue the negotiations with White. Keynes asked him to press White for acceptance of the unitas version, but White disagreed on the ground that this 'version would be regarded as involving a surrender of sovereignty and it would be thought that business would no longer be done in dollars, pounds, etc., but in a new-fangled international currency'. Despite British arguments to the contrary, White maintained that there was no essential difference between the unitas and the non-unitas versions, and, while he appreciated the political reasons the British had for pressing for the unitas version, he thought his own difficulties in trying to have Congress accept the unitas version would be insurmountable. He was open-minded about the name, but the word 'Union' in the title would be politically impossible. He suggested 'International Exchange Fund' as a possible compromise, but emphasised that, as regards Congress, it was a bad second to 'International Stabilisation Fund'.[2] Keynes suggested 'International Monetary Fund' or 'International Monetary Board'.[3]

All these discussions about what he considered small details to be decided on at the conference irritated White. He felt that, unless the conference were held in March or April and the results submitted to Congress in May, it would be too late. The coming election campaign and probable developments of the war in Europe would make it impractical to hold a large meeting of finance ministers. On 18 January 1944 Opie saw

White, and found him pessimistic about the prospect of the United States becoming party to an international monetary agreement. The press and the bankers had become antagonistic, the latter having indicated to Morgenthau that they would fight any proposal along the lines of what they understood to be the Treasury's aim. White thought the bankers were much better organised in their resistance than they were a few months earlier.[4] He wanted to move ahead, and show the Statement of Principles to the Russians, and to the representatives of a number of other countries. Keynes strongly objected to this course, 'for which we foresee no advantages but only much confusion and probable leakages'.[5] Furthermore, the Statement had not yet been considered by British ministers, was not complete, and had not even been finally agreed upon between the negotiators. White retracted, and agreed not to show the statement to anyone except the Russians.

White's pessimism was not without reason. Not only had the press and the bankers increased their opposition: Congress had recently heard the first major speech on the subject. Representative Frederick C. Smith of Ohio had presented the 'Keynes–Morgenthau plan' as a 'British plot to seize control of United States gold'. Representative Smith was a medical doctor, and a member of the Committee on Banking and Currency. He had taken a considerable interest in the monetary plans, and had written the Treasury a number of letters, asking for additional information. A thorough study of the plans had led him 'to the inescapable conclusion that the whole thing is nothing less than a plot to give Great Britain control of our gold stock and unload upon the United States an immense volume of debts owed by Britain to other countries'. 'The British', he said, 'furnished the materials for this scheme. Our Treasury officials, referred to by Mr Morgenthau as experts, worked those materials up into legislative draft form . . . .' But there was only one plan, the British plan. The sophisticated language used by Keynes was a deliberate attempt to deceive the American people. 'Here is a subtle, sly suggestion that we must not place too much confidence in the future monetary usefulness of our gold; that it might, even in the not too distant future, become altogether worthless to us.' If the United States ever became enmeshed in this grandiose scheme with its adroitly concealed purposes, 'we should be fully prepared to continue – to complete exhaustion – to pour our gold into the European bottomless pit of debt. . . . I see in it only a grave threat to our economy and to our national existence. I want to solemnly warn the Congress and my countrymen of this danger.'[6] There had been no further debate on the subject.

White and Keynes continued to explore the provisions to be included in a joint statement, in an effort to reduce their disagreements. Keynes had originally conceived the Clearing Union as an institution that would assume a considerable measure of authority and influence. This authority and influence, however, had to be defined. He now thought that it may seem alarming to entrust any wide measure of discretion to a new body which necessarily starts without tradition, under a management of whose wisdom and impartiality we have as yet no experience. Our object must be, therefore, to secure as much prior certainty as possible concerning the methods of those responsible for daily management, and to limit their initiative and discretion to cases where the rules and the purposes of the institution are in risk of infringement, thus keeping them as an instrument, entirely passive in all normal circumstances, for the facilitation of international settlements between Central Banks, with whom alone the right of initiative would lie.[7]

White, on the other hand, wanted that the new institution should immediately be given wide discretionary and policing powers. Since the United States would dominate the institution through its voting power, and since the powers of supervision would apply only to the other countries – the United States being financially strong enough never to have to apply for aid – White continued to argue strongly for a Fund entrusted with considerable authority.

Keynes had abandoned the name bancor, but pressed White to accept unitas as an international unit of account, because it would have made the whole plan more intelligible; the central banks would hold their accounts with the Fund in terms of an international unit, and this would make the procedure more straightforward. This set-up would also lend itself to future developments in the evolution of a managed international money, 'whereas the alternative is in danger of moving in the wrong direction, namely dealings by an international body in a mixed bag of national currencies'.[8] White argued that, while he himself would probably accept an international currency, the US Treasury and all the other agencies which had been parties to the discussion were strongly of the opinion that its adoption would add enormously to their difficulties with Congress. There would be considerable opposition in the United States among those who would feel that national currencies were being replaced by a new experimental currency. The non-unitas version required virtually no legislation in the United States, while it was 'arguable that the other version would require special legislation which could be presented as tying up the dollar to a phoney international unit'.[9]

Another difficulty was what definition of 'gold-convertible exchange' should be used in the joint statement. White and his assistants had not found a suitable definition. On 3 February 1944 he sent a message to Keynes, suggesting that they agree to

leave the definition of 'gold and gold-convertible exchange' for determination at the formal conference if one is held. There would appear to be no need to provide for this in the Joint Statement. If desired, we could include in the joint minutes a statement that the conference would determine the definition of holdings of gold and gold-convertible exchange although we believe this is not necessary.[10]

The exchange of views, on these and many other points, either direct or through Mr Opie, and the delay they caused in arriving at a joint statement gave White cause for apprehension. Time was running out for a discussion in Congress during the current session, and political conditions might be much more unfavourable during the next one. He was embarrassed by the requests that other countries were making for information and the public and press in the United States had begun to feel that there were insoluble differences between the United States and Britain, and that this meant that nothing would emerge from the currency discussions.

Since their meeting in Washington in autumn 1943, White had agreed to some of Keynes's proposals, and Keynes had abandoned many of his positions, one after the other. White wanted to move ahead, and resolve the outstanding issues at a conference. This, however, required an agreed joint text, to serve as a basis for the conference meetings. He could not understand the slow procedure to which the British government had to submit itself, and he kept pressing Keynes for an agreed statement 'with as little further delay as possible'.[11]

In London, the stage had now been reached where it was necessary to submit the plan to the government. One of the serious political difficulties was that the ministers considered the currency talks not in isolation, but as part of the Article VII discussions as a whole. These covered a wide field, and it was felt that the Prime Minister and the War Cabinet should discuss the subject in detail. But the war and the preparation of the second front took all their available time. Representatives of the Dominions and India had arrived in London, and discussed the plan in a number of meetings. They had made some observations which Keynes felt he should transmit to White.

On 16 March, in answer to another message from White, Keynes wrote, 'we are still, most unfortunately, not in a position to send you an official reply, and it has, therefore, seemed right that I should let you have this personal, unofficial letter to tell you how matters stand and what the explanation of the delay really is'. The representatives of the Dominions had been discussing the draft, and were concerned with the statement regarding the quotas; the ministers had not yet agreed in principle to the publication of the joint statement, and there was restiveness in Parliament and growing criticism that the proposals, 'however we dress them up, . . . are no better than a revised gold standard'. He was

exceedingly appreciative of the way in which our suggestions were met at your end. The result of this was that you and Opie were able to arrive at a text, which was complete in respect of the discussions up to that point, except the question of the Unitas version. Personally, I think it most unlikely that we shall make Unitas a condition of acceptance, but we are not yet in a position to tell you so officially.[12]

While this concession on the part of Keynes was a considerable victory for him, White was 'profoundly disturbed by the continued absence of any definite reply'. The position of the Treasury in Washington was becoming increasingly difficult, as the monetary proposals were becoming a major political issue. The strategy of the US Treasury would be to hold the international conference in May. During the election campaign, anyone who opposed the plan would be opposing international co-operation, and would brand himself an isolationist. However, before its recommendations could be fitted into an election platform, it was necessary for the conference to end. White kept stating that the decision to be made by the President whether or not to call a conference depended only on the answer from London, and the President wished to include the monetary proposals in his election platform.[13]

But White's impatience and the fact that he so often used — and even abused — as a lever the President's desire to hold a conference in May could not shake the British government into short-circuiting the normal procedure. The discussions planned between British officials and the representatives of the Dominions and India took place in London between 23 February and 21 March 1944. They covered, in addition to the examination of the Statement of Principles resulting from the Washington conversations, the problems of international investment, commercial policy, commodity policy, cartel policy and employment.

Keynes was there much of the time to inform the officials about the status of the monetary negotiations and about the meaning of the provisions of the Statement. Under the present formula, he said, a country should not alter its exchange rate unless it had good reasons to do so; it should present the facts of the matter to the Fund, which would have to accept the situation as it found it. The Americans had agreed to increase the aggregate quotas to $10,000 million, but the quotas of some of the smaller countries were insufficient. On the control of capital movements, it had been difficult to find a satisfactory formula. 'The Bank of England in particular considered it unthinkable to go back to the inter-war habit of uncontrolled capital transfers, which had been held responsible for so much aggravation of the world situation.' The scarce-currency provision allowed countries to control the inflow of American imports, thus throwing on the United States the onus for finding a solution to the problem.[14]

The use of unitas as the international unit of account would present many advantages and afford a basis for valuable future developments, but White was strongly opposed to it. Congress would be hostile to a 'new-fangled currency', and its introduction, White had stated, would require special legislative action which would not be necessary if the non-unitas version were accepted. Keynes did not think it worthwhile to risk breaking with the Americans on this point. In response to a question concerning the unit in which the Fund would express its book-keeping and statistics, Keynes said that this would be done in a unit equivalent to US$10, but that he expected that slowly an international unit would emerge. He also thought the monetary and the commercial schemes should be co-ordinated. The commercial scheme allowed a return to restrictive policies, which the monetary plan did not foresee.[15]

The Dominion delegates were not too well equipped to deal with any technical questions raised by the monetary plan. Each had its own approach to the problem. For India the most important matter was how Britain would pay for the supplies that India had made and was continuing to make during the war, and for which it was accumulating sterling balances in London, which could not be converted into other currencies. Canada was mainly concerned with the progress that the United States and Britain could make with regard to postwar co-operation. South Africa, now that gold was assured a role in the plans, could look at the whole thing with a certain amount of indifference.[16]

At the conclusion of the meetings, the committee proposed certain amendments to the Statement of Principles, including a revised table of quotas. It also formulated a number of resolutions:

> The Committee desire to place on record their unanimous preference for the monetised Unitas version of the Statement of Principles, which has many advantages over the non-Unitas version. But they also record their view that, from the technical aspect, the Unitas version is not essential to the satisfactory working of the scheme, and that the acceptance by the United States Treasury of the Unitas version could not be pressed as a condition of the acceptability of the scheme as a whole. . . .
>
> The Committee took note of the right of a country to impose restrictions on imports on balance of payments grounds on the conditions proposed by the Committee on Commercial Policy, and they affirm the importance of this right in relation to the obligations of member countries of the Monetary Fund. . . .
>
> The Committee had a full discussion of Clause 11 of the Statement of Principles which deals with the Transitional Period . . . Clause 11 is satisfactorily designed to safeguard the necessary freedom of action of member countries during the early post-war difficulties.[17]

While these meetings were going on, Keynes kept receiving messages from Washington urging him to confirm his agreement to the publication of the Statement. He began to fear that, if White was to be told that there was no answer, he might lose patience and publish the Statement of Principles with some introductory equivocal phrase that they were drawn up after consultation with the UK experts.

He felt that it was necessary to submit a realistic programme of procedure. Summoning a drafting committee by the end of May to write up a statement with government authority behind it was out of the question. Still more so was a conference of finance ministers to endorse a draft. What might be possible was a wider technical conference, at which the Statement of Principles would be discussed. Keynes felt that, if White were told officially that the British had agreed to the non-unitas concept, he might be kept quiet for a little longer. Unless some reply were given, White would probably be angry, and reject other proposals that had emanated from London. The Chancellor of the Exchequer and the leading officials at the Treasury gradually came to agree with Keynes that the monetisation of unitas was no longer of significant importance.

The Bank of England, however, continued to 'regard this as an essential principle because it is the last safeguard, in their judgment, to ensure the Fund will not possess national currencies and can therefore have no temptation to deal in them, nor can a country desiring to purchase sterling choose between the Bank of England and the Fund as the source of purchase'.[18]

The Chancellor of the Exchequer had another objection: he felt that it was not possible to move forward on the monetary scheme unless commercial policy, investment policy and other aspects of postwar reconstruction were discussed at the same time as the monetary proposals. These views were shared by others at the Treasury. Sir David Waley felt that the Fund, which deliberately excluded from its scope the problems of reconstruction, could not function until the war-damaged countries could see their way through the transitional period, and this raised the question of reconstruction loans.[19]

Consideration of postwar monetary plans was stalled for another reason. The enormous amount of attention that needed to be given to the preparation of the second front made these questions seem academic. In addition, the Dominion prime ministers were expected in London in May, and it would have been discourteous to publish a joint statement without definitely knowing their attitude.

On 3 April, however, Sir Richard Hopkins, under pressure from Keynes, suggested to the Chancellor that, given the repeated requests received from Washington, the monetary scheme should be allowed to go it alone, and that the Dominion prime ministers should discuss the statement after its publication; they might well wish to reserve final judgement until they had consulted with their governments back home.[20]

That same day, in Washington, Morgenthau called Hull, and 'asked him how he felt about calling the world monetary conference and after I pressed him a little bit he said he was favorable to calling it and he thought the chances for success were greater than being a failure'. Hull, however, had no appointment with the President, and did not know when he could see him. Morgenthau had asked to see the President 'and the President would unquestionably see him'. He told White, 'Don't worry. I haven't let you down, have I? I have it very much in mind and I promise you that I will see the President before he goes.'[21] On 4 April, Morgenthau wrote to Hull as follows.

> Dear Cordell:
> I spoke to the President and he approved the calling of a monetary conference. He said that if it is to be held, he would like to have it held in May. In view of the shortness of time left, I should like to present the situation to the Chancellor of the Exchequer through a cable to Winant.
> I want to thank you for your help in getting the President's approval.[22]

Morgenthau cabled Winant in London, asking him to call upon the Chancellor of the Exchequer. The President had given his approval to the calling of a conference and 'he wishes it convening during May. To do this, it is essential to publish the Joint Statement of recommendations within a week.' He needed the acquiescence of the technical experts of some other countries, but the British had insisted 'that we do not show even a preliminary draft . . . until its publication has been agreed between us'. He did not wish to influence the decision of the Chancellor, but only to inform him of the necessity for a prompt decision.[23]

In his answer the Chancellor explained 'why we are proceeding with what may appear to you excessive deliberation'. The questions arising out of the monetary scheme and out of the other plans for economic co-operation after the war 'affect the interest of our two countries in a rather different way. For us, these matters raise issues vital to the financial and economic position of the United Kingdom and the British Commonwealth. For you it may be that the chief question is how far you are in a position to help other nations.' It was necessary for him to look round the whole matter very thoroughly, and he hoped to be in a position 'to communicate shortly with you giving you a detailed statement of our views on the procedure to be followed for wider consideration of the Monetary Fund'.[24]

To Winant the Chancellor gave an additional reason. When the Statement was published, Parliament would demand an early debate, and it would be impossible to refuse this. During the debate, the government would have to define its attitude toward the proposals. It would be embarrassing for the British government to be obliged to take up a definite attitude while the US government still maintained an attitude of detachment. The US government would be committed only after Congress ratified the agreements.

During the meeting with the Chancellor, Ambassador Winant

came to the conclusion that there must be a strong opposition. After careful inquiry I found that a majority of directors of the Bank of England are opposed to the program and that Lord Beaverbrook is their spokesman in the Cabinet. This opposition argues that if the plan is adopted financial control will leave London and dollar exchange will take the place of sterling exchange. This argument disturbs Right Wing Conservatives such as Amery ... who represents British Imperial thinking in the Cabinet. The Prime Minister who has never felt that he had a real grasp of financial questions because of this opposition postposes decision on them.[25]

Morgenthau failed to understand why the question was being raised in connection with the publication, since at this stage he was not concerned with the attitude of the governments. Whether he understood the fundamental difference between government procedures in London and those in Washington is not clear. He cabled back that

the U.K. representatives have placed us in a most embarrassing position by their delay in indicating to us their decision on the sole matter of the publication of the Joint Statement. The anomalous position in which we are placed has made it impossible for us to keep the Congress, our public and other governments informed, has given rise to harmful rumors, and has increased the difficulty of carrying through our program. Unless we hear immediately that the Joint Statement can be published next week ... then it is my personal opinion that we shall not be able to hold a conference this year.[26]

On 12 April, London advised that

We regard it as impracticable to consider publication of statement without a provisional list of quotas. Sensible debate in Parliament and general understanding of effect of scheme would be impossible without a list and we could give no satisfactory explanation of its omission. To leave the whole issue of the size of the quotas to a larger conference would produce confusion and controversy.

The Dominions had insisted on larger quotas, and White had been asked to consider this, but had refused.[27]

When Opie transmitted this message to White, he was told that it would be a serious error to publish a list of quotas, because it would excite controversy at once. The quotas would be allotted at the conference. This decision was final, and it would be useless to bring the subject up again. He agreed, however, to delete the words stating that the quotas would be determined by a formula. In general, he felt it would be wise to issue a rather vague statement for publication, and leave it to the conference itself to work out the details. This was particularly true for the quotas, which he expected to be the most controversial problem to be settled.[28]

Keynes thought it was 'far superior tactics in our judgment to present them with a table which purports to be a *fait accompli* whilst not necessarily turning a deaf ear if it can be shown that there are two or three cases where this may not completely meet the necessities of the case'. If the revised table prepared by the British Treasury was not printed, then the table of quotas already circulated by the US Treasury should not be printed either. He would support the Dominions and India in their request for an increase of their quotas. In the event that no table of quotas was published, there should be no suggestion that the quotas would be determined by a formula. 'White must know as well as we do by now that there is no conceivable formula which will produce reasonable results all round.'[29]

For several weeks, Keynes sent one telegram after the other to Opie, with suggestions for amendments to the Statement of Principles White had prepared. Opie was to put Keynes's point to White, discuss it with him, try to convince him, and cable the answer back. Sometimes White would agree, but more often he would refuse to change the text. On a number of matters he did not feel strongly one way or the other. Keynes, on the other hand, was reluctant to yield on what he considered to be essential, before it was absolutely indispensable to do so.

On 4 April, White had asked to see Opie to tell him that he was in a most embarrassing position with the Chinese, who kept asking for a copy of the Statement of Principles. He would also be compelled to show it to several Latin American countries. He spoke with great earnestness on the necessity of getting an answer immediately on unitas, and an indication that the British virtually agreed on the Statement of Principles. Otherwise it would be impossible to hold a conference during the spring.

As long as the negotiations were carried on mainly between Keynes and White, through Opie in Washington, they were frustrating enough. Keynes, forced by objections and criticism in Parliament and in Whitehall, and by the decisions of the Dominions and India officials to correct some of his previous positions, had made a number of suggestions White would not accept. However, when Morgenthau became involved in the exchange of telegrams, he added to the confusion by working simultaneously through the British embassy in Washington and the American embassy in London, the one being unaware of what the other was doing, except when it found out through some indirect channel.

On 13 April, Morgenthau discussed with his staff the speech he was expected to make before the Committee on Foreign Relations. White said,

The problem would be simple if the British were to agree, because then you have the statement with an appropriate speech. If the British do not agree to its publication by that time ... instead of saying that it represents the consensus of all, we could say it represents the position of the American technicians and of many other countries. If they ask you how about Britain, then the presumption is, if they have not given assent to it, that you would say, simply, that they haven't agreed to it.

From experience Morgenthau knew that it was more than likely that his statements before the Congressional committee would leak out to the press. So it was necessary to tell the British that he was going to make this speech. But if he did this,

they will interpret that as a threat of bringing pressure to bear on them, because they say they are taking it up this Friday in Cabinet. Now, I don't know whether that will accelerate the thing or not, but you have always got to look at this thing from the darker standpoint, laying down the law to them and saying, 'Morgenthau goes up, win or lose, and is going to tell the Congress of the United States that we haven't been able to get agreement from the English, and haven't been able to get agreement from the Russians.' And that may be just what they want. Now, that may accelerate the thing, but in the wrong way.

White thought that this difficulty could be avoided by making the statement 'a little more delicately'. Morgenthau could say that 'this represents the agreement of most of the technicians, and the matter is still being discussed, and there is not yet an agreement. I wouldn't say they haven't agreed; I would merely say, "There isn't yet agreement, but we wanted to bring you up to date to show you the product of the discussions which have been going on in the many months since I came here last." ' If pressed, Morgenthau could also answer that the British 'have agreed on each of the points, but haven't yet agreed to the whole -- which is true'.

A new development was adding to the pressure for publishing the Statement of Principles as quickly as possible. Republican Congressman Thomas E. Dewey was ready to introduce a Bill under which, instead of an International Monetary Fund and other possible government institutions, it would be the United States private and public institutions which would grant reconstruction and stabilisation loans to individual countries, after investigation of the requirements of each case. In view of the forthcoming hearings, Dewey had lined up an impressive group of New York bankers, including the president of the Federal Reserve Bank of New York, and several economists who all were unalterably opposed to the Treasury's plans. White had told Opie that he was in a hurry to get on with the monetary discussions because

people in the New York banks are lining up to give evidence at the hearings the week after next on the Dewey Bill in Congress. The idea is to adopt a position that will obstruct any movement in the direction of the U.S. Treasury plans, monetary or bank. White repeated that the delaying tactics are being used because they think the temper of Congress will be such after November that no broad-minded international schemes will stand a chance. The Administration take this as a serious threat and think that the only answer to it is to get Congress committed this year at least to the extent of a committee endorsement of Morgenthau's proposals.[30]

In a letter to Mr Opie, the Chase National Bank had asked whether he could help them with a question which perplexed them, namely 'the amount of credit which England may require following the termination of hostilities and the reason for such credit. In other words will England need to borrow in order to build up stocks of raw materials and also to liquidate in whole or part her blocked balances.'[31] Opie advised Keynes of the bankers' approach, and about their possible willingness to open a credit, if London were interested in a loan. Keynes did not think this worth considering. He wrote back,

> the point you ought to have at the back of your head (it is probably there already), but which is not always easy to make clear to the Americans, is the following: We can in the long run only pay our debts by the export of goods. It suits us, therefore, much better to owe money to a great variety of countries, who are our natural customers, than to have all these debts canalised and consolidated into a loan from the U.S.A., which is not one of our natural customers on a large scale. If the Americans do not want us to repay and the whole thing is frankly on that basis, well and good. But, if they do expect us to pay, then we have to keep within the narrowest possible bounds what we borrow from them. This is the fundamental reason why we look gift horses in the mouth when they are of the breed offered by the New York bankers.[32]

Morgenthau and White wanted to have the Statement of Principles published simultaneously in Washington, London, Moscow and Chungking, as well as in the capitals of some of the Latin American countries. Although White had stated that 'practically' all the countries except Britain and Russia had agreed to the Statement of Principles, this was an assumption, because none of the representatives of the other countries had seen the final text. White simply took their agreement for granted.

On 11 April the Chancellor wrote a memorandum for the War Cabinet, stating that although some important questions remained unsettled, it was urgent that the government reach a conclusion about its general attitude towards the plan. He suggested acceptance, dependent upon recognition by the US Administration of three conditions:

(1) that the Fund was designed primarily for the long term, and could not function unless there were also in existence some international organisation for long-term investment, and unless the problems of reconstruction of war-damaged countries had been solved;

(2) that the Fund should come into operation during the transitional period, by stages, beginning with the supervision of exchange adjustments, and proceeding gradually and experimentally; and

(3) that Britain could not enter the scheme, or accept any of its obligations, until it was clear how the difficulties of the transitional period were to be met. For the time being it was not possible to 'see the beginnings of our path through the transitional difficulties in regard to foreign exchange'.

Despite the recommendations of the Dominion officials, the Chancellor suggested that the government agree to the next steps on the monetary scheme without waiting until the discussions on commercial policy had reached a stage where they could be formulated in a corresponding agreed statement of principles. 'The alternative of long delay would be violently opposed in Washington.' He recommended that the government agree to publication upon the basis that it would declare its attitude after a debate in Parliament. It would have been an act of courtesy first to clear the document with the prime ministers of the Dominions, but time did not allow.

'A second desideratum to which I attach importance . . . . If we are to declare ourselves on behalf of the Government, we should wish the Americans to do the same. I am not clear what Mr Morgenthau's intentions are and have telegraphed him to learn them.'[33]

On 14 April the War Cabinet decided that, in principle, subject to the settlement of outstanding points, 'we should offer no objection to the publication at a very early date'. When the Statement was published it should be accompanied by another statement making it clear that the government was in no way committed to it, and that the scheme should be the subject of informed discussion before any commitment was undertaken. It would also be necessary to make certain whether the attitude of the US Administration was non-committal.[34]

The decision of the War Cabinet was cabled to Opie in Washington, who immediately advised White, who reacted very unfavourably. White did not agree with the statement that the Fund was dependent upon the satisfactory working of an international investment organisation. He wanted to have some elucidation on the other points, but Opie could tell him no more than that they meant to put the United States experts under notice that the future was uncertain as regards both the difficulties and their solution.[35]

On 18 April London surrendered on the matter of publishing the quotas: 'We reluctantly agree that no table of quotas should be published.'

The government was, however, entirely uncommitted on the subject, and reserved the right to press for higher quotas for some of the Dominions at the conference.[36]

Keynes anticipated that this would not be the last time that London would have to yield. If Congress and the American public supported the proposals after ·their publication, and if there were an opposite development in Britain, this might 'lead to a position where Dr White, having secured widespread domestic and international support, adopts a take-it-or-leave-it attitude which will be extremely awkward and perhaps humiliating'. If the reception in the United States were doubtful, 'then undoubtedly he would attempt, and probably succeed, to put all the blame for a breakdown on us – with great prejudice to subsequent proposals'.

Whatever happened, 'Dr White is a man with a memory. We may find ourselves in a position where we are forced to accept his general conditions without any of the admirable and far-reaching safeguards which we have worked, with such immense labour and forethoughtfulness, into the present document . . . .'

It was important, as far as Britain was concerned, not to allow a hostile public opinion to develop – not because the plan itself was unsatisfactory, but because it had been inadequately explained and defended. 'If the poor thing is brought into the world baldly and quite naked with no explanation of what it means and with no-one entitled to defend it, it will not have a fair chance.' In order to mitigate this danger, he had prepared introductory explanatory notes, and suggested to the Chancellor of the Exchequer that they be published together with the Statement of Principles. He also suggested that a 'copy should be sent in advance to Dr White, but he should not be asked or expected to agree to it. He has not earned such a privilege. And, in the circumstances, we should be acting as whipt curs to offer it. There is nothing in the Notes which goes beyond the terms of the agreed document or to which he is entitled to object.'

He also asked that the Chancellor agree to let him see members of the press before publication and Members of Parliament after publication, with a view to answering questions and giving explanations. This course had been followed previously, and had proved successful. He hoped that 'others would also help in the good work. But in certain respects the fact that I am not a Civil Servant and live in a limbo (though it be, in all respects, nearer hell than heaven) makes my interposition in such a way rather easier.'[37]

On 18 April, Morgenthau sent a message to the President, advising him that he had made arrangements to appear before the appropriate Congressional committees on 21 April to discuss the Statement of Principles. Release of the Statement to the press was planned for 8 p.m. of that day, so that it would appear in the papers the following morning. He proposed to tell the committees that the Treasury wished to call a conference if circumstances permitted.

Secretary Hull and I would recommend that I be authorized to state
that you would probably appoint a delegation to be headed by the
Secretary of the Treasury, and including, among others, representatives
of both houses of Congress. . . . We both believe that such a statement
to the Congressional committees will be of the greatest importance in
getting the proposed conference off to a good start with the Congress . . . .

Roosevelt approved.[38] Morgenthau would head the delegation, but it was
still up to the State Department to organise it. Secretary Hull had been
very co-operative, but was somehow under the impression that the
conference would be held in July, not in May. The Republican and the
Democratic conventions would take place about that time, and both
Morgenthau and White knew that this would be the worst possible period,
because the newspapers would then be devoting far the greatest part of
their attention to the conventions.

Somebody had told Hull that the Treasury was aiming for July.
'Somebody over there may still be trying to cut our throat', Morgenthau
said. White was convinced that it was Pasvolsky: 'Mr Secretary, that
Pasvolsky, I think – well, I can't quite make him out. He is fighting us
behind the scenes.'

'That is it', said Morgenthau. 'Don't blame Hull. He goes in there and
tells Hull, "This isn't going to be in May; the Treasury is double-crossing
you, this is going to be held in July." '

'The campaign by Pasvolsky and some of his colleagues', White thought,
'is now being centered on the Bank to stop us from discussing the Bank.
The thing has gone too far to stop the Fund, though Pasvolsky did lead the
discussion in the State Department to prove we ought not raise the
question of a Fund before this summer. We went over there in Dean
Acheson's office, and after an hour or more of discussion, convinced Dean
Acheson that we were right and they were wrong. But Pasvolsky worked
behind the scenes.'

'You know what I think it is, behind Pasvolsky? He has been in charge
of post-war planning. The only thing he can show in the way of tangible
results is what the Treasury has produced', said Luxford.[39]

The date of publication Morgenthau had set was now approaching
rapidly, and neither the British nor the Russian nor the Chinese government had shown itself ready to express its agreement with the Statement
of Principles by joining in publishing it on that date. The Washington
representative of the Chinese Ministry of Finance had agreed to the
publication, but the final decision had to be made by the Chinese government. Morgenthau had cabled the American ambassador in China that 'The
statement will be released here irrespective of whether or not it is released
in Chungking.' Publication in the Latin American countries was only a
matter of formality, and White would handle it. White had assured

Morgenthau he could tell the Congressional committees that 'practically' all the governments had agreed, except Britain and Russia.

On 17 April, four days before the scheduled publication, while he was still waiting for an answer from London, White submitted to Morgenthau a draft cable which he wanted the Secretary to send to Ambassador Harriman. The cable said:

> I would appreciate if you would call on the People's Commissar of Finance and inform him that I have just received word from the Chancellor of the Exchequer informing us of their agreement to the publication of the joint statement of the technical experts of the United and Associated Nations recommending the establishment of an international monetary fund. It is contemplated that the publication will be simultaneous in London and Washington. It would obviously be highly desirable if the statement were also issued at the same time in Moscow.[40]

White warned Morgenthau, 'This says we have received an agreement and we haven't.'

'May I make a suggestion?' Morgenthau said. 'Why couldn't everybody perfectly well be in agreement except the English? I would go ahead with a cable to Harriman and say that we hope to get an agreement with the Russians, irrespective of what the British do.'

'We have done that', said White. He had told the Russian ambassador in Washington that 'we were practically in agreement, but not quite. There is nothing we can add unless we say the British agree. Now, the chances are ninety-nine out of a hundred they will. . . . We might call Opie up, and tell him that in order to get simultaneous arrangement, we have to send another cable off, and can we assume that his Government will agree? If he says yes, we will go ahead! If he says no we won't.'[41]

The cable went off, but the answer from Harriman was disappointing. The People's Commissar for Finance stated that he had not heard from his experts regarding the changes proposed by Russia, and which would have made the Statement acceptable. Under the circumstances, he could not agree to the text of the Statement.[42]

On 20 April, after another exchange of telegrams and messages, the Chancellor of the Exchequer cabled Morgenthau that arrangements were being made in London for publication, to fit the timing of publication in the United States. Right up to the last moment, Keynes kept bombarding Opie with cables about alterations he wanted made.

Morgenthau then decided to call Harriman over the telephone and to ask him to try again. On 20, April, at ten o'clock in the morning, while they were waiting for the call to come through, Morgenthau reviewed with White what he was going to tell Harriman. He wanted to see the cables that had already been sent. Reading the cable dated 17 April, he told White,

'You took an awful chance on that.'

The call finally came through, and Morgenthau urged Ambassador Harriman to do whatever he could to obtain the Russians' agreement. He also called the Russian embassy in Washington, to ask for their support in whatever they could do.[43]

The following morning, 21 April, the day of publication, he received the answer. Molotov had asked Harriman to call near midnight. He said that among the Russian experts there existed a major disagreement with respect to the basic conditions of the establishment of the Monetary Fund. The Soviet government had not yet succeeded in fully studying the proposal. 'If it is necessary, however, to the Government of the United States of America to have the concurrence of the Government of the Soviet Republic to secure due effect in the rest of the world, the Soviet Government is willing to instruct its experts to associate themselves with Mr Morgenthau's project.'[44]

The answer arrived just before Morgenthau was to appear before the Congressional committee, and thus allowed him to announce that Britain, Russia and the other countries had agreed to the Statement of Principles. The Statement itself was released to the press that same day, and was published the following morning.

12
The Opposition in Whitehall

In British government circles there were many who did not share Keynes's enthusiasm for the Clearing Union. The reasons for their opposition were varied. Some continued to be convinced that Britain had no choice but to continue and expand the system of bilateral agreements as the only possible method to control the balance of payments. Some feared that the dollar would completely eliminate sterling as an international currency. Others were passionately attached to Empire trade, which the obligations involved in the postwar plans would dilute. Many saw in the plans a return to the gold standard. When Keynes, under the impact of the warnings issued by the State Department, had tempered his advocacy of controlled international trade, Sir Hubert Henderson had not followed him. An able economist, he had participated in the meetings held at the Board of Trade, where the idea of a Commercial Union, intended to complement the Clearing Union, was being discussed. The group involved in these discussions was mainly concerned with the reduction of prewar impediments to international trade, such as tariffs, preferences and import restrictions. They set out to formulate rules to be followed by member countries and envisaged an International Commerce Committee to which disputes between members of the Union would be referred.

At a meeting on 24 November 1942, Henderson had suggested 'that the success of multilateralism depended on the solution of currency problems. There must be equilibrium in the balance of payments, and the Clearing Union by itself did not provide the solution'. The interdepartmental committee at the Board of Trade had introduced an escape clause which might be incorporated into the Commercial Union rules to protect countries getting into serious financial difficulties. The committee had also decided that there should be an initial period, probably of three years, during which no government should be pressed to open its borders to

imports more than it felt reasonable. It had also been agreed that
quantitative import restrictions should be allowed if they were justified by
the existing or prospective state of a country's balance of payments on
current account.[1]

In a memorandum dated 7 December 1942 Henderson wrote, 'I suggest
that it would be shortsighted in the extreme for H.M. Government to
adopt an attitude towards the technique of quantitative import restrictions
which implies that it is an inherently objectionable expedient.'[2] In a
memorandum dated 14 October 1943, he criticised several aspects of the
Clearing Union plan:

> There is strong antagonism in this country to anything in the nature of
> 'a return to the gold standard'. The antagonism is equally marked on
> the political Left and the political Right; and it is common to bankers
> and those who are suspicious of bankers. It is only natural that so
> general a feeling and so technical a subject should be somewhat
> incoherent, and should comprise elements of irrational prejudice.[3]

Under the gold standard, each country could withdraw from its obligation
to supply gold for its currency at a fixed rate of exchange, by unilateral
decision, and without notice. The Clearing Union did not state expressly
what was involved in the obligation to maintain the prescribed parity. If it
were meant that countries would have to use up all their gold or monetary
reserves to protect the parity, the obligation would be a more serious one
than a straightforward return to the gold standard, since it would be a
formal treaty obligation. If this were not the meaning of the Clearing
Union, then the undertaking would be worth very little. This was an
ambiguity which it was important to clear up.

The permission to lower the parity by 10 per cent did not meet the
difficulties of a country which found its monetary reserves being drained
away.

> Indeed this might be an aggravation rather than a remedy. A lower
> exchange rate makes the 'terms of trade' less favourable; that is to say,
> the country concerned sells more cheaply or buys more dearly. It is
> only as a consequence of this that its exports may be stimulated and its
> imports checked. But this influence on the *volume* of trade takes time
> to operate. The effect of the 'terms of trade' is more immediate, and
> this serves to accentuate an adverse balance of payments.

By subscribing to the rules of the Clearing Union, Britain would be
debarred from using measures such as import restrictions, exchange
control, and clearing or payment agreements to control its balance of
payments; it was to be presumed that the Clearing Union did not imply
the obligation to pursue a policy of internal deflation, meaning a

deliberate reduction of wages and prices, in order to restore competitiveness, which was the traditional method under the gold standard.

The temporary facilities provided for by the Clearing Union to cover the expected balance-of-payments deficit were entirely insufficient. Thus, there was the very serious danger that Britain, having signed away its right to employ any of the possible remedies, 'other than that of going cap in hand for further accommodation, or that of withdrawing from the Fund', would have to watch helplessly the drain on its monetary reserves. As a result the Fund would probably collapse, and with it any other international economic arrangements that might be based upon it.[4]

In another memorandum, 'The International Economic History of the Inter-War Period', Henderson commented,

> Stripped of their institutional trappings, the schemes which are emerging from the Anglo-American expert discussions closely resemble the policy pursued in the 1920s. Indeed, there are only two differences that seem material: The first is that it is proposed for the future that countries should be allowed, and in certain circumstances required, to control capital movements. This undoubtedly is a helpful change and a welcome concession to the teachings of experience. ... The second difference is that it is proposed in effect to replace deflation by exchange depreciation as the regulating spring of the international mechanism. That deflation can no longer serve this purpose is clear enough. Few countries would be willing in future to make the volume of their internal purchasing-power depend on the magnitude of their gold reserves. It follows that it is also right to make provision for altering exchange-rates so as to avoid large over-valuations or under-valuations of particular currencies. But the experience of the inter-war years does not support the idea that exchange depreciation might provide an efficient substitute for deflation as the regulator of a quasi-automatic system, still less the idea that alterations of exchange-rates which are to serve this critical purpose might be made the subject of amicable international decision. Of the various expedients which different Governments employed in the 1930s, none produced more unfortunate results than deliberate exchange rate depreciation. It was the least helpful to countries which tried it, and the most harmful to other countries.[5]

The apparent implication of the Clearing Union and Stabilisation Fund plans that an adverse balance of trade could best be corrected by a deliberate depreciation of the currency was almost certainly mistaken.

Shortly before, in another memorandum, Henderson pointed to the dangers of signing prematurely such an agreement. It was generally admitted that the monetary plan was not intended for the transitional period. This period would certainly last for at least three years. Congress,

and American opinion, after endorsing an elaborate international monetary plan, which was supposed to solve Britain's problems with the help of
large-scale contributions by the United States, would be reluctant to
approve further proposals entailing additional American help for the
transitional period. It would be wise to do first things first and 'try to get
satisfactory and businesslike arrangements for the transitional period
before embarking on the more complex task of building the long-run
international structure'.

Moreover, after having condemned exchange restrictions (except upon
transfers of capital) as an evil, Britain would be in 'a position of constant
humiliation and embarrassment, involving charges of bad faith', if it had to
resort to them, as it would have to. This 'might easily prove a source of
misunderstanding [and] friction', and the process of 'consultation' which
was envisaged would inevitably be stormy.

> But there is another practical danger involved. A likely outcome is that
> in order to avoid such 'discrimination' we should feel obliged to go cap
> in hands for further credits to the United States, or to the Fund. We
> should have placed ourselves in a position in which we should be
> pursuing courses which had been stigmatised as undesirable, pleading
> financial difficulties as an excuse, and having to accept gratefully
> assistance doled out along with admonitions to conduct ourselves better
> in future.[6]

Sir David Waley, who had been an early supporter of the Clearing
Union, became sceptical after attending a series of conferences at the
Treasury to consider the Draft Statement of Principles that Keynes had
brought back from Washington. From the beginning, he had felt the need
for an international organisation, provided that the rules to be followed by
the member countries were rather loosely drawn, and that 'the management of the Scheme, before acquiring formal powers, learnt its job and
moved towards a position in which it could exercise powers as a result of
experience. Managing an internal Exchange Equalisation Account is a
difficult, sensitive and technical job. To manage an international scheme of
that kind is a job that has never been tackled.'

The Americans wanted an institution with specific rules and powers.
The general economic confusion that would inevitably follow the war
made such a finely-drawn scheme for financing trade on current account
premature; 'a more empiric approach will be needed'. One of the major
difficulties was the obligation for multilateral clearing: 'this means an
obligation to convert sterling on demand into whatever currency the
holder of sterling might need. Clearly this is something beyond our powers
in the immediate post-war period.' And he added, somewhat prophetically,
that 'in the end, we shall find ourselves requiring substantial assistance
from America for which she may impose conditions, including, possibly,

adherence to the Monetary Scheme proposed, and some qualification of the exercise of our freedom under the Transitional Period Clause contemplated'.[7]

Some of the most vigorous opposition, according to Waley, came from the Bank of England:

> Up till 1931 and in a large measure also after 1931, the Central Banks of the Sterling Area and of many other countries in Europe and the Middle East looked to the Bank of England as an elder brother and this position of leadership it will be sad to lose to an untried and perhaps ill-qualified international body on which the Americans may well have more influence than we have and in which nationalistic politics may well play too large a part.

The Bank of England had 'an almost passionate interest in maintaining and restoring the position of London as a monetary centre for the sake of all the help that that position gives to the restoration of the Balance of Payments — one of our gravest problems'.[8]

The Bank was still a private institution. Before World War I, it had been the guardian and the centre of a truly international monetary system, the gold standard. The return to the gold standard, in 1925, which was mainly the work of the Bank itself, and was to restore the City to its position of financial centre of the world, had ended in disaster. Out of it had grown the sterling area, a group of countries whose currencies were linked to sterling.

In the Cabinet the spokesman for the Bank of England was Lord Beaverbrook. On 9 February 1944 he submitted a short memorandum to the War Cabinet:

> THIS is the Gold Standard all over again.
> And at a moment when the United States has all the gold, and Great Britain has none of it.[9]

On 6 March 1944 he submitted another memorandum:

> (1) The Bank of England take the view that the Monetary Plan is, in fact, the Gold Standard, subject to 10 per cent. spread and certain limitations to capital movements. ...
>
> (4) The Bank take the view that it is essential to sustain and strengthen faith in sterling. To do so, the Sterling Area must be persuaded to believe in its own currency. Any doubt or misgiving will result in a flight from sterling, with holders trying to sell for any other currency. ...
>
> (6) I am entirely in agreement with the Bank. I support their project. I look with horror on the alternative Plan because it destroys the

Sterling Area. This is all to be done at the compulsion of a Fund in Washington. Many consequences will flow, one of which will be a Black Market in sterling.[10]

Representatives of the Bank of England had handed a note concerning its position to the Committee on External Economic Policy:

The Bank's first objective must be to maintain and develop the acceptability and purchasing power of sterling. This policy is entirely consistent with the general objectives of the Fund: stability, avoidance of unruly capital movements and of speculation in currencies or competitive manipulation of exchange rates, and easy settlement of current account transactions.

But quite apart from the questions whether or when we shall be able to afford to accept the obligations of convertibility and fixed parities, the mechanism proposed by the scheme is inconsistent with our first objective in two respects:—

(1) The Fund as drafted is basically a gold fund — the whole suggestion is that gold-convertible currencies are better than other currencies. This in terms of international currencies means that the Fund will like dollars and encourage their use, but will look askance at sterling.
(2) The Fund as drafted contemplates settlement of international trade payments in the currency of each country and not in international currencies.

Therefore, if we accept the mechanism in principle, even if we defer its operation, we say publicly that we are working towards a system where sterling will be less useful. This can only make our transitional arrangements, where we are largely dependent on the credit of sterling, more difficult.[11]

Thus, the Bank, which had prospered for more than a century on the generally accepted idea that sterling was preferable to other currencies because it was gold-convertible, did not accept this theory any more, because only the dollar was now gold-convertible. Dominance of sterling over other currencies seemed natural and desirable. The Fund, however, might result in a dominance of the dollar. 'If we accept the "Gold Fund"', Lord Beaverbrook warned, 'we lay ourselves down to die.'[12]

Opposition to the Fund also came from the strong group passionately committed to imperial preference. The most effective spokesman for the cause was Leo Amery, Secretary of State for India, who, along with those of like mind, believed that the most important thing was to maintain the Empire, a group of nations closely knit together by economic, political and sentimental ties. To Amery,

Our export trade is not an end in itself. It is the means for securing those imports of food-stuffs and raw materials which are essential to the balancing of our economic system. . . . It is only by the fullest use of the bargaining power of our splendid consumers' market, whether within the Empire or with foreign countries, in order to secure special terms for ourselves, as well as by the firm control of our imports, that we can possibly hope to survive. . . . We must be free to take whatever measures we think necessary to the safeguard of our own production, to develop Imperial Preference, to use our bargaining power with foreign countries, and to strengthen that wonderful monetary instrument the sterling system. We must enter into no international commitments which in any way limit that freedom.

To Amery, joining the Fund meant a policy of imperial disintegration. To him, it seemed incredible that Great Britain, instead of strengthening and developing inter-Empire trade, should consider abandoning it or whittling it away. He warned, 'We are still technically uncommitted. But we have gone dangerously far and are apparently still disposed to drift.'[13] Prime Minister Churchill could not, and did not, ignore these warnings and criticisms. He was particularly sensitive to the position taken by his old friend Beaverbrook. As Churchill noted, there were two fundamental points to be considered: 'First: No fettering of our country, direct or indirect, to a gold standard. Second: No abandonment of Imperial Preference unless or until we are in presence of a vast scheme of reducing trade barriers in which the United States is taking the lead.'[14]

Within the Cabinet there were, of course, some who strongly supported the establishment of an international organisation along the lines that were being considered, and the continuation of the negotiations with the Americans. Among them was Richard Law (later Lord Coleraine), Minister of State at the Foreign Office, who, contrary to the opinion of the Bank of England, felt that the Statement of Principles, 'even though it is dressed up in American terminology', contained the main features of the British plan. 'Anything less like a Gold Standard can scarcely be conceived.'[15] In a note to the War Cabinet on 5 February 1944 he stated,

The new draft explicitly accepts the principle that the value of individual currencies should be changed to suit changing circumstances. It also lays down explicitly that the Fund is not entitled to interfere in any way in the domestic, social or political policies of member countries and must agree to a change which would, in fact, restore equilibrium by other means than a change in such domestic policies. . . . Countries with a seriously unfavourable balance of payments are permitted, while other countries are not permitted to restrict imports; countries with balances of payments so favourable that their currencies become scarce may find their goods subjected to discriminatory restrictions in their export markets; and there is a general principle that while exchange rates may be adjusted when this is necessary to correct a fundamental disequilibrium, they may not be so adjusted unless necessary.[16]

This was Keynes's interpretation of the principles. On a number of points, White would have a different view. Thus, the 'agreement' on principles was vitiated by a basic ambiguity, or, as Robertson put it, 'the cloven hoof in the Monetary Plan'. On the other hand, it is very unlikely that any sort of agreement could have been reached without this deliberate misunderstanding. To White, the words 'not engage in discriminatory currency arrangements' clearly meant non-discrimination in foreign trade.

Keynes's understanding, although he seems not to have mentioned this during the negotiations with White, was entirely different. Shortly before leaving for the Bretton Woods conference he noted,

The point is that currency multilateralism is quite distinct from commercial multilateralism. ... It has been extremely inconvenient to have to discuss the Monetary Proposals whilst concealing one's opinions about the commercial proposals. That is a consequence of the tergiversations of the Cabinet, which we have to submit to but which cannot affect the logical and actual independence of monetary and of commercial multilateralism.[17]

13
The Joint Statement of Principles

Sufficient discussion of the problems of international monetary co-operation has taken place at the technical level to justify a statement of principles. It is the consensus of opinion of the experts of the United and Associated Nations who have participated in these discussions that the most practical method of assuring international monetary co-operation is through the establishment of an International Monetary Fund. The principles set forth below are designed to constitute the basis for this Fund. Governments are not asked to give final approval to these principles until they have been embodied in the form of definite proposals by the delegates of the United and Associated Nations meeting in a formal conference.

After this introduction the Statement spelled out the purposes and policies of the Fund: to promote international monetary co-operation; to facilitate the expansion and balanced growth of international trade, thus contributing to the maintenance of a high level of employment and income; to make the Fund's resources available to member countries, thus giving them time to correct maladjustments in their balance of payments without resorting to measures destructive of national or international prosperity; to promote exchange stability; to assist in the establishment of multilateral payments facilities on current transactions and in the elimination of foreign-exchange restrictions hampering the growth of world trade; and to shorten the periods and lessen the degree of disequilibrium in the international balance of payments of member countries.

Members would subscribe in gold and in their local funds. The obligatory gold subscription was fixed at 25 per cent of a member's quota, or 10 per cent of its holdings of gold and gold-convertible exchange, whichever was smaller. The transactions between the Fund and the member countries were described in detail.

The par value of a member's currency would have to be agreed to with the Fund, and expressed in terms of gold. Members agreed not to propose a change in the parity of their currency except to correct a fundamental disequilibrium. Changes were to be made only with the approval of the Fund. A change not exceeding 10 per cent was allowed, and a further change of 10 per cent could be requested, the Fund having to give its decision within two days.

A member was not allowed to use the Fund's resources to meet a large or sustained outflow of capital. It was not intended to prevent capital movements provided they were in accordance with the purposes of the Fund.

When it became evident that the demand for a member's currency was such that the Fund's holdings of that currency would soon be exhausted, the Fund might declare that currency scarce and temporarily restrict the freedom of exchange operations in that currency.

The Fund would be governed by a board on which each member country would be represented, and by an executive committee of at least nine members, including the representatives of the five countries with the largest quotas.

Except for the revision of members' quotas and a uniform change in the gold value of member currencies, all matters would be settled by a majority of votes. Withdrawal from the Fund could be effected by giving notice in writing.

The obligations of member countries were: not to buy gold at a price which exceeded the agreed parity of its currency, nor to sell gold at a price lower than the agreed parity; not to allow exchange transactions in its market in currencies of other members at rates outside a prescribed range based on the agreed parities; not to impose restrictions on payments for current international transactions, restrictions on capital transfers being allowed; and not to engage in discriminatory currency arrangements or multiple currency practices without the approval of the Fund.

Since the Fund was not intended to provide facilities for reconstruction or to deal with obligations resulting from the war, a transitional period of three years was foreseen during which member countries would be allowed to maintain certain exchange restrictions on current account.

The Statement of Principles as published in London was preceded by explanatory notes stating in what way the principles agreed upon differed from or resembled the Clearing Union proposals.

Instead of being allowed to run overdrafts, members would have to make an initial subscription to the Fund, which would be diminished as it drew on the resources of the Fund. 'These two arrangements represent alternative technical setups, capable of performing precisely the same functions.' It had been easier to obtain agreement on the mechanism proposed by the Fund, because it was closer to what was already familiar.

As a consequence of this, it was no longer necessary to introduce a new international unit, since only if member countries banked with the Fund would such a unit become absolutely necessary. Although the aggregate facilities provided for in the Fund were smaller than those proposed for the Clearing Union, they were substantial, and could be increased by later agreement.

The Clearing Union proposals had been criticised on the ground that they made insufficient provision for the elasticity of exchange rates. The new proposal explicitly provided for alteration of exchange rates, while maintaining the principle that a change in the parity of a currency was a proper subject for international consultation. The Fund was required to approve any change which was essential to the correction of a fundamental disequilibrium, and would not be allowed to criticise the domestic social or political policies of a member applying for a change. If a member disagreed with the Fund, it could withdraw without notice and without penalty.

The Clearing Union proposals had included certain provisions putting responsibility for the maintenance of a reasonable equilibrium in the international balances of payments on the creditors as well as on the debtors. In the Statement of Principles these had been replaced by the scarce-currency provision, which was perhaps even more far-reaching.

After a transitional period of three years, the Fund would be entitled to make representations to member countries for the withdrawal of currency restrictions, but no member was committed as to any fixed date for the final removal of restrictions, and each country would decide for itself when it was strong enough to undertake the free convertibility of its currency, which it had accepted as a desirable aim.[1]

These explanatory notes had been prepared by Keynes, and it was obvious that the principles meant different things to different people. The Statement of Principles left some questions open: 'gold-convertible exchange' was not defined, nor was 'fundamental disequilibrium'. Provisions for the management were vague, and a number of important issues that would come to the surface later were not touched.

The Statement of Principles was, in general, well received. On 22 April all national newspapers in Britain devoted prominent news and editorial comment to the Chancellor's announcement and the statement itself. There was a tendency to sound a note of caution and to view the practical success of the plan as dependent on certain conditions, mainly the solution of the trade and tariff policies. A few papers depicted the Statement as tantamount to a return to gold, and as an American victory over British proposals.

The American press felt that the joint scheme followed the original American proposals more closely than the British, although many of the

objectionable provisions of the successive drafts of the White plan had
been considerably diluted. The *New York Herald-Tribune* noted that the
plan did away with many of the features of the Keynes plan which were
particularly subject to criticism in the United States. It followed the
pattern of the US Treasury in its emphasis on the role of gold. Although a
scheme like this was strictly limited in its functions, it could promote
international co-operation in the field of exchange dealings and correct
temporary dislocations, but it could not by itself cure the ills which were
the cause of chronically erratic currencies. The only remedy for such
conditions was a balanced trade position and sound internal fiscal
policies.[2]

An American industrialist noted that, as a result of the plan, the United
States could succeed Britain as the world's chief banking centre.[3]

Secretary Hull considered that world stabilisation of currencies and
promotion of fruitful international investment were basic to the expansion
of international trade. 'A great many things will tend to interfere with our
getting on with the reconstruction expeditiously, natural hurdles that we
have no control over. But among the greatest difficulties will be un-
certainty as to the stability of currency and as to the flow of international
investment for postwar reconstruction and development.'[4]

Congressional reaction ranged from warm enthusiasm in some quarters
to the conclusion of Representative Frederick C. Smith: 'So perilous to
the United States that no words can describe it . . . one of the most, if not
the most un-American proposal ever presented to the people of this
country.'[5] By contrast, Representative Wright Patman, Democrat, of
Texas, thought it 'the finest constructive step any government has ever
taken'.[6]

14
Towards the Conference

Morgenthau had taken unusual care to interest the press in the recommendations of the monetary experts. On 20 April, the day before the release of the Statement of Principles, he held a lengthy press conference on the subject, and discussed the matter freely and with exceptional frankness, both on and off the record. 'Harry White was there . . . and when Morgenthau seemed if anything slightly more muddled over the recommendations than his questioners White was appealed to or intervened tactfully without being asked. On one occasion Morgenthau after being corrected, gently remarked "see what a polite assistant I have".'[1]

Morgenthau was very emphatic that no advance information should be given on the Statement. Not only would it be embarrassing if Congress learned from the newspapers what he was going to tell them, but in addition he had pledged his word to thirty-four nations that no news would be released before 8 p.m. Eastern Standard Time on 21 April. Correspondents asked amid laughter if he could guarantee that the British would not, as usual, break the news too soon. Morgenthau said he hoped there would be no leaks.

There had been no leak after his appearance before the Congressional committees; despite Morgenthau's and White's fears that some information would be cabled to London and that the news would be prematurely broken there, nothing seemed to have come out.

'If it did, it would be very pleasant if we got there first, once', Morgenthau had told White.

'Four times at a bat', White answered.

As it turned out, the story was released from London two and a half hours before the correct time, and some American papers used it with a London dateline. A British observer who attended the press conference wrote in his confidential report,

Matters have now reached a point when it is hardly news that the British don't keep their word, or cause a mix-up, over release dates. The 'man bites dog' story would be if the British *did* abide by an agreement as it was understood here. These continuous breaches while angering officials don't meet with quite so strong a reaction from correspondents. Their attitude is more one of sorrowful amusement, much as they would say 'so you're drunk again' to an incorrigible friend.[2]

At his first press conference Morgenthau had to admit that the Russians had not accepted the recommendations. At his second conference, however, he was able to announce with obvious pleasure that Russian acceptance had just come in. When a reporter remarked, half-humorously, 'You mean you put the heat on them', Morgenthau protested in alarm that any such implication would be the worst possible way of treating the subject. He had cabled Moscow urging the importance of presenting a united front and thus making the maximum impact on German morale, and this had prompted Molotov to agree.

During the discussion of the part the smaller nations have played in the negotiations the Secretary exhibited a somewhat cavalier attitude. Some of the smaller nations had objected to minor points but that didn't alter the fact that the recommendations as published constituted a consensus of their views. Harry White . . . poked fun at the British for insisting upon the phrase 'consensus of opinion'. This redundancy should not be laid at the feet of the American experts. . . . Morgenthau was also somewhat off-handed in the part which the smaller nations would take in fixing the gold parities of their postwar currency. 'We'll ask their advice and then fix it for them', he remarked amid laughter.[3]

Now that the publication of the Statement of Principles was assured, Morgenthau made plans for a conference to convene about 26 May. He cabled the Chancellor of the Exchequer, 'It seems to me that if you could come to the United States at the head of the United Kingdom delegation it would provide an excellent opportunity for us to become acquainted and to go over our common problems with our colleagues of the Soviet Union and China.'[4] He was disappointed when he received an answer to the effect that Sir John Anderson would not be able to decide for two weeks whether or not he agreed to a conference at the end of May. Lord Halifax cabled London,

White unburdened himself freely to Opie and said that . . . something serious lay behind delay on our side since the Autumn discussions in Washington, and suspected that the trouble was a difference of objectives between what White chose to call the internationalists and nationalists in England, two groups which he thought were not unlike

internationalists and isolationists in America. He feared British resistance to calling a monetary conference was jeopardising the success of
international collaboration as a whole and that this transcended in
importance the relatively narrow aims of monetary proposals. The
danger arose because important United States Republican forces were
still opposed to international collaboration in the full sense, both
political and economic, the most that they would contemplate being a
partnership where Britain would be in their view decidedly the weaker
partner. Moreover many people in United States Administration
believed there was a similar group in the United Kingdom who would
like to constitute an exclusive Empire bloc for the purpose of increasing
the United Kingdom as a European power and of entering into
arrangements with individual countries in which the Commonwealth or
even the United Kingdom would play a stronger part analogous to the
part which American 'imperialist–isolationists' envisaged for the United
States. . . . The British nationalists group were, in White's opinion, by
holding up the progress in international lines playing into the hands of
American isolationists who were their and the world's worst enemies.

Halifax suggested that 'if you are clear that Conference is impossible, you
should centre your case exclusively on security grounds and corresponding
difficulty of transportation'.[5]

'White's explanation to Opie of the causes of the delay over here is a
piece of insubstantial imagining', the Chancellor cabled back. The first
definitive proposal he had heard for a formal conference of finance
ministers, which he was expected to attend personally, had been received
only a week before. In view of the pressure of financial business in London
he could not possibly keep the date suggested. Furthermore, the American
reference to an agreement of some thirty nations was ahead of the facts.
The Dominion premiers still had to give their opinion, and discussions had
just begun with representatives of the European countries, whose adherence to the plan was absolutely essential 'if it was to have any practical
meaning at all'. While war events made any commitment difficult (the
Allies were preparing for D day), he thought it might be possible to
arrange for a conference of experts early in June. Although there were
sections of opinion who regarded the monetary plans as a mechanism
which could be fully effective only if other economic policies of the major
countries were consistent with its purposes, and although delay on
commercial and commodity policy seemed inevitable, he was willing to
co-operate in a conference on the Monetary Fund alone, provided the
conference were in the form and for the purposes he described. In
addition, the War Cabinet was so preoccupied with other matters that it
had to defer for the moment a clear decision about the subsequent stages.[6]

Keynes wrote to the Chancellor that it was vital not to fall out with the
Americans over the question of international collaboration in the

economic field, which was part of President Roosevelt's immediate programme.

I do not think he wants our ardent support along these lines. Indeed, it might embarrass him. All that he requires is that we should not obstruct this line of development or retard his time-table. . . . Could not the Prime Minister and the Cabinet be persuaded to see the thing in this light? Is it not clearly in our interest to help the President along the above lines and not to obstruct him?

Those who took the line of imperial preference, including the Members of Parliament who had spoken in favour of it, did not know that the Canadians agreed with the State Department, and had so advised the Americans.[7]

Morgenthau became insistent. He cabled Ambassador Winant, 'We must have a definite response to the following question: Will the British Government send a delegation to a monetary conference at the end of May if the President issues an invitation? This matter is now before the President and we expect to call you Saturday morning with the hope of receiving a "yes" or "no" answer to this question.'[8]

Winant cabled back that he was convinced it would be impossible for the British to agree to the schedule, for two reasons. Before appointing a delegation to an international conference, it was necessary to consult in London with the Dominions, and, following such meetings, to have a debate in the House of Commons. Before the government could take such a step it would need the support of a majority in Parliament. This contrasted with the American procedure, where executive commitment could be accepted or rejected by Congress *afterwards*. British procedure ensured practical commitment to the project by a responsible delegation. Military security was another consideration. All communications and all travel from Britain had been suspended except for American and Russian officials. This meant that other governments in residence in London would not be permitted to attend the conference. He suggested a delay of two weeks.[9]

On 3 May Morgenthau cabled back, 'The Soviet Government has now advised us of their intention to participate in the conference. . . . This means that calling of the conference depends now upon your success in obtaining British participation.'[10]

When, on 4 May, Ambassador Halifax gave Morgenthau the reasons for the delay, White, who was present, said he 'wasn't terribly impressed with either of the reasons'. Halifax then discussed the distinction between a conference of experts and a conference of the character the United States was contemplating. According to White,

It was finally agreed that there was no difference. . . . It was agreed that the representatives attending the conference would be coming in a sense in their expert capacity though they need not be designated experts. Lord Halifax suggested, 'Why not have the meeting called of experts?' I pointed out the word might have a supplementary meaning. Secretary Morgenthau stressed the view that it would be much more desirable from our point of view and the State Department's point of view to have the delegates attending the conference referred to as representatives rather than experts. It was agreed that the conference should be referred to as a conference of the representatives of the governments.[11]

Early in May Keynes held several meetings with the experts of the Allied governments in London to discuss and explain the provisions of the Statement of Principles. The main concern of the European representatives seemed to be the quotas. Keynes explained that none of the formulas so far suggested had been found practical for every case, and it had been agreed to drop a specific formula at this stage. Keynes had suggested higher quotas for the smaller countries, but White had not accepted because this would increase the aggregate to too high a figure. He would, however, continue to sponsor higher quotas for some countries.

Norwegian delegate Professor Keilhau thought that the reference to the 'consensus of opinion of experts', as the Statement had been called, had been misunderstood by the press, and was in fact an exaggeration. 'Lord Keynes added that the Statement was necessarily vague in this respect, because it was not known on this side precisely who had been consulted by the Americans.' Professor Keilhau then stated, 'it would be difficult to keep the books of the Fund in a great variety of currencies, and he thought that an international unit of account would be forced on the Fund in due course. It would therefore be better to adopt one now. The difficulties of introducing such a unit were only those of denomination and exact value, and he hoped the idea had not been dropped.' Keynes thought that if the Fund had to use a common unit, it would probably be weights of gold. 'Nevertheless, if professor Keilhau was right, and they were forced towards an international unit, so much the better.'

The Dutch delegate Dr Beyen thought every effort should be made to discourage the possible inference that every sort of disequilibrium could be cured by exchange depreciation, as the Statement of Principles seemed to imply. Keynes agreed that exchange depreciation 'was no cure for many forms of disequilibrium'.

Mr Varvaressos, of Greece, pointed out that discussions on possible changes in parities had, in the past, caused a great deal of speculation, and he hoped it would be possible to safeguard the members against this. Keynes stated that the discussions must take place within a small group, and that this would assure their confidentiality.

Other delegates made constructive contributions, or expressed doubt over some of the provisions of the Fund. But they all agreed to take part

in future discussions, if and when desirable. The Europeans agreed with
Keynes that the use of the Monetary Fund for the complicated problems
of the transitional period would be limited. It dealt with current trade,
after that trade had been re-established; it did not deal with reconstruction
loans. Nor did it make any distinction between countries which had
escaped war damage and those that had suffered considerable destruction.
They did not know what conditions would be in their countries after
liberation, and could accept only with reservations the discipline and the
obligations of the Fund. They felt that in the early postwar years the Fund
should be more a medium for regular consultation than an institution
attempting to enforce discipline ahead of events.[12]

Keynes drew attention to the difference between the gold standard and
the system that was being planned. While the Statement of Principles said
that the par value of a member's currency would be expressed in gold, this
was merely a method of measurement. 'The Fund itself possesses no
international currency to whose value the values of the various currencies
could be related. Gold is the only alternative recognised international
measure.' But while fixity of value in terms of gold was the essence of the
gold standard, as it had functioned, the Statement of Principles set out the
opposite point of view.[13]

With an eye to the House of Commons debate on the Statement of
Principles, Keynes made a number of suggestions. He thought that 'the
Chancellor's speech might try to avoid technicalities except so far as the
actual course of the Debate renders them necessary', and he hoped that
the Chancellor would categorically deny that the proposals were open to
the charge of reinstating in any respect the gold standard:

> I suggest the following passage: The question has been raised whether
> the proposals would involve us in any way in what could be properly
> described as a return to the gold standard. As I understand these
> provisions exactly the opposite of this is the truth. . . . The former gold
> standard was a firm understanding approaching almost to a moral
> contract that changes in the gold value of a currency would not be
> made except in very abnormal circumstances and under *force majeure.*
> Thus there was a very strong presumption in favour of rigidity. . . . The
> proposals of the Fund . . . assume that . . . the par of a country's
> currency would be changed whenever there is a good and sufficient
> reason for this, and whenever a change would assist that country to
> reach equilibrium . . . .

The one-way convertibility of gold also differentiated the proposals from
the gold standard: 'gold can be used to buy a currency at whatever
happens to be the par of that currency at the time, but there is no
corresponding liability to turn that currency into gold'.[14]

The debate took place on 10 May. The government had been careful.

The terms of the motion described the Statement of Principles as 'a suitable foundation for further international consultation', and the debate made it clear that this phrase was to be narrowly interpreted. Almost every speaker expressed some doubts about the plan, and some were openly hostile: it meant a return to the gold standard; it would allow an international organisation to interfere with domestic policies directed towards full employment; a transitional period of three years might be too short; there was a danger that the plan would undermine the sterling area.

Mr Robert Boothby, as usual, was one of the most severe critics: it was unfortunate, he said, that the whole problem of international trade and economic organisation should have been tackled from the standpoint of currency. The fundamental dispute was between those who thought of wealth in terms of goods and those who thought of it in terms of money. Money was not petrol, it was oil, and without it the financial machinery was likely to seize up. He thought the currency discussions premature; what was needed was a sound commercial policy and a constructive investment policy, intra-imperial trade and the reinstitution of the sterling area; it was an illusion to suppose that Britain could return to uncontrolled multilateral trade.[15]

The Chancellor of the Exchequer denied that the scheme in any way involved a return to the gold standard. The attitude of the government to any suggestion of a return to the gold standard would be one of 'the most vehement opposition'. The plan aimed at keeping national currencies in relationship with gold by an adjustable link, and was designed to facilitate the adjustment of exchange rates where a fundamental disequilibrium had arisen. The government would not favour any plan likely to interfere with the interrelationships of nations in the sterling area, and there was no obligation to get rid of imperial preferences. The currency plan was one part of a broader scheme. There was nothing in it which would prevent Britain from entering into reciprocal trade agreements with other countries, either in the monetary or in the commercial field. He did not think it unreasonable to work out the technical details of a plan of this kind, while reserving final judgement until the whole picture could be evaluated. The motion was agreed.[16]

The debate in the House of Commons was a bitter disappointment to Keynes. 'I spent seven hours in the accursed Gallery, lacerated in mind and body.' Without having studied the plan, Members of Parliament seemed to be violently against it, for no other reason than that the Americans had agreed to it.[17]

He commented that 'almost incredible stupidity was shown in the debate on the monetary plan', but thought that only two or three people had instigated the agitation against it. However, while recognising that imperial preferences were the principal cause of the opposition displayed by some ministers, in a conversation with officials of the American embassy in London he pointed to the form in which the Joint Statement of Principles was drawn up as even more influential.

The central difficulty was that the exposition at a number of points in the document started out with flat prohibitions of certain practices and measures and only later introduced qualifications and limitations which indicated that the practices and measures could be resorted to in specified conditions and were not actually 'prohibited' in any absolute sense at all. Exposition in this form might appeal to American opinion, but the circumstances were quite different here.

Keynes said that in drafting the monetary plan he had kept political factors constantly in mind, and had frequently adopted a wording that would meet fears and doubts of potential critics, without making any difference whatever to the substance of the plan.[18]

A few days after the Parliamentary debate, the Statement of Principles was brought up for discussion in the House of Lords. Introducing the debate on 23 May, Lord Addison, while admitting to have no expert knowledge on the subject, contented himself by asking a number of questions which he hoped Keynes would answer. He was mainly interested in knowing to what extent the scheme being contemplated differed from the Keynes plan. Was the British quota not inadequate? Would the plan not interfere with the large-scale purchases of food the government had made from the Dominions during the war, and which it contemplated continuing after the war? Would the plan not interfere with the full employment policy of the government? Despite the assurance by the Chancellor of the Exchequer that the scheme did not involve a return to gold, he was not convinced. Neither was he convinced 'that to dig gold out of the ground in South Africa and to bury it refined in a cellar in the United States is, in fact, adding to the wealth of the world. It may be that I am so ignorant that I do not appreciate that there is some advantage in the process.' Who would determine the value of the currencies and how would the Fund be managed? What powers would it have? Recalling the 'horrid memories' of the interwar years, 'during which the management of our fate, nationally, was largely in the control of the Central Bank', he wanted to know who, under the new international organisation, would have this responsibility.

I am quite sure that it is essential in the future that national control of the major matters of finance policy should remain within the Government of the country, and must not be the business of any semi-independent private corporation. I should be glad if the noble Lord can tell us how national policy in that regard can be made effective through the organization which is proposed.[19]

Keynes regretted, he said, that 'certain features of elegance, clarity and logic in the Clearing Union plan' had disappeared. As a result, however, there was no longer any need for a new-fangled international monetary unit. He commended the new plan as being a considerable improvement on either of its parents. First, it was recognised that, during the postwar transitional period, of uncertain duration, Britain was entitled to retain any of the wartime restrictions and the special arrangements with the sterling area. Second, when this period was over, and the country was strong enough to live year by year on its own resources, 'we can look forward to trading in a world of national currencies which are inter-convertible'.

> To suppose that a system of bilateral and barter agreements, with no one who owns sterling knowing just what he can do with it – to suppose that this is the best way of encouraging the Dominions to centre their financial systems on London, seems to me pretty near frenzy. As a technique of little Englandism, adopted as a last resort when all else has failed us, with this small country driven to autarchy, keeping to itself in a harsh and unfriendly world, it might make more sense. But those who talk this way, in the expectation that the rest of the Commonwealth will throw in their lot on these lines and cut their free commercial relations with the rest of the world, can have very little idea how this Empire has grown or by what means it can be sustained.

The plan was, in his judgement, an indispensable means of maintaining the tradition whereby other countries centred their financial systems on London. Sterling being interconvertible with other currencies would make it possible to export to one country and to use the proceeds freely for purchases in other countries. But there was no compulsion, 'and if we choose to come to a particular bargain in the country where we have resources, then that is entirely at our discretion'.

Third, the wheels of trade would be oiled by what was, in effect, a great addition to the world's stock of monetary reserves, distributed in a reasonable way. The quotas, while not so large as under the Clearing Union, were substantial and could later be increased. The quotas for drawing on the Fund's resources were 'an iron ration to tide us over temporary emergencies of one kind or another'. They were not intended for the war-damaged countries to live upon during the reconstruction period, for which another phase of international co-operation would provide, and 'upon which we shall embark shortly unless you discourage us unduly about this one'.

Another advantage was that a proper share of responsibility for maintaining equilibrium in the balance of international payments was squarely placed on the creditor countries. The Americans, 'of their own free will and honest purpose', had offered a formula of protection against 'the draining of reserves out of the rest of the world to pay a country which was obstinately lending and exporting on a scale immensely greater than it was lending and importing'. If this were to happen again, the creditor country would 'release other countries from any obligation to take its exports, or, if taken, to pay for them'. This would avoid a 'repetition of a chain of events which between the wars did more than any other single factor to destroy the world's economic balance and to prepare the seed-bed for foul growths'.

The details of the management had not yet been worked out, but the Fund was to be 'an organization between Governments, in which Central Banks only appear as the instrument and the agent of their Government'. Keynes was convinced that the plan would not interfere with the full-employment policies the government planned to pursue, and Britain would not have to surrender anything which was vital for the ordering of its domestic affairs:

> Sometimes almost alone, in popular articles in the Press, in pamphlets, in dozens of letters to *The Times*, in text books, in enormous and obscure treatises I have spent my strength to persuade my countrymen and the world at large to change their traditional doctrines and, by taking better thought, to remove the curse of unemployment. Was it not I, when many of to-day's iconoclasts were still worshippers of the Calf, who wrote that 'Gold is a barbarous relic'? I am so faithless, so forgetful, so senile that, at the very moment of the triumph of these ideas when, with gathering momentum, Governments, Parliaments, banks, the Press, the public, and even economists, have at last accepted the new doctrines, I go off to help forge new chains to hold us fast in the old dungeon? I trust, my Lords, that you will not believe it.

The plan accorded to every member government the explicit right to control all capital movements. 'What used to be a heresy is now endorsed as orthodox.' It followed that the right to control the domestic capital market was secured on firmer foundations than ever before, and was formally accepted as a proper part of agreed international arrangements.

The question which had been given chief prominence was whether

> we are in any sense returning to the disabilities of the former gold standard, relief from which we have rightly learnt to prize so highly. If I have any authority to pronounce on what is and what is not the essence and meaning of a gold standard, I should say that this plan is the exact opposite of it. . . . The gold standard, as I understand it, means a system under which the external value of a national currency is rigidly tied to a fixed quantity of gold which can only honourably be broken under *force majeure*; and it involves a financial policy which compels the internal value of the domestic currency to conform to this external value as fixed in terms of gold. On the other hand, the use of gold

merely as a convenient common denominator by means of which the relative values of national currencies – these being free to change – are expressed from time to time, is obviously quite another matter.

The sterling value of gold would be fixed by the British government initially in consultation with the Fund. If the external value should be altered so as to conform to whatever change that might occur in the domestic value, 'it is made the duty of the Fund to approve changes which will have this effect'. The domestic policies which had made this change necessary would be immune from criticism by the Fund. 'That is why I say that these proposals are the exact opposite of the gold standard. They lay down by international agreement the essence of the new doctrine, far removed from the old orthodoxy.'

The prolonged and difficult consultations of the past year had encouraged him 'beyond all previous hope and expectation, about the possibility of just and honourable and practical economic arrangements between nations'. 'Do not discourage us', he asked.[20]

After paying tribute to Keynes for his clarity of argument and grace of phrase, Lord Nathan, 'speaking as a layman', asked the question, 'What is this going to mean in terms of trade and employment and standard of living? That is what matters most. Finance exists for trade, not trade for finance.' Monetary management was not a conjuring trick, it was a process. It could not make possible what was physically impracticable, but it could and must make possible what was physically practicable. While he preferred the original Keynes plan, this plan had the advantage of being an agreed plan.

It is an attempt agreed to by experts of thirty-four different countries. What an extraordinary thing but what a magnificent achievement it is that so many experts, representing such diverse interests and with such different traditions, should have come together and have been able to produce a plan such as this with substantial agreement.[21]

Not all the members of the House were convinced by Keynes's speech. Lord Perry felt the plan still amounted to a gold standard, even if gold was put to use only 'as a simple yardstick, a very expensive yardstick'. He could not see why the plan could not work without the use of gold.[22]

The Lord Chancellor, Viscount Simon, reminded the House that the resolution which was being debated was moderately phrased, and that it was only asked to confirm that the Statement of Principles provided 'a suitable foundation for further international consultation'. Lord Perry had asked what was meant by 'gold-convertible exchange'. Obviously, the American dollar was gold-convertible. Lord Perry disagreed: he had been told that the American dollar was no more convertible than the sterling banknote was. The Lord Chancellor was not aware of that, but Lord Perry 'had that on the best authority'.

At this point Keynes intervened: 'May I say that the American experts believed that the dollar was convertible? I have not checked the accuracy of their view.'

The Lord Chancellor strongly recommended that the House accept the proposition, so as to allow the continuation of the discussions. The motion was agreed.[23]

While the reaction of the press to this move was mixed, *The Times* warned that 'Unless the public on both sides of the Atlantic is given a clear idea of the precise implications of the joint statement, eventual controversy about its interpretation might well have a most unfortunate influence on Anglo-American relations.'[24] And the *New York Times* commented on Keynes's statements in the House of Lords, 'Many Americans, when they study the full text of that speech, may conclude that the very arguments that Lord Keynes offers in support of the plan are from both an American and an international point of view against it.'[25]

The German press had followed the development of the monetary discussions closely. One paper noted that, whereas in the early stages of the 'monetary duel' Keynes seemed to have taken the lead by cleverly protecting British interests under the pretext of saving the world economy, while the American plan seemed amateurish, it was now obvious that the Americans were mainly concerned with dollar imperialism, and that they were interested not in factual considerations but in imposing their will because of their superior political power.[26] The *Kölnische Zeitung* noted that Keynes had spoken in the House of Lords not as an economist, but as a man who, for political reasons, accepted as inevitable the concessions made by Britain. The paper asserted that British public opinion was being given a completely distorted view of the situation.[27]

On 11 May, after the debate in Parliament, Sir John Anderson had sent a message to Morgenthau, advising him that 'If an invitation is issued by your Government to a further conference, we will gladly do our best to respond at the earliest date at which security conditions permit, and will arrange for some of the experts of the European countries who are in London to attend.' He added, however, that 'we are not at this stage ready that our representatives should be authorised to commit the Government to acceptance of a scheme'. Therefore the conference would only draft a detailed text for subsequent consideration.[28]

Keynes had told officials at the US embassy that, because of the invasion that was being prepared, it was not practicable for any leading minister to leave the country. He expected to go to the United States personally, and was actively working on an international investment plan, a bank for reconstruction and development; he hoped that his work would be far enough advanced for the subject to be taken up at some stage in the monetary conference.[29]

On 18 May Morgenthau announced to his staff, 'I have been told that

Ambassador Winant, Baron White and Private Morgenthau are to see the
President some time today.' The purpose was to present to the President
the programme for the monetary conference. In the meantime, they would
have to consider among themselves the political and the public relations
aspects of the arrangements.

The Republican convention would be held during the latter part of
June, and there should be no overlapping of the two events. 'There is no
point in trying to get publicity out of anything during the Republican
convention, because they are going to hog all the papers.' There was not
time to make the necessary preparations and be ready before the
convention, so the conference had to be after. The Democratic convention
was going to take place a few weeks later, and, if the conference could be
held before that, there would be an opportunity of making postwar
monetary planning a matter for party politics. This meant that the
conference would have to take place early in July.

'Have you picked a place yet?' Morgenthau inquired. 'How can I if you
don't know the dates', said White. 'Have it in Maine or New Hampshire,
some place up in the mountains there', Morgenthau suggested.[30]

The meeting with President Roosevelt had to be postponed several
times, but when the plans were submitted to the President he immediately
agreed to everything Morgenthau proposed. He read the draft letter of
invitation and approved it. He thought the list of delegates was all right,
and so was the press release. Glancing at the letter by which he appointed
Morgenthau as chairman of the American delegation, he said, 'that's good,
here's where you get your medal, Henry. . . . Go right ahead.'

The President then referred to the fact that Morgenthau had been fixing
some exchange rates for liberated countries. The Secretary said that the
matter of the German rate was coming up and that he might need the
President's support. Roosevelt wanted to know why it was necessary to fix
any rate. 'Why couldn't we go in there without fixing any rate?' he asked.
White explained that it would be possible to do so, but that there were
certain difficulties. The soldiers had to be paid, and the army had to make
certain purchases. 'Why can't they do it in dollars?' the President asked.
They could, said White, but prices in Germany were all stated in marks,
and it was necessary to convert the mark prices into dollars. White noted
that the meeting lasted 'little more than half an hour and the President
seemed to be in excellent humor and interested in the conference and
approved wholly of the program presented him by the Secretary'.[31]

Morgenthau was also gratified by the fact that 'the publication of the
joint statement took the wind out of the sails of those people in Wall
Street who were lined up to give evidence on the Dewey bill'. Opie advised
London that 'the U.S. Treasury tell me that the hearings were a flop. The
U.S. Treasury are optimistic enough to have told me that if I can deliver
Randolph Burgess to them in favour of the joint statement, they believe
the battle for it will be won.'[32] Mr Opie spent some time in New York

trying to convince the bankers, but on 9 May he had to report, 'The bankers in New York with whom I have been discussing the joint statement of principles on the Monetary Fund allowed themselves to be led up to the trough, but at the last moment they refused to drink.' They were prejudiced, he said, 'partly against the present Administration and partly against what they regard as an interference with the operations of private bankers in international lending'. They were confused about many of the issues. 'Their fear that something may actually come from the proposals made them fall back on the comforting thought that, even if there were a conference, the scheme would stand no chance of getting by Congress.' They resented the fact that the Treasury officials had not taken them into their confidence, and they saw no prospect of being represented on the American delegation to the monetary conference.

Instead of a worldwide monetary agreement, the bankers had consistently recommended a generous loan to Britain, and an agreement between the two countries stabilising the rate between the dollar and the pound.[33] The idea offered some attractions. After reading Opie's letter, Sir David Waley wrote to Keynes,

> Taking a short view it is of much more immediate importance to us that we should be given the option of borrowing up to 3 billion dollars from the United States for the transition period than it is that the Monetary Plan should be accepted for the post-transition period. . . . Of course our real trouble is that we do not know whether in 1945 co-operation with Mr. Morgenthau and Dr. White or co-operation with the New York bankers will be most likely to produce the practical results which we wish.

It was as important, he thought, to stand up for the principles of the Joint Statement as it was not to alienate the sympathies of the bankers.[34]

But Keynes was emphatic. He put 'very little faith in the Bankers loan. What strings would there be to the 3 billion? A great many I should expect.' Until the situation had completely changed, he was sure that from every point of view 'the wise and prudent course is to run with the U.S. Treasury rather than with its disgruntled critics'. If Britain needed help from the United States, the chances of obtaining it would be jeopardised if 'we desert the U.S. Treasury, European Allies and everyone else to flirt with the Bankers who . . . do not know their own mind and have no power whatever to implement their promises'.[35]

Robert Brand, the new British Treasury representative in Washington, shared Keynes's views: 'I do not think that we should be at all guided in our views at the moment by Wall Street . . . I have no doubt that some enlightenment of Wall Street as to the position is desirable.' He conceived his duty first of all to establish as good as possible relations with the US Treasury. 'Wall Street's final influence will depend greatly on the results of the election.'[36]

Opie had advised the Foreign Office that Burgess had told him that 'it would have a bad effect in banking and business circles here, and also in Congress if Lord Keynes were a member of the United Kingdom delegation' to·the monetary conference. 'On the other hand it would be a smart move to make Lord Catto a member of such a delegation because it would help to instill confidence in American bankers if the Bank of England were represented. Burgess added that if the United States Treasury were wise they would include someone from the Federal Reserve Bank of New York in their own delegation.'[37]

On 24 May White called a meeting which was attended by Opie and by Russian representatives. He announced that the monetary conference would start in the first week of July. The exact date had not been fixed, because of some difficulties, including transport and finding a cool place. It was necessary, however, to have a drafting committee meet about three weeks in advance, and it became urgent to decide who would participate. He wanted Mexico, Brazil and France, and he assumed Britain would wish Canada to be a member. White said he would prefer Belgium to Holland, but did not want both. Opie suggested Australia. The Russians made no comments, but said they would have to telegraph home. White said he hoped there would be no objection 'if someone suggested Cuba. They would be silent members and their main function would be to bring cigars.'

In order not to upset the representatives of the countries that would not be invited to this drafting committee, it was decided to advise them before any statement was released to the press.[38] White knew very well that this international drafting committee was not going to draft anything, although he stated that it would do more than draft just an agenda, as the press release indicated. When Keynes learned of these plans, he felt that

Dr. White's conception of all this seems to get 'curiouser and curiouser'. 42 nations, making 43 in all, have been invited for July 1. They are to have no power of commitment or final decision and everything is to be *ad referendum*. Nevertheless it now appears that they are not even to have the semblance of doing any work, since that is to be done before they meet. ... The American newspapers have indicated that 'the Conference beginning on July 1 may last several weeks'. Unless this is a misprint for several days, it is not easy to see how the main monkey-house is going to occupy itself. It would seem probable that acute alcoholic poisoning would set in before the end.

Most of the countries invited, the majority of them from Latin America, knew little or nothing of international finance, had nothing to contribute, and would merely encumber the ground. This was to be the 'most monstrous monkey-house assembled for years'. It seemed outrageous and completely unreal to put on the drafting committee countries like Panama, Haiti and Liberia but to exclude Holland and her empire.[39]

On 26 May, Morgenthau issued a press release stating that President Roosevelt had called an international conference for the purpose of discussing proposals to meet postwar international problems. 'Invitations have been extended to all the United Nations and the nations associated with them in the war, requesting them to send official representatives to the United States for the conference which will begin July first. . . . All agreements worked out by the conference subsequently will be submitted to the respective governments for approval.'[40]

Finding, at such short notice, a place for the drafting committee to meet was a serious problem. White wanted the meeting to take place outside Washington, to avoid the inevitable interruptions. He had just received a letter from Keynes stating that, because of the heat, it would be considered an unfriendly act if he were asked to come to Washington in July. The Claridge Hotel in Atlantic City was finally selected, because it could accommodate the group and because the climate was more convenient.

While Harry White was preparing, under high pressure, and, as he said, 'despite considerable non-cooperation from the State Department', for the Atlantic City and Bretton Woods conferences, Keynes was preparing to sail for the United States, at the head of the United Kingdom delegation. While White was concerned mainly with long-range planning, Keynes concentrated on the immediate postwar period and on the problems Britain would have to face. Just before leaving he completed a long memorandum entitled 'The Problem of our External Finance in the Transition'. Compared with 1919, the problem would be greatly aggravated. After World War I, 'nearly the whole of our 1914–1918 external debt was canalised into the American debt – and that we shuffled out of. On the assumption that this time we intend to pay, the fact that we owe money all over the place . . . means that the effort required to emerge without loss of honour, dignity and credit will be immensely greater.'

As one of the three Great Powers responsible for pacifying the world, Britain would need cash and it would only have debts. Its position would be ludicrously out of proportion to its responsibilities. Britain was bearing a disproportionate share of the financial burden of the war, but was mainly concerned with appeasing its allies and the neutral countries. Keynes 'noted the more realistic and entirely successful methods of the Russians. For one then understands how little appeasement and gentleness contribute to pride and prestige.'

As far as Britain's postwar export drive was concerned, a frontal attack was needed on the American attitude towards the British programme. Whilst exports were a luxury to the United States, they were a matter of life and death to Britain. Moreover, in the race to recover export markets, Britain would start behind.

But inevitably there would remain a substantial sum for which the government must look to the United States. The Americans were likely

> to offer us considerably more than it will be wise for us to accept . . .
> we must reduce our requirements for American aid to the least
> possible — say, to $2 to $3 billions . . . ; and even be prepared, if the
> worst befalls, to do without it altogether. . . .
>
> Any accommodation we accept from the United States must be on
> our terms, not theirs. Recent discussion in the United States and
> evidence given before Congress make it quite clear that there are
> quarters in the United States intending to use the grant of post-war
> credits to us as an opportunity for imposing (entirely, of course, for our
> good) the American conception of the international economic system.

This would include the abolition of imperial preference, the linking of sterling to the dollar, and the abolition of exchange controls which prevented the sterling-area balances held in London from being spent on American exports.

It was possible, however, that the United States government was not seriously concerned about Britain's capacity to pay. 'They want to get their stuff out somehow, and our obligation is better than most.' Resenting the fact that only British exports could be purchased with these sterling balances, they might 'be quite happy to canalise a proportion of our present debt to the Sterling Area into a debt to themselves'.

What he was suggesting was 'a hard doctrine. It might mean postponement of much that the public is being led to expect.' But, if these recommendations were rejected, 'the best alternative (and one which it is ill-omened to mention, since it is so likely to be adopted) is to borrow all we can from the United States on any terms available, and in due course, shuffle out. The Americans, as we have mentioned above, may positively tempt us to this course.'[41]

15
Rehearsal at Atlantic City

The international monetary conference Harry White had been planning for two and a half years was at last within his reach. Under the leadership of the US Treasury, the delegates of forty-four Allied and Associated Nations would lay the foundation for worldwide economic co-operation. It would be the first major international conference to deal with postwar reconstruction, and would set the pattern for other conferences to follow. If successful, it would stand as a landmark in history, and bear witness to the high economic statesmanship of the participants. Many hurdles still stood in the way of final success; but, as usual, White concentrated the full thrust of his energy on the immediate tasks, while never losing sight of the ultimate goal.

A polyglot international gathering, with delegations from many countries, each with its own problems, demands and temperaments, could easily degenerate into a debating contest. The agenda was heavy, and there would be no time to thrash out the many unresolved issues, nor to resolve the conflicting interests and contradictory views of the numerous participants. Although a compromise had been reached on some matters, there remained many areas of disagreement, and new controversies would certainly come up. White's chief interest and main concern was the Fund. The preliminary work on the Bank for Reconstruction and Development was far behind, and it was doubtful that there would be sufficient time to formulate definite proposals and to reach agreement during the conference.

In order to keep control over a congerie that could easily get out of hand, it was necessary to have a small, dependable and well informed organisation constituting the nucleus of the conference and keeping it moving in the right direction. White's first task was to build such an organisation. To his closest assistants at the Treasury he added several

156

people from the Federal Reserve, the State Department and other government agencies. These people would be trained to become technical advisers to the American delegates. It was on this small group, working mostly behind the scenes, that the success of the conference, as White saw it, would depend.

A major point of White's strategy was to neutralise his most formidable and intractable opponent, the only one able seriously to upset his plans. Keynes's international prestige and his persuasive power might sway the delegates on a number of controversial issues, and this could easily lead the conference into an impasse or on an undesirable course. By appointing Keynes chairman of the commission on the Bank, he would keep him busy, so that he could not interfere too much with committee meetings where the provisions of the Fund would be discussed.

White himself would head the commission on the Fund, but, to create goodwill among the foreign delegations, the chairmen and the reporting delegates of the committees would all be foreigners. This had the advantage of giving a truly international appearance to the conference, while the impact on the outcome would be slight. What was important was to have a signed document, an 'agreement' that could be referred to, long after the noises of the conference had faded away. Writing up such a document would be the task of the secretaries of the commission, of the committees and of the Secretariat of the Conference. All the secretaries and their assistants would be Americans. They would select and propose the subjects to be discussed, count the votes, and, above all, write the minutes of the meetings and the Final Act.

It was this small group that White decided to train, and to build into a homogeneous and cohesive team that would understand the issues, defend the American position on each point, and make sure that the Final Act – the agreements – would reflect this position as closely as possible.

On 15 June this small group met at the Claridge Hotel, Atlantic City, and for two weeks they were to be the microcosm of the Bretton Woods Conference. White had not invited any of the official American delegates to this meeting. At the outset, White told the group that at Atlantic City there would be no limit to the frèedom of discussion, but that, once agreement had been reached among themselves on the position to take, they were expected to stand firm on the position of the American delegation, regardless of personal opinion.

White divided the group into four committees, corresponding to those that would be organised at the conference: 'Purposes, Policies and Subscriptions'; 'Operations of the Fund'; 'Organisation and Management'; and 'Establishment of the Fund'. Each committee was handed one or two typed sheets, called 'flimsies'. The flimsies listed the US Treasury's proposed amendments to the Joint Statement of Principles, and alternative suggestions made by foreign delegations since the publication of the Statement. The committees' assignment was to discuss two or three related provisions of the Statement, and the proposed alternatives, and to suggest modifications at a general meeting.

The topics discussed included the obligations of member countries, quotas and voting power, the charges to be imposed by the Fund, the withdrawal or suspension of members, changes in parities, and so on. For five days the group discussed these subjects intensely. Once a day they reported to a general meeting headed by White, and suggested changes. This also gave White an opportunity to familiarise them with the American position on the major points. No one except White's closest Treasury assistants was allowed to see a complete draft, although several participants repeatedly asked for it. White also insisted that no minutes be kept to which anyone could later refer.[1]

On 19 June several foreign delegations arrived at Atlantic City. The committees were expanded, and the same procedure continued for several days. White had said, however, that the discussions with the foreigners were not supposed to be 'serious' until the British arrived. One of the American participants noted: 'Everyone is dying to see a complete draft of the Fund and Bank. It is very difficult to figure out how the flimsies are supposed to fit in with the Joint Statement, whether the new provisions are to be added or to replace similar provisions in the Joint Statement.'[2]

Back in Washington, Morgenthau was becoming restless. White had gone a full week and nothing had been heard of him. On 22 June the Secretary called, and complained that he did not 'know what's going on other than I hear when you're short of bath towels'. White explained that he had been meeting 'day and night with the American group to agree on our positions . . . we're going over the various points, seeing where we're going to have disagreements or run into trouble, but it's all . . . just an exchange of view and discussion basis'. He was just whipping the complete draft into shape and would then show it to the British as a basis for discussion.

'Yeah, but look; Harry, you're leaving me completely high and dry, and all the rest of the American delegates and then you expect us to come up there and sign on the dotted line, and it won't work. It just won't.'

'Well, I was going to suggest that . . . .'

'I mean it just won't work. It's very nice. I mean, I know you are working your head off, but you're leaving . . . all the rest of us completely high and dry.'

White suggested that some of the American delegates come to Atlantic City and participate in the meetings. Otherwise he could explain to them the American position at Bretton Woods, before the conference started.

Morgenthau was not satisfied: 'Yeah, but supposing I don't like at all what's been agreed to . . . the point is, if you'd send me the stuff and kept me posted as you went along, I would know. . . . If I don't read it, it's my own fault, but if I don't have anything from you, then it's your fault.'[3]

In a memorandum to the Secretary, White explained what he was trying to achieve.

> The work of the U.S. experts in Atlantic City has been of inestimable value in preparing for the Conference. The experts are being trained to work · as a team that will give the U.S. delegates the best possible technical aid at the Conference. As a result of this preparatory work the U.S. delegates can be sure that the policy of this country . . . will be set forth clearly in the drafts now in preparation.

It was important to clarify and co-ordinate the views of the American technical advisers on all questions, and to train them 'in committee work on the tentative agenda of the Conference', as well as to prepare the technical secretariat of the conference. Previous drafts on the Fund and the Bank had been enlarged and revised, and a complete draft of an agreement for establishing an International Monetary Fund was being prepared as the basis for the work of the US delegates at the Conference. 'No attempt is being made to get agreement on these drafts. We are concerned with clarifying questions and finding out where difficulties arise.' By having the various committees discuss the draft, the experts of all countries had

> an opportunity to express their views. . . . The U.S. experts are in this way kept informed of the questions that will be pressed by the foreign delegates at the Conference. The success of the Conference depends not only on the technical preparation by the U.S. experts of the material needed by the U.S. delegates, but as well on the assurance that the Conference secretariat, staffed by technical men from the Goverment departments, will know their duties and perform them efficiently. This is what we hope to do during the period of the agenda committee meeting.[4]

While these meetings were being held at Atlantic City, the British delegation, headed by Keynes, together with the delegations from several European countries sailed for the United States. During the voyage the Statement of Principles was reviewed, and Keynes prepared a report containing a number of suggestions for the amendment of several provisions.

The agreed text did not clearly state that the individual member countries retained ultimate authority over the value of their currency. In case of disagreement between the Fund and a member country, it was better to suspend the member from the facilities of the Fund without relieving it from its obligations than to sever relations without penalty and without notice.

Keynes objected to the words 'gold-convertible' (which appeared in three sections of the Statement), on the ground that 'all our researches

into the technical legal position and the opinions of the experts we have
consulted support the view that no such currency at present exists'. He
also questioned the concept 'holdings of convertible exchange', and
Britain's ability to assume the obligation of convertibility after a period of
only three years.[5]

Also during the crossing, Keynes prepared a revised draft of 'the
Reconstruction Bank according to our own ideas, and that also we put
through to the Allies, who greeted it with some enthusiasm'.[6]

At New York, he was greeted by Mr Brand and Mr Lee, and from there
proceeded to Atlantic City.

Shortly after his arrival, he had a conversation with Mr Pasvolsky. He
was convinced, he said, that the establishment of a bank was absolutely
indispensable in order to meet the problems of reconstruction. On the way
over, he and his colleagues had discussed the matter very thoroughly with
the representatives of the governments-in-exile, and had come to the
conclusion that these countries were more anxious about their ability to
secure foreign financing for the restoration of their economies than they
were about anything else.

> Keynes also gave me a picture of some of the difficulties which he
> believed it is important for us to realize in connection with the British
> situation. When I said to him that his speech in the House of Lords had
> caused us considerable trouble here, he replied that the situation was so
> bad that he felt it absolutely necessary to say the things he had said. In
> fact, he said that just before he delivered his speech, there was an
> almost universal conviction in the parliamentary circles that the
> opposition had won out and that the proposal for the stabilization fund
> was dead as far as Britain was concerned. That situation, he said, was
> changed by his speech, but there is still much trouble ahead.[7]

Keynes exposed to the American delegation his ideas of a Bank for
Reconstruction, and the Americans immediately agreed. It also appeared
that agreement on the Fund could easily be reached, since the differences
were slight. After spending two days at Atlantic City, Keynes advised
London that

> everything at present is as smooth and friendly as it could be. Nothing
> worth mentioning had happened before our arrival. . . . White is anxious
> that not too many doubts and choices between alternatives should be
> finally settled here at Atlantic City, since it is important for him that
> there should be no appearance of asking the members of the American
> Delegation who are not here and the other powers not represented here
> to rubber-stamp something already substantially finished. At the same
> time he agrees that we and the Americans should reach as high a degree
> of agreement behind the scenes as to which of the alternatives we are

ready to drop and which we agree in pressing. Thus to the largest extent possible White and I will have an agreed text, but on the surface a good many matters may be presented in alternative versions. How this will work out remains to be seen.

And he added,

Perhaps the most striking feature of the position so far is one which I have not mentioned. Harry White is wreathed in smiles and amiability, hospitable, benevolent and complacent. . . . He also seems extremely fit and happy, and inclined to agree with almost anything which is said to him. Heaven grant that it continues but it seems too much to hope for.[8]

It was. While Keynes was being lulled into a feeling that agreement would be easy, and that the major questions would be resolved between the two of them, White saw trouble ahead.

On 25 June, after meeting with the British delegation, he sent a memorandum to Secretary Morgenthau, advising him of 'several troublesome differences between the British and ourselves which the American delegation will have to contend with at the conference'.

The chief of these are briefly as follows:

(1) The British want to increase the flexibility and ease of alterations of exchange rates. We think we should not budge one bit.
(2) They are advocating changes in the direction of making the resort to the resources of the Fund much more automatic and a matter of right as compared with our view that the resort to the resources of the Fund is always conditional upon the taking of measures for correcting the situation and always in a sense that they are implicit or explicit of the Fund.
(3) They object to what we call 'deterrent charges' on those who utilize the Fund. These deterrent charges are in effect interest rates which increase progressively with the amount purchased from the Fund by anyone country and likewise increase the longer the period before which they are repurchased. . . . We regard this as an important feature in our proposal and it looks as though the American delegation will be in for a difficult time trying to obtain agreement on this matter at the conference.
(4) The British are going to back small countries in their demands for larger quotas, particularly Australia, and are also going to back India's demand that it be accorded an equivalent position with that of China.
(5) There also appears on the horizon a technical fight on what

constitutes gold holdings and offsets and a large number of technical points of a complex though minor character. We hope that most of these minor and technical points will be ironed out before the conference so that the delegates will be free to handle the larger issues.

On the Bank, the British had submitted alternate proposals which seemed to be in accord with the general approach suggested by the American delegation. It seemed that they were not as far behind with the Bank proposal as he had thought, and it would be possible to pursue the matter at Bretton Woods.

We hold a large meeting from 10.30 to 1 in the morning and another from 4 to 6 in the afternoon, reserving the intervening hours and the evening for committee work, for meetings of the American technical group and preparation of material for the following day. Breakfast, lunch and dinner are occasions for bringing our allies in line and softening up the beachheads for D week at Bretton Woods.[9]

During the two weeks spent at Atlantic City, many of the important amendements to the Joint Statement were discussed, but no attempt was made to reach a final decision on them. They were to be submitted again, more or less unchanged, to the Bretton Woods Conference. Since these matters were not to be resolved immediately, they generally were discussed without too much heat, and only on one occasion did Keynes threaten to break off the negotiations. But even this was proof to White that the strategy he had decided on was the only one which would permit him to reach his goal.

On 26 June an important meeting was held between the British and the American delegations. Keynes had prepared aboard the *Queen Mary*, during the voyage to New York, several amendments and proposals he wanted to discuss with White before submitting them to a general meeting. He had redrafted Article IV of the Statement of Principles, after the criticism to which it had been subjected in the House of Commons and in the press. He said it was not very different from the original except on two points.

(1) Each member would retain *ultimate rights* over its exchange rate. This, he said, was not a significant difference.
(2) A country which allows its rate to deviate from the rate agreed upon with the Fund would be subject to the sanction of loosing access to the Fund's resources, while having to maintain the obligations to which it had subscribed. This might be a more severe penalty than forced withdrawal from the Fund, and had the advantage of leaving the door open for further negotiations. The contact would not be

broken.

During the debate in the House of Commons, strong objections had been made against the Statement because the Fund was given authority to accept òr reject a member's request for a change in the par value of its currency. The Chancellor of the Exchequer had replied that this was a misunderstanding, and that he would have the matter cleared up. It was, said Keynes, a point of high political importance.

White replied that he appreciated the difficulties, but that he also had a fundamental problem. The whole purpose of the Fund was to bring about greater stability of exchange rates. The intention was not to repeat the mistakes of the 1930s. In order to obtain this increased stability, the Fund would be willing to assist countries in their effort to maintain it. The *cardinal* point of the Fund was stability of exchange rates. The American position was not in favour of rigidity; flexibility was provided for. He had made a very substantial concession with respect to the unilateral change of 10 per cent. He had then made additional concessions with regard to the second 10 per cent, on which quick action was provided for. By doing so, he had subjected himself to increasing criticism on the ground that he was legitimising instability. If he went one step beyond this, it would bring down the whole structure like a house of cards. People in the United States would say the Fund was just a credit scheme and not a device to bring about stability. Much as he wanted to meet the British view, he could not do it. It was the unanimous view of the American group that they were with their backs against the wall, and that, if they retreated further, it would jeopardise the whole project. White recalled how the American Bankers Association had reacted to Keynes's speech in the House of Lords.

Keynes thought that perhaps the gap between the two positions could be bridged, and he said that he would try to find a formula that would be satisfactory to both. They all agreed that the objective of the Fund was to make the exchange as stable as possible. The British felt that the Fund would be very valuable, because it would prevent disorderly changes in rates. What the United Kingdom was concerned about was the *ultimate control of its own affairs*. It wished to keep the right to do what was in its own interest. It did not like to be in a position of having to withdraw from the Fund if it exercised that right. That sort of withdrawal would have the appearance of defaulting, and the country would be so reluctant to withdraw that it would in fact tend to maintain an exchange rate even if it were no longer considered right. Keynes thought that this would also apply to the United States, and that, if Congress really understood the Fund, it would object to this clause. The experience of 1931, when devaluation of the pound was postponed because of the international obligations resulting from the gold standard were so burnt into the public mind that nothing even remotely resembling this obligation could possibly be accepted. He had thought that there were sufficient safeguards in the plan, but this had proved not to be so; he would try to find a new form of words that would be acceptable both to British public opinion and to the Americans.

White replied that exchange stability had been the basis of all their negotiations, that agreement upon it had been reached, and that to reopen the matter now was very disturbing.

To this Keynes replied that the United Kingdom would use its right to depreciate only if it were felt that the Fund was unreasonable. British public opinion feared that the Fund could be badly managed, which made it difficult to accept in advance the obligation not to act contrary to its directives. What he would propose was that a country could not use the *facilities* of the Fund while at the same time it was using its right to depreciate.

If the British could find a satisfactory formula, White replied, he would be glad to see it. 'The British, in their new suggestion, however, are saying that the consequence of failure to comply with the exchange provision shall be merely deprivation of resources. We think this is very grave. A country may at that time have used up its credits at the Fund and not have any further interest in these facilities.' The new suggestion put forward by Keynes was 'a direct violation of our understanding'. The main purpose of the Fund was to promote stability. Members should not have a *right* to resort to the Fund, and then simply withdraw when their resources ran out. Provisions had been made for suspension, but withdrawal would be a very serious step, to be considered only in extreme circumstances.

The second point Keynes wanted to bring up was the three-year limitation of the transitional period. It was unlikely, he said, that Britain would complete the transition in three years, and other European countries would be in the same position. Their success or failure would depend to a large extent on the policy of the United States. If the United States ran a persistent large export surplus, the problem of Britain and the other countries would be made worse.

White agreed that three years might be optimistic, but Keynes said it was utopian. Although the plan provided that after three years a country might continue to apply controls with the approval of the Fund, Keynes maintained that each country must be its own judge; the Chancellor of the Exchequer had assured Parliament that this would be the case.

Did this mean *no* period, not even ten years?, White inquired. Keynes's answer was that, after a certain period, if a country decided to control its foreign trade, and if it had a good case, it was in the interest of other countries to help; if it had a bad case, it could be expelled from the Fund. But 'the time when approval is required will never come for the United Kingdom'. This was final.[10]

Keynes may have thought he had won the argument, since White did not press the point. White had correctly anticipated that agreement could not be reached by debate and discussion. He could wait until the time came when he would be the arbiter, and resolve the question in the manner he had decided. He did not appear to be taken aback by Keynes's threat to break off the negotiations, nor did he challenge him to do so.

After the meeting, Keynes reported to London on the disagreement with White, and asked for instructions. The answer was that there must be no doubt that it was the member and not the Fund which decided on the change of parity.[11]

These were not the only matters on which there was basic disagreement. Another one, which was discussed at Atlantic City and left for the conference, was that of the 'gold-convertible currency'.

On 28 June, Keynes's recommendation that the words 'gold and gold-convertible exchange', which appeared in several provisions of the Statement of Principles, be replaced by the words 'monetary reserves' was discussed at some length. When asked whether 'gold and dollars' would be satisfactory, Keynes said no. Other currencies would be convertible some time in future, and the dollar should not be given a special positon. White did not take up the matter. Professor Keilhau, of Norway, suggested once more, as he would again at Bretton Woods, that an international unit be adopted, but Keynes rejected the proposal. He did not know that, while he maintained that no gold-convertible currency 'at present exists', and while he objected to the words 'holdings of convertible exchange', White had decided that these words were simply the equivalent of 'dollars'. He and his staff had already submitted to Secretary Morgenthau a memorandum in which the references to 'gold-convertible currency' and 'holdings of convertible exchange' had been replaced by 'dollars'. The memorandum stated that the formula proposed by the American technical advisers for the determination of quotas took account of 'national income, gold and dollar holdings, foreign trade, fluctuations in exports, and the importance of foreign trade in national income'. The gold subscription to the Fund was to be '25 per cent of a country's quota or 10 per cent of its holdings of gold and dollar balances, whichever is less'.[12] No such amendment to the Statement of Principles had been submitted. Nor had the subject been discussed with the other delegations. White simply assumed that a way would be found to include this substitution in the agreement to be signed at Bretton Woods.

Although the British delegation headed by Keynes was the most difficult to handle, it was by no means the only one White had to cope with. At the committees and subcommittees, the representatives from the other countries present at Atlantic City submitted amendments intended to improve the provisions of the Statement of Principles, or to protect their own national interests. White's instructions to the American technical advisers had been to talk as much as possible with the foreign delegates, but to 'stick to the party line', and not to mention any possibility of US compromises.[13]

The most controversial question, and one in which many countries would take a strong interest, would be that of the quotas to be allotted to each member. White had decided that quotas would not be discussed at Atlantic City; nor would the table of them prepared by the US Treasury be shown to anyone outside the American group, because this would lead to endless discussion. Nor, obviously, would the formula be discussed. The delegates knew that the aggregate quotas for the Fund would be between $8000 million and $8500 million. When the individual quotas were announced at Bretton Woods, each country would also know that, if it wanted its quota increased, something would have to be taken away from another country. Thus, instead of fighting the American delegation which had set the quotas, they would have to fight each other.

China wanted to have the fourth largest quota, as a recognition of her role in the war. France wanted her quota fourth or fifth. India, as the largest importing and exporting country in the Far East, insisted that her quota should be larger than that of China. Several of the smaller nations, each for its own reasons, pressed for higher quotas.

Russia wanted to have a reduction of 50 per cent in the required gold subscription, because of the damage caused by enemy action or occupation during the war. Other European countries supported this position, in the expectation they would obtain a similar reduction. Russia also wanted a special provision for newly-mined gold. In addition, the Russian experts took the view that, because Russia is a state-trading country, her exchange rate is not of significance to other countries. Therefore they had introduced an amendment providing that, since Russia's exchange rate had no effect on international transactions, they could change the rate without the approval of the Fund. Russia also objected to linking voting powers exclusively to quotas.

Mexico, Australia and Belgium felt that no member country should have more than 20 or 25 per cent of the aggregate votes. Many countries believed that more pressure should be put upon creditor countries to secure an appropriate balance of payments, and that penalties should also be applied to creditor countries. Mexico wished to have silver recognised as a monetary reserve, next to gold, and used as a basis for the calculation of the quotas.[14]

All these requests and proposed amendments were to be finally dealt with at Bretton Woods, but the meetings at Atlantic City provided an excellent opportunity to prepare for the ultimate decision.

Many problems were still unsolved. The Statement of Principles, as published, had been considerably modified and amplified by White and his assistants at the Treasury, but the revision had not been made available to anyone outside this small group. Only once did Harry White allow the American technical advisers to see the whole document. Several of them 'had been pressing for a complete document, mostly because many difficulties arose in trying to discuss one little section of the document not knowing how the other sections would read but partly also because we all wanted to know all the cards the Treasury had up its sleeve'. When they were finally allowed to see it, the 'copies were numbered and taken back from us after the meeting'.[15] Neither Keynes nor any of the other delegates saw it at Atlantic City.

Since it had been agreed upon, the Statement had also been considerably altered by Keynes. He had suggested to White that their documents be combined, and presented as a single document to the conference, but White had not agreed to this.

Towards the end of the meeting at Atlantic City, White submitted a new proposal — namely, that the principal office of the Fund 'shall be located in the member country having the largest quota', meaning obviously the United States. Keynes immediately asked London for instructions.[16]

Shortly after his arrival at Atlantic City Keynes had cabled,

It is essential in judgment of the Americans with which we concur, that Bretton Woods Conference shall not be presented with agreement for rubber-stamping. This will mean that we must reach general understanding particularly with the Americans about important clauses but the outline presented to the Bretton Woods Conference may contain some alternatives so that the Conference will have something to debate.[17]

There would indeed be something to debate, but Keynes's mind was now set mainly on the Bank; and whatever the other delegates might contribute to the debate would not weigh heavily on the outcome of the conference.

And so, after two weeks of intense labour, the meeting at Atlantic City was concluded. On the night of 30 June the delegates boarded the special train that would take them to Bretton Woods.

16
The Bretton Woods Conference

One participant described it as 'a quiet, green and soothing garden of the gods, circled by mountain ramparts'. A press reporter grew lyrical as he surveyed the scenery:

> Viewed from this wicker chair on the curving porch of the Mt. Washington Hotel the Presidential range of New Hampshire etches zigzag indentations into the azure sky. A dark line against a twisting path of earthy green — that of the merging tracks of the world-famous cog railroad — climbs to the summit of New England's highest peak, Mt. Washington. On its crest, Tip-Top House and the radio tower stand out like a village in a mirage. In the foreground the darker greens of pine and hemlock vie with the lighter shades of oaks and birch. Set in the midst of these the brilliant green of one of the golf fairways forms a grassy floor. A sand trap glistens in the morning sun. Directly below, the wild Ammonoosuc plunges unseen but noisily on its way to join the sea.[1]

The majestic beauty of the surroundings was in striking contrast to the temporary bedlam created by the arrival of about 700 people from more than forty countries. In addition to the official delegates, there were advisers, assistants, stenographers, newsmen, observers, technicians, and so on. Many of them spoke no English at all. The trains that brought them to Bretton Woods were dubbed 'the Tower of Babel on wheels'.

The Mount Washington Hotel, one of the most luxurious summer hotels in the world, had been closed for two years. Of Spanish Renaissance architecture, the hotel was surrounded by the White Mountain National Forest, which covers nearly 1 million acres. The management had only about a month to prepare for the onrush. Painters and cleaners were still busy applying the finishing touches. Rooms were mixed up, offices for the delegates had to be hastily improvised, and there was a general feeling of ineffective goodwill. A group of Army Military Police joined in the work, and even outworked some of the hired labour in the final cleaning of the premises.

Bretton Woods, the postal address of the hotel, was only a stop on the railway. It had no store, not even a main street. The hotel was self-sufficient with its own power-plant, dress shops, beauty parlour, bowling alleys, barber shop, and stock ticker-tape. There were two cinemas, a swimming pool, tennis courts, and stables. A church was located in the hotel grounds.

The extraordinary bustle and confusion regarding the allocation of rooms, complicated by the lack of staff, hot water, beds, and so on, caused at least one casualty on the first day of the conference: the news went around that the new manager of the hotel had either drunk himself out of his job, or else had given up in despair and left.[2]

While the foreign delegations acquainted themselves with their new surroundings, Morgenthau and White set to work. Shortly after their arrival, Morgenthau called a meeting of the American delegates to prepare them for the commission and committee meetings. While some of the delegates, such as Dean Acheson and Marriner Eccles, had been exposed to the plans before the conference, most them knew practically nothing, except what they may have read in the press or heard in Congressional committees. There was Fred Vinson, 'the Judge'; Leo Crowley, Administrator of the Foreign Economic Administration; Miss Mabel Newcomer, professor at Vassar College; Representatives Brent Spence and Jesse Wolcott; Senators Robert Wagner and Charles Tobey; and Edward Brown, president of a large Chicago bank, 'a large, industrious, outspoken man who represented the tractable element of the banking community'.[3] He had been at Atlantic City.

Morgenthau asked White to explain the salient points regarding the Fund and the Bank, and to give 'a broad outline of what the American experts feel as in the interest of our country as a result of the work in Atlantic City'.

The purpose of the meetings in Atlantic City, White said, had been purely exploratory. It had been useful to ascertain the differences of opinion, the major issues troubling the various delegates, so as to provide a basis for discussion and determine the position to take on the various points. He would confine himself to the major issues and differences:

With the Fund, the first major issue is the question of quotas. . . . In the first place, all countries want larger quotas, but the countries that will give us the most trouble . . . are as follows: China insists that she shall have fourth place . . . France is insisting on fifth place and India is insisting on fifth place . . . and has sent a pretty high-powered delegation here. .... The smaller countries all want larger quotas. The most troublesome will be Australia who is participating to an extent far beyond the proper role of a country of her size and importance. .... The South American countries would like a larger quota. Now, it is the South American countries who in this are going to be important to us for reasons that we will discuss later.

The American position had been that the aggregate quotas would not be more than $8000 million to $8300 million, that the American quota would not be larger than $2750 million, and that the British Empire as a whole would have a little less. 'Russia will get third place and she will have about ten per cent of the quotas. There is no problem – I mean, there is general agreement there as long as she had third place.'

The next point of importance was the amount of gold to be subscribed. The only problem here was that Russia insisted on a reduction of 50 per cent, and argued that all other countries that had suffered war damage should have a reduction, relative to the amount of destruction suffered. All the invaded countries supported this Russian claim, and Britain, though it had not been invaded, wanted the same treatment.

Then came the question of voting power. The American delegation had taken the position that voting power and quota should approximately be the same. Smaller countries had objected, and wanted to start every country off with 100 votes. But White did not 'want to budge'.

One of the main points in dispute between the American and British delegations was the degree of flexibility of exchanges and the conditions under which a country could alter its exchange rate. The British, remembering the depression that followed their return to gold, were saying 'that they are never going to be in a position like that again, in which they are tied to the gold standard and have to suffer a depression merely to suit somebody's notions on monetary theories'. Those, like Keynes, who had warned against a return to gold, were now completely in the ascendancy, and the whole British people, with the exception of some banking groups, objected to anything that resembled the gold standard. Although the Fund provided for some flexibility, the British wanted more; 'Our position here is quite the opposite.' He wanted to prevent a return to the 1930s, with floating exchanges, unilateral decisions and exchange depreciation. He realised that, if the British delegation made too many compromises, 'Parliament will throw it out.'

Edward Brown wanted to know why Russia had to be in the Fund: 'Russia doesn't need the Fund. It has a complete system of State trading – state industry. It doesn't make any difference to them whether the ruble is five cents or five dollars. They want to get some other things; they would like to keep a market for their newly mined gold.' But White, for reasons which he would point out later, thought 'the Fund needs Russia'.

Brown also thought that many of the small countries put in claims which they did not expect to get. Morgenthau agreed: the Mexicans would raise the silver question, but only for home consumption, and would not press it too hard. 'So I mean, these fellows are good horse traders, but I think among our delegates we have a couple of pretty good horse traders, outside myself — I trade cows.' As for Keynes, he had his hands full with the British Empire. 'He has an incipient revolution on his hands and . . . we will let the British Empire fight it out without making us a cat's paw.'

The next important point of difference, White said, was the pressure on debtor and creditor countries. The other countries had suggested that pressure should be put on creditor countries, and by that they meant mainly the United States. They expected that the United States would continue to export more than it imported, and to drain the world's gold. So they wanted these creditor countries to adopt a policy which would put less pressure on the exchange of the debtor countries, and 'enable them to sell more goods here. We have been perfectly adamant on that point. We have taken the position of absolutely no, on that. And that has created a good deal of discussion and will continue to create some.' The debtor countries, on the other hand, would have to pay deterrent charges, and the more they borrowed from the Fund the higher the charges would be, so that they would be under pressure to put their balance of payments in order. To the objection of one delegate that deterrent charges might accelerate the indebtedness of a country, instead of reducing it, White answered that these charges were low, but that it was necessary to create an inducement for the country to restore equilibrium.

He also explained that there was little risk for the United States in participating in the Fund. The amount of gold would remain stable, and, if a country devalued, it would have to put up more of its currency to make up for the difference.

The British and a number of other nations, White said, had insisted that their access to the Fund's resources were a matter of right, but the American delegation had persistently taken the attitude that the Board of Directors of the Fund had the power to refuse the Fund's facilities, even though the quota might be available. That was the way the provision now read, 'but it reads in a way that is not too easy to see if you read it quickly'. In drafting the provision the lawyers had taken great care, Luxford added; 'the language gives us clearly that right, but we have tried to avoid emphasizing it more than you have to'. Although there were technical experts at Atlantic City who disputed Luxford's interpretation, White was certain that he was right.

White also objected to the allegations of those who said that the Fund would go 'bust', and that the United States would loose the money it put in. '. . . we have surrounded this thing with protective devices at every point. That doesn't mean it is without risk.' If another war broke out, and 'a country says, "Yes, you have balances here, but try and get them", nothing can protect you against that kind of relationship'. But, otherwise, 'Our lawyers have done a job', White concluded.

If the worse came to the worst, members could always withdraw: 'we did that for our own sake . . . most countries feel that it is satisfactory to them, because it enables them quite appropriately to tell their Congress they are sovereign'.

White explained some of the other matters which had not been resolved, and answered the questions of the delegates so as to prepare them to defend the American position in the commissions and committees, or wherever they were being buttonholed by foreign representatives.

Morgenthau recommended, 'So again, if we play this as a team, if we have any differences, let's have them here in the room and over the bar . . . we have gotten off to a good start. We have some very good New Hampshire sunshine and weather, and let's play this as a team, looking over a broad horizon for future generations.'[4]

THE CONFERENCE GOES TO WORK

On 1 July the delegates met in the assembly hall for the first plenary session. White had suggested that Morgenthau address the conference for the first time on some other day, so that his statements would not be lost among those of the other delegates, but Morgenthau disagreed. He wanted to get 'all the folderol over and then you can get down to work'.[5]

After listening to the message President Roosevelt had sent to the conference, the chairmen of the Chinese, Czechoslovakian, Mexican, Brazilian, Canadian and Russian delegations spoke in the name of their countries. After his nomination as president of the conference, Secretary Morgenthau stated that 'what we do here will shape to a significant degree the nature of the world in which we are to live'. The delegates were not asked to make definitive agreements binding on any of them; they would refer the proposals to their respective governments for acceptance or rejection.

We can accomplish this task only if we approach it not as bargainers but as partners — not as rivals but as men who recognize that their common welfare depends, in peace as in war, upon mutual trust and joint endeavor. . . . We are to concern ourselves here with essential steps in the creation of a dynamic world economy. . . . This is the indispensable cornerstone of freedom and security. All else must be built upon this. For freedom of opportunity is the foundation for all other freedoms. . . . On battlefronts the world over, the young men of all our united countries have been dying together — dying for a common purpose. It is not beyond our powers to enable the young men of all our countries to *live* together — to put their energies, their skills, their aspirations into mutual enrichment and peaceful progress.[6]

As had been planned by White, Commission I (International Monetary Fund), of which he was to be chairman, was to be subdivided into four committees. Commission II (Bank for Reconstruction and Development) was to be headed by Keynes. Commission III was to concern itself with 'Other Means of International Financial Co-operation'.

The four committees of commission I were as follows:

Committee 1 – Purposes, Policies and Quotas of the Fund;
Committee 2 – Operations of the Fund;
Committee 3 – Organisation and Management;
Committee 4 – Form and Status of the Fund.

All the chairmen and reporters of these committees were non-American. They were all referred to as representatives of their respective countries, with the exception of the French, who represented the French Comité. The French resented this, but in the course of the conference some of the differences between General de Gaulle and President Roosevelt were settled in Washington, and the French gradually came to be referred to as French delegates.[7]

As in Atlantic City, each committee was assigned a number of subjects which it had to discuss and, if possible, agree upon. The secretaries of the committees, who were the people White had trained, plus some new ones, trained by White's pupils, wrote up the minutes of the committee meetings and reported to the commission.

It soon became evident that some of the chairmen and reporters of the committees did not speak English, or spoke it very poorly. 'The Russian delegate ... turned the meeting over to his Canadian colleague as soon as he had made his inaugural speech (in Russian). This sensible procedure has not unfortunately been imitated by other chairmen, with the result that several of the committees moved with maddening slowness.'[8]

Dr E. A. Goldenweiser, director of research and statistics of the Board of Governors of the Federal Reserve System, and a member of the American delegation, brought back these observations:

It was very hard work. The delegates of each country usually met by themselves in the morning. There were always two or three meetings of committees and commissions and sub-committees, and later there would be the big task of having all that combined, written and distributed by the next morning. There was a large force of stenographers and multigraphers who worked day and night. They had shifts and ... did an amazingly good job in taking material that sometimes wasn't finished until two or three in the morning. ... One of the nice features of the meeting was a little group of Boy Scouts who were

acting as pages, and helped a good deal in keeping things moving and
distributing things smoothly.   . . .

It was a combination of settling various conflicting interests, and at
the same time hammering out specific provisions. I am not too familiar
myself with all of the provisions. They are inevitably complex because
of the subject, and they are written in a legal language, which I have
always found it difficult to understand.   . . .

There were a great many varieties of people and a great many
varieties of unintelligible English spoken. Most everything was said in
what was supposed to be English. The Russians didn't speak English;
neither did their interpreters. The French spoke English but always had
trouble in being satisfied that their exact meaning was properly
translated by their interpreters.   . . .

The Russians were an interesting group. I could not help feeling that
they were struggling between the firing squad on the one hand and the
English language on the other. They seemed to be very much afraid of
the reactions in their own country, and didn't dare to make a step
without consultation by 'phone or cable with their Government.

(Dr Goldenweiser was born in Russia, and spent his boyhood there.) He
gave this appreciation of Keynes:

the outstanding personality at Bretton Woods was Lord Keynes. He
shone in two respects — in the fact that he is, of course, one of the
brightest lights of mankind in both thinking and expression and in his
ability to influence people, and he shone also by being the world's
worst chairman. He presided over meetings of the Bank in a way that
was entirely intolerable because he had his own documents all fixed up
so that he could go through in a hurry. . . . He spoke while he was
sitting down in a meeting and it was difficult to hear him. He spoke
indistinctly when presiding and was impatient of any difference of
opinion. . . . His function at Bretton Woods was primarily performed in
a suite of rooms on the second floor to which everybody went for
inspiration and guidance and compromise.[9]

It might be noted here that Lord and Lady Keynes had their suite just
above the rooms occupied by Secretary and Mrs Morgenthau. The
penetrating rhythm of the exercises performed by the prima ballerina,
unaware that her routine practising could be heard through the ceiling
beneath, occasionally prevented Morgenthau, worried and tense about the
outcome of the conference, from going to sleep.

During three weeks the overcrowded hotel would be filled with the
extraordinary hustle and bustle of a polyglot conference. More than 700
people had to be accommodated. Since not enough room was available at
the hotel itself, some had to be lodged at nearby hostelries.

COMMISSION AND COMMITTEE MEETINGS

On 3 July, the second day of the conference, the plenary session was devoted to the selection of permanent officers, the creation of committees and the election of those who were to direct the activities of the conference. The chairman of the New Zealand delegation presented the nominees for membership of the steering committee and the three main commissions. All were unanimously approved.

Commission I was given the task of dealing with the Fund. White told Morgenthau that he would preside over that commission: 'The importance why we need somebody to chairman this, who knows the complete matter, is that he should prevent coming to a vote on matters which he doesn't wish to come to a vote on, and in general arranging the discussion in such a way that we are never caught with an agreement among the Commission on something that we don't want, because then it is too late.'

'I don't know anybody more competent', said Morgenthau.[10]

The secretaries of the committees, who were to write up the minutes of the meetings, were designated by White. They were all Americans. At the beginning of the conference, a memorandum had been distributed to the delegates, which said that the 'Secretaries, like all other officers of the Conference, are on this occasion international officials and for all practical purposes temporarily lose not only their national identity but their allegiance to the organizations, governmental or otherwise, with which they are affiliated.'[11] This had the ring of true internationalism. They were, in reality, the people who had been trained by White in Atlantic City (or had been trained by people who had been trained there).

Senator Tobey, in his own state of New Hampshire, made a moving speech:

> It is our common aspiration, I believe, that, assembled here among these eternal hills, we shall, under a deep conviction of the needs of humanity, discard trivia and refuse to be turned away from our great purpose to give to the people of the world new hope and courage through the constructive results which we pray may come from this historic conference. . . . Every great effort in human history has had its saboteurs, men who utter critic peep and cynic bark. There are some of these around the perimeter of this Conference. . . . As we confer together here today, amidst the eternal hills, inspired by the sublime beauty around us, and as the shadows of passing clouds above leave their impress for a moment on the slopes of yonder mountains, may the contemplation of the tragic sufferings and sacrifices of every nation bind us together in brotherly love. . . . Two thousand years ago Christ was hanged on a cross, a spear thrust in his side. . . . There are nations represented here today who, too, have had their sides pierced and a crown of thorns pressed upon them by the sufferings of war. . . .

Gentlemen, we must not, we cannot, we dare not fail. The hopes and aspirations of the common people of each of our countries rest in us.[12]

With the first committee meetings due to take place on 4 July, the American delegation discussed the strategy to follow. The first and most important question that would be brought up, and in which practically every country was extremely interested, was the table of quotas. No satisfactory formula had been found, and no complete list had been published, although many nations had been told what their quota was to be. The British had been working on it in an effort to increase the quotas of the Commonwealth countries. No delegation could go back home, after a table had been published, and meet the charge that they had been bad negotiators. So it was necessary to come to some agreement with the British before announcing the list of quotas. Australia, said White, was 'very rambunctious and almost belligerent in the attitude that she should have a much larger quota. . . . There will be a cat-and-dog fight, anyhow, because every country will want to change. Our safeguard is, however, that if the maximum is fixed, any increase that any country gets has to come out of some other country. . . . It will be a struggle between countries.' One good idea was to hold back a kitty: 'They will make strong arguments . . . and if you can give them a little something, they feel that they have negotiated . . . and I think they feel better.' Dr Goldenweiser did not think it was a dignified situation for America to be bargaining 'with all these people about little items of twenty-five or fifty million dollars'. Why not give them a figure and say 'This is where we stand', and if there is any change the whole American delegation will have to decide.

'It would make them mad at us, though', said Luxford. 'Why should we be the scape-goat for thirty-nine countries?'

'That is right', said White.

The foreign delegates would be told that the total was $8000 million, but the real total would be $8400 million dollars. 'They have got to fight around a couple of days and get nowhere.' If you told them in advance that the total would be increased, they would 'prolong the discussion interminably because they wouldn't believe that is your final figure'.

The next point concerned the rules under which the committee meetings were to be held. White said he had prepared many alternatives, which usually did not change the substance, but were formulated in more appropriate language. It was not necessary for the United States delegates to take much part in the discussions, 'but the boys that will be with you will be able to indicate whether they think something ought to be said, but I think you will find that most of the others will want to talk'.

Would the rules of the committee be some 'catch as catch can'?, Vinson asked. No, they would be very informal, he was told.

'Just make one general rule', Dr Goldenweiser suggested, 'that anybody can talk as long as he pleases provided he doesn't say anything. Separate the business of the Committee from the talk.' He thought his remark might be facetious, but it was rather close to what White wanted.

'You have got to go through the motions', someone suggested; 'the Chairman should go through the motions, at least of asking whether there are any alternatives because, after all, these are the alternatives of Atlantic City and there were thirty countries not represented'.[1][3]

The committees met twice every day. The meetings were staggered, to enable all national delegations to be represented adequately. The committees on the Fund devoted most of their time ironing out technical differences rather than establishing broad lines of agreement. The basis of all discussions was the joint statement and the alternatives submitted by the various countries. Keynes, after he saw the results of the Atlantic City conference, as they had been drafted by White and his group, thought he would have to submit a separate draft, but recognised soon that this would have mixed things up considerably, and gave up the idea.

This was the first international meeting of its kind and importance in which the US Treasury had taken a leading part. It soon became evident that some method had to be devised in order to achieve what had to be achieved, within the time limit available.

'You can argue and argue', said Luxford, 'and we haven't good arguments for some of the things we have to push through.'

'There is no question that you can't vote on every provision', White thought, 'but pursue the same tactics on others. Speaking of legalities for a moment, supposing the chairman, after hearing the discussion, four or five for and one against, and he says that the chair rules that the sense of the meeting is as follows, can at some time subsequently the British say there was no vote and that wasn't the sense of the meeting, and re-open the thing?'

Acheson did not have the rules for international conferences with him, but he thought that delegates could ask for a roll-call vote. Luxford did not think that would be satisfactory: 'But the trouble is, you are going to find so many of these countries so very articulate who are in opposition, whereas the Latin Americans will just sit there until they vote.'

'I think what you could do', Acheson suggested, 'is to have a yea and nay vote if you can't tell by the noise, and ask them to raise their hands.'

But White did not like that. He preferred to ascertain the sense of the meeting by the general attitude of the delegates. 'It is much safer . . . if it is legal.'

'That is perfectly all right', said Luxford, the lawyer, 'if they don't object.'

The procedure White had in mind also made it possible for him, as chairman of the commission, to delegate to a 'special committee', which would hold no public debates, any question on which it seemed difficult to reach agreement. This allowed the matter to be settled behind closed doors, within the group of technical advisers.[14]

For about two weeks the committees and the commissions met, and reviewed the provisions put before them, making suggestions, recommending changes, and putting forward new proposals. The level at which these discussions were held was, in general, very high. In addition to economists of international reputation, there were many government and central bank officials of outstanding competence in monetary affairs. There were Professor Robertson, Professor (later Lord) Robbins, Mr Redvers Opie, Mr Robert Brand, and several officials from Whitehall and the Bank of England. There were Mr Louis Rasminsky from Canada, Professor Mossé from France, Mr Varvaressos, governor of the Bank of Greece, Dr Beyen from Holland, Mr C. Gutt from Belgium, and many others who were counted among the best brains in the world on international monetary relations. They participated in the various specialist committees looking at the provisions on such matters as the following: conditions of membership, subscriptions, time and place of payment of quotas, revision of quotas, the obligatory gold contribution, the transactions of members with the Fund and with non-member countries, the scarce-currency clause, members' obligations, the pressure to be exerted on debtor countries, the conditions under which a change in parity would be authorised (although the term 'fundamental disequilibrium' was never defined), the charges to be paid to the Fund, control of capital movements, management of the Fund, publication of reports, where the Fund's gold should be held, withdrawal from the Fund, the transitional period, and even the liquidation of the Fund. The secretary of each committee wrote the minutes of the meeting and passed them on to the commission, pointing out where agreement had been reached, and where there was disagreement. White took up the problem from there.

These discussions were of the greatest importance. Mr Istel probably expressed the general feeling of the delegates when he said, 'We have worked so hard in examining the detailed texts that it is difficult at the present juncture to get an over-all picture.'[15] Every day, the 'Journal' of the conference would keep the delegates advised of the main decisions and events of the previous day. It was hard work, and very useful.

Obviously, each delegation had its own special interests and problems. The Mexican delegation kept insisting that silver be considered, next to gold, as a monetary metal: Mr Suarez stated that 'a large part of humanity will continue to believe in silver', and said that the problem was 'small in economic dimensions, but large in human implications'.[16] The South African delegate stressed the importance of gold, but he could relax about the subject. The Indian delegation wanted the conference to take up the matter of the sterling balances India had accumulated in London, and that were frozen there; the American delegation refused to consider this matter, on the grounds that it concerned only the British and Indian governments.[17]

But, whether the delegates were aware of it or not, the important decisions were made behind closed doors, between the American delegation and the foreign delegation involved. While Harry White and his small group of 'technical advisers' kept absolute control over the text of the articles to be included in the agreement, the powerhouse of the conference was in Morgenthau's office, where some of the most difficult and troublesome issues had to be settled. It is to the most important of these that we now turn. The technicalities of the subjects debated in commission and committee meetings are of interest only to specialists.

THE QUOTAS

As expected, the allocation of quotas, which involved practically every delegation, was a very difficult and dangerous subject. From the beginning, White had indicated that the aggregate quota should not exceed $8000 million, with a possible margin. Russia's quota was to be not less than 10 per cent, and China's was to rank fourth. The total voting power of the British Commonwealth as determined by the quotas should not exceed that of the United States.

The ranking of the major nations having been thus determined, this still left the field open for a scramble for quotas by the delegations of the smaller and less powerful countries. Britain supported the demands of India, Australia and others for an increase of their quotas. During the early days of the conference, however, the Russians threw a spanner into the works by informing the Americans that they could not accept a quota less than the British. Such a major adjustment was obviously impossible if the aggregate was to be kept to $8000 million. This piece of information was leaked to the press, adding to the annoyance of the American delegation. Keynes had a confidential discussion with White, Acheson and Vinson on the subject. It was difficult to see any solution without decreasing the United States quota or increasing the aggregate. The Americans, in addition, felt themselves under the necessity of allowing increases to Brazil, Mexico and Cuba. Keynes balanced their demands 'by pressing vehemently for a further increase for India and saying that we hoped something could be done for Australia also'. Such a position could obviously not be supported publicly, and an agreement had to be reached behind the scenes; otherwise, the floodgates would be thrown wide open. Keynes advocated an increase of the total quotas.[18]

Delegations from the smaller and less powerful countries, spurred by national and personal considerations – the matter of prestige in the ranking of one's country and its economic importance relative its rivals, and the delegates' desire to earn grateful acknowledgement of their own performance and achievements at the conference – manoeuvred with the American delegation to obtain satisfaction. On the allocation of quotas, as on practically everything else, the American delegation was the ultimate arbiter.

Although Committee I was supposed to discuss and decide about the quotas, it was obvious that such a controversial matter, which for almost every delegation was the one of principal concern, could not be handled there. On 4 July the committee 'agreed to postpone temporarily the discussion of quotas until a paper on this subject had been distributed'. The American delegation then went on to consult separately each of the other delegations.[19]

The question of the quotas was crucial and central. When, at one meeting, some of the delegates refused to consider one matter because they said they could not consider it intelligently unless they had their quotas, White immediately solved the problem. As he explained to the American delegation, he appointed a quota committee. 'This is a formal Quota Committee, which presumably will report the quotas to the Commission, but we won't call them to meet. United States is chairman. We won't call them to meet until we have the quota settled, but at least we met the requirements of the moment.'[20]

On 5 July, Morgenthau being in Washington for a few days, Vinson presided over the meeting of the American delegation to discuss the quotas, and asked White to report how things stood. White replied,

I have done a little calculation. If we give the various increases which the U.K. stated they felt were essential, and if you give the increase to the U.S.S.R. that you have suggested, then we are well within the eight point five ... before you grant Australia, you might consider the desirability of U.K. assuring that Australia lay off some of the difficulties she has been making for us, I mean, if we are going to give it, that is the least we can expect in return. She is very troublesome on issues.

In general, he felt that, except in a few cases, principally that of Russia, the negotiations on quotas had been less difficult than he expected. He also thought that they were underestimating the difficulty they would have with the Chinese. Part of the problem there was that India wanted to be on a par with China, and Britain tended to back her up. White stated,

France will have to have more than India, and it is a twenty-five million increase, and India, they want four hundred. So we'll put France ahead of India, which is all I think that France would ask for. And it would satisfy India ... if you give them four hundred million, she will be through. And if you give France twenty-five million more, I think, I am not sure because we have not discussed it with her, she will be satisfied there. That leaves the two major issues of China and Russia. China, we don't know.[21]

Members of the American delegation meeting with the other delegations, trying to reach agreement on the quotas with each country individually, met with varying degrees of reluctance and protest. Although it was felt that in some cases the foreign delegations 'were just going through the motions', some of them proved difficult to handle and persuade. On the other hand, it was important to reach 'unanimous' agreement.

On 9 July Morgenthau reviewed the position on the quotas with his delegation. Collado, who had been mainly in contact with the Latin Americans, reported that

> The principal trouble lies in Cuba, Chile, and Colombia. It is very difficult. The Cubans want to be third, and by the existing statistical and other standards, they are probably correct in being third. The Chileans would like to be equal with the Cubans, and that is probably a little excessive for Chile. But the real problem is that Colombia will be satisfied with forty, but insists on being equal with Chile. . . . There is not too much logic in any of this . . . the Venezuelans don't want to put up so much. Venezuela, Uruguay and Bolivia all requested that they be a little lower than the top figures that we suggested they might wish.

Vinson recalled that it was thought important not to reduce the Latin American quotas: 'Brazil, a hundred million. But it was increased to one hundred and fifty million . . . the Mexican quota should be in proper relationship with the Brazilian quota. . . . Of course, we had in mind the voting strength of the Latin Americans.' Congressman Spence wanted to know why some countries wanted a reduction, and White explained that it was because of their gold and exchange position. 'It makes it too expensive for them.' Venezuela, in fact, was not much interested and would have to be talked to.

The question of the French quota, which it had been promised be fifth, was still open. As for the Netherlands, White said, 'We allotted [them] two hundred and fifty . . . . They are going to make a strong fight for three hundred. I think that from the tradition in history and the caliber of the country we ought to up that to 275.'

Dean Acheson reported about a 'controversy which has been raging in the last thirty-six hours about elections to the Executive Committee'. The Latin Americans, not knowing their quotas, were fearful that they would only have one representative, and they wanted two. He suggested that the members of the Executive Committee be increased from eleven to twelve, with the guarantee that the Latin Americans would have two votes. '. . . we can solve this thing in a hour', said Acheson.[22] The following day he reported,

> I spent several hours with the Chileans with Mr. White. The Chileans are quite unhappy and they make the sole point that they want to have the same quota as Cuba. They don't care about having it raised, but they would like to have Cuba lowered. They said we ought to do that. We couldn't raise Chile because then we would start raising everybody and we would come to the end of the money and would have a lot of trouble. We said the same thing over again for about three hours, at the end of which they said they would telegraph their Government, but I think they have accepted it.[23]

On 14 July, Morgenthau reviewed the quota situation with Judge Vinson, Harry White and Congressman Wolcott.

Vinson: 'Here is exactly the score. The score, if South Africa is dropped fifty and that fifty is split between Poland and Czechoslovakia, the Netherlands goes up to two hundred and seventy-five and Mexico goes up twenty, to a hundred.'

Morgenthau: 'That is ninety-five by my figuring. You are increasing them by ninety-five and reducing them by fifty. That is plus forty-five.'

Vinson: 'That is right, but the way I was doing it — '

Morgenthau: 'Is that right?'

Vinson: 'That is right.'

Morgenthau: 'See, Jesse, that is why I am Secretary of the Treasury. I can add and subtract.'

The total, said Vinson, was well within the limits, 'and we will have a few million that could be added to any place we wanted to'.

But Morgenthau wanted to bring up a political problem he was faced with. The Administration was asking China and France to pay for all supplies to their own civilian population, 'and they are kicking like hell. So if we can do a little something here that doesn't come out of the taxpayers, for France and China, why — '

Vinson: 'Well, you can up China twenty-five, to fifty-five; fifty-five wouldn't affect this at all.'

White: 'We had fifty-five.'

Morgenthau: 'You couldn't give them five seventy-five?'

Vinson: 'Not if you give Poland and Czechoslovakia twenty-five apiece.'

Morgenthau: 'Why do that?'

White: 'Give them fifteen each. Particularly Czechoslovakia deserves a hundred and you have to give Poland the same thing.'

There were those devastated countries, and they too deserved a little more, Vinson thought; 'it has a heart appeal for me and for you, too.'

White: 'You don't think we could squeeze a hundred more off the total and settle all our problems? What the hell — go to eight hundred and fifty.'

Vinson did not think that would be practical, because, as it stood, there was only $1250 million left for the neutrals.

'Have one hundred million less for them', White suggested.

The group agreed that they had to make a final decision, and announce the results to the other delegations. So they had to do some more reckoning.

Morgenthau: 'Let's just say tentatively twenty-five for Poland and twenty-five for Czechoslovakia.

But this was conditional upon getting fifty off South Africa, and they would have to be talked to, Vinson thought.

Morgenthau: 'I think Mexico is important. I would leave that.'

Vinson: 'Now, the Netherlands – you told them two hundred and fifty.'

Morgenthau: 'I would stick to it.'

Wolcott: 'Two hundred and twenty-five for the Netherlands was predicated upon a decrease of the total to eighty-five.'

Vinson: 'The Netherlands is two hundred and seventy-five, so we pick up twenty five, and that twenty-five can be used with France or China.'

White: 'And give France what you can pick up – what is left.'

Morgenthau: 'If you are going to do something for Poland and Czechoslovakia, you have got to do something for France, because those countries talk together and they work together.'

White: 'We cut France's formula more than any other country.'

Morgenthau: 'If you are going to give twenty-five to Poland and twenty-five to Czechoslovakia, then I recommend twenty-five for France.'

Vinson: 'If the Netherlands stands at two hundred and fifty, we can give that to France.'

Morgenthau: 'After all, today is Bastille Day.'

White: 'That is a good time to tell them.'

That evening the table of quotas was put together.[24] The commission was unanimous in adopting the quotas reported by the special quota committee, except that reservations were expressed by the delegations for China, Egypt, France, India, New Zealand and Iran, all of which felt that they should have larger quotas. None of the delegations indicated that they would not support the plan when submitting it to their governments.

THE PRESS IS TAKEN INTO CONFIDENCE

On 2 July, during the morning session, Morgenthau discussed with the American delegates how to handle the press. 'The best plan in the world is no good if you can't get Congress to accept it', said White. It was necessary to meet the opposition that still prevailed in some influential papers, and get public opinion on the side of the Fund. On the first day of the conference, every accredited representative of the press had received the full text of the master document that was to be the basis of all the

discussions, and they were told that they would be given all facilities to
remain informed about the proceedings of the conference. This was an
innovation in the conduct of international conferences, and the reporters
liked it. But Morgenthau felt that this was not enough. Senator Tobey said
that he had met 'some saboteurs at this hotel doing all they can to stick a
knife into this thing'. Representative Wolcott had just been told 'that this is
throwing money down a rat hole'. As Republicans, they had been
opposing the Fund, and were now expected to continue their opposition,
which they did not want to do. 'If we are going to be successful', Wolcott
said, 'we have to have public sentiment with us because public sentiment
will control whatever action is taken by the Congress, and I think we have
got to begin and start building public sentiment right today and now.'
Utilising the medium of the press to beat the opponents to the punch and
to take the edge off their criticism seemed the most effective way of
building up public sentiment. The Congressmen obviously did not know
enough about the subject to answer the questions that were asked by press
reporters; they suggested that White hold a press meeting every afternoon
to explain the purposes of the Fund and to answer questions. 'Let them
have it with both barrels', Tobey recommended.[25]

The method was extremely effective. The *Chicago Daily News* reported,

> Every afternoon at 3 Harry White, the dynamic assistant secretary of
> the Treasury Department, holds a 'seminar' for the press, at which he
> relates what progress, if any, has been made by the various committees,
> and discourses freely on the dark science of international finance. White
> is a medium-sized man with a trim mustache, rimless eyeglasses and
> thinning hair.
>
> He formerly taught college economics, and as he gets into his stride
> with the 40 or more reporters who attend these sessions he seems to be
> back in the classroom. A reporter stumbles through a complicated
> inquiry, and White shakes his finger at him and says vigorously, 'That's
> a very intelligent question.' The reporter, who is a little in doubt about
> it in the first place undergoes a lifting of the spirit and begins to take
> notes furiously as White goes into rapid-fire account perhaps of the evils
> of unilateral action in the manipulation of foreign exchange.[26]

On 6 July, Keynes appeared at one of these press conferences – the
only occasion on which he did so. As usual, White was present. So far as
the press was concerned, the event was obviously one of the highlights of
the whole conference. For an hour and a half, Keynes and White answered
questions fired at them by the correspondents. Keynes warned that, if the
Fund were rejected, Britain might have to resort to bilateral barter
agreements in order to protect its economy. He ridiculed the 'key
currency' proposals, which would 'let the rest of the world go hang'. The
Fund would make gold 'a monarch subject to constitutional limitations'.

No one with any practical sense would make the gold reserves of the world worthless, but gold should not exercise 'tyrannical powers over the world'.

'It is thought here', said a reporter, that the purpose of the Fund is to eliminate foreign exchange restrictions, but in your speech — a great point was made that the Fund will allow each country to control all capital.'

'The object of the Fund', Keynes responded, 'is to remove exchange restrictions as soon as possible. It provides that capital movements must be controlled, and indeed that is an essential condition. . . . I think you will find there is no possible doubt about that in the provisions of the Fund.'

At that point White intervened to state that countries which chose to impose restrictions on capital movements were allowed to do so, but 'the United States does not wish to have them and they do not exist'.

Keynes explained that, in the long run, there had to be for every country a balance between imports and exports. If the United States went on exporting more than it imported, there was no remedy. 'The Fund can't solve continuing problems of this sort. It can just give the opportunity for settling it in an orderly way.' If he wished to criticise the Fund, he could make 'quite a good job of it'. But all the alternatives he had seen were very much worse.[27]

Using the material provided by White during his seminars, by the daily conference journal, and by rumours and leaks, and the statements by delegates or prominent visitors, the press reported daily about the proceedings of the conference. Some correspondents were able to obtain confidential information about the attitude of the Russians, the conflict between Keynes and the American delegation about where the Fund should be located, and many other matters. Comments were generally neutral or favourable. Despite all the available information, much of what went on, however, remained mysterious. Walter Lippmann commented, 'It has been impossible for the general public to obtain any idea of what the Bretton Woods conference is about. Though it is concerned with questions which will affect men's lives deeply, the language of monetary policy is understood by very few men in any country.'[28]

The *Christian Science Monitor* noted that 'Fundamentals behind the monetary conference were partly hidden by the controversies over quotas, gold subscriptions, and other technicalities.' The monetary plans were a 'game between debtors and creditors, between the United States and Great Britain, or between Wall Street and Washington'. Although White had taken great pains to convince the press that the commercial banks would profit from the operations of the Fund, which would deal only with government agencies, the papers which had opposed the Fund were not convinced.[29]

The *New York Times* commented, 'The proposed agreement sets up a huge machinery and ignores all basic principles which must be adopted if such machinery could hope to be successful. American money poured into supporting weak foreign countries will be worse than wasted.'[30]

Another critical comment was that, instead of compelling a debtor nation to put its affairs in order, the Fund merely provided a breathing spell. While there was no objection to a breathing spell, the money provided would be wasted unless the breathing spell were used by the debtor country to strengthen its economic structures, so that it would not only get back to a sound monetary basis, but stay there.

As usual, the German press closely followed the monetary discussions. And so did the German government. Speaking to a group of economists and business leaders, Walther Funk said on 7 July 1944, while the Bretton Woods Conference was in process, that this was the wrong way to handle the problem. Instead of providing a complicated machinery to restore equilibrium in the balances of payments, it was much more effective to make sure that they did not get out of equilibrium. International commerce could not be maintained in orderly condition by monetary plans, but currencies had to be maintained in stable relations through commercial planning. If the Americans advocated a return to currencies backed by gold, this was only to make the dollar the international currency of the system. As for the Russians, they must be following the struggle between the two major capitalist countries with diabolical pleasure. In practice, the Russians were interested in the conference only because it assured them a market for their gold production, for which, because of the poverty of the Russian population, they had no internal use.[31]

THE FRENCH: TERRIBLY UPSET

In the early days of the Conference, the French delegation was referred to as the 'Comité', and it bothered the French delegates. President Roosevelt was furious at de Gaulle, and fed up with the general's manoeuvres to become the sole and undisputed leader of the French Committee of National Liberation. While the Bretton Woods conference was going on, the President, in Washington, modified his position, and became more favourable towards de Gaulle. By the end of the conference it had become customary to refer to the 'French' delegates, and they had become a little happier; but their problems were not over.

Mr Mendès France had flown from Algiers to the United States, and had briefly met Morgenthau on the stairs of the hotel. Morgenthau had understood that he was 'terribly upset' about the attitude of the American delegation: 'he can only draw one conclusion – that we are unfriendly to his Government'. Mendès France had not threatened a French withdrawal, but the case was serious, and Morgenthau had another crisis on his hands. He promised to see the Frenchman in the evening. White reported that at a committee meeting Mendès France had warned that, because of the French quota, his government might not participate, and White thought it 'inexcusable for a country like France to make that statement'. Vinson, however, thought 'he had to make a strong statement, because, as I saw it, there is hostility in this group, and if he didn't put a strong speech in, it might be others around that might replace him. I didn't take his statement seriously. . . . I think he is a pretty fair poker player.'[32]

One of the problems of the French delegation, causing them great anxiety, was the fact that Holland, Belgium and Luxembourg had recently signed the Benelux agreement. The combined quotas of these three countries was slightly larger than that of France, and the French feared that Benelux might get even closer together, and be given the fifth rank in the table of quotas, qualifying them automatically for a seat on the executive Committee of the Fund.

Morgenthau had agreed to see the French delegates on the evening of 15 July, at nine o'clock. He was there, but the French were late for the appointment, and everyone was becoming restless. Morgenthau suggested that White, Vinson and the other delegates wait for another five minutes and then go on with their own work, but soon afterwards Mendès France and Istel at last arrived. Morgenthau asked them to speak their mind. Mendès France explained that France had hoped to be number four, but that for political reasons China had been given number four, and France number five. This was understood and accepted. He had hoped, however, to be more successful on other matters, but, 'since we are here, on all questions we were interested in, we were refused'. In April he had been assured that, since France was considered a devastated country, it would have to pay only 75 per cent of its gold contribution. 'Then this thing was wiped out and we didn't receive it.' Morgenthau replied that France had not been singled out, and that this would apply to all countries. He was worried because Mendès France had told him that he would go back to Algiers saying that the Americans were against France.

Istel indicated that he was aware of the deal that had been made with the Russians, for whose sole benefit a special clause on newly-mined gold had been granted. At Morgenthau's request, France had earlier backed the proposal behind this, not knowing that in fact it would work to the disadvantage of France.

'But I don't want to discuss again all this question', said Mendès France. 'What I wanted to tell you is that, that I wanted to give you a few examples, and it is bad, but I can give you a lot of them. I wanted to give you a few examples to show you that every important decision was taken since we are here, and all this decision is without you willing it and without you and of course an enemy of my country, but these questions are always settled against our interest, and I give you the first example, which was this question about devastated countries. A second example is the example about quota. I am sure, and I don't say it to be polite, because I am sure you think it, I am sure you like my country and you want to be good with it, and I saw this morning when I spoke with you, that of course you were willing to find a solution and I am grateful to you, having made what you could, but in fact what happened, that in this situation, we didn't get what we hoped for and why – because when we started this question two or three days ago with Mr. White, we thought we would have a talk between us and he would have an agreement and this morning you told me it is too late.'

Morgenthau interrupted him: when this was discussed, the committee meeting was still going on, and the French delegation could have argued its case.

'No,' said Mendès France, 'because what happened, I went to this Committee this morning and we were suddenly given a list and we saw on this list we had four hundred and fifty and I spoke and said we don't accept it. Then Lord Keynes said it is too late. "You can not change these things, it is a total which is eight and seven fifty and if somebody gets more, then it is necessary to take it to another man, because the total must not be changed." Then what was to do at this moment – I understood it was very difficult. Then I came to you and I saw you were willing to find something, but the direct difficulty, you told me, is that you have given a promise to the Chinese they must always be a hundred more than us and if you give us, for example, fifty, you have to give fifty to the Chinese, and the result is instead of having increased the fifty, you have increases of a hundred. But this promise you make to the Chinese, and if you made this promise, I have nothing to say against it, but this promise you made has a result that you give to the Chinese of course more thán they have to receive, because you know, as well as we all know, that wasn't correct calculation with the correct quota, with the formula. We all know if China will not get so much than she has, then we have not to be a victim of this situation and when you told us, not you, but Mr. White, one month ago, that we will have five hundred, we thought it will be so, and now we only have four hundred and fifty.'·

White had had to leave the meeting, and while Mendès France admitted that this had not been a firm commitment, he still wanted five hundred. White had promised to talk to the Secretary, but nothing further had been heard. The Frenchman had wanted to talk to Acheson, but that had not been useful. 'And then this morning when we received this sheet it was too late. . . . That is another example.'

'But', Morgenthau wondered, 'I asked you whether twenty-five million dollars would do any good. You said no.'

'You see, I am not a bargaining man.'

'I am not either, but I asked you if it would help any and you said it would be of no use.'

Vinson intervened: 'Now it seems to me in all friendliness that you are making a mountain out of a molehill.'

'And how will it look', said Mendès France, 'when I come back to my people and explain to them, "I went some months ago to Bretton Woods, and explained our position. I told them we want to ask this, this, and this, and in all these questions I have to tell you I come with zero." That is the fact. Then comes another example. Yes, it is very bad, as you know it is. Now, we have spoken with the Fund. Now we speak with the Bank. You have a council of Executive Directors in the Bank, the same kind as the Fund. That is to say, a council in which five permanent countries will be represented. And as our quota is the fifth, we thought that, like in the Fund, we will have the fifth seat. Now what happened today? We heard for the first time that only three permanent seats would be given.'

None of the American delegates had heard about this. It might have been suggested, but no position had been taken, and nothing had been decided.

'But please,' said Mendès France, 'but sometimes I come too early and sometimes I come too late. Then I prefer to come now too early as too late, because it is very expensive in these last days when I come too late.'

Morgenthau asked the American delegates whether France would have a seat if there were five members on the Executive Committee. Luxford thought that 'If there were five appointed members and France subscribed the fifth quota, she would have a seat.'

'But I don't want to speak about technical questions', said Mendès France. 'I want you to understand this. I must tell you frankly I have not an easy position in Algiers. I understand why you are laughing now. . . . Then when I go back to Algiers and have to explain all these things, my colleague will say, "You have lost on the quota, you have lost on the devastated countries, you have lost on these, and these, and these — then what do you bring back to us? What is the good news you bring back? What do I have to understand?" Then what I said this afternoon to the Commission — and I said it because it is true — it is not that I am leaving the Conference, but what I said — and it is worse — that if there are those I am describing now, my Government will not accept it, and I don't want to be in such a position.'

'If you don't mind my saying so,' Morgenthau remarked, 'I think your statement is a little bit too strong.'

'It is strong like the truth', the answer came back.

Morgenthau asked whether the request for a seat on the Executive Committee was the last one.

'It is the last one I wanted to give you, but if you want to have some others, I can give you — '

'It is enough', said Morgenthau. 'Let me ask this. I think that, Mr. Mendès France, about the Government and the little threat there which I don't like — '

'It isn't a threat. You must not think so. I give you my word it isn't a threat. It is an exact position. I have explained this morning about Belgium and Holland and Luxembourg.'

But Morgenthau had learned all about the customs union; he had learned his lesson. What worried the French was that the Benelux quotas would amount to 510, as against 450 for France.

'This was really the new fact which changed the position', Istel explained.

Vinson asked what was the position of Belgium, the Netherlands and Luxembourg 'in respect of France having a seat among the mighty'.

'It is very simple', Istel started to say, but Mendès France ordered him, 'Don't speak.'

'I will speak to you afterwards. You know the position of Luxembourg' was all Istel could add.

Morgenthau wanted the Frenchmen to understand how difficult it was, when you have 'forty-four nations to juggle and put together into a picture puzzle'. The thing that had bothered him, and which had now been corrected, was that the French delegates might have had the impression that anything he had done would be directed at France. 'I don't know who is handling this thing, but let's throw our weight to five Directors', Morgenthau suggested.

This satisfied the French delegates. 'Mr. Secretary,' said Mendès France, 'I must tell you, you spoke with me about this, and I thank you very much for having put five countries, and I told you, of course I would back it and I told you I am grateful. But, please, you must understand that taking this position was not so easy with us, because on issues with Belgium and Holland it was not quite easy, but as I had promised you, I did it and I thank you for the idea you had for us.'

Luxford thought they had already asked for this at Atlantic City.

'Yes, and we thank you for it', said Istel.

'And I thank you for it', Mendès France echoed.

'Once is enough', said Morgenthau.

'But you had the feeling I had some bad idea', Mendès France wondered.

No, Morgenthau was simply concerned that there had been this impression that the American delegation had been unfriendly to France, and 'I told you I would not go to bed until I tried to correct that impression. Now you say you have not got that impression and I can go to bed.'

Thereupon the French delegates left, and Mrs Morgenthau, who had followed the conversation, asked, 'Does he feel happier?'

'Yes,' said Morgenthau, 'he said tonight that he did not feel that the American Delegation and the Conference were opposed to France. Now I understood him to say this. That is the only thing that bothered him and the man is a very smart, intelligent fellow and I think, a very sincere fellow. And I certainly didn't know it, because you can't know all these things, but it never occurred to me that when we were fighting the Russians on the twenty-five percent that France was one of the most devastated countries and that they were affected. It never occurred to me.'

'Well,' said Morgenthau, 'let's call it a night.'[33]

THE RUSSIANS: TOUGH CUSTOMERS

The position of the Russians had been anomalous from the beginning. Why, with their system of state trading and absolute government control over imports and exports, they should become part of an international organisation that would not allow restrictions on current transactions, but would be ready to assist governments whose citizens, by their multitude of unco-ordinated decisions, had led the country temporarily to live beyond its means, was hard to see.

White had insisted all along that 'the Fund needs Russia', and Morgenthau shared this view, though, to get the reluctant Russians to Bretton Woods, they had all but had to drag them there. In the end Russia had sent to the conference a strong delegation, headed by Mr M. S. Stepanov, Deputy People's Commissar of Foreign Trade.

Within the American delegation there was disagreement on how far to go along with the Russians, particularly because they were demanding that provisions applicable only to them be written into the Final Act. They wanted, for instance, to be able to change the value of the rouble, if the change in parity did not affect international transactions, without having to refer the matter to the Fund. White had agreed, although he could not

figure out what purpose it could be and neither could the Russians. We have asked them time and time again to cite us a single illustration of what they would wish to accomplish in parities that would not affect international transactions. They couldn't give an illustration, but you might conceive a hypothetical circumstance in which they would want to call their gold a different unit or something for domestic book-keeping and still keep their exchange rates the same.

The provision, White thought, might save us a lot of trouble, because if this phrase isn't there, Congress might take the position, do we understand we can't alter the gold content of the dollar, which has always been our right, unless it is appropriate to correct a fundamental disequilibrium. If we could be able to answer 'no, you could do anything you want as long as it doesn't affect international trans-actions', we are talking at the kind of nonsensical level, but that is the level at which those discussions take place.

'What reason would we have, Harry, to change the gold value of the dollar if it didn't affect international transactions?', Marriner Eccles wanted to know.

'No reason', said White. 'It is nonsense.'

Brown, the banker, thought that putting in this provision 'would be an invitation to every other country to monkey with it and get them in trouble with the Fund.' The surest way to have the whole thing rejected by the American people, was to put it in. 'I think you have to meet the Russians head-on on this.'

Eccles thought that 'the Russians have . . . determined to have more than it is possible to give them, without breaking up the Conference'. The outlook was not very bright, and their interest in the success of the conference was entirely different from that of capitalistic countries. 'Their interest is openly to get this credit.'

'What is China's interest and Poland's interest and Greek interest?', White asked. He thought it was necessary to make concessions to Russia.

To Brown, the Russian attitude proved that for them this was not a stabilisation fund, 'and as I see it, it is a grab-bag'.

This made White angry. He went into a long speech: 'No. I don't think that is an appropriate supposition. . . . A Stabilization Fund is a fund to provide exchange to take care of the cyclical swings in the demand for foreign exchange. Those cyclical swings may be caused by harvest failures, depreciation abroad, certain breakdowns of one kind or another when you are unable to export . . . your goods at a price which will enable you to keep the imports you want. . . . USSR has advantages which no other country has. She has large gold production, she has tremendous productive capacity, and last and most important, she herself can determine how much she is going to sell. No capitalistic country can do that, because they have to sell at a profit. Now then, when USSR says, very frankly, "We are going to use this Fund to buy things because this is a time of need and this is what a stabilization fund is for and we will pay you back after five, six or seven years", I say that is a stabilization operation and no different than what happens in any other country. . . . The reason why I go into detail here is because there is a tendency completely to distort the analysis and to point a finger at USSR, because they are saying frankly what the other countries are going to do anyway. What do you think Poland and the Netherlands or France or Belgium or China are going to do? If they didn't do it, in my judgment, their financial ministers would be stupid. That is what they should do, and that is what the Fund is for, and the only consideration that we have to bear in mind is, can they repurchase that within the period we are thinking of, within the four, five, six, seven year period. If a country cannot repurchase it, then she has no business in getting some money from here, but should get it in thirty or forty year loans, and it is even questionable whether she should get it there. . . . From the point of view of the ability to repurchase foreign exchange which she buys from the Fund, I put USSR on top of the list and instead of giving her one billion dollars you could give her two billion and the Fund would operate still better and your exports would do a lot more business. That is quite a speech, but I think it is necessary in the light of the misunderstanding which is prevalent not only here but outside on what the nature of the Stabilization Fund is.'

'That is an honest difference in point of view', said Eccles. 'I don't agree with you. Your speech hasn't changed my point of view a particle.'

Neither did Brown like the agreement that had been made on the technical level 'that Russia should get eight hundred million. That was not published but you gave them an agreement to give them twenty-five per cent off in gold payments which isn't important, which wasn't published, just as the eight hundred million wasn't published but which is very important when you take the world as a whole as to the amount of gold you are going to get . . . you are going to hurt yourself. The newly-mined gold . . . two hundred million more than the eight hundred million that was agreed . . . twenty-five per cent. . . . Now I think . . . the Conference is stalled absolutely stalled by these Russian demands. I think the time has come when unless it is resolved that the Conference will fail just because it can't complete its task within the two weeks, that it is necessary for us at this time to show our teeth, something which I dislike to do.'

'Not unless they are good teeth', said White.

Tell the Russians that the Fund is more to their benefit than to ours, Congressman Wolcott suggested. 'I don't like to say, "Take it or leave it", but that should be our attitude anyway.'

'I think the delegation should make up its mind and instruct the negotiators', Judge Vinson said.

But to Eccles, 'the question of negotiations is over. I think you have reached the point where you say this is taken up, this is the position and that is final. Let's adopt their tactics.'

White had been warned. He thought there was a chance in attempting to bargain. 'It is kind of a ticklish situation in which I really think we have the final cards, but they may not break out that way. You see, they may not turn it down that way. They will say, "We will consult with Moscow", maybe. And we sit and sweat and wait.'

'That will give us some time to go up to the mountain and play some golf', Wolcott concluded.[34]

The Russians were tough negotiators. On 3 July the Soviet delegate had privately indicated to Morgenthau that he hoped the Russian quota would be only slightly less than the British quota, which meant $1200 million instead of the $800 million which had been discussed before. Morgenthau thought there must be some misunderstanding, but 'In spite of this regrettable misunderstanding . . . the delegation of the United States will associate itself in any efforts by the Soviet delegation to obtain an increase at this Conference in the quota for the Soviet Union.'

According to White, 'they are basing their desire to have a billion two on the grounds that from an economic point of view, from their economic potentialities, from the fact that they are a rapidly expanding economy and expect to play a major role in international monetary and economic affairs'. On the other hand, the Russians wanted a very substantial reduction in their gold contribution, 'because they say that during the next years they cannot get dollars or other currencies because they are not in a position to export anything until they restore their factories'.[35]

On 11 July Morgenthau asked the Russians to come down and see him, because this was 'the first time I have had this experience in dealing with your government'. There had been an honest misunderstanding about the $800 million, but White had suggested two alternatives: either a $1200 million quota, or a $900 million quota with the right to reduce by 25 per cent the amount of gold contributed.

But the Russians wanted $1200 million *and* a 25 per cent reduction. Morgenthau was 'quite shocked that two great nations should begin what we call "to horse trade". . . . That isn't the spirit which my Government has approached this problem with; it isn't the spirit expressed by Mr. Molotov to me; it isn't the spirit of your Minister of Finance, where he said we would do this thing side by side, which means like partners.'

Stepanov did not understand English. The interpreter translated Morgenthau's words, and gave Stepanov's reply: 'Mr. Stepanov's idea is such that our Government really consented not to object against the positions which were made by your technical experts, in spite of the position of ours, because it was regarded to the mutual benefit and we didn't interfere, but wanted to collaborate with the Government of the United States.' Stepanov was of the opinion that 'there would be no difficulty in settling these problems if we try to understand each other properly. The Russian questions which we are not entitled to decide in case they have been already decided and agreed upon in Moscow – among these questions is the question concerning the loans of twenty-five per cent.' By 'loans' the interpreter meant something different, but Morgenthau understood what he wanted to say.

The quota suggested by White was very tentative, very approximate, the interpreter continued. But in Moscow 'those people who are in a position to see more clearly the data available for them concerning our financial position, they say that the amount which was just mentioned is approximate to that amount which we are entitled to get. And the American Delegation would see very clearly that we were right in this respect after we will give you the data concerning our financial position, including the national income.' Stepanov could not decide anything without the consent of Moscow.

Morgenthau was puzzled by this method of negotiation: 'I am not a diplomat, I am not a lawyer, I am just a farmer', he said. The interpreter answered: 'Mr. Stepanov says he is no diplomat himself – no lawyer, no financier, just a businessman.' And he went on to say that Russia would be 'glad to support the position of your country and your personal proposition . . . we simply would like to occupy the place which we regard we are entitled to, according to the calculations which we have'.

Morgenthau said that he would be glad to recognise the importance of Russia in the world, 'but we have no real data about Russian resources and therefore that is why I said we had to do this largely based on your military successes. We have not been furnished any data, you see?' After the Fund came into operation, Stepanov said, Russia would be glad to present all the data required, 'and you would see very clearly that this sum is very approximate to the exact sum you have arrived at on the basis of the American formula'.

Two days later, since nothing had been heard from the Russian delegation, Morgenthau saw Stepanov again. Unfortunately, no word had been received from Moscow. Mr Stepanov 'is not sleeping too well at night waiting for the answer', the interpreter said. He had sent another cable but received no answer. 'What I would like to say to Mr. Stepanov, with all courtesy, is that the whole conference is being held up', Morgenthau remarked. Ambassador Harriman had cabled from Moscow that the Russian delegation had received instructions but he had not been able to find out what the instructions were. There was going to be a meeting in the afternoon, and the American delegation would have to take position publicly on the Russian attitude. Morgenthau made the suggestion that the American delegation would support the $1200 million quota, and would also agree that the newly-mined gold would not have to be counted as part of the national reserves. This, he thought, was more important than a 25 per cent reduction in the gold contribution. Since the position of Russia was unique, in that it was the only country that had suffered devastation from the war and was at the same time a gold-producing country, by taking this position the American delegation would keep out of trouble with the other countries that had been devastated. If Russia received a special treatment because of the war damage, 'then all the other countries who have also been devastated will want the same treatment'.

The meeting where the quotas were to be announced was being held shortly, and it was necessary to make a decision.

'Now, we feel very sorry that we have to do this thing publicly, and that we can't wait', said Morgenthau; 'and we don't want to be discourteous. But we must go forward, and therefore at this two o'clock meeting when this question on the quotas comes up, that will be the position of the American Delegation. And I sincerely hope that when Mr. Stepanov gets word from Moscow that he will be able to concur.'

'Mr. Stepanov wants to thank you, sir, sincerely', said the interpreter, 'for your very good attitude towards our position.'[36]

Having obtained about all they wanted, the Russians came to see Morgenthau the following day. They wanted to bring up again the point that a country would be allowed to change the par value of its currency if this did not affect the international transactions of the other members of the Fund. White had already gone a long way to meet the Russian demand, and had changed the paragraph which now said that the Fund would 'concur' in a proposed change, if it was 'satisfied that the proposed change does not affect international transactions of the member proposing the change'. The Russians wanted this to read that the country could, in that case, change the value without the consent of the Fund. Stepanov suggested that just the USSR should be given that right.

But White objected, 'If we did, it might be clear to the technicians, but it would create a storm of protest and suspicion on the part of the people who do not understand – in Congress and with the public.'

This was becoming too complicated for Morgenthau and he asked White to carry on the discussion. White said that, as a result of the redrafting they had agreed upon, the two provisions were almost identical. There was no difference of substance.

'Mr. White finds that both languages are identical, then Mr. Stepanov proposes to take our wording', said the interpreter.

'Not identical; almost identical. The substance is the same', White answered.

'It is the "almost" we want to liquidate, do you see?'

White explained again that, since the Fund must agree, there was no difference in substance. But the Russians wanted their wording, which said that they would only have to inform the Fund of the proposed change: 'We have studied the American proposal very carefully. . . . Still, we think that our proposition is the one that is feasible and that it will be accepted.'

There followed an intense discussion, each sticking to his own position. 'We will go in the other room and you just relax', Morgenthau told the Russians.

After a while the American group came back; White told the Russians that 'we have a suggestion that will meet you and probably please you'.

Luxford, the lawyer, started reading: ' "A change in the par value of a member's currency affecting the international transactions of members may be . . ." – you don't have to propose it, it doesn't affect it.'

'That is identical with yours', said White.

'And what about the changes that do not affect those transactions?', Stepanov wanted to know.

'Don't raise them', said White. 'That is identical. The reason why we have a little preference for that is because it doesn't highlight the change, do you see? But you don't raise the question. . . . Probably that is equally good, or better from your point of view; but it is better from ours, because it doesn't stand out.'

As far as Stepanov could see, there was no more disagreement on substance. He agreed to it. But since the question was of great importance, Moscow would have to agree also. Therefore, he insisted on the wording he had proposed at the start of the conversation, since there was no difference of substance.

Morgenthau was exasperated: 'Mr. Stepanov has said two different things. First he said he would like time to consider the language of Mr. Luxford; then in the next breath he has changed his mind and has gone back to his own language.'

The interpreter explained that Mr. Stepanov had not changed his mind, but that he only wanted to point out that since there was no difference in substance, it would be easier for everyone to take his wording, since in that case he would not have to refer to his government.

'You mean you have to cable?'

'Cable. Mr. Stepanov says to avoid loss of time, he is offering his proposal.'

'I am laughing because he knows when he says "Cable" to me, I go like this!' said Morgenthau, gesturing.

'Same reaction on our side. It is a point of primary importance concerning our domestic affairs. There is no disagreement about the substance.'

'What is the use?' asked White.

'Well, look, on this particular issue,' said Morgenthau, 'I think it will be easier for the Conference to accept the language Mr. Luxford suggested, but we also like to be reasonable and therefore we will accept your language.'

'Thank you very much.'

'You tell Mr. Stepanov I am afraid it is the last time he is going to say thank you at this Conference!' responded Morgenthau, laughing.

There were more points to be discussed. The Russians wanted to know where the Fund's gold would be stored. Then there was the matter of the information that the Fund requested: Russia had never published many detailed statistics regarding newly-mined gold, national income, the index of prices, and so on, but it was ready to accept a programme such as the one proposed by the American delegation.

The Russians also thought that the rates of interest to be charged by the Fund were too high, and they were ready to discuss again the 25 per cent reduction in the gold contribution for devastated countries, bearing in mind that, since Russia had suffered the heaviest devastation, she would have the full reduction. They also had a few more points to make about the Bank. 'May I say this to Mr. Stepanov?' Morgenthau asked. 'He has brought up enough questions to take us ten hours to discuss, and Mr. White has a Commission at ten o'clock. What meeting is there now?'

'Why do they bring up all these things?' Morgenthau asked. There was no answer.[37]

THE BANK FOR RECONSTRUCTION AND DEVELOPMENT

From the beginning White had fully identified himself with the Fund. It was *his* idea and was to be *his* contribution to a better world. Keynes, while not losing interest in the Fund, had recently come to believe that the Bank was more urgent and important, and the European governments in residence in London tended to agree. While White was the driving force for the Fund, Keynes moved swiftly in Commission II to complete an agreement on the Bank.

Before his departure from London, and on the boat sailing to New York, he had prepared a proposal which had been received with enthusiasm by the Europeans. He had discussed it with White at Atlantic City, and White had approved of it. But Keynes had to move fast, and some of the other delegates attending the Commission II meetings had complained about the fact that he was running what was practically a one-man show.

On 8 July Keynes had cabled London that it had been reported to him that the British press was expressing pessimism about the outcome of the Bretton Woods Conference.

> I believe this is a misreading of the position though a natural one. In fact great progress on most contentious and difficult issues is being made behind the scenes. In open Committee 44 nations are of course capable of wasting as much time as is at their disposal. But in the course of coming week I believe we shall be in a position to crystallize quite suddenly on concrete and agreed conclusions.
>
> We are only now beginning to work seriously on the Bank. But that appears surprisingly free from controversial issues. There are several improvements needed to make set-up really workable from a practical point of view; but nothing so far as I am aware controversial between Delegations.[38]

On 13 July, however, Morgenthau opened the meeting of the American steering committee by stating, 'Theunis was so mad he shook. Souza Costa was just furious. The head delegate from India was just as furious as he could be.'

Acheson, who was the chief American delegate to the commission on the Bank refused to continue the role in which he was cast. One of the problems was that Keynes, having started working on the Bank much later than White on the Fund, was in a great hurry. 'Keynes' performances . . . are completely understandable, and although tactless . . . all he could do.'

White said that there was no comparison between the two projects, and, while Acheson did not want to 'waste time by arguing', Morgenthau asked him to explain what he was concerned about. 'Let's be very frank for a minute. If I may be frank, when Dean gets irritated, it is so rare; I realize the cause must be grave.'

'The first problem about the Bank', Acheson said, 'is that the commission meetings on the Bank, which are conducted by Keynes, are being rushed in a perfectly impossible and outrageous way. Now, that comes from the fact that Keynes is under great pressure. He knows this thing inside out so that when anybody says Section 15-C he knows what it is. Nobody else in the room knows. So before you have an opportunity to turn to Section 15-C and see what he is talking about, he says, "I hear no objection to that", and it is passed. Well, everybody is trying to find Section 15-C. He then says, we are now talking about Section 26-D. Then they begin fiddling around with their papers, and before you find that, it is passed.'

Morgenthau, as president of the conference, was perfectly willing 'to go and call on him and in a very nice way tell him that at least half a dozen people have come to me perfectly livid and I think he is making a mistake, and I am going to ask him very respectfully if he wouldn't do the thing at half speed'.

Acheson, of course, understood Keynes's problem, and suggested that 'when you are asking him to slow up this thing you are still making it possible for him to finish by Wednesday when the train leaves'.

White thought that Acheson should not let things go on like that: 'Just because Keynes is an autocrat doesn't mean that you have to take it. You stand up and you say you don't like the way things are running.' He would attend the next meeting and get up on his feet. 'Nobody talks to him. They are either too scared to talk to him or too nice to talk to him, but I am sure that if he is called to task strongly, and you have the crowd behind you, he will modify his procedure.'

'Could you do it privately rather than publicly?', Morgenthau asked.

'Maybe', said White.

There was another and more serious problem, said Acheson, and that was the problem of the American delegation. When they went to a meeting of the commission, they did not know what their view was, so they could not present it forcefully and clearly. They simply had no organisation to do it. There had been a committee meeting where the American delegate had agreed to something which was the direct opposite of what everybody had said was the policy of the United States. 'Up comes Angell and says, "He is a liar, we never agreed." So I got up and said this was all a mistake, we never agreed to this, whereupon somebody else came rushing up and handed me a report. Another committee had agreed to the opposite. I was going almost nuts.'

In Commission I, White had a tremendous organisation, and all the experts were working on the Fund. But in Commission II, 'as far as I can see, all the decisions to make judgements on the merits and which I am wholly incompetent to make judgments on is thrown on me. The whole business of negotiating and talking with people is thrown on me. The whole burden of being Chairman of the Drafting Commission is thrown on me. The whole burden of presiding at these Commissions is thrown at me, and this afternoon when Commission Two met, there was not one single person in the room from five o'clock, when the Commission met, until a quarter of seven, when you came in who had ever been in a single meeting or knew what the dickens was going on. Now, I will go on and do anything that I am asked to do, but the responsibility which is in somebody's mind is one which I am not discharging and cannot discharge.' Acheson went on to say that in fact he knew nothing about the Bank; 'I am playing this by ear.'

What Acheson wanted he was going to get, said White. He had every intention of giving him all the expert help he would need, once he was through with the Fund. Most of the people Acheson was using were very helpful in specific tasks, but they had not been involved long enough, and it was impossible to build an organisation in a few days.

There was another problem, however. Acheson thought that the procedure adopted by White had got the commission and committees on the Bank 'in the most chaotic mess in the world. The only way I believe you can iron it out is to get the Steering Committee together and find out what we are doing. The thing is buzzing around in a perfectly nonsensical manner. We appointed *ad hoc* committees, section committees, drafting committees and all kinds of committees. A draft comes in from somewhere and nobody reads it, so it gets referred to somebody else; the delegates are going crazy.'

White did not think it was that bad. 'To some extent it is, Harry', Acheson insisted. Most of the people who were there knew only one-tenth or one-hundredth of what he knew himself. Vinson seemed to agree with White that the procedure was really very simple. The Russians had come down at noon, and they were very much concerned about the exchange rates, but they did not want to bring it up in an open meeting; so the matter was settled between the American and the Russian delegations. When there was disagreement on some point, 'instead of referring it back to the committees or instead of discussing it at any length in the committees, we let a few people discuss it, and immediately referred it to the ad hoc committees, created especially for that purpose, to refer back to the Fund Commission, and not to the committees', White explained. 'The procedure is very simple, Dean.'[39]

'GOLD AND THE US DOLLAR'

Putting the dollar next to gold at the centre of the postwar monetary system had been uppermost in Harry White's mind ever since he started thinking about the subject. Early in 1943, before any plan was published, he had told a group of economists, 'The dollar is the one great currency in whose strength there is universal confidence. It will probably become the cornerstone of the postwar structure of stable currencies.'[40] In the early drafts of his plan, however, he stated that any attempt to make an existing currency the international unit of account 'would be opposed on the grounds that it would seem to give the country possessing that currency some slight advantage either in international publicity or in trade'.[41]

As we have seen, in September 1943 Keynes told White that the United Kingdom did not contemplate going on to a gold or a dollar standard, but might be prepared to accept a unitas standard. Whenever the matter was brought up, he categorically rejected the idea that the dollar should be given a special status, and he continued to take the same line at Atlantic City, when the subject briefly cropped up there. There seems to be no evidence that the Americans discussed the subject with any other delegates. However, though the Statement of Principles, as it was submitted to the Bretton Woods Conference, clearly stated that 'The par value of a member's currency ... shall be expressed in terms of gold', White knew that the international bankers were extremely anxious to see the dollar become the international currency of the future.

A few days before leaving for Atlantic City, he made, in the face of persistent opposition by a few large banks, a statement to the press. He said that he had just spent a day in discussion with bankers, and that this showed 'differences of points of view on some matters.' 'A great part of the bankers' fears', Dr White said, 'arose from their lack of understanding of the plan, and not knowing all the other things we have in mind. The statement of principles is a mere skeleton, but there will be a lot of flesh on those bones before we are through.'[42]

To put the flesh on the bones took three simple operations, of which only White and his closest assistants at the Bretton Woods Conference were aware. It is doubtful that even Morgenthau was involved. While it made White a little nervous, until the process was completed, it was in fact the easiest hurdle to overcome during the conference, and the one that had the most far-reaching consequences for the future. Since only a small group of 'technicians' were informed, it did not become a point of general debate.

The first move was made on 6 July, at the 2.30 p.m. meeting of Committee 2. Many provisions and their alternatives were discussed that day. Professor Robertson was the British delegate. Also present were Professor Mossé from France, Mr de Iongh from Holland, and several other monetary experts. The consideration of a Mexican proposal about silver was postponed. The Dutch delegate proposed that the wording 'offer to' appearing in one provision be replaced by 'buy the currency'. There was a discussion about scarce currencies. The Greek delegate, Mr Varvaressos, suggested that the reports made by the Fund should be communicated, since they were confidential, to a 'member government', and not to the country, as it was stated. This was referred to the language committee.

Then came Alternative A, p. 16. This alternative, submitted by the American delegate, provided that 'The par value of the currency of each member shall be expressed in terms of gold, *as a common denominator, or in terms of a gold-convertible currency unit of the weight and fineness in*

effect on July 1, 1944'. This alternative was later presented in the official
record of the conference (p. 1651) as an American and British proposal,
which is not accurate. It was, in fact, one of the numerous alternatives
worked out by White and his group. Keynes obviously would never have
agreed to the proposal, and he was not aware of it.

The American delegate explained that the purpose of this alternative
was 'insignificant', and that it dealt with several problems. It was 'so
worded to show no obligation to sell gold was implied'. He assumed 'there
will exist a gold-convertible currency by definition within the terms of this
agreement'. There was no further discussion, and the alternative was
approved. It became part of the mass of material the committees and
commissions were piling up day after day, and it does not seem that any of
the delegates had noticed its implications.[43] On 12 July the British
delegation cabled London, 'Norwegian resolution proposed that books of
Fund and Bank should be kept in figures for international monetary unit
equivalent to 10 dollars in present gold value of United States currency.
This revives the proposal that accounts should be kept in Unitas and we
regard it as already dead.'[44] Having been approved by the committee, the
provision then went to the commission.

The second move was made a week later, during the 2.30 p.m. meeting
of Commission I on 13 July. Harry White was chairman. Just before the
meeting he had told Morgenthau, 'The commission meeting this afternoon
is extremely important. This is where we either fish or cut bait on most of
these things.'[45]

The agenda again was heavy. One of the points to be discussed was the
date on which countries joining the Fund should make their initial
contribution of gold and gold-convertible exchange. This was a minor
point, and, since the 'delegations did not have time to consider the
matter, the Committee agreed to refer this question directly to your Commission'.

The Indian delegate asked for a definition of gold-convertible currency,
which had been discussed, and of which Keynes had said it did not exist.
The question as put related to the gold-convertible contributions only, and
not to the par value of currencies.

Robertson, against Keynes's instructions, but as the responsible British
delegate, suggested that the words 'gold and gold-convertible currency' be
replaced by 'net official holdings of gold and U.S. dollars', and remarked
that this would involve several changes elsewhere. This was White's opportunity. Using his authority as chairman, he referred the matter to a special
committee, which took it out of any further discussion.[46]

That evening he was satisfied. He told Morgenthau that the commission
on the Fund 'covered quite a little material. A good deal of it was passed,
and some of it was referred back to a special committee which is to
consider it tonight'.[47]

The special committee was the group of technicians headed by White. It prepared for inclusion in the Final Act a number of provisions that were never discussed, nor even brought up. The argument (referred to earlier) between Acheson and White over procedure took place after White had expressed his satisfaction.

'You have a very complicated procedure', Acheson said. 'First of all, you get a report of the Drafting Committees, Committee One, and Committee so and so. Those things are all brought up. People think they are about ready to vote on something. Then they discover that it isn't true because it has to be referred to an *ad hoc* Committee or a Special Committee, and then it has to go to the Drafting Committee . . . .'

As far as the Fund was concerned, all Acheson's confusion was in his own mind, said White. The commission on the Fund was 'running as smooth as silk, and I don't know where you get your idea. There is no confusion as far as the Fund is concerned. All the important problems have been settled. They have either gone then – '

'I am sure they have been settled,' snapped Acheson, 'but I don't think the delegates know that.'[48]

They didn't; but, except for Keynes, what difference would it have made? After the meeting, White joined his group of technicians, and worked with them until three o'clock in the morning. He reported to Morgenthau the next day that the draft on the Fund was in excellent shape.[49]

The change from 'gold' to 'gold and US dollars' was lost in the ninety-six page document the chairmen of the delegations would sign a few days later. Whether or not any of them noticed it, or understood its implications, it seems that none of them expressed any reservations about it. Keynes would not find out until later, when he studied the Final Act.

Henry Ford, who celebrated his eighty-first birthday shortly after the end of the Bretton Woods Conference, told press reporters that he had not followed what had happened at the conference, but that he had always favoured a universal currency. 'That currency', he added, 'should be our own dollar.'[50]

LIQUIDATION OF THE BANK FOR INTERNATIONAL SETTLEMENTS

On 10 July, Commission III examined a proposal submitted by the Norwegian delegation:

BE IT RESOLVED that the United Nations Monetary and Financial Conference recommends the liquidation of the Bank for International Settlements at Basel. It is suggested that the liquidation shall begin at the earliest possible date, and that the Governments of the United Nations now at war with Germany, appoint a Commission of Investigation, in order to examine the management and transactions of the bank during the present war.[51]

White had been informed about this proposal immediately, and was obviously in favour. He said that Norway, France and Belgium supported it, 'and I think they could line up a majority. But England has been very busily at work, trying to get them to withdraw, and they tell me that the State Department here is also supporting the English'.

But Acheson thought it would be undesirable to discuss the Bank for International Settlements (BIS) at the conference.

'McKittrick would be forced to resign', said White. 'I would support the motion of the Norwegian delegate. I think it would be a salutary thing for the world.' Morgenthau agreed: following the invasion of Czechoslovakia, the BIS had turned over to the Germans the Czechoslovak gold. Luxford felt that the dissolution itself would not be too important, but it would be a symbol, since the bank was 'by virtue of the Nazi occupation of the countries of Europe, now . . . in the hand of the Nazis'.

Edward Brown, the banker, was embarrassed. At the request of the Hoover Administration, his bank and three New York banks had participated in the foundation of the BIS, and shares had been distributed to the public. The Norwegian delegate, Keilhau, had just made an attack on the president of the bank, McKittrick; the BIS ought to be dissolved, said Brown, but this was not the place to discuss it.

Acheson was of the same opinion: this concerned foreign relations, he said, and it was up to the Secretary of State to express his opinion. 'I would be delighted to talk with Cordell Hull about this', said Morgenthau. 'I am fairly confident what his answer would be.'[52]

The Norwegian proposal was strenuously opposed particularly by the Dutch delegation, whose chairman, Beyen, had been president of the BIS when the Czech gold was turned over to Germany. On 19 July the Norwegian and Dutch delegation communicated to the press a new proposal that they were submitting, recommending 'the liquidation of the Bank for International Settlements at the earliest possible moment'. It would be considered in commission the following day.[53]

When he learned about this new resolution, which was milder than the first, Keynes wrote to Morgenthau, 'We are entirely in accord with the general purpose . . . What we cannot manage is a recommendation from Commission III to Commission I to write some specific agreement into the International Monetary Fund. For technical reasons this . . . would inevitably prevent us from participating either in the Fund or in the Bank until after the expiry of an indefinite period.'[54]

Keynes delivered the message personally. Morgenthau told his staff,

Lord Keynes came in here at about seven-forty, and the man was livid over this BIS thing, and said that if this thing went through at nine o'clock he was going to get up and leave the Conference. He didn't use the language that he had been double-crossed, but he said that this was the first time this has happened, but the inference was that he had been double-crossed and this thing had been given out in advance of the meeting . . . to the press, which he thought most unfair. . . . He said that he thought the people responsible should be rapped over the knuckles. What he said is just amongst the people here in the room and I don't want it to go any further. So I told him please to quiet down, that I would see my people and we decided that we would let the thing go over until tomorrow morning . . . he really was very much disturbed, and I don't think he was putting on an act. He said the BIS, politically, is just as unpopular, if not more so, in England than in America.[5 5]

This may have been so, but Keynes was aware of the fact that Britain was bound by the obligations to which it had subscribed in joining the BIS, and could not simply repudiate them. He had suggested that, at the date of the constitution of the Fund, 'the necessary steps will be taken to liquidate the Bank for International Settlements'. But White and his staff had seen to it that the proposal put forward was stronger. They wanted the Bank liquidated as quickly as possible. In addition, lining up the Fund with the BIS, 'in the way Keynes suggested, I think, would be most unfortunate', said White. 'It would make it appear that that is a direct competitor.'

Morgenthau was puzzled that Beyen should have associated himself with this proposal: 'I am not sure that fellow Beyen didn't pull a fast one on us too', he said. 'Getting us to do something which he knew that Keynes would object to.'

Luxford gave the explanation: 'No, he didn't get us to do it. He fought it tooth and nail. We forced him to give us the right technical language against his will.'[5 6]

White was very much disturbed that it had not been possible to pass the first Norwegian resolution. 'They will try very much to get this to look just the opposite of what we want. They will try to give the BIS status and a clean bill of health by saying it should continue in operation until the Fund comes and then it ought to pass out because it is doing approximately the same work. In the first place, it makes it more difficult for us in the Fund, because they can say, "Why don't you give the BIS more powers?" In the second place, it would look as though they were a perfectly good institution, it is just that the Fund has a little broader powers. And in the third place, it would be a public recognition of the fact, by forty-four nations, that the BIS is a good institution and should continue until the Fund . . . .

'Well, I am confident', Morgenthau interrupted, 'that if we can get Keynes down here face to face and make him agree to something on the spot, that I can be successful . . . .'

Shortly afterwards. Keynes walked in with several members of the British delegation. Morgenthau handed him the proposal about the liquidation 'at the earliest possible moment'.

'I don't quite know what the earliest possible moment is', said Mr Bolton, who accompanied Keynes.

'Not very early!' was Keynes's reply. He then came back to his own proposal, which recommended the liquidation after the establishment of the Fund. 'The only difference', he said, 'is that that says it is contingent upon the establishment of the Fund. This says it shall be liquidated whether there is a Fund or not. I don't think we want to keep the damned thing alive, do we?'

'Amen, brother!', said Vinson.

From the conversation that followed, in which Keynes said it was 'very wrong' that the proposal had been revealed to the press though it had not been passed by the committee, it became clear that White and his staff had in fact engineered the whole manoeuvre, using the Dutch and Norwegian delegates as a front.[57]

The recommendation for the liquidation of the Bank for International Settlements 'at the earliest possible moment' was agreed upon by the conference and included in the Final Act. Once more, Keynes established himself as a prophet. The liquidation would not come 'very early'.

LOCATION OF FUND AND BANK

During the meeting in Atlantic City, White had indicated that he wanted the head offices of the Fund and Bank to be located in the United States. Keynes had advised London, and the answer had been that this would not be acceptable. White had prepared for submission to the conference a proposal to the effect that 'The principal office of the Fund shall be located in the member having the largest quota.' Keynes had submitted a proposal suggesting that the decision about the location be made at the first meeting of the board of governors.[58]

London had not quite understood Keynes's motives; after all the emphasis that the Fund would be a technical and not a political organisation, it would be a pity if the first task of the board of governors were to be to settle a highly political and controversial matter such as the location of the Fund. The question would have to be settled behind the scenes.[59]

Keynes wrote White a 'personal and private' letter, dated 9 July, advising that he had tabled a proposal about the location of the Bank's headquarters, and that this was similar to his proposal about the location of the Fund's. This was a most difficult matter to settle, and he had just received a telegram from the Chancellor of the Exchequer stating that no agreement was to be made without his express authority.

'The only comment I would like to make on this', White told the American delegates, 'is if you don't get this settled in the Conference, it certainly is reduced, and that is why they want to postpone. Maybe they hope to get some arrangement whereby they will get some and we will get others. I think it is important enough for us to push the issue here in the Conference where I am sure we will get a favorable vote.'

Morgenthau asked the Congressional delegates how they felt about it. It would have a material effect, said Wolcott; 'there has always been a certain jealousy that the financial center of the world is London, England'. If the United States were going to participate, it should have the head offices. The other Congressmen agreed. Senator Wagner thought that if the United States did not have the head offices it would be almost impossible to obtain Congressional approval of the Fund.

'Then the answer is that we have got to fight it out here and now', Morgenthau concluded.[60]

Several delegations were on Keynes's side. 'Canadians, Dutch and Belgians all tell us that if London wants to remain in business even our present proposal goes dangerously far', he cabled. There was no hope of securing agreement on any location outside the United States during the time at their disposal. He asked that the Chancellor give him clear instructions. The Americans were emphatic that the matter should be settled at the conference. 'But if we are to be defeated on this perhaps we should retire with dignity by withdrawing our amendment.'[61]

The Chancellor asked Keynes to make it clear to the American delegation that the considerable opposition the government would have to face would be gravely augmented by any decision that the Fund be located in the United States. He asked Keynes to hold the proposal, irrespective of the result, for the time being. If it were not possible to obtain a decision in favour of London or Amsterdam or some other appropriate European centre, opinion would be able to express itself. If it were possible to have the Fund in London or in some European capital, 'then we should raise no objection to the location of the Bank being in the United States'.[62]

On 13 July Morgenthau discussed with the American delegation a letter he had just received from Keynes. The decision about the location of the Fund was a highly political matter to be decided by governments, and not by a monetary conference. The question could not be considered without reference to the location of other international bodies with which the Fund would have to co-operate. He hoped that the participating governments could reach a decision on the matter before the first meeting of the board of governors. 'But I must particularly emphasise in this letter that in the opinion of my Government it would not be a proper course to settle a political matter, such as this, by equal voting of the financial or technical Delegates from the wide variety of nations here assembled.'[63]

White thought that the British wanted the headquarters of either the

Fund or the Bank to be in Britain. 'They don't care, as long as they have one, because they feel otherwise there are important things to follow. I think we are strategically in an invulnerable position to get it now. If you wait, I don't know what you will get, because they can't back out on the basis that they don't like where the head office is. Their public won't stand for it and the world won't stand for it. So the thing to do is to put it through on a vote here. If they don't like it, it is too bad.'

The Congressional delegates again confirmed their position. Also, many South American and smaller countries would feel more comfortable if the gold of the Fund were stored in the United States.

'New York has become the financial center of the world. These British are just fighting up-hill. There is no question about that', said White. He did not even think that Morgenthau should answer Keynes's letter: 'he isn't saying anything he didn't say before. . . . Moreover, we are putting in twice as much money as anybody else, three times as much. On the face of it, it is preposterous that the head office should be any place else. We can vote it any place we want, by members, by votes, and we will win. They know it, and that is why they don't want to come to a vote. I don't see why we should put ourselves in a position to be subject to political manipulation.

'And if Churchill called Roosevelt, requesting a postponement of the decision?', Luxford wondered.

The President would not answer such a question without first contacting the American delegation at the conference, said Morgenthau.

'The vote will take place tomorrow', White decided. 'If the President should call up, we will say we are very sorry, but the Delegates have all voted on it. That will give him a good answer to Churchill. We can't hold up everything.'

'That is no answer,' Morgenthau concluded, 'but anyway, we have taken care of the meeting for tonight.'[64]

During a previous meeting White had suggested: 'Rather than bring that on with the British, why not postpone it until the last meeting of the Fund – just dodge it. . . . They are almost licked. What do they do? Publicly say "We object because of some other reason?" ' But Morgenthau did not want to postpone it, and Luxford thought that 'If we are willing to take this thing to a vote basis, we can clean up the whole works.'[65]

The following morning Morgenthau went up to Keynes's suite, and told him that the American delegation was emphatic that Congress would not accept the Fund unless it were located in the United States; that a proposal for postponement would not be understood; and that in any event the ultimate decision must be regarded as a foregone conclusion. This problem arose out of the peculiar relationship between the Administration and Congress. He had regarded it as essential to associate Congress closely with the drafting of the agreement. So far, he had had an extraordinary and almost miraculous success. All Congressmen present at the conference, including not only Republicans but also old-time isolationists and hostile critics had been brought round to enthusiastic support for the Fund and the Bank. The Republican senators were even telling Senator Taft, who had issued a critical statement, that he was not speaking for the party. Morgenthau begged Keynes to ask London not to upset the present mood of his team and pleaded that Whitehall should appreciate the special nature of his problem, which arose wholly from the relationship of Congress to the Administration, irrespective of politics. In passing on this message to the British government Keynes commented, 'I believe that we are on a losing wicket here.' He hoped that the Chancellor would instruct him either to withdraw the amendment or to argue, but not to press the matter. 'Eady, Brand and Ronald reluctantly concur.'[66]

In the light of Keynes's advice, the Chancellor agreed not to press the proposal, but to withdraw it. He wanted, however, to make it clear that British public and Parliamentary opinion were very sensitive on the point, and that the government was not debarred from making it a condition of acceptance of the plan that the head office of the Fund be located in Europe.[67]

Morgenthau once more submitted the issue to the American delegation: 'I know you have expressed your opinion once before and I would like some sort of direction from the Committee. . . . It is a question of New York versus London.'

'I stand pat', said Senator Tobey.

'I haven't changed', added Senator Wagner.

Congressman Spence was 'unalterably opposed to it and I am not going to change. I think you ought to talk to him as plainly as diplomacy will allow. I don't know how plain that is.'

'Well, I am not a diplomat', said Morgenthau; 'I can talk pretty plain . . . I think this is the time to wave the flag. . . . It is the unanimous opinion . . . that we should not accede to Lord Keynes's request that this matter of location be postponed.'[68]

The next day White reported that Professor Robbins of the British delegation had strongly urged him that the question of the location of the Fund should not immediately be raised at a public meeting, but should be left a few days, until the British had had an opportunity to obtain a reply from London. Vinson added that Robbins had said, 'We know we will be beaten and we hope to avoid being humiliated.'

'We can wait', said White.[69]

In order to keep the American embassy in London informed, Morgenthau and Acheson sent a telegram stating that 'The most controversial point which we have had with the British during the course of the Bretton Woods Conference has been the location of the head office of the Fund. We have taken the position all along that the head office must be located in the country which has the largest quota. In a conversation yesterday with Mr. Morgenthau the President instructed our Delegation to insist on this point.' Keynes was ready to give up his objections and would make a purely formal statement for the record. The decision on the matter had been postponed until 17 July.[70]

On 17 July Keynes wrote to Morgenthau that the Chancellor had authorised him to withdraw the British amendment, 'but in doing so to place on record that in the view of His Majesty's Government the question where the headquarters of the Bank should be situated ought not to be considered without reference to the location of other international bodies'. He also mentioned the public and parliamentary opposition to the Fund that the decision about its headquarters was likely to create in Britain, and gave a reminder that the whole plan would eventually have to be put before the British government for its approval. Keynes said that, in order to avoid incomplete or inaccurate press reports, he would issue a statement announcing the withdrawal of his alternative, but making it clear at the same time that the location of the headquarters of the Fund was a matter for governments themselves, and not just a rather technical conference to decide.[71]

The following day, the United States proposal that the headquarters of the Fund be located in the country having the largest quota – in other words, the United States – was adopted. That evening, Morgenthau discussed Keynes's press release.

The reservation by the United Kingdom was no different from any other reservation, said Luxford. 'It simply means that they object to it, but in the final analysis there is no choice as to whether they accept the Fund or not accept it, and they can't be rewriting the document. . . . We can be very gracious. We are getting what we went after. We ought to let them do as much as they can do.'[72]

At an earlier meeting Acheson, who had always been concerned about keeping strictly to the correct international procedure, had asked Morgenthau whether he could see Keynes's letter, because 'It ought to have some powerful consideration.' No one shared his view. It had been discussed and the American delegation was unanimous, 'more completely unanimous than it has ever been'. White did not think it necessary to bring the matter up again. 'Who is to determine where the head office is in an international conference? I should think it would be the conference. The governments are represented by the delegates. After they decide it, like any other point, any government can accept it or reject it.'

Acheson did not want to argue about it, he just wanted to ask a question.

'The question has to be argued about in order to come to a decision', said White.

Acheson was not scared of an argument; he was 'just too tired to make an argument, but I do want somebody to understand the question'.

'I see. Well, you restate it', said White.

The question that Keynes had raised, said Acheson, was whether a major policy decision that would normally be made among governments could be left to the groups meeting at Bretton Woods or postponed for a vote by the board of governors of the Fund after it had come into operation.

Morgenthau had sensed the intention of Acheson's question: 'What he is saying is that this is a matter between governments, or foreign offices.'

Keynes had brought up the same question in Atlantic City, said White, saying that he hoped it would not be put in the draft on which the conference would vote, because the most appropriate time to determine where the Fund would be located would be after it got started.

'Are you through?' asked Morgenthau. 'May I simply say this, Dean, that whether it is done between governments or whether it is done here, this thing is a matter of postponing the day of reckoning. . . . Now, to me it boils down to this – and I will be willing to face this thing – these groups – once and for all – that the financial center of the world is going to be New York and we don't want to postpone this thing until another day where we may not be in as advantageous a position and maybe have them to get in a horse-trading position and maybe end up by having it in London. Now the advantage is ours here, and I personally think we should take it.'

'If the advantage was theirs, they would take it', said White.[73]

THE FUND IS BORN

After two weeks of negotiations, Secretary Morgenthau issued a statement to the press:

> The International Monetary Fund has been born. The achievement has been an unusually fine demonstration to the world that forty-four nations can get together to iron out their differences and decide how they will work together in post-war monetary matters. Not all countries have received all they hoped to get, but the spirit of give and take is the best kind of omen for international cooperation and for what we may expect when we get around the peace table. The few matters still outstanding are not of supreme importance.[74]

In the morning session on 17 July, Keynes, Morgenthau and other delegates discussed a possible extension of the conference. Keynes had raised the question. In matters of fundamental difficulty or disagreement, he said, most questions had been resolved. 'But the technicians and draftsmen can handle the detail properly only when you have settled what it is all about, and I am afraid they are dreadfully behindhand. They are doing a grand piece of work. It is not easy to keep track of it because none of us are seeing it as a whole, but in bits and pieces.' If they were hasty, errors and inconsistencies might slip in, and this would be dangerous. The British delegates concerned with the details were 'quite breaking up under the strain ... their efficiency is getting very seriously impaired'. And so was their health. Then there was another consideration:

> There are certain final technical matters we haven't considered at all, what the lawyers call the final act, which embodies the results of this Conference. No attempt has yet been made to draft that, and it hasn't been considered by anybody. At present, no one has seen, as a continuous narrative, the work that has been done, and I think it is not quite fair to the Delegations that they should be expected to pass so quickly on things they have never had a chance, really, of reading as a consecutive narrative.

There was unanimous agreement that the conference should be extended.

'We have certain mechanical difficulties which I won't bore you with', said Morgenthau. 'We may have to get the President to get out an order to seize the hotel as of Wednesday night, and put troops in here to run it ... we may have to carry the manager of the hotel out with two soldiers! If that is necessary, Judge Vinson will give the orders ... we ought to fix a date and then not postpone it again, because we will be in considerable litigation here with the hotel.'

'We want to do as good a job as we can,' said White, 'because when it is available the whole world is going to examine this document. There will be lawyers and technicians and writers. They are going to go through this with a fine-toothed comb and find out and interpret every phrase, and as Lord Keynes has said, some of them may give rise to substantial problems.' Several of his people were 'getting irritable and a little inefficient. I felt myself cracking up last night and I went to bed at 10 o'clock, had some sleep, and I feel fine now.' He thought it would be possible to get through by Saturday night. 'So I would strongly urge that you don't leave here until Sunday.'

'As a technician,' said Luxford, 'I don't believe that you can promise that this job will be done by that time.'

'Well, you just have to', Morgenthau told him; 'you can't stay on here forever. ... Why last night did it suddenly dawn on you that you couldn't do it?'

Judge Vinson intervened: 'Lord Keynes' men last night – Sir Wilfrid Eady and Mr. Robertson were just fagged. I am just merely saying that for Mr. Luxford.'

White also wanted time for a plenary session, 'a rather formal night occasion – in which the world can be informed of the successful conclusion of the Fund, and an indication that the Bank is going forward'.

Keynes suggested that the rest of the day 'be a whole holiday. ... Everybody wants to stop and think. I haven't been able to get hold of my technicians for three days.'

There was unanimous agreement.[75]

Two days later, Keynes walked upstairs to his own suite after dining with Morgenthau, and suffered a mild heart attack. Lady Keynes mentioned the fact to a friend she had met at the conference, and who was the mother of the Reuters correspondent. The news leaked out.

Keynes advised the Chancellor of the Exchequer that the conference would be extended.

> The procedure of this conference is enormously complicated, the subjects under discussion are difficult and intricate, we are constantly sitting under chairmen who barely understand English and opportunities for the minor powers to waste time are unlimited. In the end we shall I believe produce satisfactory and workable document but here again there are lessons to be learned for future occasions.[76]

In another telegram he said, 'With the exception of the Russians, who have pursued an unbroken policy of contracting into all benefits but out of all duties and obligations and a hesitation probably temporary by the Netherlands, all of the major delegations have agreed to subscribe to the Bank an amount of not less than their quota with the Fund.'[77]

THE FINAL DAYS

Secretary Morgenthau asked the chairmen of several delegations who were members of the steering committee to see him on 19 July at 9 p.m.

'I think we will start', he said, 'and maybe Lord Keynes can catch up.' He introduced Mr Frank Coe, the technical secretary-general of the conference, and asked him to explain the purpose of the meeting. Coe explained that it was necessary to constitute a co-ordinating committee to compile the documents of the conference. Because the commissions had been so careful in their work, the co-ordinating committee would have practically nothing to do. Therefore he suggested that it would not be necessary to call it together, 'unless some confusion should develop which would require such a body'. There was general agreement that authority for this job should be delegated to Secretary Morgenthau.

'The next piece of business is the resolution on the Final Act', said Morgenthau.

Frank Coe read a statement to the effect that the conference secretariat, of which he was leader, would be authorised to prepare the Final Act, containing the definitive texts of the conclusions approved by the conference, and that no changes would be made at the closing plenary session. The co-ordinating committee could review the text, and submit it to the final plenary session. 'The signature, therefore, of the Final Act would be essentially, or entirely, a statement by the signer that he had attended the Conference and had witnessed these things being done', Coe added.

Mendès France wanted to know when the plenary session would take place. It had tentatively been arranged for 10 p.m. on Saturday, after the farewell dinner, he was told.

'At what time do we get the last papers?', Mendès France inquired.

'That will depend, of course upon the time that the Commissions complete their work and the Executive Session is held. It might be explained that each of those articles and resolutions will be considered twice by the plenary session; one, in Executive Session where there can be free discussion, and the last a mere formal approval.'

This too was agreed. 'If there is no other business, we could make this a record meeting', Morgenthau said happily.[78]

The records seem not to contain any evidence, and probably never did, of whether Keynes was asked to attend the meeting.

The meeting over, White and his group could go ahead and write up the Final Act; the co-ordinating committee would not be called together, and there would be little time for anyone else to read much of the text. White and his group worked day and night at combining the provisions that had been adopted by the various committees and commissions, plus those that had been secretly agreed upon in bilateral negotiations, and including those that had been prepared by the special committee and not been referred back to any commission meeting. The completed Final Act contained ninety-six pages and was written mostly in lawyers' language, practically unintelligible to the layman; the chairmen or other chosen representatives of the delegations were to sign it by noon on the day following the closing plenary session (held at 9.45 p.m. on 22 July). Before that could happen, however, the conference went through some of its most dramatic moments.

On 21 July, Keynes took the time to write a long letter to Sir John Anderson, the Chancellor of the Exchequer, who was preparing for a visit to the United States:

> You should appreciate that you will be coming into an atmosphere of the greatest possible friendliness and good will. The Americans are inclined to be intolerably tiresome in method and in detail and with the execution of plans and in the mode of pressure they bring to bear. . . . One can and should approach them as a band of friends and brothers. They have their own difficult psychology and a dreadful tendency to suspicion and all the rest of it. But underneath, what I have just said is the real truth. . . .
>
> The fact that we have been able to work in such intimacy and for so long a period with the Americans, and more especially with the

American Treasury, more as colleagues on the same side of the table, helping them to common ends and to make a good job of a piece of work, than trying to get something for ourselves has, as I think all of us agree, produced a relationship of intimacy and confidence which has never previously existed. We have tried most scrupulously to be reasonable and not to be greedy. We and we alone of the other Delegations have spent 90 per cent of our time trying to help them and not to make trouble for them. This is deeply understood and appreciated. . . .

As I have already reported, one of the surprises has been the intimate and friendly relations with Morgenthau personally. As you know, I myself have known him for a considerable time. But until Bretton Woods I had never spent a minute with him that was not sticky. Now all that is completely changed. I have seen a good deal of him, and increasingly as time went on. Most of the interviews have been *tête-à-tête*. For the first time I have been able to discuss serious matters of business with him in quite long interviews without his getting into those moods which used to be so obstructive to proper relations. He could not have been more consistently kind and friendly, and even expansive. . . .

The pressure of work here has been quite unbelievable . . . carried on in committees and commissions numbering anything up to 200 persons in rooms with bad acoustics, shouting through microphones, many of those present, often including the Chairman, with an imperfect knowledge of English, each wanting to get something on the record which would look well in the Press down at home, and one of the most important Delegations namely the Russians, only understanding what was afoot with the utmost difficulty and expense of time. . . . We have all of us worked every minute of our waking hours practically without intermission for what is now four weeks. . . . I have resolutely refused to go to any committees after dinner (except once only against orders which promptly led to a heart attack, so that I suffered from guilt not less than from bodily discomfort!); whereas the others have been sitting in committees night after night up to 3.30 a.m., starting again in the committee at 9.30 a.m. next morning. How people have stood it all is a miracle. . . .

Our personal relations with the Russians have been very cordial and we have seen quite a lot of them socially. We like them exceedingly and, I think, they like us. Given time we should, I believe, gain their confidence and would then be able to help them a good deal. They *want* to thaw and collaborate. But the linguistic difficulties and very poor interpretation are a dreadful obstacle. Above all, they are put in a most awkward, and sometimes humiliating, position by the lack both of suitable instructions and of suitable direction from Moscow.

Well we have survived. In my opinion the final products are clear and

even aesthetic in presentation. I hope you will like the substance and
we feel that we have protected your position not too badly.[79]

One of the knottiest problems the conference had to deal with was the
Russians' attitude on the quotas. It had been stipulated that the quotas of
each country would be the same in the Fund, where they meant access to
the facilities, as in the Bank, where they had to be contributed and would
be used by the neediest. All major countries had agreed to this, except the
Russians, who insisted on a $1200 million quota in the Fund, but wanted
to contribute only $900 million to the Bank. After protracted negotiations
the American delegation had accepted this, and the press had become
aware of it.

In order to break the deadlock, Judge Vinson asked the chairmen of a
number of delegations to meet during the morning of 21 July. Several
delegations indicated their willingness to increase their Bank quota, in
order not to change the aggregate, while subscribing the part the Russians
refused to take. Keynes appealed to the Soviet delegate, who was present
but had not yet spoken: 'He has heard in the course of the last few
minutes that Poland and China are prepared to make increased contributions to meet something that Russia cannot afford.' The risks involved
were limited, but, owing to language difficulties, this probably had not
been understood by the Soviet delegation. The delegate from India had
just remarked that, if the Russian contribution remained at $900 million,
the Indian contribution 'will be half the Soviet contribution, which he
would find difficult to justify. I do urge, most sincerely, that it is scarcely
consistent with the honor and dignity of a great country to remain so
uncompromising at this stage.'

The Soviet delegate was 'deeply moved by the willingness of other
delegations to reach the goal which was mentioned'. He had, however, no
authorisation to propose any other figure. In international organisations
each country has to determine its contribution by its circumstances, and
he could not see the necessity for taking into account other countries'
circumstances too. Russia had suffered more from the war than India. He
did not want to influence in any way any other delegation; it was up to
each country to make its own decision.[80]

That afternoon the same delegates met again, and Vinson had to
announce that the Russian delegation had received no further communication from Moscow. China, Poland, the United States, Canada, and even
the Latin American countries had all shown themselves prepared to
increase their own contributions. Thus the total remained unchanged.
Keynes suggested that the final table of contributions be presented at six
o'clock that evening. There was unanimous agreement.[81]

At seven o'clock that evening, the two principal Russian delegates
came to see Morgenthau.

'Mr. Stepanov would like to tell you that he has the answer from Mr.

Molotov', said the interpreter, 'and the answer is that he is happy to agree to your proposition.'

'Yes', was all Morgenthau could say.

'Mr. Molotov says that we will agree to increase our quota', the interpreter repeated.

'To how much?'

'To $1,200,000,000.'

'Mr. Molotov agrees to that?'

'He said that he agrees with Mr. Morgenthau.'

'Well, you tell Mr. Molotov that I want to thank him from the bottom of my heart. Now, I don't know what we will do, but I will have to send for Mr. Vinson and the others right away, and we will have to get busy.'

'Yes, Mr. Stepanov says that it is all right.'

'Just so I understand', said Morgenthau, 'would you mind saying it once more?'

Mr. Stepanov repeated the message and the interpreter formulated it once more: 'Mr Molotov gives us the right to agree to a quota of $1,200,000,000 in the Bank. He said that he agrees with Mr. Morgenthau, and I should like to mention this too. Mr. Molotov says that he agrees to the size of the quota because Mr. Morgenthau asked the Soviet Delegation to do it.'

'I want you to say this to Mr. Molotov. This confirms the long time respect and confidence that I have in the Union of Soviet and Socialist Republics.'

'Mr. Stepanov says that he will telegraph what you told him just as it was said by yourself.'

'Well, this makes me very, very happy. The Conference was almost a success and now it is a complete success.'[82]

Before the Russian decision became known, Keynes had sent the following comment to London:

At the final discussion of subscriptions . . . Russia stood pat on 900 and lost much honour and dignity in the process . . . . The Americans have been outstandingly anxious to meet Russia on every point. The Russian stonewalling tactics have been successful in getting nearly all concessions for which they have asked. Nevertheless they have overplayed their hand and seriously diminished their prestige before every delegation here present.[83]

Another problem that came up at the end of the conference resulted from the fact that the representatives of China, France, the USSR, Greece, Ethiopia, Yugoslavia, India, Australia, Egypt and New Zealand, while they agreed to sign the Final Act, wanted to express reservations of one sort or another, most of them about their quotas.

At the executive plenary session on 20 July, Keynes took up the subject and wondered

> whether there is not a possibility of some misunderstanding in the minds of the Delegates who wish to make reservations on particular points. So far as the U.K. Delegation is concerned we, in common with all other Delegations, reserve the opinion of our Government on the document as a whole and on every part of it ... we are at the present stage in no way committed to anything. ... We do not even recommend our Governments to adopt the result.

By expressing reservations on part of the document, the countries concerned seemed to suggest that the rest was in some sense accepted, and this might create some misapprehension of the position of those countries that expressed no reservations. He suggested that the reservations be retained in the minutes of the commission, but not be made part of the Final Act.

Judge Vinson appealed to the delegations that had made reservations not 'to make the task of friends more difficult'. He assured the Chinese delegates that the United States was not unmindful of the 'historic friendship that has existed throughout the years between China and our country; tell me that the United States does not recognize the glorious courageous effort that China has made'. As for France, 'we learned it at our mother's knees that France came to us years ago when we were in need. 1917 when millions of our sons joined common cause with France and others of her kind a historic statement was made by an American when he stood before the tomb of Lafayette, saluted and said, "Lafayette we are here." ' He trusted and prayed that all delegations that had expressed reservations on the question of quotas would reconsider their position.

Following these appeals, the reservations were withdrawn. They remained recorded in the minutes of the commission, but were not included in the Final Act.[84]

During the morning of 22 July, the American delegation met for the last time. Morgenthau was happy. The previous night, at 11 o'clock, he had 'got the idea that it might be nice if the President sent a message of congratulations to the Conference on the conclusion'. He did not know where the President was, but around midnight he had sent him a proposed draft for a telegram, and the President's approval had arrived in the morning.

He thanked everybody for the splendid work the American delegation had done. 'It has been a team. It has been the most successful group I have ever worked with, the most pleasant, and I think it has demonstrated to me that on this sort of thing it is the way we should work with Congress.'

One after the other the delegates complimented Morgenthau on his 'splendid leadership', on 'your remarkable patience and your genius in directing the Conference'. The members of Congress, both the Democrats and the Republicans, promised to do the best they could to 'carry this thing forward to success'.

Ned Brown the banker promised to 'do what I can to sell it to the bankers of the country', although he 'didn't give any guarantee'. The Republican senators, Morgenthau felt, could take care of the opposition in Congress: 'I will leave Taft to you', he told Senator Tobey. 'He is your personal meat. I think you could take him apart and put him together again so that you would not recognize what he looks like.'

Senator Tobey, in turn, paid tribute to 'something that has impressed me tremendously, and it is the genius of these two men, Luxford and Bernstein. I have watched them in action and it is wonderful the work they have done here and I want to compliment them and I appreciate all they have done.'

Now that the conference was coming to an end, there was general agreement that 'every one here has to work as hard as they have been working to sell it. Our job isn't done until it is sold.' Morgenthau suggested that the delegation meet in Washington from time to time, and 'go along step by step', as a permanent body, to organise the campaign that would have to be conducted in Congress and with public opinion.

'Speaking of continuing our conversations in Washington,' Morgenthau concluded, 'I think the New Hampshire air has contributed much to the clear thinking of everybody. . . . Believe me, if the United States Government had a summer capital, I think it would increase the work by a hundred per cent.'[85]

A formal dinner marked the closing plenary session. When almost everyone was already seated, Keynes's chair was still empty. He came in a little late. 'Tired, pale as a sheet, he was walking round the long table to his empty seat. Spontaneously everyone in the room stood up in complete silence while he made his way to his chair. It was an unspoken moving tribute to the master, the true prophet of this gathering.'[86]

The message from President Roosevelt asking Morgenthau to convey his heartiest congratulations to the delegates on the successful completion of their difficult task was read: 'They have prepared two further foundation stones for the structure of lasting peace and security.'

Keynes had been asked to address the conference for the last time, and to submit the motion to accept the Final Act. He rose and said,

I feel it a signal honour that I am asked to move the acceptance of the Final Act.

We, the Delegates of this Conference, Mr. President, have been trying to accomplish something very difficult to accomplish. . . . We have had to perform at one and the same time the tasks appropriate to the economist, to the financier, to the politician, to the journalist, to the propagandist, to the lawyer, to the statesman — even, I think, to the prophet and to the soothsayer. Nor has the magic of the microphone been able, silently and swiftly perambulant at the hands of our attendant sprites, the faithful Scouts, Puck coming to the aid of Bottom, to undo all the mischief first wrought in the Tower of Babel.

He paid tribute to Secretary Morgenthau's 'wise and kindly guidance', and to 'the indomitable will and energy, always governed by good temper and humour, of Harry White'. But it had been teamwork, such as he had seldom experienced.

And for my own part, I should like to pay a particular tribute to our lawyers. All the more so because I confess that, generally speaking, I do not like lawyers. I have been known to complain that, to judge from results in this lawyer-ridden land, the Mayflower, when she sailed from Plymouth, must have been entirely filled with lawyers. . . . Too often lawyers busy themselves to make commonsense illegal. Too often lawyers are men who turn poetry into prose and prose into jargon. Not so our lawyers here in Bretton Woods. On the contrary they have turned our jargon into prose and our prose into poetry. . . . I have only one complaint against them. . . . I wish that they had not covered so large a part of our birth certificate with such very detailed provisions for our burial service, hymns and lessons and all.

I am greatly encouraged, I confess, by the critical, sceptical, and even carping spirit in which our proceedings have been watched and welcomed in the outside world. How much better that our projects should *begin* in disillusion than that they should *end* in it![87]

The end of his address, in which he stated his hope that the brotherhood of man would 'become more than a mere phrase', is quoted at the beginning of this book.

One of the most dramatic moments of the conference occurred when Secretary Morgenthau announced that the Russian government had agreed to increase its quota in the Bank from $900 million to $1200 million. The delegates applauded when they heard that the telegram from Moscow announcing this decision had just arrived. The Russian delegate expressed his gratitude to Secretary Morgenthau and stated,

The stabilization of the currencies of the various countries, the expansion of world trade, the balancing of international payments, long-term capital investments intended for the reconstruction and development of the democratic nations and especially for the restoration of economy of those countries who suffered severely from enemy occupation and hostilities — all these aspirations will have exceptional importance for the postwar organization of the World and for the maintenance and strengthening of peace and security.[88]

Mr J. L. Ilsley, chairman of the Canadian delegation, hailed the results of the conference as 'a great and even historic achievement'. He paid tribute to the technical competence of Harry White and his associates, to Morgenthau, and particularly to Keynes, who had so eloquently and fittingly presented the motion.

We find a happy fitness also in that delegate being Lord Keynes. Throughout the Conference, as indeed throughout his life, he has showered his ideas upon us and has occasionally nourished some of ours. His sudden insights, his revealing phrases, and, if I may say so, his passionate striving for what is reasonable and emancipating in human affairs, have contributed greatly to the progress and wisdom of our deliberations.[89]

Mendès France, recalling the failures of the numerous economic and monetary conferences held between the two wars, stated that the delegates to the conference of Bretton Woods

may be proud of having inaugurated a new era in the history of these conferences. ... Because, as it is impossible in the modern world to circumscribe wars, it will be impossible to avoid the spread of unemployment, economic stagnation, excessive economic fluctuations from one country to another with all their train of miseries and sufferings.[90]

As president of the conference it fell upon Secretary Morgenthau to deliver the farewell address. He stressed the fact that nations at the conference had 'had to yield to one another not in respect to principles or essentials, but in respect to methods and procedural details. The fact that we have done so ... is a sign blazoned upon the horizon ... that the peoples of the earth are learning to join hands and work in unity.' The American delegation, like all other delegations, 'has at all times been conscious of its primary obligation – the protection of American interests. And the other representatives here have been no less loyal or devoted to the welfare of their own people.' But the only genuine safeguard for the national interests lay in international co-operation.

To seek the achievement of our aims separately through the planless, senseless rivalry that divided us in the past, or through the outright economic aggression which turned neighbors into enemies, would be to invite ruin again upon us all. Worse, it would be once more to start our steps irretraceably down the steep, disastrous road to war. That sort of extreme nationalism belongs to an era that is dead. Today the only enlightened form of national self-interest lies in international accord.

He took it as an axiom that governments would not tolerate prolonged and widespread unemployment any more. A revival of international trade was indispensable if full employment was to be achieved in a peaceful world, 'and with standards of living which will permit the realization of men's reasonable hopes'.

What are the fundamental conditions under which commerce among the nations can once more flourish?

First, there must be a reasonably stable standard of international exchange . . . .

Second, long-term financial aid must be made available at reasonable rates to those countries whose industry and agriculture have been destroyed. . . . Objections to this Bank have been raised by some bankers and a few economists. The institutions proposed by the Bretton Woods Conference would indeed limit the control which certain private bankers have in the past exercised over international finance. It would by no means restrict the investment sphere in which bankers could engage. On the contrary, it would greatly expand this sphere by enlarging the volume of international investment and would act as an enormously effective stabilizer and guarantor of loans which they might make. . . . The effect would be to provide capital for those who need it at lower interest rates than in the past and to drive only the usurious money lenders out of the temple of international finance. For my own part, I cannot look upon this outcome with any sense of dismay. Capital, like any other commodity, should be free from monopoly control, and available upon reasonable terms to those who will put it to use for the general welfare. . . .

This monetary agreement is but one step, of course, in the broad program of international action necessary for the shaping of a free future. But it is an indispensable step and a vital test of our intentions. We are at a crossroads, and we must go one way or the other. The Conference at Bretton Woods has erected a signpost — a signpost pointing down a highway broad enough for all men to walk in step and side by side. If they will set out together, there is nothing on earth that need stop them.[91]

A band played the 'Star-Spangled Banner'.

All eyes were on Keynes, and, as he rose and moved to leave the room, the delegates stood up again and sang 'For He's a Jolly Good Fellow' and applauded.

Some chairmen of the delegations moved to room B to sign the Final Act. Others signed it the next morning.

The delegates then boarded two special trains, bound for New York and Washington.

17
'Self-Contradictory or Hopelessly Obscure'

Shortly after his return to London, Keynes became involved in a public controversy over Bretton Woods. *The Times*, in a series of articles written by 'a special correspondent', launched a broad attack on the agreement. Whoever the author was, his ideas were very similar to those Hubert Henderson had expressed in several memoranda. Among other criticisms, the credit facilities of the Monetary Fund were judged insufficient to meet Britain's postwar problems.

The mechanism provided for maintaining the balance of payments was crude and ineffective. The only method of adjustment envisaged was an alteration of the rates of exchange. The causes of disequilibrium, however, were numerous and varied. In some instances, a disequilibrium might be corrected by a devaluation or a revaluation, but in many circumstances, because of the immediate effect on the terms of trade, the imbalance might be increased.

The basic assumptions of Bretton Woods flew in the face of much recent experience: in the interwar period a freely working multilateral system had been successful for only a short period and had ended in disaster. Contrary to the legend, the Depression had grown out of a period of economic liberalism, and 'economic nationalism' had been the consequence of the Depression. A necessary condition for the balanced expansion of world trade was that individual nations accept responsibility for keeping their balance of payments in equilibrium. This might call for the application of quantitative import controls, bilateral agreements, barter arrangements and other devices implying 'discriminatory practices' condemned at Bretton Woods. It was clearly specified that payments, once due, must be made at agreed rates of exchange, and must be freely convertible into any other currency. Bretton Woods, however, was concerned only with money. No rules for commercial policy had been elaborated. No country was asked to refrain from planning its trade or controlling its balance of payments. Did this mean that the 'money side' of international transactions could be wholly separated from commercial policy?

The series of articles ended with the question, 'How far can these necessary or desirable facilities be accommodated within the Bretton Woods framework?'[1]

Keynes's answer was immediate, and, considering the document he had signed at Bretton Woods, somewhat surprising, but unequivocal. He stated that the 'Bretton Woods plan would be consistent with our requiring a country from which we import to take in return a stipulated quantity of our exports.'

> The most effective means of carrying out such a policy would be to supply the country taking our exports with a certificate which importers from that country would be required to produce as a condition of receiving an import licence into the United Kingdom. If such a policy were to commend itself to us and if it were consistent with any commercial agreements we might have signed, there is nothing in the Bretton Woods plan to prevent it. Equally there is nothing to prevent other countries from requiring us to take their imports as a condition of receiving our exports.[2]

This brought in a number of critical letters, contesting Keynes's interpretation. Thomas Balogh reminded Keynes that 'Nazi Germany . . . utilized a similar method in her drive to secure certain South American markets. . . . Is it not precisely these "malpractices" which the Bretton Woods agreement is intended to preclude?'[3] Another correspondent stated that 'Lord Keynes assures us that "there is nothing in the Bretton Woods plan to prevent it" (such a policy). We can only devoutly hope that someone will prevent it.'[4] In a sarcastic letter, rejecting Keynes's 'glib answer of August 23', a US army officer stationed in Britain reminded Keynes of the provisions in the agreement specifically in contradiction with his interpretation.[5]

Clearly exasperated, Keynes maintained his position:

> The Bretton Woods proposals are concerned solely with currency and exchange and not with commercial policy.
>
> They are consistent equally with the more moderate methods of planning foreign trade which we are likely to need, at any rate so long as we have balance of trade difficulties; with more elaborate measures about the advantages of which it is not so easy to make up one's mind; and also with the more extreme proposals which, if applied all round, would be destructive of trade.
>
> Whether we adopt any of these methods, and if so which, will have

to be determined by our own common sense and by the commercial treaties which we find it to be in our interest to sign because they offer compensating advantages. All this falls outside the ambit of the Bretton Woods discussions.

Some of your correspondents press me to admit (a) that forms of commercial policy, permissible under the Bretton Woods currency proposals, may nevertheless be very foolish; (b) that forms of commercial policy, permissible under the Bretton Woods currency proposals, may be so destructive of multilateral trade that, if they are adopted, Bretton Woods will have been rather a waste of time. Both of these contentions are, in my opinion, correct.[6]

At Bretton Woods, representatives of the forty-four delegations had signed the agreements without having had the time or opportunity to read them. It took some while before the text was made public in London. But, when it was finally made available to the press, several financial writers submitted it to detailed analysis. One of the commentators noted that the provisions and the wording were so complicated that a specialist with a lifetime's experience in international monetary questions had to read it many times before he could even begin to understand it. And, even then, the contradictions between the various provisions left many questions unanswered.

It was essentially a lawyers' document, going into minute details about the obligations of member countries, subscriptions and quotas, voting rights, conditions of membership, withdrawal, relations with non-member countries, and even the administration of the liquidation of the Fund.

Before ratification of the agreement by the United Kingdom could be properly considered, there had to be authoritative answers to the many questions. *The Times* noted that 'Legitimate anxiety has been expressed over the possibility of a divergence of interpretation and consequent misunderstanding on what may be a matter of vital concern to this country.' Despite Keynes's emphatic assertion, the question remained of whether countries were permitted to make commercial arrangements for a balanced exchange of stipulated quantities of imports and exports. Would such agreements not fall under the Bretton Woods ban? The free-trading system which Bretton Woods wanted to restore was desirable, but was it practicable? This question had been insufficiently explored. 'A scheme which treated as uniform and completely separate entities national units of utterly divergent size, wealth and power, and discouraged any kind of grouping or combination between them for currency purposes on a regional or any other basis, might well be found to sacrifice practical opportunities of expansion for the shadow of theoretical perfection.'[7]

It was Paul Einzig who submitted the provisions of the Final Act to the most searching scrutiny and the most devastating criticism. In the *Daily Express* of 10 August 1944 he warned,

If the public were to realise what it is being led into it would raise its voice in a powerful protest, instead of allowing the experts a free hand to do their worst, as they did in 1925. Some weeks ago, Lord Bradbury ... complained that the previous joint statement ... so far from being plain English, was hardly even English at all. Yet that document was clarity itself compared with the tangle of tricky technical clauses contained in the final draft of the experts' plan of the new gold standard.

These clauses concealed from the British public the fact that, for the second time within the life of a generation, sterling was going to be linked to gold, but this time much more rigidly than in 1925. 'Once the plan is translated into intelligible English and is denuded of all camouflage, every layman of normal intelligence is bound to realise that it is the gold standard, the full gold standard and nothing but the gold standard'. Far from paying heed to the objections of Parliament, the British delegation to the Bretton Woods conference had agreed to fundamental modifications to the Statement of Principles in exactly the opposite sense. 'Is it really conceivable that Parliament could pass such a suicidal measure?'[8]

In the *Financial News*, Einzig submitted the Bretton Woods agreements to further scrutiny. One of the most controversial issues sprang from the provision that 'The maximum and the minimum rates for exchange transactions between the currencies of members taking place within their territories shall not differ from parity ... by more than one per cent.' It was not stated how this should be done. Einzig noted that two diametrically opposed interpretations of this provision emerged from discussions in the press. According to one, it would be the duty of members to prevent transactions outside the official limits by controlling and forbidding them. According to the other school, the governments, by selling 'strong' currencies and buying 'weak' currencies, must prevent the exchange rates from rising or falling beyond the official limits. The first interpretation, however, meant the adoption of exchange restrictions, which would be contrary to the letter and the spirit of the Final Act.

But there was more. One of the most remarkable clauses of the Final Act, Article IV(4b), clearly implied that dealing in currencies outside the official limits must be prevented not by means of restrictions, but by means of official intervention. This meant, for example, that if American exporters to Poland chose to offer zlotys in London, and there were no private buyers who were prepared to pay the official price, the British authorities would have to support the zloty—sterling rate by buying up the unwanted zlotys. This was incredible.

American exporters may want to offer in London weak currencies, or, what amounts to the same thing, the American banks, having bought weak currencies from American exporters may want to resell them in

London . . . as a result of the operation of IV(4b), weak currencies will tend to be cheaper in New York than in London. Under that clause the obligation to support weak currencies at the official rates does not apply to 'a member whose monetary authorities, for the settlement of international transactions, in fact freely buy and sell gold within the limits prescribed by the Fund'.

Now, while the United States is in a position to buy and sell gold freely, Great Britain is hardly likely to be able to do so. . . . As a result, while weak currencies will have to be supported in London, they may not be supported in New York, and will then decline below their London cross rates.

While the rules of the Fund applied only to current transactions and not to transfers of capital, it was germane to ask how it would be possible for member countries to ascertain whether a transaction was a genuine current transaction or not. If the transaction originated abroad, this would practically be impossible. Thus, Britain 'would finance by the acquisition of frozen balances the exports of financially strong countries to financially weak countries. The idea seems absurd, yet it is based on the letter of the "Final Act".'[9]

The controversy over the interpretation of the Bretton Woods agreement was not limited to outside economists and financial writers in the press. Within the Treasury, there was disagreement between Keynes and Professor Robertson over the meaning of certain provisions of the Final Act. As we have seen, it was Robertson who was the British delegate at the Commission on the Fund, while Keynes was busy with the Bank. Unknown to Keynes, he had agreed with White that, for the initial contribution of member countries, 'gold-convertible currency' and 'US dollars' were synonymous. But there was more to come.

The controversy over the interpretation of the Bretton Woods agreements forced Keynes to re-examine the text, and after doing so, he was 'of the opinion that, on all the main points which have been raised as doubtful, the strict interpretation is what I intended and thought it to be, and that therefore all is well'. He was disturbed, however, that on the most important points, Professor Robertson took a different view. 'If Professor Robertson's interpretation is correct, then, in my opinion, the draft is not one which the Chancellor is justified in commending to the House of Commons.'

Article VIII(2a) stipulated that, except during the transitional period, and, later, if a currency had been declared scarce, 'no member shall, without the approval of the Fund, impose restrictions on the making of payments and transfers for current international transactions'. Keynes had understood this clause to mean that there was an obligation *not to block balances* resulting from current transactions. 'It does not carry with it any obligation of convertibility. The obligation "not to impose restrictions"

does not carry with it an obligation "to provide positive facilities".'
Professor Robertson, however, disputed this interpretation. He considered
that this clause carried with it an overriding obligation 'to *provide facilities*
to convert sterling, whether held by residents or by non-residents, into any
desired foreign currency, in all circumstances, subject only to the exceptions specified' — that is, during the transitional period, and when a
currency had been declared scarce.

Robertson agreed that this entirely destroyed the effect of the safeguards, 'on which we spent so much time and heat, rendering it unnecessary and valueless'. It meant that, even when a country was cut off from
the facilities of the Fund, the obligation of convertibility was maintained.
If Robertson was right, 'a country would be promising to maintain
convertibility in circumstances in which it had been deprived of the power
to do so'.

There was disagreement with Robertson on another major point, 'which
cuts at the whole philosophy of the Fund as I have understood it'. From
his first draft, in September 1941, and throughout the negotiations, one of
Keynes's fundamental concepts was that Britain would continue to
exercise a government monopoly on exchange transactions, and that there
would be no free currency markets. Private persons could obtain convertibility only through the good offices of their own central bank.

Robertson maintained that Article VIII imposed an overriding obligation to provide any private person, on request, with any currency in the
world. According to his interpretation, 'The very existence of the Government monopoly constitutes the imposition of a "restriction on the making
of payments and transfers for current international transactions" to the
United States, unless the monopoly is in fact so operated as *not* to hinder
the making of such payments and transfers.' After the end of the
transitional period, the government would have to stand 'ready to sell
dollars against sterling to anyone (whether British or American) who
desires to make ... payments or transfers' for current international
transactions.

Although Robertson had not participated in the final formulation of
the Articles of Agreement, he had participated in all the discussions of
Commission I, and Keynes had not been there. It was not until after the
conference was over that Keynes became aware of any doubts of interpretation. If Robertson's 'interpretation is held to be correct, I think we must
ask to have the matter re-considered. If the interpretation is merely held to
be open to reasonable doubt, I suggest that I should personally write to
Dr. White to discover how the Americans understand it.'[10]

Paul Einzig, in the *Financial News*, had raised another doubt which, if
admitted, 'would have much the same effect as Professor Robertson's
contention'. The agreement provided that 'Each member undertakes,
through appropriate measures consistent with this Agreement, to permit
within its territories exchange transactions between its currency and the

currencies of other members only within the limits prescribed' — that is, within 1 per cent over or under parity. However, 'A member whose monetary authorities, for the settlement of international transactions, in fact freely buy and sell gold within the limits prescribed by the Fund . . . shall be deemed to be fulfilling this undertaking.'

Einzig had interpreted this clause as though the word 'permit' meant 'facilitate', and thus arrived at the same, or even a more far-reaching conclusion than Professor Robertson. His argument was that Article VIII 'forbids exchange restrictions, and to render a black market illegal would be an exchange restriction. Therefore the only way of preventing dealings outside the permitted range is for the Exchange Control itself to provide convertibility to all comers in terms of all currencies within the permitted range.' Einzig argued that, since the United States was able to freely buy and sell gold, it was free to allow within its territory exchange transactions outside the prescribed limits. He inferred

> that only in the U.S. is a black market to be allowed in a weak currency, which is also correct (and is an oversight on our part). And he infers further that *we* shall be under an over-riding liability to absorb weak currencies in order to prevent them from depreciating in our market (and here his contention goes beyond Professor Robertson's), even in circumstances when we cannot pass them on to the Central Bank to which they belong. If his initial contention is granted, this also seems to be correct and is, indeed, its *reductio ad absurdum*.

This interpretation, said Keynes, had never occurred to anyone at Bretton Woods. The intention had been to require members to make black markets illegal, 'whereas, according to Dr. Einzig, Article VIII . . . has done just the opposite — it has put members under an obligation to keep black markets legal'.

Another point which troubled Keynes was the controversy over the article concerning relations with non-member countries. This article had been hastily compiled, without much discussion. 'No one paid much attention to it because it was regarded as affecting only a few recalcitrant or objectionable countries which declined, or were not admitted to, membership when, or shortly after, the Fund is set up.' It had not occurred to Keynes, or, he thought, to anyone else, that 'non-members' included 'ex-members'. The agreement provided that 'Any member may withdraw from the Fund at any time by transmitting a notice in writing.' This made that country a non-member and raised the question of whether, after its withdrawal, it was immune from the jurisdiction of the Fund. More specifically, if a member withdrew from the Fund because it could not agree on its exchange rate, would members of the Fund be prevented from dealing with this 'ex-member' at a rate of exchange that it had decided to establish, but to which the Fund had objected? Keynes thought this would be absurd: 'There is nothing "contrary to the provisions of this agreement and the purposes of the Fund" in a non-member having any exchange rate it likes. Perhaps the lawyers will offer an opinion. If they do not confirm my reading, the text may require reconsideration.' He felt that it would be sufficient 'to call the attention of the United States Treasury to this inadvertence of drafting which is easily remedied'.[11]

On 6 October, Keynes wrote a letter to Harry White concerning the questions of interpretation which had been raised. The intention of the clause permitting exchange transactions only within the prescribed limits, Keynes suggested, was that member countries 'were authorised, and indeed required, to render illegal dealings outside the prescribed range'. Some critics, however, had argued that this would be inconsistent with the clause prohibiting restrictions on payments and transfers for current transactions. 'For it is said that to forbid a black market would be a restriction on current payments. Much capital has been made out of this by Paul Einzig who, as perhaps you know, is one of the chief thorns in our flesh.' It seemed that there had been a slip in drafting. Keynes also pointed out that the provision by which the United States could contract out of this clause by freely buying and selling gold was illogical.

> For, whilst gold convertibility prevents the dollar from depreciating, it does not prevent *other* currencies from depreciating in the New York market. Thus unless you legislate to the contrary, New York will become, as Einzig has been eager to point out, the chartered black market where all dubious transactions and weak currency deals will be concentrated. Let us hope that in spite of the Statue of Liberty pointing to New York as, under the Constitution, the proud home of black markets as the symbol of Freedom, you will in fact legislate!

The next point, namely the inconsistency between the provision prohibiting restrictions on current transactions and the obligation of convertibility of foreign-held balances was more serious. According to Keynes, there was no suggestion of any obligation on the part of the monetary authorities positively to support the exchanges or to stand

> ready at all times with an offer to provide any foreign currency to any private applicant'. The obligation of convertibility only existed between 'pairs of Monetary Authorities or Central Banks. . . . Our view is, as you know, that we cannot conveniently maintain an effective control of capital transactions except by a monopoly of all foreign exchange dealings by an official Exchange Control. It is argued that such a monopoly would be a 'restriction' . . . and would, therefore, be disallowed, unless, perhaps, the practical effect of the monopoly was offset by the Exchange Control standing ready at all times with an offer to all-comers of any desired foreign exchange at a rate within the

prescribed range, though even then it is not clear on a strict reading that the monopoly would be in order.

Keynes suggested that

> we might get round the difficulty by some technical device. For example, all proposed exchange transactions might be required to pass through the Central machine which would not then handle them itself but would grant licences (*inter alia*) to *all* requests relating to 'current' transactions allowing them to be dealt with by the open market, leaving the applicant to take his chance whether or not the open market can find a counter-party for him at a rate within the prescribed range. This would have the same practical effect as an official monopoly of exchange dealings, but in a more clumsy and less convenient way.

Britain would either be forced to adopt an inferior technique, such as he suggested, or accept an obligation of convertibility, which Parliament would almost certainly reject. If White agreed that this dilemma was not intended, but was the result of inadvertent drafting, 'owing to the haste in which a most complicated piece of work had to be done', this could be corrected by drafting amendments which would be incorporated in a revised text.[12]

White never answered or even acknowledge the letter.

In November, Keynes was back in Washington to discuss what the financial relations between Britain and the United States would be after Germany had been defeated and the common war effort was directed against Japan. He was told that Secretary Morgenthau intended to bring both the Fund and the Bank before Congress as soon as possible, and would try to 'railroad both plans through as an indivisible whole incapable of amendment'. Opposition would support the Bank as an immediate necessity, but urge that the Fund be postponed. 'If I was in the place of Mr. Morgenthau and Mr. White, I should accept this compromise. But that is not their present intention, and I do not believe that they will ever accept it, except under political orders from above.'[13]

Since it was important to clarify the questions which had been raised, Keynes asked to see White. On 18 November the meeting took place. White was accompanied by his legal adviser, Mr Ansel Luxford, and his economic adviser, Mr Edward Bernstein.

White immediately agreed that Keynes's interpretation of the clause concerning the obligation of members to permit exchange transactions only between the prescribed limits was correct, and he even offered to confirm this in writing. He promised to vote in favour of an interpretation to this effect as soon as the Fund was set up.

The second and more important point, however, caused serious trouble. White had not been aware of the inconsistency until Keynes drew his attention to it, and it took some time to make him understand the problem. Bernstein and Luxford, 'on the other hand, knew all about it and strongly supported, in substance, the interpretation sprung on us (or, at any rate, on me) after our return by Professor Robertson'.

White, when he understood what the point was, remarked that he attached very little importance to it, but that, on the other hand, he could not agree to Keynes's interpretation. In addition, there was no procedure for amending the agreements. This was the way it should be, because otherwise every legislature could make amendments. His intention was to submit the document to Congress for acceptance or rejection *as it stood*. If he now agreed to an amendment, his plans would fall to the ground. He therefore urged Keynes, in view of the small practical importance of the matter, to accept the text of the agreements as it was.

To this I replied that if the matter had not been already raised publicly, this might have been at least considered. Unfortunately the question had been raised prominently by the critics of the scheme; the Chancellor could not possibly avoid explaining to the House of Commons what he understood the clause to mean; and I, at any ate, could not advise him to defend on its merits the meaning put to it by Mr. Bernstein, nor could I take it on myself to say or imply, which would not be true, that I had consciously accepted at Bretton Woods a clause having the effect which Mr. Bernstein claims for it. I added that I believed most of the other signatories would be extremely surprised if the alleged effect of what they have signed were to be pointed out to them. (We, all of us, had to sign, of course, before we had had a chance of reading through a clean and consecutive copy of the document. All we had seen of it was the dotted line. Our only excuse is the knowledge that our hosts had made final arrangements to throw us out of the hotel, unhoused, disappointed, unaneled, within a few hours.)

Well, said Mr. White, we must take time to think over what can be done, and I will let you know later; upon which we broke up after a very exhausting afternoon. Even that man of iron, Mr. White, enquired sympathetically as we went out, whether *we* were such men of iron that we did not find such a discussion tiring.

Was White right when he stated that the issue had small practical importance? Keynes felt that, at any rate, the doctrinal importance was too great to be disregarded, and also the inner consistency of the document:

The essential point is this. If a country gets into exchange difficulties two types of remedy are open to it. It can depreciate the rate of exchange; or it can restore the limited and discretionary convertibility of its currency into foreign currencies such as we have now. We took

great pains to ensure that our discretion to use the former should not
be unduly fettered. I thought that we had taken equal pains to retain a
discretion in emergency to use the latter also, by accepting under
Article VIII 4 an obligation of free convertibility which was limited in
the sense that the obligation accepted in VIII 4(a) lapsed in the event of
any of the circumstances set forth in VIII 4(b). . . . For this meant that
our obligation lapsed as soon as we had run through, or had been
deprived of, our right of drawing on the Fund; so that we were not
compelled to go on accepting convertibility until we had run down our
gold reserves to the level at which the Fund might choose to let us off. I
argued that there were reasons of politics and war which made it both
reasonable and essential that we ourselves should retain the discretion
to decide at which point we should call a halt to the further depletion
of our gold reserves.

Would Britain be prepared to hand over to the Fund the power to decide
to what point the country would have to reduce its gold reserves, having
already run through, or been cut off from the resources of the Fund,
before the obligation of free convertibility for current transactions was
suspended? 'I say, on merits – No. The matter is important because, if we
do get into difficulties, we are much more likely to want to suspend free
convertibility than to depreciate.'

In addition, the Chancellor would be in a poor position if he had to
explain to the House of Commons that the apparent let-out which had
been written into the agreement was a pure deception, because the British
representatives at Bretton Woods had not been wide-enough awake to
notice that the provision had been made ineffective. As far as intention
was concerned, this related to only very few individuals, those who had
written up the Final Act; the question had never been raised in a main
committee. What had been secured after much open debate, had been
'quietly removed and cancelled out'.

Then there was the question of legal interpretation. The agreement did
not impose on a member a positive obligation to provide any exchange
required for current international transactions. The most it did was to
forbid certain means of preventing it. But it would not be difficult to set
up a system of control which fell far short of free convertibility, and yet
did not obviously infringe the clause. 'What the lawyers do when two
clauses of an instrument contradict one another I do not know. But I
should have supposed that they would give the benefit of the doubt to any
interpretation which avoided the contradiction.' White had argued 'that we
could always dodge Mr Bernstein's intention by import controls. There is
something to this'; but such controls in peace time would fall a good deal
short of covering all types of current transactions as they were defined in
the agreement.[14]

Shortly after his meeting with White, Bernstein and Luxford, Keynes received a telegram from London suggesting that he suspend the discussions, pending receipt of a letter containing a revised version of the clauses. The letter arrived when he was about to sail, and he left Washington without reaching an agreement. Upon his return to London, he submitted to the Chancellor of the Exchequer a memorandum about his unsuccessful conversation with White.

Time was running out. Keynes suggested that the Chancellor write to Secretary Morgenthau calling his attention to the discrepancy which Keynes, in the haste of the concluding days, had failed to notice. Would the Secretary advise which, if any, of the contradictory clauses prevailed? The Chancellor would state that he proposed 'to inform Parliament that there is here a plain error of drafting and that our adherence must be subject to the difficulty being cleared up in due course'. Keynes then suggested again two alternative redrafts from which the Americans could choose. He concluded his memorandum: 'We cannot be expected to sign an instrument which is either self-contradictory or hopelessly obscure.'[15]

Keynes not only suggested that the Chancellor write to Secretary Morgenthau, but in addition he prepared a draft letter in which he stated the 'difficulty and perplexity' caused by the differences of interpretation. 'The truth seems to me to be that we have here a piece of inconsistent, ambiguous, faulty drafting, which is not surprising in view of the inevitably hurried work of the last days of the Conference.' He realised that it would be difficult to amend the text now, since it would open the door to additional changes. However, it was necessary that the two governments agree that the matter be corrected in due course, 'so that no greater obligation is required than clearly appears'. Otherwise, 'we here must put ourselves on public record, not only with you but with all the other participants in the Conference', concerning the inconsistency and faulty drafting of the agreements, and as regarding 'the satisfactory clearing up of this matter in the meanwhile as one of the essential conditions pre-requisite to our being in a position to accept eventual convertibility' after the end of the transitional period. He hoped that it would be possible to avoid this, but 'it would be a bad and dangerous precedent to seek by subtle interpretation to impose any obligation which did not appear, clearly and unambiguously, on the face of the document, or which had not been understood or accepted by those who signed it'.[16]

In a letter dated 1 February 1945, the Chancellor of the Exchequer passed these observations on to Morgenthau, who did not answer, but asked White to handle the problem.

On 22 February, White told Brand and Opie that the interpretation given to the clauses by the Chancellor was very different from the interpretation given to them by the US Treasury. The clauses had been discussed over and over again, and their meaning fully understood. There was no ambiguity in them. The Treasury's position was that, if for any reason a member country was not entitled to draw from the Fund, it was not allowed to reimpose exchange restrictions except with the approval of the Fund. White himself did not consider the matter important, but the Federal Reserve and the State Department had taken a very strong position. Moreover, the American public would be alarmed if it were told that member countries would be free to impose exchange restrictions after they had exhausted the facilities of the Fund.

If the Secretary was to send an official answer, it would have to be that the United States government's interpretation was different from that of the British government. This could be extremely damaging to the chances of obtaining Congressional approval of the Fund. There had already been enquiries concerning alleged differences between the two governments. If, during the forthcoming hearings, the Secretary, under pressure, was forced to admit the existence of correspondence on the subject, this 'would provide strong ammunition to enemies and might destroy the hope of Congressional approval'. White therefore suggested that the Chancellor agree to take the letter back, so that it should not be part of any official record. The existence of it would not be revealed to any other departments. If the Chancellor did not agree to this, then, White suggested, the matter should be held in abeyance until after the Congressional hearings. He hoped, however, that the Chancellor would omit any reference to the ·hurried work of the Conference'.[17]

A week later, the discussions were continued. White, however, stating that he had not had 'a moment to give thought to the problem, suggested that Luxford and Bernstein explain the US Treasury's position'.

'I think myself this was very convenient,' Brand reported to Keynes, ·since we were at least able to hear a very full, though you may think unsatisfactory, account of the U.S. Treasury's view from Bernstein.'

Contrary to White, Bernstein admitted that the issue had never been fully and openly thrashed out, except 'on the fringe'. He 'was taking for granted that supervision of exchange transactions (in contrast to exchange *restrictions* . . .) would be exercised, as indeed would be necessary to control capital transactions, and that the municipal rules would be respected by other monetary authorities and upheld by the Fund.'

It would be impossible however, 'to tell Congress that the Fund proposed to "pay" countries not to impose exchange restrictions, but that when the facilities of the Fund were exhausted by a member, the latter should have complete freedom to do whatever it wished in the way of imposing exchange restrictions'. The United States had no intention of setting up a monopoly of foreign-exchange dealings, as existed in other countries.

Dr Bernstein explained that 'It was essential so far as they were concerned to secure that no country should place restrictions on an exporter from the United States being able to secure dollar remittances for his sale without the Fund having agreed that such restrictions were reasonable and necessary.' The US Treasury could not agree to Keynes's interpretation that the obligation of convertibility lapsed when a member had exhausted its facilities with the Fund. There were many critics in the United States who claimed that the Fund 'was simply a big bag into which other countries could dip', and impose exchange restrictions, even in respect of current transactions, as soon as they had run through their facilities with the Fund. 'In other words, any member who liked could turn the Fund into a piece of machinery which gave him privileges without corresponding obligations. This was a position which it would be impossible for the U.S. Government to accept or get through Congress.'

'Mr. Bernstein's whole effort was to prove that we need not fear the consequences of leaving the document as it stands . . . all that they were talking about referred not to the transition period but to some period thereafter. It was even possible, he thought, that the transition period might never in actual fact be formally brought to an end. A country like the United Kingdom might indicate that it was prepared to return to convertibility for current transactions, but was not prepared to regard the transition period at an end. In other words it would try convertibility, retaining the right to go back on it if circumstances proved too strong for it.' 'Mr. Bernstein also argued, as I understood', that the obligation not to impose restrictions might be limited from another side: 'Every trading transaction was complicated by the fact that both money and materials were concerned. We might protect ourselves on the side of materials. We might put on import restrictions, quotas, etc. We pointed out that in this sphere we should meet with difficulties from other U.S. departments.'

The conclusion to be drawn from the discussion was that the United States would not agree that members had the right to impose exchange controls on current transactions; that the clauses in question 'might well have been more clearly drafted, but he would certainly not agree that they could be re-drafted to meet the above claim'. The dangers the British feared were unreal, it would be expected that the Fund would be reasonable, and there were many ways of dealing with the problem.[18]

Keynes was 'particularly interested in Bernstein's suggestion of the possibility that the transition period might never be formally declared to be at an end. . . . We are grateful to him for this suggestion, which may very well be the best way of solving the difficulty which has arisen.'

But he disagreed with the interpretation of the US Treasury. 'Indeed, the more the detail in which he explains what he would wish the text to mean, the more obvious does it become that this is not in fact its meaning, even if it were to be conceded that the meaning could be stretched a small way in the direction he wants.' It was true that the fundamental principle of convertibility had never been fully discussed, but it would be 'unreasonable to expect us to feel ourselves bound by a highly sophistical and

elaborate gloss, going far beyond the clear meaning of the words, on a
matter which had admittedly not been elucidated by those concerned in
the drafting'.[19]

In a telegram to Brand, Keynes restated his position. He had never
disputed that 'we are prevented in all circumstances from blocking the
proceeds of current transactions except with the approval of the Fund'. It
would not be allowed to prevent the transfer of funds resulting from a
current transaction. 'But this does not in our view carry with it any
positive obligation on the monetary authority to convert such holdings
into any desired external currency.' What he sought to avoid was some
subtle interpretation of the text 'which goes far beyond the plain meaning
of the words' by implying an 'obligation of convertibility to every private
person which over-rides the obligation of convertibility between members,
i.e. between monetary authorities'.[20]

At Keynes's request, Brand tried again, but in vain, to persuade White;
nor would Keynes accept the interpretation put forward by the US
Treasury.

> That we did not openly and fully thrash out this issue was, of course,
> the initial mistake. As we all know, both the reason and the excuse for
> this is simply that we were not given time to do so. I myself had never
> seen the final text of the clauses now under discussion at the time when
> I signed the paper, since they had not emerged from the drafting
> committee soon enough for a complete text to be circulated.[21]

When White was told that the Chancellor did not agree to his suggestion,
he was very much concerned. 'He claimed that there was a great likelihood
that when he went before [the] Senate he would be asked questions which
would force him to produce [the] Chancellor's letter.' The fact that the
US Treasury had received the letter early in February, and would reveal
the differences of interpretation only when forced to do so, would be very
damaging. But the most damaging part of the letter would be the
statement twice repeated that the drafting of the plan was deficient
through hurry and haste. This would throw doubt on the whole plan, and
White felt the consequence might be fatal. He therefore asked that the
date of the letter be changed from 1 February 'to the present date', and
that the references to haste and hurry should be eliminated.[22]

White's fears were not without foundation. Several weeks before,
during the hearings of the Committee on Banking and Currency of the
House, he had been asked by one of the Representatives whether there was
any truth to the statement made by a British Member of Paliament that
'Nothing could be more deleterious to the future of Anglo-American
relations than that the two countries should sign an agreement, each
thinking that it means something quite different.'

White had answered that it was entirely possible that there were some provisions which might mean slightly different things

> to each of the 40 countries, in the same way that there are provisions in our Constitution that apparently mean different things to various members of the Supreme Court. . . . That does not mean that the Constitution was a bad document. . . . The Bretton Woods document was drafted, however, by a large number of lawyers, in addition to economists, and one of their objectives was to remove, as much as possible, the grounds for difference of interpretation.

It might well be that the Member of Parliament — Mr Boothby — who was not at Bretton Woods and who did not participate in any of the negotiations, was confused, 'but that is quite a different thing from assuming that there is a difference of interpretation on major points between the two Governments'.[23]

The Chancellor of the Exchequer did not see how he could consent to changing the date of the letter. 'The difficulties of interpretation which formed the subject of the Chancellor's letter were raised by Keynes in writing shortly after our return from Bretton Woods, and subsequently while Keynes was in Washington last Autumn. Therefore, to alter the date would imply that this is a last minute reflection on our part, which is not correct.'

The Chancellor recognised, however, that 'although it can scarcely be disputed that the final drafting was rather rushed and may reveal other imperfections, it might be embarrassing to the United States Treasury to have such criticism on record if there is any risk of the letter having to be produced or published'. He therefore agreed to delete the reference to haste and hurry, in order to 'spare Mr. Morgenthau embarrassment so far as he can'.[24]

On 3 May, 1945, Sir John Anderson sent to Brand in Washington a slightly revised letter, dated 1 February 1945, which was to be substituted for the original letter. The reference to faulty drafting owing to haste was eliminated. But the basic question about the interpretation of the provisions of the Agreement was still there. The Chancellor asked that Brand make the substitution by a personal visit to Morgenthau, and he 'hoped that this action on his part will be found helpful'.[25]

By that time the hearings on the Bretton Woods Agreements Act before the House had been completed several weeks earlier, and Morgenthau and his staff were preparing themselves for the hearings before the Senate committee. They had made it abundantly clear to the members of the House that the Act would have to be passed without any change. Any amendment to it would require another conference, and this was neither possible nor even desirable.

18
The Treasury Campaigns

Flattered by the unusual attention granted them by Harry White, the press reporters covering the conference had generally sent back to their editors favourable, or at least neutral, comments on the proceedings. When the text of the agreement became known, the attitude changed. The *New York Herald-Tribune* noted, 'It is regrettable that the distinguished international experts . . . have employed a language as difficult to understand as the Latin in which physicians used to write their prescriptions.'[1]

Very soon, the papers were also being supplied with critical comments. The *Commercial and Financial Chronicle* reprinted an analysis prepared by the National Economic Council:

The 'Stabilization' Fund has nothing to do with stabilization. It is a machine for turning worthless foreign paper currency into dollars. The 'Bank' is not a bank at all but a machine to 'guarantee' foreign loans so that they can be sold to gullible Americans. Both 'schemes' are mixed up with the fantastic debt theories of Lord Keynes. . . . The delegates did not reach an 'agreement'. They merely signed a paper which looked like an agreement. But on the minutes they entered reservations that destroyed the agreement.[2]

The prediction by the Guaranty Trust Co. that the Fund would be a failure was widely reproduced:

In the Aug. 29 issue of *The Guaranty Survey* . . . the International Monetary Fund is assailed as 'an attempt to enforce exchange stability without striking at the causes of instability', and the prediction is made that if the project is established and then fails, it 'could easily throw international currency relationships into chaos from which the entire world might suffer for years to come'.

240

The Bank was criticised as 'a plan to supplement private credit agencies in the international lending field by making, participating in, or guaranteeing long-term loans. . . . Whether such credit functions could be performed better by an international bank organized and financed by governments than by private agencies operating in accordance with established credit practices is very doubtful.'[3]

For Secretary Morgenthau, the establishment of an International Stabilisation Fund would be the victorious consummation of his years of struggle to move the financial centre of the world from London and Wall Street to the United States Treasury, and to create a new concept for international financial dealings. The new organisation would be an agent as between sovereign governments, granting financial help when and where justified. The purpose was not profit, but the promotion of international co-operation. He knew that conservative business circles were successfully spreading the idea that, despite bureaucratic harassment, business was winning the war by producing the tools. He also knew that the New Deal was in decline.

The New York bankers were in a position to cause considerable trouble. Their reports and their public speeches were generally well prepared and given considerable coverage in the press. The public, and many Congressmen, looked at them as professionals of finance whose statements carried considerable weight. The bankers had not been involved in the preparation of the Stabilisation Fund plans and had not been consulted on them afterwards. The publication of the Keynes and White plans had, however, stimulated considerable interest among them.

Morgenthau and White knew that, in addition to the direct action they could exert on Congressmen, individually or as a group, they would have to carry their campaign on two fronts: an uncomprehending but malleable public opinion, and a small but influential group of bankers who, through seemingly neutral organisations with prestigious names and considerable information power, were ready to fight the Treasury with all the means available.

Several correspondents of the Office of War Information had covered the Bretton Woods Conference and made a study of its impact on public opinion. The Office submitted a report to the Treasury:

> There is virtually no public opinion about the Bretton Woods conference according to our correspondents. There is no general discussion of it because there is no interest; and there is no interest because there is no comprehension of the issues involved and the plans proposed, or of their importance. Bankers and business circles are believed to be more informed than the general public, yet even these are often 'surprisingly ignorant' of the subject. Much of the ignorance is blamed on inadequate publicity, which is criticized both for quantity and quality. There should have been more, say these correspondents; and it should have

been more simple, more direct, more educational, more compelling.[4]

There were several reasons why the Treasury had refrained from an intensive publicity campaign before the Conference, and White had given an explanation:

> Most of the discussions in the press and most of the criticism in the press springs from a complete ignorance of the plan, or misunderstanding. And I think that is largely our fault, and designedly so. We haven't attempted to supply to them very much . . . because we have been waiting until there was agreement – a measure of agreement among ourselves and among the other countries, so we won't be explaining and defending some kind of proposal which we ourselves would want to back away from.[5]

There was another reason. Marriner Eccles, chairman of the Board of Governors of the Federal Reserve System had stated it very simply: 'Harry, your plan is so darned complicated I asked our people to put down briefly in layman's language so I could understand the darned thing, just what it means. . . .'[6]

If the New York bankers could be neutralised, or even induced to support Bretton Woods, the battle for public opinion would be won. Morgenthau thought that they should be approached first. The occasion arose when Winthrop Aldrich, chairman of the Chase National Bank asked to see Morgenthau about a loan not exceeding $100 million that the Dutch government had requested from his bank.

The meeting took place in Morgenthau's office on 25 August 1944, a few weeks after Bretton Woods. Morgenthau immediately agreed that commercial banks should have first opportunity for such loans. He then came to the subject he really wanted to talk about: 'I have a request to make of you, you see. You have been reported to be opposed to what we have been doing up at Bretton Woods, and I would like you to give our people sufficient time to sit down and have a very frank talk and give you a first-hand expose of what we have done up there.' Morgenthau suggested that Aldrich and White make a date, 'and spend half a day. . . . I hope to get your support.'

Aldrich was willing to meet White, but 'It doesn't look to me as though you can actually get my support.' He had felt that the approach at Bretton Woods was from the wrong angle, that the stabilisation of currencies should be postponed 'until we know a little bit more clearly where we are going'. To him the nub of the problem was the British position, and he 'would like to see if I can't sell to the opposition the idea of going to that nub of the problem and facing it squarely with the idea of doing the things that the British say are impossible to do'.[7]

In a memorandum dated 18 August 1944, Luxford wrote to Morgenthau that the public and Congress were ignorant on the subject of Bretton Woods. It was important to move forward as rapidly as possible in educating them about the Fund and Bank proposals. 'I mentioned that one sympathetic Congressman (Voorhis) had told me that "Congress had no opinion on subject because Congress did not understand it".'[8]

Under the Constitution of the United States, international agreements are not valid unless they are ratified by Congress. Couched in a language which professional economists admitted they did not understand, already subject to controversy over the meaning of certain provisions, the Bretton Woods agreement, full of abstruse technicalities, was far above the head of practically every Congressman. Morgenthau knew that some members of Congress would oppose the bill simply because the Roosevelt Administration was for it. But there was a vast number among them who were undecided and could be won over. At luncheon on 8 January 1945, Morgenthau told Senator Wagner and Congressmen Spence and Wolcott that he wanted to retain the non-partisan character of the Bretton woods agreements. All agreed. There was a discussion of the nature of the legislation that would be needed, and Morgenthau said that he would have it done in whatever way Congress preferred, even if it meant more work for the Treasury. Senator Wagner said he expected long hearings, and Congressman Wolcott thought it would be very helpful if the President could make a statement about Bretton Woods, in order to bring it to the attention of the public and gain public support.[9]

The Treasury's effort to interest American opinion in Bretton Woods had been slow. Harry White had made a few speeches. In November he addressed the National Foreign Trade Convention, and made a strong bid to gain endorsement by the foreign traders. The *New York Times* noted,

> Endorsement of the plan, it was felt by these traders, would have been 'too much of an encomium to the present Administration'. . . . However, other traders pointed to the foreign trade bankers as the 'restraining force'. . . . the alternative plan by Aldrich . . . militated against any general approval by this section of the foreign trade fraternity and thus stayed the endorsement of manufacturing exporters to whom the agreements are generally acceptable, it was said.[10]

On 13 November, Dr Bernstein told a New York audience,

> We cannot expect to see a balanced expansion of international trade or adequate international investment, if countries maintain fluctuating exchange rates, if they depreciate their exchanges to secure temporary competitive advantages, if they restrict exchange transactions for current trade, and if they block the proceeds of international investment. Given orderly, stable and free exchanges, other measures can be taken to assure a balanced expansion of trade and investment.[11]

Such isolated statements, while they received some publicity, were not
sufficient to influence public opinion. White became convinced that it was
necessary 'to push our program more forcefully in preparation for
Congressional action'. He asked Morgenthau to meet some leaders from
labour, industry, and the peace foundations; and also to make speeches
about the programme. White had prepared a good deal of material, and
had placed articles in several journals. A group of 100 leading economists
were preparing a statement urging Congress to approve the Fund and
Bank. Contact had also been established with various associations, councils
and universities.[12] All this was obviously intended to influence public
opinion, not for its own sake, but so that the climate in Congress would be
favourable.

On 1 March, 1945, Harry White discussed with his staff the strategy to
adopt. A professional public relations organisation had been hired by the
Treasury. It was decided that the secretary's speech for the hearings would
be

> on a high and broad plane, with no details or figures, and should end on
> the note that this is a critical period in history ... and that economic
> security and political security are inseparable. It should also be
> emphasized that neither the discussions nor the Conference have been
> on a partisan basis, that it is not an Administration or Treasury plan,
> but rather the demand has sprung from the whole country, with the
> exception of the isolationists 'who would do it differently, do it later
> and do it alone'.

The idea that the Treasury is against the bankers should be denounced.

For Secretary Morgenthau a very heavy programme had been prepared:
invitations to commentators and columnists to lunch at the Treasury;
filming of newsreel-theatre releases; telephone calls to prominent people,
asking them to make speeches or to testify; participation in a 'Town
Meeting of the Air' broadcast; and several speeches. Others would contact
shipping people, leading businessmen and economists, and prepare material
for Congressmen, banks, and a number of other organisations.[13]

For several months the country was showered with statements about
Bretton Woods. Over-praised by some, over-condemned by others, it
became a very important matter. In learned journals and in public
statements, economists explained why it would be unacceptable to the
United States and a grave danger to the world economy, or why they saw
it as the only road to salvation.

The *Wall Street Journal* reported on 13 April, 'Clergymen of four big
Protestant denominations were welcomed to Washington this week ... for
off-the-record "educational" sessions ... every effort is being made to
keep what was said ... out of the papers. ... Some of the ministers left
this city full of enthusiasm and determined to preach the gospel of Bretton

Woods in their churches.' This, the paper added, was part of a 'super-charged and sustained promotional campaign, conducted by the Treasury and State departments and other agencies, to build a fire under Congress'.[14] 'It can do nothing but harm to both Church and State', the *Journal* commented a few days later.[15]

Professor Kemmerer condemned the agreements as an 'embodiment of numerous compromises, of glossed-over differences on matters for which clear-cut compromises could not be reached, of weasel-worded phrases and of numerous escape clauses'. To counter the statement made by an economists' 'Committee on Bretton Woods', who gave a 'distorted picture of economic opinion', Kemmerer conducted a survey, by telegraph, of the members of the Economists' National Committee on Monetary Policy. Of those who replied thirteen approved of Bretton Woods, eight approved with reservations, and thirty-seven rejected the agreements.[16]

The US Chamber of Commerce joined the ranks of those who disapproved of the Fund. In its report, it stated that British experts talking to Britons would stress the aspects of the Fund which fitted Britain's particular needs, while American experts talking to Americans would stress the features which served the special needs of the United States. It was possible to speak of 'flexibility' and 'stability' of exchange rates in the same breath without being contradictory. The Chamber recommended that Congress defer action on US participation in the Fund, and let the Bank temporarily assume responsibility for stabilisation activities.[17]

By contrast, the Independent Bankers Association, representing 2000 banks in forty American states, recommended that the Bretton Woods proposals be acted upon 'at the earliest possible date and without crippling reservations'. In their report the bankers stated, 'while we can hardly claim to speak for Wall Street, we do believe we can speak for Main Street.'[18]

The Treasury's campaign induced influential groups to adhere to its cause. This brought the following comment from The *New York Herald-Tribune*:

We venture to predict that if the Bretton Woods program dies, it will have died not at the hands of its 'enemies', but at the hands of its overzealous sponsors. The high-handed tactics of these latter, their intolerance of criticism and devious strategy could hardly be better calculated to alienate the support of disinterested observers who, though in sympathy with the objectives sought, believe that they have not only a right but a duty to insist upon a thorough airing of the several mechanisms that have been proposed.

Nor was the paper convinced that the Fund would do the job: 'any institution set up prior to a general commitment on commercial policies would be a house built upon sand'.[19]

In the face of such criticism, coming from a small but powerful and

well organised number of individuals, supported by the theoretical arguments of some of the most highly regarded economists in the country, the
Treasury campaign had to be a professional job. It was. Mr Randolph
Feltus, who had been retained by Morgenthau to organise the campaign,
explained his strategy to an official of the British embassy. The essence of
his programme, he said, was to emphasise 'conservative' support for
Bretton Woods; 'they have the Left solidly with them anyhow, and in
order to impress the Center, must open with some good guns from the
Right'. His principal difficulty, said Feltus, would be to keep some papers
'from damning the whole business by too vociferous support of it'. He
would emphasise

(a) That Bretton Woods is good business for the U.S., good business for
American business, good hard-headed business, good Yankee trading
business, (b) Bretton Woods will be hitched to the star of Yalta. It will
be fitted into the San Francisco conference picture. It will not stand
alone but will be pictured as the first step in the implementation of the
Yalta agreements. The Treasury must have publicly as little to do with
the campaign as possible. 'The Treasury is suspect. The Treasury is New
Deal looney.'

The technical side of the Bretton Woods proposals would be soft-pedalled.
'It's Feltus' idea that most people won't bother to understand them
anyhow. When they're sick they do what a doctor tells them without
knowing why. If we can sell this as business and get businessmen to shout
for it, they'll want to do what the businessmen say — without knowing
why.'[20]
Whereas public opinion and Congress were rather amorphous and apt to
be influenced, the international New York bankers knew what they
wanted. One paper sized up the matter in the following terms:

I suppose at the heart of the matter is the fact that this machinery
would be put in the hands of public servants, paid executives of the
governments involved, rather than in the group of private and powerful
international bankers in 'The City' in London, and in lower Manhattan
in New York. You can see at once why there is a row involved. It
depends on whether you think public servants can do the international
job better than big private banks — largely creditor-minded — who have
been doing it in the past.

It was 'one of those battles among the financially and intellectually mighty
in which the merits of the contending positions usually remain for the
most part obscure to the vast audience'.[21]
A British observer at the embassy in Washington, with close contacts in
the Treasury as well as with the bankers, kept London advised about 'the

skilful blend of attack on Bretton Woods and on full international approach to economic problems'. The bankers, he said, 'desire to keep American lending in American hands'. He wrote,

> From talking to Burgess and other people in New York, I have the impression that the bankers are sincere in advocating that a start should be made with the Bank, suitably amended, if necessary, to extend its functions. It is true that Burgess is cautious, but on the other hand he has a difficult job in leading the more ignorant and conservative members of the banking community in the direction he wants them to go, and he is probably right in believing that they cannot be driven – at least not by him. He knows very well that our friends at the Treasury accuse him of being insincere and regard him as a broken reed. Burgess, on his part, thinks that the people in the Treasury are themselves unfairly biased in their attitude to the banking community.[22]

On 4 January, 1945, Secretary Morgenthau and his staff met with several bankers, representative of the various banking groups. He asked Burgess, who had requested the meeting, how he wished to proceed. Burgess read the conclusions of a report that had been prepared by the American Bankers Association and the Reserve City Bankers Association and that recommended that, because it would give credit automatically to countries which were not creditworthy, the Fund should be rejected. The report also recommended that the functions of the Fund be given to the Bank, and that the Bank be empowered to make stabilisation loans. The American governor and director of the Bank should be appointed by the President with the advice and consent of the Senate. The report also recommended that the capital of the Export–Import Bank be increased to $2000 million.

The Secretary went on to say that his relationship with the banks had always been cordial, that he had secured fine co-operation with them on war bonds, and that as a consequence the bankers had risen in public esteem. They now had the confidence of the public in a much higher measure than they had ever had before. He feared that the report they had prepared would affect the esteem in which the bankers were being held. Bretton Woods was the first international agreement on vital economic matters. The problem was urgent. Forty-four countries had agreed to it, and if one country started changing the agreement it would start a similar movement in other countries. The Bretton Woods agreements represented long and careful work; the best experts in the world had co-operated. If the bankers pursued the policy they had indicated, the public would suspect that they were attempting to wreck the agreements. He had listened carefully to all that had been said, and he did not think that the suggestions made by Mr. Burgess were important enough to justify the opposition. It was of little significance whether they had one or two institutions; some of the provisions were not perfect, and experience would possibly show that some changes should be made. But Bretton Woods was of international significance, and to endanger the success of the programme was a grave responsibility.

Speaking from a position of power, Morgenthau again presented what he regarded as the proper approach for the bankers. He saw no reason why they should not make a full statement of their suggestions. But, after making whatever technical suggestions they believed desirable, the conclusion of their report must be that they would approve the agreements because of their importance for international monetary and financial co-operation. Burgess said that, 'if it were this or nothing, he would take this'. The other bankers present agreed.

Morgenthau emphasised that it *was* this or nothing, and that the report the bankers would issue ought to be based on recognition of this fact. He thanked them for coming to the Treasury to discuss the question with him and his staff, and he expressed the hope that their report would show the effects of the meeting.[23]

Early in February the American Bankers Association issued its report, which stated, 'We find much that is desirable in the objectives and in certain features of the Bretton Woods plan; but we also find provisions which, in our opinion, are financially unsound and, if adopted, might retard rather than promote enduring recovery.' The report recommended 'that the plan for the International Bank for Reconstruction and Development be adopted with minor changes, but that the plan for the International Monetary Fund not be adopted, as it embodies lending methods that are unproved and impractical. In lieu of the Monetary Fund we recommend that certain of its features be incorporated into the provisions for the Bank.' The Fund was too big, too elaborate, too complicated, too difficult for the public to understand. The language of the agreement was so vague as to be susceptible to widely different interpretations. It did not stipulate that the loans should be good loans. It might tempt borrowing countries to continue on the easy political way, instead of making the maximum effort to put their economic affairs in order.[24]

The *New York Times* hailed the report as 'constructive and statesman-like'.[25]

Morgenthau was furious. On 5 February he discussed with his staff the strategy to adopt in order to counter the bankers' report.

'What do you think, Herbert?' asked Morgenthau, looking at Mr Herbert Gaston, who was among his oldest, most faithful and trusted assistants.

'I feel that the question is whether the monetary policy and the relation of the dollar to other currency should be governed, as far as the United States is concerned, by the Government of the United States or by a few New York bankers', Mr Gaston suggested.

'I think there might be something of that kind', said White.

'That will get the headlines', said Bell.

Mr Gaston continued, 'The position of the American Bankers Association has been dictated by a small group of large banks who have handled the bulk of foreign exchange in the past, and who resent the United States Government in the matter of mutual stabilization of currency.'

'You want also to say, like the grand old party, they never learn anything and they never forget anything', someone remarked.

Morgenhau felt sure that most of the country's bankers would support the government, and that it was only a small clique that opposed it.

'You might say', Gaston suggested, 'I doubt whether this represents bankers throughout the country.'

'On the contrary,' said White, 'we know it doesn't.'

'They were against the Federal Reserve System', Luxford recalled.

Morgenthau had made up his mind: 'I think Herbert ought to lock himself in a room and give me something if I am going to hit it. We might as well hit them hard.'

White approved: 'If you are going to hit it, it ought to be at that level, because any attempt to hit it from the technical point of view will be dull and take a lot of time . . . the public is never going to examine the merits of this proposal. They are merely going to be impressed by the fact that the American Bankers Association, Federal Reserve City Bankers and the New York State Bankers, are all against it. That is a very impressive roll call.'

'We might distort it', White suggested, 'and say the speculators are against it.'

Morgenthau was determined not to compromise: 'The forty-four nations have to come to an agreement that can't be a perfect instrument. It has to have mistakes, we agree on that. It is this or nothing, and this is the first thing, and this is the first thing that is going to go before the world, not just before the American people, to looking forward to a better world in business, and it is the same thing that I made on one of the speeches on the Government. It is up to the Government to take the risk on the interest rates and not up to the individuals. Remember I used that thing? It's up to the Government in taking the risk. Sure, we are taking the risk. Is it better for us to take the risk and spread it among forty-four partners, or to have five banks in New York dictate foreign exchange rates – with the five banks in line, and having London lead us around by the nose, which they have done in the last one hundred years?'[26] This was a fight between the international bankers and the government. The cards were down and the fight had begun. Having determined the strategy, public opinion had to be informed. Later the same day, Morgenthau announced to the press reporters his uncompromising opposition to the suggestions advanced by the American Bankers Association. If Congress followed these suggestions, he said, the agreements would be killed. The Treasury had been in contact with thousands of bankers all over the

country, and had found them in favour of the Fund. He had pleaded with
the American Bankers Association not to issue their report. Small liberated
countries could not survive without the Fund, he said.

For several weeks the public debate over Bretton Woods occupied the
news. Several groups bought space in the newspapers to advocate the plan;
others, mainly the banks and insurance companies, to recommend rejection of the Fund.

19
Congress Debates

Although the Bretton Woods agreements had been signed by the Secretary of the Treasury, the final decision rested with Congress. International monetary policy and, even more so, the agreements themselves were too intricate to be legislated on the floor. It would be necessary to hold Congressional hearings. Morgenthau and White knew that Congress would follow the lead of the Administration, or reject the agreements, not on technicalities but on the mood prevailing at the time of voting. Congressmen's opinions would be influenced by the campaign for and against, and, in particular, the arguments presented by the witnesses at the hearings.

On 28 December 1944, Morgenthau asked President Roosevelt to recommend White's promotion to Assistant Secretary of the Treasury: 'He will have to carry the brunt of the fight of the Bretton Woods legislation and the additional prestige of being Assistant Secretary will be most useful. He has earned his reward many times over. . . . White has been more than a match for people like Lord Keynes. I strongly recommend his promotion.' The President answered immediately that he would send up Harry White's name.[1]

On 12 February 1945, the President submitted to Congress a special message in which he urged the immediate adoption of the Bretton Woods agreements, as concrete evidence that the United States was in favour of international economic co-operation. Three days later, legislation was introduced in both houses of Congress, suspending the Johnson Act for countries joining the Fund and Bank. This would allow European countries which had not paid their debts from the First World War to become eligible for American loans.

Congressional opposition would obviously come from the Republicans. Those who till then had led the campaign against the Treasury were the older Senators who had consistently fought Roosevelt. To win over those who were undecided would require skill, patience and correct timing. Morgenthau and White felt that a first step might be to explain the agreements to younger Senators, both Republicans and Democrats. They did so, and apparently with success.

A few days before the Congressional hearings were to start, a meeting took place, attended by about half of the Republican members of Congress. Senator Taft was in the chair, and asked Leon Fraser to make a statement. Acheson, who was also there to speak in favour of Bretton Woods, told Morgenthau after the meeting that 'Fraser made a very effective and very powerful and utterly unscrupulous misrepresentation of the thing.'

'For heavens sakes!' said Morgenthau.

'It was really very shocking. ... Old Dr. Goldenweiser was trembling with rage when he got through.'

'For heavens sakes!' said Morgenthau again.

'Yes. It really was a demagogic appeal to every prejudice they have. ... And he did it very ably. He's no slouch. ... And he took cracks at me on the way through, and ... he just represented this as the damndest silly thing that a bunch of crazy people could do. ... And then they gave me half an hour, and I went into the thing, and I was polite to Fraser but I got stories which illustrated what I thought was the exaggerated and unfair presentation he'd made. ... And then explained the terms as well as I could, and then Goldenweiser by that time had collected himself. At first, I think if he'd followed me, he would have been so mad, he would have had a stroke. ... But he ... was very good ... moderate ... and he said he was terribly unhappy — very unhappy about what Fraser had said. ... And he said the trouble with Fraser is that he's got on creditor glasses, and he wants to run the whole world as a creditor.'

'Yeah', said Morgenthau.[2]

CONGRESSIONAL HEARINGS: THE HOUSE

Secretary Morgenthau opened the hearings before the Committee on Banking and Currency with the statement that the Bretton Woods agreements were good for every American citizen. While they dealt with rather technical questions, they represented a very simple issue, 'stability and order instead of insecurity and chaos'. Political security in the midst of economic chaos was impossible. Morgenthau explained the purposes of both the Fund and the Bank, and how they would prevent another series of depressions culminating in war. The world was at a turning point, and the task of Congress and of the government was to act so that future generations would say, 'Thank God, they took the right turning.' He then answered numerous questions asked by the members of the committee. So did Dean Acheson, after making his statement.[3]

Then came White's turn, to explain some of the more technical details. He briefly recalled how the Treasury had been working on the plans for several years, and how the Fund and Bank, which had considerable and specific powers, would affect the well-being of people in every country. While the technical material was 'dull, boring, and intricate', it affected Congress in many ways. He described how, in the 1920s, countries had gone back to the gold standard, and how they had been forced or had gone off it. He explained how the isolated action of one country affected conditions in others: 'All economic phenomena are interacting; they are like a pool ball that you have hit hard; it bounces back and forth, striking other balls which in turn hit others.' He recalled how in the early 1930s world trade had dropped from $65,000 million to $22,000 million, how farm prices had more than halved, and how this had affected general business conditions. Even though foreign trade was less important to the United States than to other countries, it was important because of the effects it had on sections of the population, which in turn affected the general economy. Reduced farm exports, for instance, depressed prices on the home market far more than the relative percentage of export loss.[4]

Every member of the committee was given a chance to ask questions. Some members, such as Representative Crawford, from Michigan, were decidedly not in favour of the Fund. He wanted to know whether there was 'anything in this agreement which interferes with private operators'. He also asked whether there was any truth in the statements, made in Britain, that, if Britain and the United States signed the agreement, they would do so 'each thinking that it means something quite different'.[5]

Representative Folger, of North Carolina, wanted to know whether there was any significance to the fact that the par value of each currency would be expressed in terms of gold or in terms of dollars of the weight and fineness in effect on 1 July 1944. White answered, 'Well, to us, and to the world, the United States dollar and gold are synonymous. We stand ready to buy and sell gold for appropriate purpose at that fixed rate, and so wherever we put gold we put our United States dollars of that fund. It is a mere matter of convenience of expression rather than significance other than the reiteration of the fact that dollars and gold are virtually synonymous.'[6]

Then came Representative Frederick C. Smith of Ohio, and the tone of the debate sharpened. Dr Smith was probably the only committee member who had carefully studied the document and tried to understand it.

To Smith's objection that the Bretton Woods proposal was a 'highly complicated and involved document', White replied that it may seem so to the layman, but not to an expert in the field of international finance – 'in the same way that certain questions of surgery or medical science seem involved to the layman but not to the physician'.

'I practised medicine for 30 years and I must say to you that I have never seen anything in the field of medicine that equals this', said Smith.

As an economist, White had occasionally dabbled at reading medical books, but when trying to decide on the course of a treatment, he felt it was better to consult a doctor.

'The document contains something like forty to forty-five thousand words, does it not?', asked Smith.

'I have not counted them, but I can tell you the number of pages.'

'It has 31 chapters, 100 subjects or more, and a hundred or more cross references.'

'I see you have studied it carefully. How much does it weigh?'

'It weighs very heavily upon our people. Now, you recognize that there are some fundamental differences of opinion respecting the fund proposal.'

'Well, I think it is fair to say I recognize that there are fundamental differences of opinion about almost anything of any significance, whether it is in the field of economics, anthropology, government, or in the field of medicine.'

'May I ask you this question, Mr. White? Do you know of any other proposal ever to come before the Congress of the United States so intricate and all-embracing as the one before us now?'

'Why, I could not possibly answer that, Dr. Smith.'

The point that Smith wished to make was that, with all the study that he had undertaken on the proposal, he could not say that he understood it. 'Of course, that is no reflection on my colleagues.' Occasionally, White, who was very careful not to show any impatience with members of Congress, would answer rather abruptly. When Smith asked him a question about the value of currencies in terms of gold, he answered, 'I am not sure I understand that question, so let me answer "Yes".'[7]

On 16 March, Judge Vinson made an eloquent statement about the need for international co-operation in dealing with economic problems, and the need for the United States to secure foreign markets for some of its products. Bretton Woods would also help other countries. The conference itself had been a model of democratic action, and the American delegation had included both Republican and Democratic Congressmen.

Mr Edward Brown assured the committee that many bankers and businessmen throughout the country favoured Bretton Woods, just as he did. He was in favour of stable exchanges, and his bank did not make any speculative profit on its exchange position. He thought that, 'if a fund and bank had been in operation in the early twenties, the present war would probably not have occurred ... it would have prevented the break-down of currency systems', and 'the lending of money for unproductive purposes, of great sums of American money, which enabled Germany to build up its armament industries'.[8]

Mr Randolph Burgess, president of the American Bankers Association, agreed with the objectives of Bretton Woods, but not with the methods. The Fund should not be created, but should become a department of the

Bank. The Bank's loans were made on sound principles. 'Long experience
has shown that poor loans are as bad for the borrower as for the lender.'
Once the money was put in the Fund, it was in the hands of a board of
directors in which the United States had a minority vote. And countries
had a right to borrow under conditions which were not difficult to fulfil.
If dollars became scarce, the tariff policies of the United States would be
blamed for it, and the country would again be branded 'Uncle Shylock'.[9]

The statement made on 22 March by Mr Leon Fraser, president of the
First National Bank of New York, was probably the most powerful and
convincing against the institution of the Fund. Mr Fraser was in favour of
the Bank, because it was 'built on constructive financial principles', but
against the Fund. He objected to its 'terrific size', and to the multiplicity
of its purposes, some of which seemed conflicting. 'The fund has a great
advantage of meaning different things in different countries.' He also felt
that having one institution, the Bank, would work better. Countries were
'entitled' to draw from the Fund, under very elastic conditions, and made
no promise to pay back the sum.

> We are told that, by a happy fiction, they do not borrow anything; that
> they purchase some other kind of exchange with their own exchange.
> They put in lei, lits, lats, and rubles, and they take out dollars. We are
> entitled to use the lei, the lits, the lats, and the rubles. . . . We are told
> that 44 nations agreed to this. I think a more exact statement would be
> that 3 or 4 groups of very expert chaps got together and wrote a plan,
> and then took it up with 44 other technicians, stating that this is what
> the United States and Britain are willing to stand for with you.

The Fund agreement was ambiguous. Whatever it said about changing
currency rates, Britain had warned that, even if the Fund disagreed, it
would alter the value of sterling as it pleased. One of Lord Keynes's ideas
was to have impersonal borrowing, a place where people could dip into a
common pool, without feeling that they were indebted to one country.
The United States had a minority position, 'which is odd, for the person
who puts up the real money'. Instead of giving countries money so that
they could buy wheat, it was better to stop the pretence that they were
paying for it, and to give it to them.[10]

Before the House hearings were over, White had to submit himself to
another interrogation by Dr Smith, who brought up a large number of
subjects: the reservations that several delegations had expressed at Bretton
Woods; the methods that the Fund would use in order to guard against the
causes of deflation; the scarce-currency provision; and so on and so forth.
It appeared that Dr Smith knew the Bretton Woods agreements better than
White himself. When White was confused about one point, he told him,
'You are a monetary expert and you are supposed to know more about
this proposition than most of us.'

He then referred to the incompatibility between Keynes's and White's statements about the meaning of Bretton Woods. Who had written the original plan, and who had conceived the idea? White did not know: 'Competent people, studying the same facts, have frequently arrived at somewhat the same conclusions. That happens among chemists, physicians, and even economists.' There existed a 'climate of opinion'.

'I believe I have heard that expression "climate of opinion" before', said Smith.

'It is a good phrase, it is very descriptive.'

'It is one that Lord Keynes uses.'

'I would not at all be reluctant to copy a phrase that he uses. He is a brilliant phrase maker.'

Dr Smith then read a few sentences of the Clearing Union plan, 'because, as you know, it is my contention, Mr White, that this whole plan was copied from Lord Keynes's original clearing union scheme'.

'Dr. Smith, that is a statement that I think you want to reconsider', said White. He knew precisely where he had originally come by his ideas, and Dr Smith was 'departing from your usual reasonable, cautious self into the realm of, shall I say, imagination'.

Why then should the United States place itself in a position where any country could invoke a sanction against it: either bring its exports and imports into balance, or give the goods away?

'That question reminds me of a story, which I would like to tell off the record', said White. Whatever was said off the record, we do not know. When the discussion resumed, Dr Smith continued his interrogation, sometimes taking White out of his depth. The restraint to be shown in answering the questions, in order to avoid antagonising any Congressman, made these sessions even more gruelling.[11]

Although those who opposed the bill had taken most of the time in the discussions, they were unable to sway the committee. On 24 May the Bretton Woods legislation was approved, by twenty-three votes to three. The amendments that had been agreed upon between the Treasury and the bankers were written into the bill. Representative Spence confirmed, however, that this 'does not change a word or alter a punctuation in the basic agreements'. It was 'just window dressing'.[12]

CONGRESSIONAL HEARINGS: THE SENATE

The hearings before the Senate Committee on Banking and Currency opened on 12 June 1945 with an eloquent statement by Secretary Morgenthau, who again emphasised the relation of the Bretton Woods agreements to peace. 'Peace and prosperity are two sides of the same problem. We can't neglect one without endangering the other.'

It was immediately obvious that Senator Taft was to lead the opposition. Unlike Dr Smith, however, he had not studied the agreements very carefully, and most of his statements were easy to refute. Much of the discussion between Taft and White centred about the gold at Fort Knox. The Senator thought that 'as long as we have this gold we can do as we please with it', but that in the Fund it would be 'at the discretion of a board we cannot control in any way' and who could 'dispose of it as they see fit'.[13]

A spokesman for the New York State Bankers Association commented on a report prepared by a special committee on international monetary matters. The committee concluded that the establishment of the Fund would not result in the achievement of economic stability or the elimination of exchange controls; that the safeguards were not adequate to assure the sound use of the fund's resources; that, if dollars became scarce, the Fund might not be able to function effectively; that there was lack of agreement on the interpretation of the Fund's provisions; and that stabilisation of each currency must be treated individually. While the American Bankers Association called for the elimination of the Fund, the New York State Bankers Association recommended its postponement.[14]

Speaking only for himself, Allan Sproul, president of the Federal Reserve Bank of New York, was 'in opposition to part of the agreements, for postponement of part of the agreements, and for adoption of part of the agreements'. While everybody agreed with the purposes of the institutions, there were too many people who allowed a yearning for international co-operation to give them assurance in advocating things they did not know much about, because they agreed with hopeful preambles. Whereas the Bank had become almost uncontroversial, he did not believe that the Fund would work during the first years after the war. While the idea of a fund might be workable in the longer term, its use during the transitional period would lead to distortions and eventual breakdown. There was too much emphasis on the responsibility of the creditor country to correct an unbalanced position, and on the use of depreciation by a debtor country to achieve the same result. 'We have Article IV of the fund agreement,' he said, 'which makes devaluation of currency little more than question of consulting with the fund before devaluing.' He suggested selective and controlled longer-term stabilisation loans, to be granted by the Bank, and above all a solution to the British problem.[15]

John H. Williams, professor of economics at Harvard and vice-president of the Federal Reserve Bank of New York, had been asked by Senator Taft to state his views before the committee. He had specialised in international monetary economics, and had studied for many years 'the workings of international monetary forces'. He thought 'the historical study of these problems is essential. We need perspective on the problem. Problems are not so new as we are apt to think they are.' He had been writing about the subject ever since the publication of the Keynes and White plans. To him, the main question was what should be done to solve 'England's special problems'. He doubted that the mechanism of the Fund would eliminate the imbalance between chronic debtors and chronic creditors; he expected some countries would misuse the Fund. Since it could not operate during the transitional period, he suggested waiting until circumstances were favourable. He expected that the Fund would soon run out of dollars. He was afraid that 'we will descend into legalism, each country setting forth its own interpretations of the provisions and then defending them on legalistic ground'. The easiest, but the worst, bargain to be made was to adopt Bretton Woods promptly, and 'be left with the discriminatory trade and exchange practices and without the basis for genuine cooperative efforts. ... We are now embarking upon a great and difficult experiment in a field in which, up to now, the record has been one of failure.' He recommended that the relationship between the dollar and the pound be firmly established. Most of the world's trade was carried out in these currencies. The way to achieve this was to grant Britain a credit of $3000 million. As far as gold was concerned, it was 'all right' because a lot of people believe in it; but 'One can set up a standard which he calls the gold standard and not have any gold in it at all, and yet it would be what we essentially mean by a gold standard.'[16]

About twenty of the nation's leading bankers, economists and business men appeared before the committee, which listened attentively to their expert testimony for and against the Fund and Bank. It was up to Harry White to close the hearings, and much of the session was taken up by arguments between him and Senator Taft. After one exchange of views White said, 'Well, Senator, you are entitled to your opinion. The technicians and the experts, most of them differ with you.'

'Most of them agree with me; those who have any — '

He was interrupted by Senator Downey: 'The gentlemen having reached an agreement to disagree here, then I would like to ask another question, if I may, please, Mr. White.'

'Do you want to add to the confusion?', Senator Barkley asked.

'I am going to ask another question to create more confusion', said Senator Downey amidst laughter. But, despite the criticism and some confusion, a majority of the Senators passed the bill.[17]

THE HOUSE DEBATE

Before the actual debate in the House opened, Representative Buffett protested against the fact that members had not had an opportunity to study the hearings. Several representatives who had tried to obtain a copy had been turned away. Only 'a large piece of bulky propaganda' was available, and it was impossible to decide, after a debate that had been limited to two days, about 'the most intricate international agreement that has ever come before the House of Representatives of the United States'. This was not a parliamentary procedure he could agree with.

One representative wondered, however, 'if the House would really understand it if they had plenty of time to consider it'.

Representative Sumner of Illinois warned that this 'swindling, war-breeding Bretton Woods proposal would . . . throw away our chance to do the good things we want to do in the future. This is forcing the American people to pay tribute to foreign governments. It will make the American people, the American taxpayers, the economic slaves of foreign governments.'

Representative Patman, on the other hand, thought it was 'the finest, the longest, and the best step that has ever been attempted by the American Congress to secure peace in the world in the future and to encourage and restore international trade'.

Representative Spence, as chairman of the Committee on Banking and Currency, opened the debate by asking the clerk to read a letter from President Truman expressing his confidence about the prompt enactment of the Bretton Woods legislation, and his interest in seeing that it would continue to have full support from both Republicans and Democrats.

Another letter, from Randolph Burgess, stated that the new bill was a substantial improvement over the original, 'and will aid in the effective accomplishment of the purposes of the whole program which is, after all, what we most desire'.

'I am wondering now who is against this bill', said Spence. 'While the people of America do not understand the technical details, in their hearts all of the men and women of the liberty-loving nations of the world hope that we may do something to prevent future wars, for the next war will be so indescribably horrible that no man living can envision it.' He then inserted the report of the committee, which was a remarkable analysis of the problem, and takes up sixty-eight columns of the *Congressional Record.*[18]

Republican Representative Wolcott, who had started out as a sceptic, stated his support for Bretton Woods. He also felt that anyone who was willing to take the time and study the agreement, the volumes of hearings, the committee report and the reams of other publications on the subject could get a pretty good understanding of what was intended. The success of the legislation depended almost wholly on the way in which it was administered: 'Any good act can become a bad act by mismanagement, and *vice versa*.' He then gave a remarkably clear and concise description of the Fund and Bank, and the reasons for voting in favour of the bill.[19]

Representative Brown, of Georgia, a recognised expert in farm products, recalled how cotton farmers had, in the past, suffered from disorderly currency practices, how exchange controls and clearing agreements had kept American cotton out of many countries. 'Who knows better than each one of you that unless you stabilize your currency in some form you cannot do any more world trade.' He could not see why there should be a single vote against 'these proposals which will help bring prosperity and peace in our country'.

Republican Representative Buffett took to the floor a sheet of American dollar bills caught in a mousetrap, and waved it periodically as he urged that Congress postpone action on 'the most intricate economic document that has ever come before Congress in the history of the country'. The government was capitalising on the desperate longing of the people for peace, and the claim that those who opposed Bretton Woods were isolationists was 'a cunning trick of political terrorism and it has fooled a lot of people'. They said it would stabilise currencies, but in Britain the Chancellor of the Exchequer had declared that Whitehall would alter the value of the pound whenever it considered this necessary. In the United States the advocates of Bretton Woods called it a return to the gold standard, but in Britain Lord Keynes had said that it was just the opposite. If any member of the House had 'any inferiority complex as you try to understand this, just remember that you have good company. The Chancellor of the British Exchequer and Leon Fraser, and other experts admit their confusion.' Therefore, the only reasonable decision was postponement.[20]

Representative Outland made an eloquent and documented defence of the proposals, and branded those who attacked it 'a certain small but vociferous number of classical economists, most of whom are thinking in terms of a *laissez faire* economy of the early nineteenth century, all of whom bow down in obeisance to the great god gold', and 'the last remnants of the isolationist gang'.[21]

Several members of the House regretted that the agreement had been written in forbidding language. One of them stated, 'I admit to having read the agreement and admit to know something about finances; still I will have to admit that it is not altogether Greek but almost Greek to me to read the agreement itself.'

Another Representative thought that, if the terms were unfamiliar to the layman, 'so are the terms used by the engineers who build the bridges over which we all drive'. The question was whether or not there was going to be international co-operation and exchange stability. The total subscription to the Fund and Bank was the equivalent of the cost of the war for twenty-three days. It was worth taking the risk.[22]

To Representative Flood of Pennsylvania, Bretton Woods was 'no mystery thriller from financial wizards', but

a reasonably workable plan and agreement among the several nations to stop once and for all this traditional and staged rise and fall of the different monies of the world. ... With world money markets and standards the subject of economic warfare, anyone trading on the world market never could tell, from one moment to the next, where his business was. The only profits made in this type of financial piracy were made by the small handful of economic freebooters who un-scrupulously manipulated the rates of exchange, sending the value of all moneys affected up and down in a sea of chaos and money madness. Is it any wonder war followed? Small wonder, indeed.

Every objection made during the hearings turned out, after careful examination, to be a point in favor of Bretton Woods.[23]

As was to be expected, Dr Smith's speech was long and passionate. He was opposed to the Bretton Woods proposals 'because I am an American, love my country, and refuse to surrender any part of it to foreign powers'. He confessed, 'I am old-fashioned enough to believe in the gold standard, which only means that I believe in liberty and am against slavery – that prices should be made in the market and not by the state.' He doubted that among monetary economists who devoted their lives to the study of money and finances there were two individuals who could agree as to the meaning of the text. The government tried to obtain legislation by pressure, and had organised what was 'perhaps the most colossal program of propaganda to force Congress, at taxpayers' expense', to pass it. The pressure mechanism invented by Lord Keynes would compel the United States to maintain equilibrium in her balance of payments with the rest of the world, 'or failing in this, penalize her by compelling her to give her goods away, or preadventure compel her to lower or abrogate her tariffs'. Capital transfers would be subjected to authoritarian restrictionism, which meant 'censorship of mails, telegrams, telephone calls, cablegrams. Foreign travel must be restricted. Persons wishing to travel abroad must be searched.' He and the others who opposed these proposals were 'as an American citizen, fighting for all those principles that have made this country great'.[24]

Representative Hill, from Colorado, suggested that the currencies of the world be stabilised on the basis of an international gold–silver standard.

While Representative Lemke saw in Bretton Woods 'twin octopuses – international octopuses designed to suck the lifeblood and energy out of the American people', Representative Hays thought that the real question was 'whether we are to have economic nationalism as the term is generally defined or economic collaboration'.

Representative Voorhis had devoted considerable time and effort to studying the proposals. He would have liked to see Bretton Woods 'come before us as a real declaration of the adulthood of mankind with all reference to this gold superstition stricken from it'. But between the two World Wars the United States had accumulated gold. 'We got plenty of gold. Indeed, we got so much that when our delegates went to Bretton Woods they were up against a very difficult dilemma. If this gold was going to be worth anything at all, it was necessary to get the other nations to recognise it in some way, but they could not obviously be expected to recognise gold unless they had at least a little of it.' Having all this gold

stored at Fort Knox, the United States now had to go through the reverse
process. 'It all seems a bit silly to me and it brings us back to the
fundamental point which is that the only way over the long pull that a
nation can expect to sell is if it buys to a corresponding volume to its
sales.' He was in favour of Bretton Woods, however, because it 'will put
international exchanges for the first time on an orderly basis, bring them
out into the light of day and take control of them away from private
manipulators and place it in the hands of representatives of the governments of the world'. Bretton Woods would prevent 'the international
financial fraternity' from reaping 'huge profits while at the same time
causing economic convulsions in the different countries'. Bretton Woods
provided for 'a controlled change of exchange rates and their orderly
management', thus removing the halo of sanctity which had surrounded
the gold standard, and eliminating the extreme rigidity which had
prevailed in the past. Under the gold standard, 'creditor groups throughout
the world have always been prepared to subject their own country and
other countries to deflation with falling prices and growing unemployment
rather than to sanction a change in monetary policies to accord with the
truth of industrial and economic conditions'. Bretton Woods was not yet
'the kind of scientific monetary system which one day the world must
have', but it was 'an important forward step along the sometimes slow
path of human progress'.[25]

Representative Wright Patman of Texas stated that he was proud of the
fact that the government had had the foresight to prepare for the difficult
problems of currency stabilisation and reconstruction which would confront the nation after the war. The vote of the House would be 'a
recognition of the businesslike and statesmanlike job done at Bretton
Woods, to get countries to work together in providing an economic basis
for a lasting peace'.[26]

Although the problems involved were highly technical and could be
argued intelligently only by those who were familiar with them, the debate
in the House was generally of a high calibre.

On 7 June the House voted, by 345 to eighteen, in favour of US
participation in the Fund and Bank. The eighteen members who voted 'no'
were all Republicans, but 138 Republicans joined with 205 Democrats, a
Progressive and a member of the American Labour party, in support of the
legislation. President Truman said he was exceedingly happy over the
vote.[27]

THE SENATE DEBATE

Whereas in the House the discussion had generally been factual, in the
Senate oratory tended to conquer analysis. Senator Taft had announced
that he would make the first speech for the opposition.

Senator Wagner started the debate by discussing in detail the main features of the Fund and of the Bank. He described the painful experience of the period between the two wars, and the reasons why the Treasury had prepared proposals 'to establish the rule of law and reason in international currency relationships'. He explained the reasons for accepting both institutions and answered some of the criticism that had been made of them. He had some difficulty in finishing his speech, because of Senator Taft's interruptions.

Taft's main objection to the Fund was that it would not and could not stabilise unstable and worthless currencies: 'if we try to stabilise conditions with this fund it will be like pouring money down a rat hole'. These countries could not balance their budgets and could not export; their population had no confidence in their own currencies.

I said the United States will put in $2,750,000,000 in gold. American dollars are equivalent to gold. The fact that they are equivalent to gold is shown by the fact that all through this fund it is always American dollars or gold that is specified. In other words, the world recognises that the American dollar alone is worth gold. . . . Now we come to the currencies. Canadian currency is good today. South American currencies are good. Is the British currency good? Mr. President, why do you suppose the British pound is worth $4 today? It is worth that much because the United States Government has supported it for the last four years . . . there are $15,000,000,000 worth of them all around the world, but no one can cash them, because the British Government is unable to cash them. Is the paper pound good? It is just as good as the United States chooses to make it, and no better. . . . The same thing is true of the currencies of every other European country; they are just as good as we choose to make them, and no better.

Because the subject was technical, and few people had studied its provisions or its effects; the Treasury propaganda efforts had concentrated on the emotional aspects. Taft appealed to every Senator to study the plan, which could 'easily be understood by reading the articles and analyzing the proposals. . . . The truth is, there are very few experts on this subject. Most of those who are quoted here have no more brains and no more knowledge than the average Senator.' He thought that, instead of establishing a fund, 'we can restore that equilibrium of the world through the development of trade and by loans which are directed primarily to the problems of the particular countries.' The proposed institutions might work later, when currencies were stabilised; but at the present they would be useless.[28]

Senator Thomas, of Oklahoma, brandished a handful of bank notes from various countries, to 'demonstrate to the Senate the need of the stabilisation of world currencies'. Here was one from Nicaragua. Did

Senator Taft know the value? The senator did not even know the name, he said. Then there was the lira; what about the value of the lira?

> I am merely exhibiting this currency to show that it is the kind of currency we would deal in, it is currency of leading nations, which is now practically worthless in terms of dollars. ... I challenge any Member of the Senate to take this pile of bills, which is worth on its face 700,000,000 in the currencies of the various countries, and go downtown in Washington and get his shoes shined with this whole bunch of bills, although in the hands of some monetary expert they might be worth two or three dollars in American money. That is a condition we confront when we create this fund and try to stabilise this sort of money.[29]

All these countries had to do, said Senator Taft, was to print money, and put it in. And by joining the Fund, said Senator Wherry, they could take out dollars in exchange.

Senator Barkley thought it was unfair to exhibit such banknotes, because conditions in those countries when the notes were issued were not what they were at present. The countries in question had unstable governments, or had just been liberated. There had been inflation. It was not that kind of money that would go into the fund. And, if every currency was stabilised, there would not be a need for the Fund and the Bank.

Senator Tobey reminded the opposition of the fact that every country had to contribute some gold and that the Fund's holdings of currencies were guaranteed against depreciation in terms of gold.[30] He spoke in favor of Bretton Woods, and reaffirmed his 'faith in the potency of the provisions of both the fund and the bank toward promoting economic security in a troubled world'. The United States had spent vast sums and sacrificed many lives to win the war; it would be 'unthinkable that we should permit economic war to engulf the world, or that we should withdraw within ourselves'. The Bretton Woods agreements had grown out of the experience of the two decades between the wars, and were the result of three years of careful discussion. The methods tried before had led to anarchy and disorder; bitter experience had shown that international problems could be dealt with only through international co-operation. He described the purposes and the operations of both institutions and answered some of the criticism. The United States should set an example and be the first to ratify the agreements.[31]

As he had been a member of the American delegation at Bretton Woods, Senator Tobey's speech was very effective. There followed a long and useful debate, in which Senator Taft found himself being contradicted by a growing number of supporters of the agreements. He even had to admit that on a number of points he had been wrong.

The debate was occasionally sidetracked by senators who had their particular interests. Senator Thomas of Oklahoma made a long speech pleading for the use of silver, next to gold, as the monetary metal of the system. He warned that, unless this was done, 'there will be an insufficiency of media for the settlement of international balances, and the use of silver as money will be undermined'.

The arguments of those who pointed to the financial risks involved were countered by statements that the risk of repeating the experience of the 1920s and 1930s was even greater.

Several amendments introduced by the opposition were defeated. On 19 July, by sixty-one votes to sixteen, the Senate passed the Bretton Woods agreements bill.

20
A Fund for a Loan

The original Keynes plan had been greeted in Britain with considerable enthusiasm. Even the White plan was regarded as better than nothing. The Bretton Woods agreements had, from the outset, been subject to very critical analysis. It had been generally assumed that the document finally agreed upon would not diverge substantially from the Statement of Principles, but the financial writers noted several amendments of major importance. While in the United States the plan was considered as a return to a gold standard, British spokesmen had tried to convince Parliament and public opinion that it did not mean a return to gold. It was generally noted that the text of the plan was sufficiently obscure to lend itself to conflicting interpretations, and that there was in fact a wide discrepancy between the British and American interpretations. The Bretton Woods conference, noted a correspondent of *The Times*, had been true to tradition: 'an international conference almost invariably begins with an unholy scrap and ends in cordial agreement upon an ambiguous formula'.[1]

The British government's first public statement on the agreement, following its signature, was made early in October 1944 by Sir John Anderson, Chancellor of the Exchequer, at a Lord Mayor's luncheon:

This Conference produced a document called the Final Act. It is, I confess, a difficult document, inevitably long and technical. There are some obscurities of language in it which have led to misunderstanding and must be clarified. The time for detailed exposition will come when the whole matter has to be debated by Parliament ... if we find that the United States and other countries important in international trade and finance decide that it is acceptable to them, we must not reject it lightly.

Some of the critics of the plan, said the Chancellor, claimed that it would prohibit Britain from entering into discriminatory commercial and currency agreements, and that it would do so not just as a temporary measure, but permanently. 'Now I think it is doubtful whether the Final Act is decisive on this point.' In the matter of changing the parity of currencies, Bretton Woods followed a middle course between rigidity and instability. Britain would have to bring its exchange policy under review by an international body. However,

> We would not surrender any ultimate right to follow our own policy, but we would accept an obligation to recognise that the adjustment of the exchange value of sterling, or of any other major international currency, is a two-ended process, and that we owe it to the general interests of international trade, to consult with an international institution before we make a change which will affect our commercial, as well as our financial relations with other countries.[2]

Keynes himself was convinced that the Fund and the Bank combined would not solve Britain's postwar problems. In a memorandum dated 28 September 1944 he wrote,

> We cannot police half the world at our own expense when we have already gone into pawn to the other half. We cannot run for long a great programme of social amelioration on money lent from overseas. Unless we are willing to put ourselves financially at the mercy of America and then borrow from her on her own terms and conditions sums which we cannot confidently hope to repay, what are we expecting? Are we looking forward to a spectacular bankruptcy (not, altogether, a bad idea) from which we shall rise the next morning without a care in the world? Or are we following some star at present invisible to me?[3]

After his return from Bretton Woods, Keynes did not stay long in England. He had to return to Washington, and spent two months there during the latter part of 1944. The object of his mission was to discuss British–American financial arrangements in the period that would elapse between the defeat of Germany and the surrender of Japan. The British, who expected this period to last for about eighteen months, called it Stage 2, while the Americans referred to it as Phase 2. This was Keynes's fourth wartime visit to the United States, and, although he did not expect to obtain all he wanted, the Americans showed genuine good-will and magnanimity. He was assisted by a group of very capable men, and his mission was a success. It seemed that as a result Britain could look forward with less anxiety to Stage 2, and tackle the problems of reconversion while continuing to receive Lend–Lease from America. On his way back to

England, aboard the SS *Nieuw Amsterdam*, Keynes wrote a long report to
the Chancellor of the Exchequer describing the experience he had 'picked
up after spending nearly a year . . . stepping like a cat over the hot tiles of
Washington', a place frantic with frustration in every quarter, where,
owing to 'the encircling flood of personal and political and departmental
jealousies and indecisions and uncertainties which never are and never can
be resolved or finished' and the plague of the lawyers who seldom
considered 'that what is administratively sensible is also lawful', 'it is not a
question of how much you can do but how much you can stand'. All this
required 'That we must stand unpropped, or be laid low.'[4]

During the two months Keynes spent in Washington, opposition to
Bretton Woods had considerably increased in London. The Federation of
British Industries had recommended that ratification be postponed, and
the London Chamber of Commerce had published a report that was very
critical. Monetary technique was not an end in itself, but a means to an
end. '. . . the International Monetary Fund does nothing to bring pressure
to bear on nations to balance their accounts with the world in terms of
goods and services, but its provisions are directed to assuring a balance in
money; and yet there cannot, in the long run, be a balance in money
unless there is a balance in trade.' If a country is unwilling to take goods
and services in exchange for its sales of goods and services abroad, 'any
financial system which permits them to profit by this unwillingness and to
use the proceeds of their sales to depress the exchange rate and threaten
the internal stability of the country to which they have sold, or
alternatively, to invest the proceeds in that country, thereby gradually
acquiring control of its fixed assets, must in the long run lead not to
co-operation but to chaos'. Moreover, whereas in the past a country could
impose exchange restrictions or use other methods to prevent imports
from entering the country, such action would be held contrary to the
purposes of the Fund. 'It is the gravamen of the Chamber's criticism that
the International Monetary Fund does, in fact, seek to deprive the nations
of their defences whilst failing to remove the perils which called them into
use.'[5]

Faced with the opposition of influential business organisations and with
growing criticism in political circles and in the press, the position of the
Chancellor of the Exchequer became very difficult and delicate. The
government had promised that the Bretton Woods agreements would be
discussed 'in due course'. But the debate had to be postponed as long as
possible, because the agreements would certainly be subjected to severe
criticism, and this might have serious repercussions on the proceedings in
Washington. The Chancellor had finally recommended that the government face a debate on a resolution which would not commit it to final
acceptance of the agreements. These delaying tactics exasperated the
critics in Parliament.

Late in January, and in the absence of the Chancellor of the Exchequer, a group of Members of Parliament had tried to force a surprise debate on Bretton woods, in he hope that the opposition would have the floor all to itself. Ambassador Winant, who had learned about it, advised Washington that the reactionary elements,

> the tory empire preference group are determined to destroy this. I felt that taking advantage of the absence of Eden and the Prime Minister from the country with failure to give notice to the Chancellor and trying to argue a basic monetary policy under a parliamentary procedure which is questionable indicates a backroom procedure and an indirection of method worthy of note. The Amerys, the Hudsons, the Beaverbrooks, the Brackens and the commercial and financial forces by whom they are supported are today and will in future be opposed to a United Nations economic policy which is basic to world recovery to my personal opinion.[6]

In a conversation with Hawkins and Penrose, Keynes had said that much mutual toleration would have to be exercised during the transition period. For that reason, it was important that long-term commercial policies be worked out that would keep in proper perspective the expedients to which Britain would have to resort. 'Much nonsense has been written and said', Keynes added, 'in favour of bilateral bargaining and restriction by a vocal minority in Britain who have a somewhat open field because of the absorption of economists and administrators in government.' He and others would soon organise a counter-offensive, and he expected that there would be no difficulty in getting the Bank approved in Parliament. As for the Fund, he said that it was preferable to wait until it had been approved by Congress.

While in London the government delayed taking action on Bretton Woods, Keynes followed very closely the Congressional hearings and debate. On the changes Congress had made to the bill as a result of the compromise with the New York bankers he wrote,

> the United States shall appoint the same individual to be their representative as Governor of the Fund and as Governor of the Bank. . . . The Governors of the two Institutions are, so to speak, ornamental personages, who receive no salary and only function on occasions. . . . The operative officials in both Institutions are the Executive Directors. . . . Here, therefore, there has been no more than window-dressing.

However, he thought, 'The technique adopted by Congress deserves attention in case we wish to imitate it.' Also, Britain might be reluctant to give its last word until there had been some progress in discussions on

Stage 3, the period following the surrender of Japan, when Britain would continue to need American aid.[7]

Britain would continue to receive Lend-Lease assistance until the end of the war with Japan. It took almost a year for the Allied troops, after their landing in Normandy, and with massive Russian offensives helping in the destruction of the German army, to achieve victory in Europe. It would take some time for the Americans to defeat Japan, whose soldiers controlled vast areas on the Asian continent, and many strategic islands in the Pacific.

The British government was careful not to declare its official attitude; while some ministers favoured ratification of the plan, under certain conditions, others remained unalterably opposed to it. For those who examined the question on its merits, and without too much prejudice, it seemed that, as a matter of plain economics, there was a clear balance of argument against membership of the Fund. But, as a matter of politics or of amicable relations with the United States, much was to be said in its favour. 'How much economic hazard is a reasonable price for continued American generosity and friendship — or at least for the avoidance of American disappointment and resentment? This is not a question to which a precise answer can be given. It all depends — depends on the size of the hazard and the intensity of the friendship.'[8]

A loan from the New York bankers was out of question. The *Financial News* noted, 'The slightest acquaintance with the trend of British public opinion (or the economic thought of the past twenty years) makes it safe to say that such an offer would be rejected outright and without hesitation by this country.' Sterling tied to the dollar, which in turn would be tied to gold, was not even to be considered as a remote possibility.[9]

Public discussion by government officials was extremely difficult: the Bretton Woods agreements were like the tip of an iceberg, visible but subject to conflicting views about which direction it would take, while hidden beneath the surface were the much bigger, fundamental questions of the management of Britain's enormous war debts, the possibility of another depression, and the like. These questions could not be canvassed in public, partly because of the reaction it would cause in countries holding large balances of blocked sterling, and partly because the subject was so complex. Another reason was that elections were coming, and no one knew which party would be in power when the decision came to be made.

Early in July, Sir John Anderson, in what was to be one of his last public statements as Chancellor of the Exchequer, spoke at a luncheon of the American Society in London. He warned his audience not to assume that Bretton Woods was a panacea. Explaining British caution in coming to a decision on the plan, he contrasted the economic positions of Great Britain and the United States. The British government, he said, had been watching with the keenest interest the passage of the Bretton Woods legislation through Congress. 'Some of our friends on the other side may have been surprised and perhaps even a little disappointed that we have been so slow in declaring ourselves upon these matters.' He promised two things: 'There is still a part of the war to finish. We shall be with you, at your side, during that struggle, to its victorious end.' And to a cheering audience he added, 'We shall never appear anywhere in the guise of suppliants and we shall not accept any obligation that we cannot see our way clearly to fulfil.'[10]

The July 1945 general elections put the Labour party in power in Britain. Labour, led by Mr Clement Attlee, was as divided on the question as the Conservatives; but the objectives of the Labour party's economic programme were perhaps harder to reconcile with expeditious and rigid stabilisation of currencies and with agreements to remove exchange restrictions. In the press, the debate intensified.

Some commentators thought the government would try to use Bretton Woods as a bargaining counter to try to extract more favourable terms from the United States in such matters as Lend—Lease, trade, civil aviation, and merchant shipping. *The Economist*, said it was 'obvious nonsense' to expect any country to commit itself in 1945 to the par value of its currency, within a limit of 10 per cent. This provision would have to be amended. Strong objections were also raised against setting any definite time limit to the transitional period.[11]

None of the alternatives the new government faced were very attractive. Ratification with crippling reservations would be little short of outright rejection. Even worse would be ratification solely for political expediency, in the belief that the obligations assumed under the Bretton Woods agreements were only paper commitments. That would be an act of bad faith more destructive in the long run than outright repudiation.

THE END OF LEND—LEASE

While the Attlee government and the British press debated over what action to take concerning Bretton Woods, events entirely changed the context of the debate. President Roosevelt died, and was replaced by President Truman. Atomic bombs were dropped on Hiroshima and Nagasaki. Japan surrendered; the war was over. Shortly afterwards the White House issued a press release:

The President has directed the Foreign Economic Administrator to take steps immediately to discontinue all Lend—Lease operations and to notify foreign governments receiving Lend—Lease of this action.

The President directs that all outstanding contracts for Lend—Lease are cancelled, except where Allied governments are willing to agree to take them over or where it is in the interest of the United States to complete them.[1][2]

Britain was not ready for this bombshell from one of its closest friends. The government had not received any prior indication that this was being considered. Churchill described the decision as 'rough and harsh', and did not believe it was the last word of the United States. Attlee stated in Parliament that the President's decision put Britain 'in a very serious financial position'. In the United States there was hardly any sympathy for the reaction of the British. Congressmen and the press expressed surprise at the statements of British politicians, especially since the Lend—Lease Act had made it perfectly clear that this was going to happen. While the British felt they were being treated harshly, the Americans felt they had been very generous for a long period of time.[1][3]

THE BRITISH LOAN

Shortly after Lend—Lease was abruptly cut off, Keynes left for Washington again. He would ask the United States Administration to place at the disposal of Britain a sum of $5000 million, in three instalments. In the absence of any support, Britain would run through the whole of its available gold and dollar reserves within less than a year. The government had accumulated considerable sterling debts during the war, and now it needed to import food and raw materials so that it could reconvert and restore its economy.

A joint press conference was held on 12 September by Ambassador Halifax and Lord Keynes. The ambassador outlined developments in Britain during the past few weeks, and then led to the objects of Keynes's mission. It was an admirable performance and it gave Keynes a good kick-off.

The following day the negotiations started in the boardroom of the Federal Reserve Board. They would last for almost three months. Keynes was convinced, and had been able to persuade Whitehall, that he could obtain a substantial outright gift from the United States and settle whatever questions were left open regarding Article VII. His natural optimism, his faith in his persuasive power and his belief that in the end justice would prevail had gradually made him confident that he could achieve all this. At the request of the Americans, he presented Britain's case, forcefully, with his customary eloquence, and in an exhaustive manner.

He did not wish to draw any invidious distinctions, he said, but in order to give greater vividness to the presentation of the facts, he had to compare the relative war efforts of the Allies. The sacrifices made by the British people in the common cause, the austerities and the suffering endured by them, exceeded those of any other country. The external difficulties that the United Kingdom would have to face after the war were the direct consequence of the absorption of the national energies in the prosecution of the conflict. He did not make any specific proposal as to how the United States could help Britain overcome these difficulties, but the Americans gained the impression that Britain was not interested in a commercial loan.[14]

> This was received with consternation by the Americans. The idea that we should justify any request for assistance from them on the ground that we had suffered and perhaps even achieved more than they, both annoyed and horrified them.
>
> Keynes expected the offer to come from the other side. It never came. Before we knew it, we were discussing, not the terms of a grant, but those of a loan.[15]

Keynes and the other British delegates quickly became convinced that their original hopes were unrealistic, and changed their position accordingly. 'Unfortunately, the Ministers and officials in London were still repeating and buoying themselves up with the poetic cadences which Keynes had left in their hearts and minds before he went to Washington. It was a full month before London began to get this notification of a change.'[16]

Night after night, Keynes would sit up late and draft telegrams to London. This, along with the strain of the meetings, caused a great deterioration in his health, and occasionally he was near to physical breakdown. When it became evident that help would not be forthcoming in the form of a grant, Keynes 'advanced a renewed plea in the very strongest terms why both on financial and on political or psychological grounds at least a part of the assistance say two billions should take the form of a grant'. He had been urged to do so by London. But Vinson and Clayton 'remained outwardly adamant that neither a grant nor a loan free of interest was practical politics for them'.[17]

Not only were the negotiations made difficult by the wide gulf between British and American public opinion, but in addition the two main negotiators, Keynes and Vinson, had nothing in common that would have helped to ease the strain of their discussions. Vinson, a lawyer by profession, concerned mainly with working things out so that they would be acceptable to Congress and to American public opinion, wanted to help Britain to the extent he deemed possible.

If Vinson showed little interest in the refinements of economic analysis he showed even less appreciation of the shafts of wit which Keynes now broke about his brows. In vain did members of the British delegation warn Keynes that he was dealing with a different type of man than Morgenthau or Acheson. 'Please try to remember', one associate pleaded, 'that you are dealing with Kentucky.' 'Well', said Keynes defiantly, 'Kentucky will have to like it.' Indeed, the more he was warned, the more unmercifully he ragged his adversary. One exchange was particularly memorable. Vinson, to illustrate some point, had grown rather rhetorical. He demanded to know whether Britain's capacity to service a loan would not be enhanced 'if suddenly, tomorrow, you found currency in a cave'. 'Why, of course', Keynes exclaimed. ' "Any currency found in caves" — we'll have that in the agreement.' There was a roar of laughter at this *riposte*. Vinson turned black with rage. He did not quickly forget the incident.[18]

On 21 November, Keynes cabled London that 'Personally I am now rather near the end of my physical reserves.' A few days later, however, the attitude of the Americans suddenly became 'more conciliatory than at any meeting this delegation have attended since they came to Washington'. Keynes called London, pressing for a quick decision. While he was being assured 'please believe that we are not trying to sabotage your efforts or being more stupid than nature has made us',[19] he warned that 'If we miss taking advantage of the present mood, my judgement is that things will move backward and not forward.'[20] This put the British government on the spot concerning the ratification of Bretton Woods, which had come to be inextricably linked with the loan.

Before he had left for Washington in the hope that the Americans would spontaneously offer an outright grant, Keynes had expected that such an offer would be made subject to various conditions: elimination of currency restrictions and liberalisation of the sterling-area arrangements. He was prepared to accept the conditions.

The offer of almost immediate convertibility of sterling, that is the acceptance of the Bretton Woods agreement without the protection of the transitional period clauses, was in fact made by our side. So was the undertaking to pursue a policy of non-discrimination in imports. That meant abandoning discrimination in import licensing and not abandoning imperial preferences. But these promises were made in the context of a retrospective Lend–Lease adjustment, or assistance disguised in some similar cloak. The promises, having been made in one particular context, we were held to them when the scene changed and we began talking in terms of a semi-commercial line of credit of considerably smaller amount than what we had hoped to get.[21]

On several occasions the British negotiators were reminded that the loan would be subject to British ratification of the monetary agreements. On 13 November 'Secretary Vinson reiterated that the granting of a credit to the U.K. was dependent on the British agreeing to Bretton Woods. He stated that it had been made clear to the British that they would have to ratify Bretton Woods before the credit proposal was put up to Congress.'[22]

While the Americans tied the loan to Bretton Woods, the British government held out as long as possible with the purpose of using ratification as a lever in obtaining financial assistance. Shortly after the Cabinet made the decision to submit the Bretton Woods bill to Parliament, the Prime Minister and the Chancellor of the Exchequer cabled the embassy in Washington, 'The Americans must realise that time is running very short if they wish for action on Bretton Woods. They must also be got to understand that we have difficulties on our side, and it has not been easy to get agreement here.'[23]

When Keynes advised London that Vinson regarded it as 'essential that Congress should know when it considers the financial proposals that we are proceeding with Bretton Woods',[24] the Chancellor replied that, even if Parliament ratified the agreement, this would not necessarily commit the government to signing it. 'This precaution is merely tactical, for unless the financial talks break down, I should assume that signature would be given before the operative date of 31st December. If, however, we are refused sufficient dollars we shall have to refuse all Bretton Woods commitments.'[25]

The Anglo-American Financial Agreement was finally signed on 6 December 1945. Ambassador Halifax cabled London that he was aware of the difficulties the government faced; '. . . we have all done our level best to move Americans to meet them. I am sorry we have failed.'[26] The amount of the credit was established at $3750 million. Detailed terms of the loan were listed and one of the conditions was the ratification of Bretton Woods. In addition, Britain committed itself, unless the United States agreed to a temporary extension, to remove within a year all restrictions on the convertibility of sterling for current transactions.

On 8 December, Keynes and Lady Keynes left Washington for New York, from there to sail home on the *Queen Elizabeth*.

BRITAIN RATIFIES BRETTON WOODS

The British government and press had watched with anxiety the developments of the financial discussions in Washington. When the terms of the Anglo-American agreement were made public, the reaction was generally unfavourable. 'Beggars cannot be choosers. But they can, by long tradition, put a curse on the ambitions of the rich', *The Economist* exclaimed.[27] The press debated the pros and cons.

The government, having secured the loan, had to obtain Parliamentary approval. The Financial Agreement, Bretton Woods and the settlement of Lend–Lease, as well 'Proposals for Consideration by an International Conference on Trade and Employment', which had been made public by the Secretary of State, would be linked. On 6 December, the day the Financial Agreement was signed in Washington, Prime Minister Attlee announced in the House of Commons, at 10.30 p.m., 'owing to the need for synchronisation with the announcement in the United States of America', that there would be an early debate on all these matters.

Mr Boothby, who had been one of the most vocal critics of Bretton Woods, recalled the repeated pledges given by successive governments that there would be an extended debate. 'Some of us have been pressing for a discussion on this for the last ten months. We have never been allowed to have a discussion. Now we have a pistol pointed at our heads, and are told that we have to pass the whole thing in three days.'

Another member asked the Prime Minister whether, in view of the fact that many people in Parliament and in the country regarded Bretton Woods 'as economic strangulation for the British Commonwealth of Nations', the government would remove party discipline on occasion of the debate. Attlee answered determinedly, 'No, Sir. The fact that certain people hold certain opinions does not necessarily mean that, therefore, we should take the Whips off.'[28] By imposing party discipline, the government could expect a positive vote from all but a few, recalcitrant party members. And since Labour had a comfortable majority in Parliament, approval was practically certain.

Mr Hugh Dalton, Chancellor of the Exchequer, and other members of the government stated very plainly that, in order to obtain the American loan, Parliament would have to ratify Bretton Woods. Deprived of American aid, the country would have to face a drastic cut in its living standards, and its programme of reconversion and reconstruction would be endangered. In addition, rejection of Bretton Woods would seriously jeopardise the country's close relationship with the United States, and would prevent the further development of plans for economic co-operation in other fields, such as the establishment of an International Trade Organisation, then under discussion. The Chancellor confessed that the government had accepted the obligation to eliminate exchange restrictions within a very short period of time 'with very great reluctance', and this commitment had been made only to avoid the breaking off of negotiations.[29]

The debate was short, passionate and bitter. Mr Boothby submitted that 'it would be an outrage if this House were asked to pass this Bretton Woods Agreements Bill, which is a vital Bill affecting the whole future of the country, without discussion'. But the Speaker stated, 'The House must abide by the Rules of Order. It is perfectly clear that the House having accepted the Motion, the Bretton Woods Agreement cannot be discussed after that. . . . There are certain matters which can be discussed on this Bill, but not on the Bretton Woods Agreement.' One member expressed the view that, if the decision had 'to be taken tonight, with no opportunity of debate, some of us who are rather apprehensive about it will have no alternative but to vote against it'. And Mr Boothby again wanted to know how the government 'squares the gagging of the House on

Bretton Woods, with the repeated undertakings of the Government that we should have a full and free discussion?' He was told that the remark was 'perfectly untrue and gratuitous', and that the House would be given 'the widest opportunity for discussion of the principles involved'.[30]

Although time was short, much of it was spent on Parliamentary oratory. On 13 December the debate started out with a long-winded speech by Lieutenant-Colonel Sir Thomas Moore, who was 'certainly conscious of lacking any specialised qualifications'. He was

> speaking as a man in the street, for the common citizens of this country, with no political complex, no inhibitions, anti-nothing, as the men of Britain generally are, except when there is a shortage of beer. I am, indeed, even speaking for the charlady who so kindly and competently cleans my flat, and who said to me yesterday morning, 'We are accustomed to hardships, we are used to hardships. Tell those gentlemen in the House of Commons to stand up for Britain and not trail after the Americans and their spam.' I believe that those are the views held by the majority of the people of this country, irrespective of their walk of life.

One of the good reasons the Chancellor had given for accepting the bill was that otherwise Britain might have to do without some luxuries such as tobacco. 'I hold that we can change our tastes. Turkey and Greece have been trying for the last five years to persuade us to buy their tobacco.' What he could not understand was why Bretton Woods was tied to the loan. When he first read the report of the Bretton Woods conference, he had

> rashly formed the conclusion that it was merely a useful extension of the prewar sterling area into a world currency area. I also had the impression, not being an economist, that currency had to be tied to or based on something; whether it was gold, or marbles, or shrimps, did not seem to matter very much, except that as marbles are easy to make, and shrimps are easy to catch, gold for many reasons possessed a more stable quality.

But now he realised that since 1931 British currency had 'no such basis of gold'. He did not feel that Britain should surrender 'the British integrity area . . . for the doubtful and unknown blessings of this World Monetary Fund'. Britain should show 'that we are not crawling to get this loan' the harsh terms of which 'take no account of the toil, sweat, blood and tears suffered by us', and of the fact that Britain waged war, not because it was attacked, but 'on account of an ideal which it believed to be right'.[31]

One of the advocates of the bill said, in rejecting the argument that removal of exchange restrictions would put undue pressure on the balance of payments and remove the possibility of safeguarding the procurement of essential supplies, that 'the safeguards for State trading are as complete as they could be. . . . There is a provision for those who wish to plan parts of the national economy, a provision for those who want to establish monopolies in a particular list of commodities, provision for those who wish to plan the whole of their international trade.' If the equilibrium of the foreign-exchange position was endangered, 'we resume freedom to impose quantitative restrictions to the extent necessary to restore equality between our purchasers and ourselves. No safeguard could be more complete.'[32]

Mr Stanley refuted the argument that Britain was assuming obligations which it knew very well could not be carried out, and that this was dishonest: 'I have no doubt at all about our ability and willingness to pay.' However, 'we are doubtful whether America is prepared to receive it'. He could not vote against the agreement, but he would not vote for it. Unlike the Labour Members, who 'have got to vote, whatever they think about it, whatever their views', the Opposition Members could vote or abstain as they wished.[33]

Miss Jennie Lee felt compelled to confess that some members of the Labour party 'may be in a mood this evening for a little flutter of rebellion' against those who said that Britain did not want a trade war with the United States. '. . . whether we want a trade war with America or not, we have got it, and no matter what our voting position is tonight, we still have got that trade war.' As for the terms of the agreement, 'There is no wisdom in this loan, and there is no kindness in it. There is nothing in the terms of this loan which gives us any reason to suppose that an administration which could offer a niggardly, barbaric, antediluvian settlement such as this, can solve the unemployment problem in their own country much less help the world.' She could not possibly vote in the government lobby, and, when answers had been given to some of the basic questions involved in the debate, she would decide whether to vote against or abstain. Someone had said that there were two interpretations of the Bretton Woods agreements, but the debate so far indicated that there were twenty interpretations.

Mr David Eccles, while he regretted that, apart from the settlement of Lend–Lease, the terms of the agreement were 'harsh, and, I regret to say unworthy of two allies who have just saved the world by their exertions', felt that without a dollar credit the country would be unable to get out of the financial straits to which the war had reduced it. The loan was indispensable. Under the circumstances, it was the best that could be obtained. The Bretton Woods proposals threw down in front of the British people a tremendous challenge. A small nation, 'standing between the revised imperialism of Russia and the commercial aggression of America', had to be 'ambitious and realistic'. 'I think we ought to place the united experience of this country, which in these commercial matters is far greater than that of any other country in the world at the disposal of America and Russia and show them just how they can and should contribute to a real multilateral trading system as much as we have been asked to contribute in these onesided and obscure proposals.'[34]

Mr Max Aitken taunted the government for threatening to restrict transatlantic flights, because the Americans wanted to reduce the rates, 'when we have not even a service running across the Atlantic'. 'Then we turn to the Americans and say, "Will you please lend us some money?" Of course the terms are harsh.' If the government had told the Americans that it would not take the loan, but 'pull our belts', in three months' time the Americans, with their warehouses almost filled up with goods, would come and say, 'All right, what are your terms? What do you want?' The trouble would not come from refusing the loan, but from defaulting on it. And that was inevitable, according to many eminent economists. Britain's future lay in its Empire.[35]

There were several excellent speeches for or against the bill. Then Winston Churchill, Leader of the Opposition, rose. There was deep misgiving, he said, 'of our ability, however hard we try, to discharge successfully the obligations now to be imposed upon us'. It was a pity that a commercial transaction should be mixed up with other agreements, such as Bretton Woods. He did not like the mixture. 'As it is, we seem to have the worst of it both ways.' The proposal to make sterling convertible within fifteen months was 'too bad to be true'. He resented the 'indecent haste with which these most serious complex matters are thrust before us, and have to be settled'. Rather than vote in different lobbies on a question of this kind, he thought it better and wiser for the Conservative party to abstain.

He recalled the invaluable aid given by the United States through Lend—Lease, 'that most unsordid act in the history of nations'. Whatever the misgivings about the present proposals, 'both their generosity and the championship by the United States of the cause of freedom will ever stand forth as a monument of human virtue and of future world hope'. He was glad that 'no one of the slightest responsiblity, speaking in the debate, has used any language likely to reflect upon the noble deeds of the people and Government of America, to make ill-will between our two countries, or mar the splendour of the story of the past'. The Americans had burdened themselves with an enormous debt; they saw, across the Atlantic, political conceptions and ideologies very different from theirs. Those who had been victorious in the elections had held out to the British people 'dazzling expectations . . . which are not only of a far higher standard of life, but of a far easier life, than any that has existed in Britain before'. The Americans had undoubtedly read about this. If the American terms were severe, what about the attitude of Egypt, which had been saved from being ravaged and pillaged by the Germans and the Italians, but had charged all expenses against Britain? Neither had India made any proposal to reduce the debts owed by Britain. By freeing themselves from the responsibility of passing these proposals, on which they had never been consulted, the members of the Conservative party did not in any way weaken public faith in the word of the British people. The financial obligations, once entered into, were binding upon all parties. The country would have to do its very best to carry the heavy load. 'If we fail, it must not be from any lack of sincerity or exertion, but simply because the weight that is being placed upon us may be far more than our exporting power can sustain.'

The Secretary of State for Foreign Affairs, Ernest Bevin, answered Churchill. The government had done all it could to obtain the best possible terms. They had hoped for a gift, then an interest-free loan. They had to settle for 'the third method and borrowed money. . . . I do not know of anybody who ever came away from a moneylender's office and calculated the repayment who ever felt comfortable.' But Britain had been a moneylender for a long time and lived on foreign investments 'in which others have toiled to produce interest on the money we have lent, and so contributed to the wealth of this country'. When Churchill said his government could have obtained better terms, that was 'a libel on the Administration of the United States'. If the Opposition wanted to abstain, let them abstain, 'But do not let us have any cowards on this side.' After all, the government had obtained that Lend–Lease could be cleared up at a cost of only $650 million. Whether or not Britain could pay its debts would depend on 'whether we are able to satisfy our creditors with sterling goods'. Whether or not there would be another repudiation 'is in the hands of the United States, and nobody else. . . . If the debts are allowed to be worked off, both with the United States and internationally, then this few billion dollar loan will not matter very much.' He called on the House to 'Carry the Bills as soon as you can . . . the country is up against an economic position very much like it was militarily in 1940 . . . now is the time for us to put our shoulders to the wheel and help this old country through as we did on that occasion.'[36] The House voted: 345 ayes, ninety-eight noes.

In all this, Bretton Woods had faded into the background. Mr Boothby rose after the vote to recall the repeated pledges that had been given 'that we should have an opportunity of a full and free discussion of the Bretton Woods Agreements as such'. This had not been granted, and it was a serious precedent. The Speaker answered him that 'a discussion on it in connection with this Bill is ruled out entirely'; 'after all', he said, 'this Bill is conditional on Bretton Woods being accepted, and Bretton Woods, being a treaty, is not debatable by this House. Therefore, I can find no grounds at all for the observations the hon. Member has made . . . this House cannot debate a matter on which it has already come to a conclusion.' Mr Boothby tried again, but was told there was no more time for questions. Thereupon he gave up: 'I do not think I can do anything more than make a vehement, violent and vigorous protest, and say that if I were not of such genial disposition, I should be almost tempted to challenge your Ruling and be removed by force by the Serjeant-at-Arms from the House.'[37]

The bill was read a second time: the ayes were 314, the noes fifty.

DEBATE IN THE HOUSE OF LORDS

Keynes landed in England after the debate in Parliament was over. Bretton Woods had been approved by Parliament because the government controlled the majority, and because party discipline had been maintained. The House of Lords, however, was in the hands of the Conservatives. Government representation was weak, and Lord Beaverbrook had been agitating vigorously against all the agreements. It was not quite certain what the effect would be if the Lords withheld their approval. This could delay legislation for two years, except if the bill was a 'money bill'. In that case, it became an Act after one month, even if the Lords failed to pass it. It was not certain whether the bill was a 'money bill'. Rejection, however, would automatically mean the expiration of the 31 December deadline. It had already been suggested that, if the Lords did upset acceptance, the Bretton Woods bill could be reintroduced in the House of Commons, and be repassed as a 'money bill', in which the Upper House would have no part.

Keynes landed on the day on which the debate in the House of Lords opened. He was exhausted. He immediately became aware of the helpless hostility to the agreement he brought back from Washington. He reached the House just in time to hear Lord Pethick-Lawrence put the government's case. Several speakers criticised the agreements very severely.

Viscount Simon thought it was no disservice to Anglo-American friendship to state that he regarded the financial agreement as 'a disappointing adjustment and, as some would say, a hard bargain'. Being compelled to make sterling convertible into dollars within a year, the British government would further American exports and put another difficulty in the way of British competition. The documents before the House left the matter in a confused state. It was doubtful whether the commitments resulting from the agreement could be kept. Repayment had to be made either in goods or in gold. Rejection, on the other hand, would mean depriving the country of immediate dollar resources imperatively needed.[38]

The dilemma the House faced was expressed by Viscount Samuel: 'To accept this scheme is to accept the possibility of grave future troubles; to refuse it is to bring the certainty of immediate disaster.' To Lord Woolton it was a bad agreement. This was really the hour of disillusion and degradation. This was not a financial Dunkirk, as *The Times* had qualified it, because 'we fought at Dunkirk, but to-day we are surrendering what I conceive to be our just rights. We are surrendering them to the power of the dollar, because those responsible for the affairs of this country do not dare to retreat on the economic fastnesses of the Empire.' When the negotiators had realised that they could not obtain reasonable conditions, the government should have called them back and should also have consulted Parliament and the governments of the Empire. Lord Woolton was 'fearful of the name of my country being placed on a bond which we may not be able to honour'. The United States would be compelled, by economic circumstances, to make credit available sooner or later. In addition, while the war had left Britain the largest debtor nation in history, America had 'become rich beyond her dreams. I ask the American people, whether in justice and in honour, they ought not to return to us, and without conditions, those securities that we were compelled to deposit with them in 1940. I do not ask for a loan. . . . I do not ask for a gift. I ask for rightful restitution of the dollars we paid in advance of what became a common cause.' The Americans were now saying they wanted endorsement of Bretton Woods before the end of the year; otherwise there would be no loan. 'That is not the way that I like to think of this country being treated.'[39]

Lord Strabolgi was not impressed by the argument that rejection of the loans would mean a tightening of the belts, and giving up some luxuries. The people, if appealed to, would face any hardship for what they believed just and right.

Lord Altrincham, while he was prepared to vote for Bretton Woods, stated, 'Never has an Executive used its power with such disregard for public opinion and such undemocratic contempt for Parliament.' Lord Pakenham rose to speak in defence of the commercial proposals. When Lord Beaverbrook, after an unsuccessful attempt to clarify some definitions, remarked, 'I thought you were here to give us advice', the noble Lord answered, 'No, my humble function is only to provide entertainment.'

Lord Kenilworth, who had been engaged for many years in business, said,

> Examining these documents . . . it seems to me that they are the products of economists and financial experts lacking the touch of practicability. . . . The people with whom they were negotiating are the sort of people who, in the early difficult days, took over the Courtauld interest in America for a sum of money which was so ridiculous in comparison with the value of the business that it cost the British taxpayer nearly £30,000,000 to compensate Courtauld's for their property − nearly a year's payment for this new loan.

He also felt that Bretton woods and the financial agreement were 'bound to cause a weakening of the bonds of Empire'.[40]

The following day, 18 December, Keynes resumed the debate. On the boat back he had carefully prepared a speech, but, after listening to the criticism to which the agreements were subjected, he decided to change his notes considerably. Two days in Westminster, he said, were 'enough to teach one what a vast distance separates us here from the climate of Washington. Much more than the winter waste of the North Atlantic and that somewhat overrated affair, the Gulf Stream, though that is quite enough in itself to fog and dampen everything in transit from one hemisphere to the other.' How difficult it was for nations to understand one another, even when they had the advantage of a common language. Things appeared differently in Washington from the way they did in London, and it was easy to misunderstand one another's difficulties and the real purpose behind each one's way of solving them. Everyone talked about international co-operation, 'but how little of pride, of temper or of habit anyone is willing to contribute when it comes down to brass tacks'.

In lucid terms Keynes explained the various agreements, and how each was complementary to the rest: the blueprint for long-term organisation of world commerce and foreign exchanges, the short-term proposals for early reconversion of the sterling area, and the offer of financial aid from the United States to overcome the immediate difficulties of the transition. He wondered whether this first great attempt at organising international order out of the chaos of the war was viewed in its right perspective in Britain. He had tried to present the British case on past service and past sacrifice, but he soon discovered that the Americans were interested only in the future prospects of recovery.

> Nor, I venture to say, would it be becoming in us to respond by showing our medals, all of them, and pleading that the old veteran deserves better than that, especially if we speak in the same breath of his forthcoming retirement from open commerce and the draughts of free competition, which most probably in his present condition would give him sore throat and drive him still further indoors.

If some of the noble Lords had led the mission to Washington, they would not for long have continued to speak in the vein they did. The financial agreement, though imperfectly satisfactory, was very far removed from what the Americans had at the outset considered reasonable. Negotiations in which technical requirements and political appeal had to be satisfied were immensely difficult. Moreover, the world was clamouring unanimously for American aid, and many members of Congress were concerned about the cumulative consequences of being too easygoing.

'On the matter of interest, I shall never so long as I live cease to regret that this is not an interest-free loan.' But one should not forget the fatal consequences 'if the Administration were to offer us what Congress would reject'. The terms of the loan were considerably better than those the United States was currently asking from the other Allies.

Lend—Lease had been settled on very favourable terms. 'Has any country ever treated another country like this, in time of peace, for the purpose of rebuilding the other's strength and restoring its competitive position?'

Several critics had laid stress on the obligation to release the current earnings of the sterling area within about a year. It would be very satisfactory if the sterling area could be maintained until that time. 'We cannot force these countries to buy only from us, especially when we are physically unable to supply a large quantity of what they require.' Canada was insisting even more than the United States on liberating the current earnings of the sterling area. He was now working out the Commercial Policy Paper which was under discussion. He reassured the House that 'Both the currency and the commercial proposals are devised to favour the maintenance of equilibrium by expressly permitting various protective devices when they are required to maintain equilibrium and by forbidding them when they are not so required.' For the first time in modern history, the United States was going to exert its full influence in the direction of reduction of tariffs, not only by itself but by all the other countries. Britain could be competitive: American wages were now twice as high as British wages.

Therefore, much of these policies seemed to be in the prime interest of the country. They aimed at the restoration of multilateral trade, which was the system upon which British commerce essentially depended. The alternative was bilateral barter and every kind of discriminatory practice, separate economic blocs, and friction and loss of friendship; 'it is surely crazy to prefer that'. 'Some of us, in the tasks of war and more lately in those of peace, have learnt by experience that our two countries can work together. Yet it would be only too easy for us to walk apart. I beg those who look askance at these plans to ponder deeply and responsibly where it is they think they want to go.'[41]

Keynes's speech was a masterly performance, but not all were convinced. Viscount Swinton, while expressing his appreciation for the tenacity and skill in negotiation, and thanking him for the brilliant and clear exposition, thought 'his dialectic was most brilliant where he was skating over the thinnest ice'.

But Keynes had swayed a large number of the members of the House whose decision had been delayed by the complexity of the problems, and who had vacillated between two equally disagreeable alternatives. Viscount Bennett probably summarised their position when he said, 'There are terms in those Agreements to which I should object, but I am not an expert in these matters, and I content myself with saying that the best possible arrangements, according to the views of those who are supposed to be experts, have prevailed.'[42]

Lord Beaverbrook made a last plea not 'wantonly and wickedly' to throw away the Empire.

When it came to voting, their Lordships divided: contents, ninety; not-contents, eight. Many had abstained.

Thus, thirteen days before the deadline, Britain ratified Bretton Woods.

21
Savannah: Pax Americana

Driven through the US Congress by what was described in the *New York Herald-Tribune* as 'the most high-powered propaganda campaign in the history of the country',[1] and reluctantly agreed to by the British Parliament because they were tied to an indispensable loan, in most other member countries the Bretton Woods agreements had been ratified without debate or opposition. Parliaments had hardly, or not at all, been involved in the negotiations, and did not know what they were all about. In most cases, it was a simple formality.

The agreements were to come into force when they had been signed on behalf of governments having 65 per cent of the total of the quotas, and were to remain open for signature in Washington until 31 December 1945. On 27 December the representatives of twenty-eight nations signed the documents, confirming that their governments had ratified the agreement, and deposited the nominal initial payment toward the expenses of the organisations. However, although the Treasury and the State Department had until the last moment expressed optimism that Russia would join the Fund and Bank, nothing had been heard from Moscow.

The new Secretary of the Treasury, Fred M. (Judge) Vinson, had organised an impressive, even solemn ceremony for the signing. At the conclusion of the ceremony he declared, 'The birth of these two great international financial institutions is not an end in itself but only a means to the end of international peace and prosperity. Our task therefore, has but just commenced.'[2]

On 28 January 1946 the United States sent out to the thirty-four nations whose governments had ratified the Bretton Woods agreements (among the countries that had not were the USSR, Australia, New Zealand, several Latin American and a number of other small countries) invitations to attend the inaugural meeting of the boards of governors of

286

the International Monetary Fund and the Bank for Reconstruction and Development. The site selected was Wilmington Island, near Savannah, Georgia, and the purpose of the conference to set up the organisations of the two. institutions, and to decide on such matters as regulations, the location of head offices, the appointment of executive directors, and the admission of new members.

One and a half years had passed since the Bretton Woods Conference, and deep changes had taken place in world politics. The wartime alliance against Nazism had disintegrated and had been replaced by mutual suspicion and antagonism, rapidly developing into an ideological confrontation between the Americans and the Russians. Three days before the opening of the Savannah conference, Winston Churchill, then on a visit to the United States, had made a speech in Fulton that caused a sensation: 'From Stettin in the Baltic to Trieste in the Adriatic, an iron curtain has descended across the Continent.' He voiced his fears of Soviet intentions, and warned that Russia aimed at an 'indefinite expansion' of its power.[3]

Harry White had watched these developments with grave concern. He wrote,

It is becoming apparent, even to the man in the street, that the international situation has deteriorated sharply since the death of President Roosevelt. So disillusioned, cynical and discouraged is the public from developments of the past few months that even though the most costly and destructive war in history is but four months ended, people speak of the next war as a probability. . . . I am confident that it is possible to change the trend of affairs . . . there are only two possible major opponents in the foreseeable future, one is the United States and the other is Russia. . . . The major task that confronts American diplomacy . . . is to devise means whereby continued peace and friendly relations can be assured between the United States and Russia. . . . It matters little what our political relationships with England become. . . . Let us, therefore, examine the situation anew.[4]

White did not have the intellectual ascendancy and influence over Vinson which he had acquired over Morgenthau. He had lost his self-assurance and his power to make decisions by himself. More recently, the relationship between the new Secretary of the Treasury and his assistant had deteriorated for reasons of which White was not aware. He wanted, above all, to become the first managing director of the Fund. His nomination as executive director for the United States had been sent to the Senate, and the Committee on Banking and Currency had approved his nomination on 5 February 1946. The following day President Truman sent secretary Vinson a copy of a report by the Federal Bureau of Investigation (FBI). The director of the FBI had brought to the attention of the President that

As a result of the Bureau's investigative operations, information has been recently developed from a highly confidential source indicating that a number of persons employed by the Government of the United States have been furnishing data and information to persons outside the Federal Government, who are in turn transmitting this information to espionage agents of the Soviet Government. ... The Bureau's information at this time indicates that following persons were participating in this operation or were utilized by principals in this ring for the purpose of obtaining data in which the Soviet is interested.[5]

There was a list of names. Harry Dexter White was second on the list. The President asked Vinson to confer with Secretary of State Byrnes and 'find out what we should do'. There were lengthy conferences attended by Truman, Hoover, Byrnes, Vinson and others. Vinson no longer wanted White to serve on the Fund or continue as Assistant Secretary of the Treasury. The problem was how to remove him. Dismissal or forced resignation would bring up awkward questions, probably even in the press. Making a secret arrangement with White was impossible, because this might alert the spy ring that an investigation was in process. It was decided that White would be the US executive director of the Fund, but that he would be 'surrounded with persons who were specially selected and who were not security risks'. Truman had also asked that the surveillance be continued.[6]

Keynes wanted Harry White to become managing director of the Fund. He said that 'unless the Fund had a really good manager it would not make very much difference whether the executive directors were good or just mediocre.' Keynes thought the executive directors would only spend a portion of their time in Washington, and that, as far as Britain was concerned, 'the U.K. Treasury representative in Washington would be designated as the British alternative to carry on routine functions'. He looked forward to spending part of March in a warm climate, and he thought that the Savannah meeting would 'be just a pleasant party'.[7]

Most of Savannah's population lined the streets as more than 300 delegates, observers, secretaries and newspaper men, having arrived on a special train from Washington, were driven to their hotels in 100 private cars assembled by the mayor of the city. They cheered the procession as it wound along a route lined with blazing azalea bushes and beautiful trees. This was true Southern hospitality.

The inaugural meeting was held at the General Oglethorpe Hotel, Wilmington Island. Several countries whose representatives had been at Bretton Woods, but who had not ratified the agreements, sent observers: Australia, New Zealand, the USSR, Denmark and Venezuela.

At the opening session, on 9 March, the secretary-general of the conference read a message from President Truman:

Bretton Woods ... was a cornerstone upon the foundation of which a sound economic world can — and must — be erected. Whether such a sound economic world will be realized will depend very largely upon your individual and collective endeavors. For the great institutions provided for at Bretton Woods must now become living operating organisms. To breathe life into these institutions is your challenging task.

In this task I wish you Godspeed. You must not fail.[8]

Secretary Vinson welcomed the delegates with these words:

In greeting you here today, I cannot — and I would not — escape the nostalgic memories of our other meeting, that remarkable conference at Bretton Woods .... one of the most outstanding achievements of that conference was never recorded in the documents emerging from that historic assembly ... the mutual trust and genuine understanding between the representatives of forty-five nations achieved at Bretton Woods springs not from the words of men — but from his heart. So too, on this occasion, the final measure of our success will never be found in the words we speak but in the inarticulate feelings and spirit buried within our hearts.

When we were together before, in that cloistered New Hampshire village, I remember that our minds and hearts were as one as we forged the Bretton Woods Agreements. The International Monetary Fund and the International Bank for Reconstruction and Development, long a dream of our respective peoples, became more than words and phrases. When that document was finished, when the last syllable was written and the ink had dried, we were confident men. Steadfast in purpose and united, we had mentally taken leave of the battlefield, doffed our uniforms worn ragged in a mighty war, put on our white shirts and had written an economic Magna Charta. And we did write it. There is no question about that. ...

We have the Bretton Woods Agreements right here with us. Truly, I feel humble in the presence of those Agreements. They are great documents. They permeate this room with their honesty, their virtue and their truth. We sat down together and wrote them, with our hands and our hearts and our minds. Here they are, just as we wrote them. And here in this room are most of the men who wrote them. ...

There is a simple axiom written in history. It is written in rock for everyone to read, written and rewritten when the blood of men who die in battle washes off the stone. It is: If we want a better world we must be better people. How many men, since the first tick on the clock of time, have handed down that wisdom in a thousand languages. We were, when we gathered at Bretton Woods and when the sacrificial altar of tyranny was being pushed backward across the Rhine, actually better

people. For a short space of three weeks we were making a better world
by being better people. I hope, I believe, we still are better people.
Until I saw these earnest humble faces of every color and culture I
might have been apprehensive. But you set my mind at ease. When I
look I see the same compassionate, honest men I saw before, and
although I cannot read your inner thoughts, I am sure that the hearts of
better men beat within you. This peace must not be a prelude. It must
be solemn and continuing, compassionate and wise. We knew this at
Bretton Woods — and we know it today.'

He also wished to reuse 'some of the words I used while we were forging
these Agreements: 'We fight together on the sodden battlefields. We sail
together on the majestic blue. We fly together in the ethereal sky. The test
of this conference is whether we can walk together down the road to peace
as today we march to victory.'

The Chinese delegate expressed his hope that the establishment of the
Fund and the Bank would mark the opening of a new era of successful
international co-operation and prosperity.

The delegate from Czechoslovakia said, 'It is a test of life or death of
our generation whether we find a way to trust each other. . . . I believe
that the Fund and the Bank are a proposition able to help a great deal in
creating a mutual confidence through a continuous cooperation in what is
one of the most important sectors of human activity. A lot will depend, of
course, on how much understanding of realities is displayed.'

Analysing the Bretton Woods agreements Mr Mendès France stated, 'we
are aware that these resolutions are not perfect. They are the result of
transactions, and like all transactions, include provisions which do not
thoroughly fit together.' These texts were not supposed to settle all the
problems, but they constituted a first firm basis for action. France, in
joining, had been willing to assume inherent charges and responsibilities. In
contributing to the common effort with a gold payment, the most
important one next to the United States, France made a severe sacrifice.
It also accepted wholeheartedly the limitations of sovereignty inherent to
the agreement, although, for all the countries whose economy had been
disrupted by war, this limitation constituted a heavy and serious risk.

The Mexican delegate said, 'We celebrate today one of the greatest
human achievements in history. Many, many men before us had tried to
achieve a worldwide covenant on monetary and financial policy. Our
forerunners suffered disillusionment. But today in this hour of elation we
pay our humble tribute to them for their unstinted devotion to this noble
ideal.'

Then came Keynes's turn. Just before leaving for Savannah he had been
to Covent Garden, where Tchaikovsky's 'Sleeping Beauty' was being
performed, and he used the theme for his speech: a christening with good
fairies and propitious gifts:

Mr. Chairman, Governors, Alternates, Advisers, and Observers, like several others here present, I have been intimately concerned with what will, I think, always be known as the Bretton Woods plans. The gestation has been long; the lusty twins are seriously overdue; they will have put on, I hope, as a result, a weight and strength which will do credit to their mixed and collective parentage. At any rate it is a privilege I would not have readily foregone to be present at the hour of birth, in some capacity whether as Governor or Governess, along with the midwives, nurses, doctors, and persons ready to christen (and, personally, I shall always hold to the view that the christening has been badly done and that the names of the twins should have been reversed).

Hidden behind veils or beards of Spanish moss, I do not doubt that the usual fairies will be putting in an appearance at the christening, carrying appropriate gifts. What gifts and blessings are likely to be most serviceable to the twins, whom (rightly or wrongly) we have decided to call 'Master Fund' and 'Miss Bank'?

The first fairy should bring, I suggest, a Joseph's coat, a many-coloured raiment to be worn by these children as a perpetual reminder that they belong to the whole world and that their sole allegiance is to the general good, without fear or favour to any particular interest. Pious words exceedingly difficult to fulfil! There is scarcely any enduringly successful experience yet of an international body which has fulfilled the hopes of its progenitors. Either an institution has become diverted to be the instrument of a limited group, or it has been a puppet of sawdust through which the breath of life does not blow. Every incident and adjunct of our new-born institutions must be best calculated to emphasise and maintain their truly international character and purpose.

Now, the second fairy, being up-to-date, will bring perhaps a box of mixed vitamins, A, B, C, D and all the rest of the alphabet. For the children may faithfully wear their many-coloured raiment, yet themselves show pale, delicate faces. Energy and fearless spirit, which does not shelve and avoid difficult issues, but welcomes them and is determined to solve them, is what we must demand from our nurslings.

The third fairy perhaps, much older and not nearly so up-to-date, may, like the Pope with his cardinals, close the lips of the children with her hand and then open them again, invoking a spirit of wisdom, patience, and grave discretion, so that, as they grow up, they will be the respected and safe recipient of confidences, of troubles, and of perplexities, a reliable and prudent support to those who need them in all times of difficulty. For if these institutions are to win the full confidence of the suspicious world, it must not only be, but appear, that their approach to every problem is absolutely objective and ecumenical, without prejudice or favour.

I am asking and hoping, you will see, a great deal.

I hope that Mr. Kelchner has not made any mistake and that there is no malicious fairy; no Carabosse, whom he has overlooked and forgotten to ask to the party. For if so, the curses which that bad fairy will pronounce will, I feel sure, run as follows: 'You two brats shall grow up politicians; your every thought and act shall have an *arrière-pensée*; everything you determine shall not be for its own sake or on its own merits but because of something else.'

If this should happen, then the best that could befall — and that is how it might turn out — would be for the children to fall into an eternal slumber, never to waken or be heard of again in the courts and markets of mankind.

Well, Ladies and Gentlemen, fairies or no fairies, this looks like being a very pleasant party and a happy christening, and let the omens be good.

While the delegates who could understand the subtle humour of the speech applauded vigorously, Vinson was furious. He thought that the reference to the malicious fairy was intended for him. One participant heard him mutter, 'I don't mind being called malicious, but I *do* mind being called a fairy.'[9]

The light touch Keynes chose to give to his address to the Savannah Conference barely covered the unspoken words over his bitter disappointment that his original concept of a Clearing Union had turned out so different from what he had hoped it would be.

THE REGULATIONS OF THE FUND AND BANK

The main purpose of the inaugural meeting was the adoption of the regulations of the Fund and the Bank. The draft had been prepared by the US Treasury, and discussed with representatives from a number of countries. It had been decided that the boards of the Fund and the Bank would meet jointly at the inaugural meeting.

As chairman of the board of governors of both institutions, Secretary Vinson had requested the delegates not to engage in 'intellectual and academic warfare' about nuances of meaning in the Bretton Woods agreements, but to get right down to work so as to put the Fund and the Bank into operation as quickly as possible. Otherwise, he cautioned, some 'stray atom bomb' might interrupt the delegates' work and blow up the Fund, the Bank and everything else. 'Ours is a race against time for sanity', he warned. Vinson was a lawyer and a politician. The Treasury was only an interlude in his legal and political career. He had not been involved in the formative stages of the institutions, and to him the Fund and the Bank were political rather than monetary and financial organisations. His concern was Congress, where the Anglo-American financial agreement was still pending, and American public opinion.

It soon became evident that the press would not be given the treatment it had received at Bretton Woods. It was indicated that because of confidential problems and their political implications, open sessions would be held only in exceptional circumstances, but that the reporters and the public would be kept advised. There were rumours of controversial issues dividing the British and American delegations. But, noted the *New York Herald-Tribune*, 'The United States, led by Mr. Vinson, appears to be demanding and getting its own way on every question. . . . One foreign delegate described Mr. Vinson's operations here as "bulldozer" tactics.'[10]

Many questions required discussion but were uncontroversial. India brought up the matter of automatic membership of the board. Since Russia had not ratified the agreements, India, which had the fifth largest quota, was given the seats that would normally have gone to Russia. What would happen if Russia, at a later date, decided to join? This eventuality had not been foreseen, and the matter was remitted to an *ad hoc* committee, which suggested that members having one of the five largest quotas at the date of a regular election or at any date between regular elections were entitled to appoint an executive director who would hold office until the next regular election, without prejudice to the right of a subsequently admitted member to appoint a director if it had one of the five largest quotas.

It was decided that the fiscal year should run from 1 July to 30 June, and that the first annual meeting of the governors should be held in September 1946.

Applications for membership received from four countries not represented at Bretton Woods, namely Italy, Syria, Turkey and Lebanon, were remitted to the executive directors. Greece and Yugoslavia raised the question of whether a former enemy country — Italy — which had not yet signed any peace treaty, should be admitted.

The United States proposed that Russia and the other countries that were present at Bretton Woods but which had not ratified the agreements be given an additional six months to join. The Russian observer, Professor Bystrov, who became noted among reporters for his liking for Southern cooking, said that he would cable his government for instructions, but added that in the meantime he could not comment on whether Russia would accept the renewed invitation.

The voting procedure provided by the Bretton Woods agreements was very complex, and it soon appeared that there was a tendency for the ballots to result in an impasse. A new rule was invented. A candidate for the post of executive director who under the Bretton Woods rules, did not obtain sufficient votes to be elected, would be considered elected if he obtained more votes than any other candidate.

These questions and many other matters needed to be decided. But the really controversial questions were the location of the head offices of

Fund and Bank, and the salary of their managing director and other senior officials.

LOCATION OF THE FUND AND BANK

It had been agreed at Bretton Woods that the headquarters of the Fund and Bank would be established in the country having the largest quota, which was the United States. Keynes had suggested New York as the site, but the Americans wanted Washington. On his way to Savannah, and in the early days of the meeting, Keynes was told clearly that the choice would be Washington. Encouraged by the attitude of other delegations, he decided to put up a fight, even though he knew that it was lost in advance.

He stated that his government preferred New York for four reasons:

(1) the Fund and Bank should appear international and independent;
(2) no single government should be in a position to influence unduly the directors and the staff;
(3) there were technical advantages in being located in New York, which was the financial centre of the United States; and
(4) co-operation with the Economic and Social Council would be easier.

The American position was as follows:

> The Fund, as an intergovernmental institution, should be free of any possible influence from economic, financial, or commercial private interests. In recent years there has been a shift from New York to Washington of international financial policy making. The judgment of the government of the country in which the Fund is located should be given substantial weight. Washington, D.C. affords a better opportunity for the members to communicate with the representatives of their respective governments. In Washington the officers of the Fund would have ready access to data and material relating to the economies of many countries.[11]

Mr William Clayton, then Assistant Secretary of State, said that the British position was inconsistent with their own view that executive directors should represent the national interest and spend part of their time at home. He also said that there had been a shift in recent years from New York to Washington on international financial matters; the loans were now being made in Washington. The United States government had put in a large amount of money, and had a great interest in having both institutions located in Washington, to improve the confidence of the American people and to prevent private influence in New York from being too important.

China preferred Washington because it would be easier to get in touch with the embassies. Canada preferred New York because of the psychological influence the institutions would be subject to in Washington. France preferred New York for similar reasons. Czechoslovakia suggested that the views of the host country should be respected. The Dominican Republic, Mexico, Poland and Ethiopia preferred Washington, because information about the economic position of the various countries was more readily available there, and also because the United States preferred it that way.

The British, French and Indian delegations withdrew their objections, and Washington was selected.

In a memorandum which he wrote after the Savannah meeting, Keynes described how this point had been irreversibly decided upon before it was even brought up:

> Passing through New York on our way to the Conference we discussed these ideas at the Federal Reserve Bank of New York, and found them in complete sympathy. No rumour had reached them of any site other than New York. No rumour reached us until a day or two before we left Washington for Savannah, when Mr Vinson told me that the American Delegation had decided that both institutions should be placed in Washington and that this was a final decision the merits of which they were not prepared to discuss. The U.S. Administration, he said, was entitled to decide for themselves what location within the U.S. was to be preferred.
>
> At Savannah we soon found that a majority of other Delegations (China, Poland and perhaps some South Americans were on the other side) shared our view that this was an unfortunate, indeed a very bad, decision. It also appeared that it was primarily a personal decision of Mr Vinson supported only by the Federal Reserve Board (which would find itself strengthened against the New York Federal Reserve Bank by the Washington location), and not supported on its merits by the rest of the American Delegation. Unfortunately Mr Vinson, before warning us or seeking our views, had thought fit to take his proposition direct to the President and to obtain his authority to make this an absolute instruction to the American Delegation from which they were not to be free to depart in any circumstances. This made it impossible for Mr Clayton, for example, to listen to our arguments, however much he recognised their force.[1] [2]

THE FUNCTIONS AND THE SALARIES OF THE DIRECTORS

Whether or not it was worthwhile fighting the battle at that stage and in that form, and whether or not it was reasonable for Keynes to fritter away his last energies on a lost cause, he decided to put up a last-ditch struggle

for a Fund as he had conceived it. While the most bitter clashes and the
most sarcastic remarks made during the Savannah meeting were over the
salaries of the directors, the question went much deeper:

> The most important discussions at the Savannah meetings were on the
> functions and remuneration of the Executive Directors and of the
> Managing Director and President. Two philosophies of management
> clashed in these discussions. The British had always been interested in
> creating a Fund that would involve a minimum of interference with
> national policies and programs. They wished to have international
> assistance available in case of need, and they would always be prepared
> to consult with an international organisation in whose personnel they
> had confidence; but they did not want political representatives of a
> dozen countries to be active in such an organisation and to use it as a
> means of prying into their affairs. If a thoroughly able and discreet man
> could be put at the head of the Fund to run it day in and day out, a
> man who would have the confidence of the directors and of the
> member countries generally, the directors would remain in the back-
> ground, meeting only occasionally to determine broad policies of the
> Fund and to protect their respective national interests. The men best
> fitted to perform these functions of executive directors when called for
> it would be top flight men active in the affairs of their own central
> banks or governments. Such men could be made available on a
> part-time basis. But they could not be spared for the daily work of the
> Fund and, even if they could, they would not find enough to do unless
> they proceeded to interfere with the management of the Fund itself
> and make it a football of international politics. [13]

Keynes's view was that the objectives of the Fund could be integrated with
those of the governments and Central Banks of the member countries only
if high officials from those countries participated in the management of
the institution. By spending much of their time at home, these men would
be thoroughly acquainted with the current problems confronting their
own governments, and through regular consultation at the Fund they
would develop a spirit of internationalism among their colleagues in
government or in the central bank. Full-time directors would know only
from what they were told what was really going on in the member
countries; they would be operating too much in isolation.

> The Americans, on the other hand, envisaged the Fund as an instrument
> for helping to correct the national policies that were disturbing the
> balance of international transactions. For this purpose they felt that the
> Managing Director of the Fund, who was not a policy-determining
> official, could never speak with the authority of those who made
> policy. It was necessary for those who made policy, i.e. the Executive

Directors, to live on the job if they were really to understand the variety and range of the problems with which they were asked to deal and if they were to make their full potential influence effective. The Americans hoped that in thus working together day after day on the problems of the Fund the Executive Directors would develop a strong international viewpoint and would be able to interpret the policies of the Fund to their respective national Governments. They would constitute an international force, even though not divorced from the realities of national interests.[14]

The American position was that the executive directors would be very busy, and that they had to be men of great competence.

We asked the Americans what these fourteen full-time executive directors and their equally full-time alternates would do to kill time in Washington. Harry White's monotonous answer was 'they will be kept busy following trends'. This was said so often that one of the Canadian delegates told us one morning that he had just had a nightmare in which he had been pursued by a trend — and in a vicious circle at that.[15]

At the meeting of the Committee on Functions and Remuneration, Will Clayton for the United States and Keynes for the United Kingdom expressed the positions of their respective countries. White intervened and

said he thought the most important thing was that the Executive Directors should be devoting their thoughts and time to studying world problems rather than the problems of their individual countries. ... They should not consider themselves as representing only their individual governments, and they should not come with instructions from their governments. They should consider themselves as members of an international organization.

The South African delegate supported Keynes's views, but several Latin American and other delegates sided with Clayton.

During the second meeting a compromise was agreed upon: the executive director and his alternate should devote all their time and attention to the Fund, and one of them should be continuously available at the Fund. This formula allowed a measure of flexibility, but Keynes thought that twenty-four highly-paid executives for the Fund would be too many. The Canadian delegate commented that 'he thought it was a happy compromise but that the question of remuneration would be difficult'.

The salary proposed for the managing director was $30,000 per year; the maximum salary for the executive directors would be $17,000, and their alternates would draw $11,000, all free of taxes.

On 16 March the report of the committee was put before the board of governors. Keynes was first to speak. He said that he had consulted the Chancellor of the Exchequer, and regretted that he could not support the recommendation on salaries. He felt that it would 'lead to severe and well-justified public criticism to load the budgets of these new bodies with such high emoluments for so large a body of officials'. And he continued,

> It is not uncommon to find that one mistaken decision leads to another. If we had foreseen at Bretton Woods what was going to happen – and it has turned out widely different from our expectations – we should certainly have proposed that the remuneration of the Executive Directors and their Alternates, who, as distinct from the staff, are National Delegates, should be provided or shared by the Governments appointing or electing them and not by the institutions themselves. This would have allowed the necessary elasticity for adjustment to the widely differing levels of official salaries in different countries. Unfortunately that course was not followed. The difficulty facing us has been greatly increased by the decision to provide for whole-time service by Directors, a decision which we believe to be inconsistent with the best efficiency of the institutions; and still further aggravated through the wholly unexpected provision for whole-time services by Alternates, not merely in the absence of their principals, but in addition to them. Nor do we believe that most countries can wisely spare from their own pressing problems the services of so many individuals of the calibre indicated. These decisions, however mistaken in our opinion, have nevertheless been made. The difficulty of the resulting dilemma which faces us is obvious. A more unpleasant duty than that which falls to me today I have seldom experienced. I do not wish to deprive any man, especially old and respected friends, of their due and proper reward. But, in our view, so large a body of persons cannot properly be remunerated on the very high level proposed, which equals or greatly exceeds the highest remuneration available in most countries for public service.

He concluded that his country could not share 'in any way the responsibility of this decision'.[16]

Mr Martin, for the United States, recommended that the report be accepted. 'We feel that its provisions are necessary in order to get the competent personnel which will be required.'

The worries of the representative of El Salvador were 'entirely different from the worries of the distinguished representative from Great Britain. .. The higher the remuneration, the greater assurance we have that the Executive Director will really be sticking to his work'.

The representative of the Philippine Commonwealth said, 'We want a high-type man. We feel we would like to have a man to stay on the job and for that reason we believe the salaries are not excessive.'

The Chinese representative felt 'very strongly that every effort should be made to attract and keep men of the highest competency'. It seemed 'a very unwise economy to try to save a few dollars in dealing with this question. We must not be penny-wise and pound foolish.' The Canadian delegate, while he felt that the individual salaries were not excessive, was concerned about the sum totals involved by the number of individuals multiplied by the remuneration.[17]

Harry White then rose for what was to be his last major, and victorious, confrontation with Keynes:

> I rise to speak on this matter with no small sense of embarrassment, for obvious reasons. My justification, however, is that I do not think the issue that is before us is one of salary. I do not believe that the matters which have been brought into the discussion relate to a question of whether a salary is a few thousand dollars more or less. There is implicit in the document something far more fundamental and that, I say, is my justification for speaking on this issue.
>
> I am quite confident that my most esteemed colleague, Lord Keynes, is wholly sincere, completely sincere, in stating that it was an unpleasant duty for him to seem to oppose the salaries which have been suggested. I know how he feels about adequately paid competence. I know how he feels about many of his colleagues. And I am sure that in taking the position he has he wished to be clearly understood that in no way was he making any invidious comparison or any suggestion as to what an adequate compensation was for particular individuals who might be considered for this position.
>
> I believe that his views and those of his Government stem from something that goes very far back, from something that ran right through the discussions with regard to the proposals that are before us from the very beginning, from the very first conversation that we had with our British friends several years ago, when early drafts were being considered. The point of view that they expressed and held then they continue to hold, possibly in slightly modified form but basically the same. Throughout the discussions at Atlantic City, throughout the Bretton Woods discussions their views have had a high degree of virtue with respect to consistency on matters of theory and policy, so that I believe they still hold the same views with respect to these basic matters now that they held then.
>
> Those views happen to be different from those that were held by the United States and those that were held by a good many other countries present at Bretton Woods and present here. The controversy stems from the issue as to what is the major role which the Fund and the Bank, and particularly the Fund, shall play. It has been our belief from the very beginning that the Fund constitutes a very powerful instrument for the

coordination of monetary policies for the prevention of economic warfare and for an attempt to foster sound monetary policies throughout the world. . . .

The British view, in my judgement, was based more on the concept that the Fund should play a role somewhat similar to that indicated in the International Clearing Union, that the greater emphasis should be upon provision of short-term credit, that it should provide the necessary funds whereby a country, when it felt the need of foreign exchange, would be able to acquire it. . . . They believed that there should be as little discretion as possible in . . . the role of the Fund to determine whether or not policies pursued by any member governments were or were not in accord with certain principles.

However, as the Articles of Agreement indicated, the majority of the member countries assembled at Bretton Woods shared the American view. The powers of the Fund were to be broad, and in order to accomplish its mission, it would require full-time executive directors of the highest competence.

We believe the Fund cannot wait until confronted with a critical matter upon which decision ought to be made, whereupon various executive directors would be called upon to vote. We believed then and we believe now that the Fund can do much to postpone and possibly prevent the emergence of critical affairs, but . . . only if there is a careful following of events and trends and policies in various countries and, infinitely more important, a constant consultation around a table amongst men of good will, amongst economic statesmen. . . .

We feel that any attempt to weaken that aspect of the Fund's operations is a threat to the Fund. We do not believe that the Fund, no matter how wisely managed by a managing director, could begin to achieve the objectives that we hope. And we do not believe, further, that it is wholly to be expected that once an issue has been decided by various conferences that the issue should be again raised in various directions and by various indirection. We submit that the thesis that salaries shall be lower than are necessary to attract competent men is not only a blow at the prestige of the group, not only a threat to the competence of the group, but may become, I hope undesignedly, an instrument to divert the purposes and divert the general policy of the Fund so that it will become closer akin to the hearts of those who foresee in the Fund little else than a source of credit and an automatic source.

Possibly, I do some of our colleagues a little injustice in setting forth the differences in black and white. I am sure I do. I am sure that our British colleagues could make a very excellent case for their position. I am sure that they would say, and I am sure they feel justly, that they agree with many things I have said. None the less, I would point out that there is a difference in approach and that that difference is an important difference. The question of salaries which is before us is one that merely is a facet of that difference. The problem of salaries which is before us, whether a few thousand dollars more or less, as I said before, is not the real problem. The real problem is, shall you have a Fund which is competent to meet these various problems which are before us or shall you have an automatic source of credit. That, I submit, is the real question that is before us on this salary issue.[18]

The governor from Poland stated he had come to the conviction that 'we must support the proposition of the Committee'. Keynes now found himself alone:

> Mr. Chairman, I do not think it is necessary to add more than a few words to the statement I have already made, but it is perhaps necessary in view of some part of Mr. White's statement, and particularly his concluding words, that I should reaffirm that we were and remain in accord with the functions of the Fund as set forth in the Bretton Woods final act, which took, in our judgment a sufficient account of our views about the limitations within which it was advisable that the Fund should work. These are clearly laid down. . . .
>
> On the issue before us today, we are solely concerned with the most efficient working of the Fund and Bank and the confidence and respect with which these new institutions would be viewed throughout the world.

The governor from Poland said that 'a salary such as the one that has been proposed seems to me right'. And the Ethiopian delegate contented himself by saying that he fully supported the adoption of the committee's report.

When it came to a vote, Keynes asked that the provision on the salaries be treated separately. He did not want to vote against the whole report, but he could not vote for that one recommendation. This was agreed to. Keynes alone voted against Section 3. Paul Bareau later said,

> It was a harsh fight in which Keynes, for the first time in his dealings with Americans, found himself faced not by arguments but by the big batallions of voting blocks. . . . We felt convinced that to follow the American line on this issue would condemn the Fund to a slow process of debilitation and ultimate atrophy. . . . We lost on every issue, not by the process of rational argument in debate but by the solid massing of the cohorts which voted automatically with America, mainly South American states, whose representatives could be depended on to read sometimes with considerable difficulty the speeches prepared for them

by the Secretariat of the United States delegation. . . . in all this there
was no suspicion of conscious abuse of power by the United States.
Their delegates were sincere in the objectives they wanted to reach.
They still visualised the Fund as a new revolutionary active intruder
into the international monetary relations of its member countries. They
were inheritors of the New Deal suspicion of the private commercial
banker and were therefore intent on keeping not merely the control but
the day-to-day organisation of the International Monetary Fund in the
hands of governmental representatives. There were many countries
represented at Savannah which thought as we did on these issues. But
they never carried their view to the point of voting against the United
States. We were the only ones to do so. The lobbying for votes, the
mobilisation of supporters, the politics of the lunch and dinner table,
were not arts in which Keynes excelled or indeed which he attempted
to cultivate. All the more reason for his bitter disappointment at the
manner in which a trip he had anticipated as a pleasant interlude, a
voyage to Savannah when the camelias were in bloom, an opportunity
of meeting so many of his friends, should have turned out as it did. 'I
went to Savannah to meet the world', he said, 'and all I met was a
tyrant.'[19]

While he foresaw the danger of the International Monetary Fund 'becoming one of the minor desks at the U.S. State Department', and fought
bitterly to put it from the beginning on what he considered the right
course, he lost.

ELECTION OF THE MANAGING DIRECTOR

It had been generally considered before Savannah that Harry White would
be the first managing director of the Fund, an institution with which he
had identified himself for more than four years, and which was his
brainchild. Keynes had vigorously supported White's candidacy, and said
so openly. It is unlikely that anybody at Savannah other than Judge
Vinson knew the real reason why the US government suddenly decided
that the president of the Bank should be an American, and that the
position of managing director of the Fund must therefore, as it would
hardly be acceptable that that also should go to an American, be given to a
foreigner.

The decision about White was not announced until the meeting, and
there were no other official candidates. After some discussions, it appeared
that Camille Gutt, Belgian Minister of State, would be a suitable managing
director. He was approached by Keynes, and indicated that, if the other
executive directors asked him to serve, he would do so.

A few weeks after the Savannah meeting, on 6 May 1946, the

International Monetary Fund made a flying start by electing Mr Gutt less than two hours after the first directors' meeting had started, behind closed doors.[20]

Epilogue

On the train from Savannah to Washington Keynes had a very severe heart attack. After laying on a couch for some two hours, he recovered. On the boat to England he took some rest. Back in London, he wrote a long and very critical memorandum on the Savannah proceedings. Shortly after his arrival he went to his home, Tilton, in Sussex. On Easter Sunday he had another heart attack. Within a few minutes all was over.

At the House of Lords, Viscount Swinton paid tribute to his memory. Keynes was, he said, 'a prophetic teacher and a great public servant.... Keynes preached a faith which in important aspects challenged long-established doctrine and dogma.... He gave all he had, his great gifts of mind and character and more than his strength, to the service of his country and of the world.'[1]

The *Economic Journal*, of which he had been editor for many years, noted that the death of Lord Keynes was a loss the full immensity of which it was not yet possible to measure:

> The world has lost one of the very few with the imagination, courage and leadership needed to restore civilisation and build a firm economic base for peace and happiness. Britain has lost the chief architect of the economic policy which made victory possible, her chief advocate in economic negotiations, the brain which more than any other was shaping her economic future. His friends have lost one who embodied for them not only all that was finest in liberal civilisation and learning, but also all that was firmest in moral strength, human affection and intimacy. Economics has lost the inspiration of one who for a generation has been the centre of every controversy, the fountain of new ideas, the iconoclast who destroyed to build better, the thinker who more than any other in the history of our science has helped to

make man master of his fate.[2]

Keynes did not live to see the results of the policies he had advocated to eradicate the 'enormous anomaly of unemployment in a world full of wants'.

However, the age of leisure and abundance which he contemplated, not without dread, as a possibility for future generations – the era of the fifteen-hour week, which he considered 'quite enough to satisfy the old Adam in most of us!' – has not yet come to be. This, he expected, would require great changes in the code of morals, but we must expect them to come.

> We shall be able to rid ourselves of many of the pseudo-moral principles which have hag-ridden us for two hundred years, by which we have exalted some of the most distasteful of human qualities into the position of the highest virtues. We shall be able to afford to dare to assess the money-motive at its true value. The love of money as a possession – as distinguished from the love of money as a means to the enjoyments and realities of life – will be recognised for what it is, a somewhat disgusting morbidity, one of those semi-criminal, semi-pathological propensities which one hands over with a shudder to the specialists in mental disease.[3]

The world today is, in many ways, different from the one he knew. 'We are all Keynesians now.' The gap opened by his death has not been filled. Thirty years have passed, and he still dominates. How would he have approached the new problems that have forced themselves upon us? Although they may not be aware of it, hundreds of millions of people around the world who have enjoyed during the past three decades an unprecedented degree of well-being owe their good fortune to a large extent to Keynes, and to the revolution he wrought in economic thought and practice.

Bretton Woods had carried Harry White to the summit of prestige and influence in the Treasury. He was now one of the most influential and powerful men in Washington. Two weeks after the conference, Secretary Morgenthau and White left for London. Shortly after their arrival, they discussed with General Eisenhower the plans for the treatment of Germany after the war. They were opposed to the directives, which they considered much too soft, prepared by the State and War Departments. After their return to Washington, White and his staff worked feverishly on their own 'post-surrender' programme: Germany would be dismembered, its mines closed down and its industries destroyed. It would become a nation predominantly of small farmers, unable to prepare for another war. Because of his close contact with President Roosevelt, Morgenthau was in

a position drastically to modify the plans prepared by the other government agencies. Many of the punitive provisions of his plan were written
into the directives for the occupation of Germany signed by President
Truman. Two years later they were to be considerably revised.[4]

In May 1946 White assumed his new responsibilities as the American
executive director of the Fund. He resigned abruptly on 31 March 1947.
He rented an apartment in New York, and set himself up as a private
'economics consultant'. He also bought a small farm in Fitzwilliam, New
Hampshire. It became known later that a Federal grand jury had been
convened to hear evidence on Communist activities in the United States.
The principal witnesses had designated White as an important source of
information for a Russian spy ring. But, after a year and three months of
investigation, the grand jury did not indict anyone for espionage. The
House of Representatives Committee on Un-American Activities then
made an extensive and public investigation. The tension of the 'cold war'
had increased considerably and Communists were being hunted. Most
people had to be dragged before the committee, and once they were there
they refused to answer many questions, invoking the fifth amendment.

White asked the committee for a chance to clear his name. He was
called to appear on Friday 13 August, 1948. There followed one of the
most unusual and dramatic scenes in US history.

Pulling a scrap of paper from his pocket he embarked on what appeared
to be a spontaneous masterpiece of eloquence. He had read in the
newspapers, he said, the charges made against him, and he thought it was
important that the truth be made known to the committee and to the
public.

> I should like to state at the start that I am not now and never have been
> a Communist, nor even close to becoming one. . . . The principles in
> which I believe, and by which I live, make it impossible for me to ever
> do a disloyal act or anything against the interests of our country, and I
> have jotted down what my belief is for the committee's information.
>
> My creed is the American creed. I believe in freedom of religion,
> freedom of speech, freedom of thought, freedom of the press, freedom
> of criticism, and freedom of movement. I believe in the goal of equality
> of opportunity, and the right of each individual to follow the calling of
> his or her own choice, and the right of every individual to an
> opportunity to develop his or her capacity to the fullest. . ,. I am
> opposed to arbitrary and unwarranted use of power or authority from
> whatever source or against any individual or group.
>
> I believe in a government of law, not of men, where law is above any
> man, and not any man above law.
>
> I consider these principles sacred. I regard them as the basic fabric of
> our American way of life, and I believe in them as living realities, and
> not as mere words on paper.

These were the principles, 'I have been prepared in the past to fight for, and am prepared to defend at any time with my life, if need be'.

The crowd at the committee hearing burst into applause. As he had done so often before, White dominated the assembly.

> Bolstered by the tribute, White lost the last trace of nervousness. He relaxed sideways in the witness chair, draping one arm over the back. He never once lost his composure when the questioning brought out that at least eight men and women named as Communist spies had worked for him at the Treasury and two others were his close friends. . . . All in all the White appearance was a *tour de force.* . . . He had the audience laughing and sympathizing by turn. He was not really answering any of the questions, except insofar as he was admitting that many of the accused Communist conspirators were his friends, and he was making even his friendships seem noble.[5]

When one of the exasperated committee members asked the chairman to instruct 'the witness that it is obvious that he is a great wit, that he is a great entertainer . . . but I would ask you to instruct the witness to answer the questions', the comment did not perturb White at all. Richard Nixon was his most persistent questioner.

White had won the audience and had become a hero. His inspired words of patriotism would be printed with praise by some newspapers the next day.

On Sunday, exhausted by the effort, he was back at his little farm in Fitzwilliam. His heart gave way again. He lingered for a while in semicoma, and the next day he died. A hearse carried his body back to his native Boston, and he was cremated a few miles away from his birthplace.[6]

During the election campaign of 1953 President Truman's critics caused a furore by throwing Harry White's name into the political arena. And then he faded into the background.

But his monument, the Bretton Woods agreement on the International Monetary Fund, would stand during a quarter of a century as the foundation upon which world trade, production, employment and investment were gradually built. As such, he deserves to be remembered, next to Keynes, by future generations.

List of Abbreviations

Proceedings	*Proceedings and Documents of United Nations Monetary and Financial Conference, Bretton Woods NH, July 1–22, 1944* (Washington DC: Department of State, 1948) 2 vols.
Diary	Morgenthau Diary, Franklin D. Roosevelt Library, Hyde Park NY.
White Papers	The Harry Dexter White Papers, 1930–1948, Princeton University Library, Princeton NJ.
Fed. Res.	Board of Governors of the Federal Reserve System, Washington DC. Files: Bretton Woods Institutions.
US Treasury Records:	Files on Bretton Woods.
Pasvolsky Papers	National Archives, Washington DC, RG59, Leo Pasvolsky Office Papers.
Berle Papers	Berle Papers, Franklin D. Roosevelt Library, Hyde Park NY.
Roosevelt Papers	Roosevelt Papers, Franklin D. Roosevelt Library, Hyde Park NY.
Goldenweiser Papers	Emanuel Goldenweiser Papers, Library of Congress.
NA.RG59.800	National Archives, Washington DC, RG59, State Decimal File 1940–1944.
Havlik Papers	National Archives, Washington DC, RG59, General Records of the Department of State, Lend–Lease and International Finance Files of Hubert Havlik.
For. Rel.	Foreign Relations of the United States, Department of State, Washington DC.
House Hearings	Bretton Woods Agreements Act, Hearings before the Committee on Banking and Currency, House of Representatives, 79th Congress, 1st Session, on HR2211.
Senate Hearings	Bretton Woods Agreements Act, Hearings before the Committee on Banking and Currency, Senate, 79th Congress, 1st Session, on HR3314.
Public Record Office Papers:	
Cab. 66:	War Cabinet Minutes.
FO371:	Correspondence of the Foreign Office.
T160/1281/F18885:	Treasury. Anglo-American Consideration Agreement (Article VII) Clearing Union Plan.
T247	Lord Keynes's Files.
T177	Phillips Papers.
T175	Hopkins Papers.
HL Deb.	House of Lords Debates.
HC Deb.	House of Commons Debates.
Bareau Lectures	'Anglo-American Financial Relations', lectures given by Paul Bareau at the London School of Economics.

Notes

Prologue
1. *Proceedings*, p. 71.
2. Ibid., p. 81.
3. Ibid., p. 76.
4. Ibid., pp. 73–4.
5. Ibid., pp. 1214–45.
6. Ibid., p. 1225.
7. Ibid., pp. 1240–2.

Chapter 1
1. W. Funk, *Wirtschaftliche Neuordnung Europas* (Berlin: M. Müller und Sohn, 1940).
2. P. Einzig, *Hitler's 'New Order' in Europe* (London: Macmillan, 1941) pp. 2–34.
3. FO371/28899, Keynes memoranda 1 Dec 1940 and 13 Jan 1941.
4. Ibid., Keynes to Ashton–Gwatkin 25 Apr 1941.
5. Ibid., Keynes, undated amendment to memorandum of 13 Jan 1941.
6. FO371/28796, Churchill to Halifax 10 Apr 1941.

Chapter 2
1. FO371/25209, Treasury to Phillips 19 Dec 1940.
2. T175/122, Keynes to Hopkins 18 Mar 1941.
3. Ibid.
4. T175/122, Keynes to Hopkins 14 Mar 1941.
5. T177/57, Keynes to Waley and Hopkins 7 Apr 1941.
6. R. F. Harrod, *The Life of John Maynard Keynes* (London: Macmillan, 1951) p. 507.
7. FO371/28798, Foreign Office to Washington embassy 18 Apr 1941.
8. Diary, 397, pp. 221–4.
9. Diary, 397, pp. 306–10.

10. Diary, 399, p. 145.
11. Ibid., p. 407.
12. Ibid., pp. 409–11.
13. FO371/28798, Keynes to Treasury 17 May 1941.
14. Diary, 412, pp. 200–5.
15. Diary, 410, pp. 103–11.
16. Ibid., pp. 104–5.
17. Ibid., pp. 184–97.
18. White Papers, Box 6, Item 16a.

Chapter 3
1. For. Rel., 1941, vol. III, p. 5.
2. FO371/28799, Telegram Halifax to Foreign Office 28 May 1941.
3. Ibid., Telegram Keynes to Treasury 29 May 1941.
4. For. Rel., 1941, vol. III, pp. 11–13.
5. D. Acheson, *Present at the Creation* (New York: Norton, 1969) pp. 29–30.
6. For. Rel., 1941, vol. III, pp. 11–13.
7. Ibid., pp. 21–2.
8. R. N. Gardner, *Sterling–Dollar Diplomacy* (New York: McGraw-Hill, 1969) pp. 1–23.
9. Cited ibid., p. 19.
10. Roosevelt Papers, Secretary's File, Box 78.
11. For. Rel., 1941, vol. III, pp. 16–17.

Chapter 4
1. Harrod, *Life of Keynes*, p. 512.
2. 131 HL Deb. 778, 16 May 1944.
3. *The Collected Writings of John Maynard Keynes*, vol. I, (London: Macmillan, 1971) p. 25.
4. Ibid., vol. V (1971) pp. xxi–xxii.
5. Ibid., vol. IX, (1972) p. 358.
6. T247/116 Postwar Currency Policy, 8 Sep 1941.
7. Lord Robbins, *Autobiography of an*

Economist (London: Macmillan, 1971) p. 196.
8. Harrod, *Life of Keynes*, p. 528.
9. T247/116, Proposals for an International Currency Union.
10. T247/121, Waley memorandum 21 Sep 1941.
11. T247/122, Thompson—McCausland memorandum 25 Oct 1941.
12. T160/1281/F18885/1, The International Clearing Union, 4 Aug 1942.
13. E. F. Penrose, *Economic Planning for the Peace* (Princeton NJ: Princeton University Press, 1953) pp. 33–43.

Chapter 5
1. Diary, 473, p. 16.
2. Diary, 470, pp. 82–3.
3. Diary, 470, p. 87.
4. David Rees, *Harry Dexter White, A Study In Paradox* (London: Macmillan, 1973) is an excellent biography.
5. Interlocking Subversion in Government Departments. (The Harry Dexter White Papers). Hearing before the Subcommittee to investigate the Administration of the Internal Security Act and Other Internal Security Laws of the Committee on the Judiciary, United States Senate, 84th Congress, first Session. Part 30, p. 2570.
6. Ibid., p. 2587.
7. US Treasury Records, memorandum 29 Dec 1941.
8. Ibid., White to Welles 6 Jan 1942.
9. White Papers, Box 8, Item 24a.
10. Ibid.
11. Diary, 408, pp. 12–33.

Chapter 6
1. Harrod, *Life of Keynes*, p. 528.
2. FO371/32450, Baring to Ronald 6 Feb 1942.
3. FO371/32492, Keynes to Hopkins and Wilson 10 Feb 1942.
4. FO371/32492, Halifax to Foreign Office 25 Feb 1942.
5. Ibid.
6. Penrose, *Economic Planning for the Peace*, p. 33.
7. FO371/32492, Ronald memorandum 23 Apr 1942.

8. For. Rel., 1942, vol. I, pp. 163–5.
9. Ibid., pp. 166–8.
10. Cab. 66/23, memorandum by Paymaster General 10 Apr 1942.
11. Ibid.
12. Diary, 526, p. 111.
13. Diary, 527, pp. 235–6.
14. For Rel., 1942, vol. I, pp. 171–2.
15. Diary, 529, p. 7.
16. For. Rel., 1942, vol. I, p. 190.
17. Diary, 545, pp. 35–7.
18. Diary, 529, pp. 115–17.
19. Diary, 545, pp. 90–114.
20. NA.RG59.800.515/555, Department of State memorandum 11 July 1942.
21. For. Rel., 1942, vol. I, pp. 196–7.
22. FO371/31516, Phillips to Foreign Office 15 Aug 1942.
23. For. Rel., 1942, vol. I, pp. 199–200.
24. FO371/31516, Campbell to Foreign Office 20 Aug 1942.
25. T160/1281/F18885/1, Phillips to Foreign Office 8 July 1942.
26. T160/1281/F18885/1, Waley to Hopkins 14 July 1942.
27. T160/1281/F18885/1, The International Clearing Union, 4 Aug 1942.
28. FO371/31516, memorandum 21 Aug 1942.
29. Sir Frederick Leith-Ross, *Money Talks* (London: Hutchinson, 1968) p. 298.

Chapter 7
1. *Pasvolsky Papers*, 1942 file, Berle memorandum 10 Sep 1942.
2. T160/1281/F18885/1, memorandum 10 Sep 1942.
3. Ibid., Keynes to Phillips 28 Sep 1942.
4. NA.RG59.800.515/536, Berle memorandum 6 Oct 1942.
5. FO371/31516, Phillips to Treasury 8 Oct 1942.
6. T160/1281/F18885/1: note by Brand 7 Oct 1942.
7. Penrose, *Economic Planning for the Peace*, pp. 48–9.
8. T160/1281/F18885/1, Halifax to Foreign Office 13 Nov 1942.
9. Ibid., Opie to Ronald 20 Oct 1942.
10. White Papers, Box 8, Item 24e.
11. T160/1281/F18885/1, Keynes to

Phillips 16 Dec 1942.

12. T160/1258/F18003/020, Henderson minority report, 31 Dec 1942.
13. T160/1281/F18885/1, suggested amendments to Clearing Union proposals, 31 Dec 1942.
14. For. Rel., 1943, vol. I, p. 1054.
15. T160/1281/F18885/1, Keynes to Eady 21 Jan 1943.
16. Ibid.
17. Ibid., Treasury to Phillips 30 Jan 1943.
18. FO371/35330, Berle to Opie 1 Feb 1943.
19. T160/1281/F18885/1, Treasury to Phillips 5 Feb 1943.
20. T160/1281/F18885/1, Waley to Hopkins 13 Feb 1943.
21. Ibid., Keynes to Waley 16 Feb 1943.
22. FO371/35330, Phillips to Treasury 17 Feb 1943.
23. T160/1281/F18885/1, Keynes memorandum 18 Feb 1943.
24. Ibid., Waley to Chancellor 19 Feb 1943.
25. FO371/35330, Phillips to Treasury 23 Feb 1943.
26. FO371/35330, Keynes to Ronald 25 Feb 1943.
27. FO371/35330, unsigned and undated, memorandum.
28. H. D. White, 'Postwar Currency Stabilization', *American Economic Review*, XXXIII, no. 1, part 2, supplement (Mar 1943).
29. *The Economist*, 6 Feb 1943.
30. Ibid.
31. *News Chronicle*, 22 Feb 1943.
32. FO371/35331, Casaday to Waley 24 Mar 1943.
33. NA.RG59.800.515/566, Berle memorandum, 15 Mar 1943.
34. Diary, 617, pp. 123–26.
35. FO371/35331, Phillips to Treasury 24 Mar 1943.
36. Ibid.
37. FO371/35331, Treasury to Phillips 26 Mar 1943.
38. Diary, 622, pp. 8–9.
39. T160/1281/F18885/3, Keynes to Catto, Eady and Proctor 2 Apr 1943.

Chapter 8
1. Diary 622, pp. 242–46.

2. T160/1281/F18885/7, unsigned memorandum to Padmore 11 Nov 1943.
3. *Daily Mail*, 6 Apr 1943.
4. T160/1281/F18885/3, note by Hodson 7 Apr 1943.
5. Ibid., Keynes to Phillips 16 Apr 1943.
6. *The Times*, 13 May 1943.
7. 127 H. L. Deb. 527–37. 18 May 1943.
8. T160/1281/F18885/3, Keynes memorandum 16 Apr 1943.
9. Ibid., Phillips to Keynes 22 Apr 1943.
10. Ibid., Keynes to Eady and Waley 29 Apr 1943.
11. Berle Papers, container 69.
12. FO371/35334, Phillips to Keynes 20 May 1943.
13. FO371/35335, Halifax to Foreign Office 18 June 1943.
14. For. Rel., 1943, vol. I p. 1070.
15. Diary, 632, pp. 24–26.
16. FO371/35335, Halifax to Foreign Office 18 June 1943.
17. Berle Papers, containers 69 and 70, memoranda 22 and 24 June 1943.
18. FO371/35335, Keynes to Eady 19 July 1943; to Jebb, 1 July 1943.
19. T160/1281/F18885/6, Keynes to Eady and Playfair 5 Aug 1943.
20. Ibid., Foreign Office to Halifax 7 Aug 1943.
21. FO 371/35334, Halifax to Foreign Office 13 June 1943.
22. FO371/35334 Foreign Office to Halifax 17 June 1943.
23. J. K. Horsefield, *The International Monetary Fund*, vol. III, (Washington DC: International Monetary Fund, 1969) pp. 103–118.
24. Pasvolsky Papers, 1943 file, memorandum 24 June 1943.
25. Diary, 657, p. 117.
26. *New York Times*, 9 May 1943.
27. Diary, 656, pp. 53–5.
28. T160/1281/F18885/6, Foreign Office to Halifax 14 Aug 1943.
29. Cab. 66/40, Campbell to Eden 18 Aug 1943.
30. Cab. 66/40, note by Chancellor 27 Aug 1943.
31. Diary, 654, p. 95.
32. T160/1281/F18885/6, Campbell to

Foreign Office 20 Aug 1943.

Chapter 9

1. *News Chronicle*, 22 Feb 1943.
2. *New York Times*, 30 Mar 1943.
3. FO371/35331, telegram Phillips to Treasury 1 Apr 1943.
4. Ibid.
5. *Christian Science Monitor*, 7 Apr 1943.
6. *New York Herald-Tribune,* 30 Apr 1943.
7. *New York Herald-Tribune,* 27 May 1943.
8. *Daily Herald*, 8 Apr 1943.
9. *The Times*, 8 Apr 1943.
10. *The Banker*, Aug 1943, p. 58.
11. *New York Herald-Tribune,* 27 Aug 1943.
12. *The Banker*, July 1943, p. 2.
13. For. Rel., 1943, vol. I, pp. 1081–2.

Chapter 10

1. FO371/35336, Keynes to Treasury 15 Sep 1943.
2. FO371/40583, minutes of meeting 17 Sep 1943.
3. T160/1281/F18885/6, Keynes to Treasury 17 Sep 1943.
4. Harrod, *Life of Keynes*, pp. 557–8.
5. Information provided by Dr E. M. Bernstein.
6. FO371/40582, note of meeting of 15 Sep 1943.
7. Ibid., note of meeting of 17 Sep 1943.
8. Ibid., note of meeting of 24 Sep 1943.
9. Ibid., note of meeting of 28 Sep 1943.
10. Ibid., note of meeting of 4 Oct 1943.
11. Ibid., note of meeting of 6 Oct 1943.
12. Ibid., note of meeting of 8 Oct 1943.
13. Information provided by Mr L. Thompson-McCausland.
14. FO371/40582, note of meeting of 9 Oct 1943.
15. Cab. 66/41, note by Chancellor 2 Oct 1943.
16. FO371/40583, meeting of British delegation 22 Sep 1943.
17. FO371/40583, meeting of British delegation 23 Sep 1943.

18. FO371/40582, discussion at plenary meeting 1 Oct 1943.
19. T160/1281/F18885/6, Monetary Policy, 13 Oct 1943.
20. FO371/40583, meeting of British delegation 21 Sep 1943.

Chapter 11

1. T160/1281/F18885/7, Keynes to White 19 Dec 1943, and Foreign Office telegrams to Washington 19 Dec 1943.
2. FO371/40583, Halifax to Foreign Office 7 Jan 1944.
3. T160/1281/F18885/7, Keynes memorandum 17 Jan 1944.
4. T160/1281/F18885/8, Opie to Foreign Office 18 Jan 1944.
5. FO371/40583, Foreign Office to Opie 13 Jan 1944.
6. *Congressional Record – House*, 1 Nov 1943, pp. 8964–75.
7. T160/1281/F18885/7, Keynes, Draft Section on Monetary Policy, 26 Jan 1944.
8. Ibid.
9. Ibid.
10. T160/1281/F18885/8, White to Keynes 3 Feb 1944.
11. T160/1281/F18885/10, Washington embassy to Foreign Office 23 Mar 1944.
12. Diary, 710.
13. T160/1281/F18885/10, Grant to Foreign Office 23 Mar 1944.
14. T160/1281/F18885/8, discussions with Dominions 24 Feb 1944.
15. T160/1281/F18885/9, discussions with Dominions 2 Mar 1944.
16. T160/1281/F18885/10, Waley memorandum 3 Apr 1944.
17. Cab. 66/48, minutes 6 Apr 1944.
18. T160/1281/F18885/10, Waley to Hopkins 24 Mar 1944.
19. Ibid., Waley to Hopkins 3 Apr 1944.
20. Ibid., Hopkins' note 3 Apr 1944.
21. Diary, 717, pp. 63–4.
22. Ibid., p. 185.
23. Ibid., pp. 186–7.
24. FO371/40586, Chancellor to Washington embassy 7 Apr 1944.
25. For. Rel., 1944, vol. II, pp. 110–11.
26. Diary, 719, pp. 208–9.
27. FO371/40586, Foreign Office to Opie 12 Apr 1944.
28. FO371/40586, Opie to Foreign

Office 13 Apr 1944.
29. T160/1281/F18885/10, Keynes draft reply to Opie 6 Apr 1944.
30. Ibid., Opie to Keynes 13 Apr 1944.
31. Ibid.
32. T160/1281/F18885/11, Keynes to Opie 23 Apr 1944.
33. Cab. 66/48, memorandum 11 Apr 1944.
34. FO371/40587.
35. FO371/40586, Opie to Foreign Office 15 Apr 1944.
36. FO371/40586, Foreign Office to Washington embassy 18 Apr 1944.
37. T160/1281/F18885/10, Keynes to Chancellor 16 Apr 1944.
38. Diary, 722, pp. 323–4.
39. Ibid., pp. 26–45.
40. Ibid., p. 48.
41. Ibid., pp. 26–45.
42. Diary, 723, pp. 35–6.
43. Ibid., pp. 1–7.
44. Ibid., pp. 37–8.

Chapter 12
1. T160/F18003/021, minutes of meeting 24 Nov 1942.
2. T160/F18003/020, Henderson, Quantitative Import Restrictions.
3. T160/1281/F18885/6, Henderson, Notes on the Monetary Plan, 14 Oct 1943.
4. Ibid.
5. FO371/40584, 20 Jan 1944.
6. T160/1281/F18885/7, The Monetary Plan, 14 Jan 1944.
7. T160/1281/F18885/7, Waley to Padmore 14 Dec 1943.
8. T160/1281/F18885/8, Eady memorandum 19 Jan 1944.
9. Cab. 66/46.
10. Cab. 66/47.
11. Cab. 66/47, WP(44) 121, p. 6.
12. Ibid.
13. Cab. 66/47, WP(44)129 and FO371/40585.
14. Cab. 66/47, WP(44)145.
15. FO371/40584, memorandum 7 Feb 1944.
16. Cab. 66/46, WP(44)75.
17. T247/28, Robertson to Keynes 22 May 1944, and Keynes to Robertson and Eady 31 May 1944.

Chapter 13
1. T160/1281/F18885/11.

2. *New York Herald-Tribune,* 24 Apr 1944.
3. *New York Times,* 29 Apr 1944.
4. Ibid., 23 Apr 1944.
5. *New York Herald-Tribune,* 22 Apr 1944.
6. Ibid.

Chapter 14
1. T160/1281/Fl8885/11, newsletter for week ending 25 Apr 1944.
2. Ibid.
3. Ibid.
4. T160/1281/F18885/11, Morgenthau to Chancellor 25 Apr 1944.
5. FO371/40587, Halifax to Foreign Office 30 Apr 1944.
6. FO371/40587, Chancellor to Halifax, 2 May 1944.
7. T160/1281/F18885/11, Keynes to Chancellor 24 Apr 1944.
8. White Papers, Box 9, item 24h.
9. Ibid.
10. Ibid.
11. Diary, 727, pp. 143–6.
12. T160/1281/F18885/11, meeting 1 May 1944.
13. Ibid.
14. T160/1281/F18885/11, Keynes to Eady 9 May 1944.
15. *Financial News,* 11 May 1944.
16. Ibid.
17. Harrod, *Life of Keynes,* p. 573.
18. White Papers, Box 9, item 24h.
19. 131 HL Deb. 834–83, 23 May 1944.
20. Ibid.
21. Ibid.
22. Ibid.
23. Ibid.
24. *The Times,* 23 May 1944.
25. *New York Times,* 21 June 1944.
26. *Deutsche Bergwerks Zeitung*, 8 June 1944.
27. *Kölnische Zeitung*, 26 May 1944.
28. T160/1281/F18885/11, unsigned and undated memorandum.
29. White Papers, Box 9, item 24h.
30. Diary, 733, pp. 18–25.
31. Diary, 735, pp. 152–4.
32. T160/1281/F18885/11, Opie to Waley 4 May 1944.
33. Ibid., Opie to Waley 9 May 1944.
34. Ibid., Waley to Keynes, Brand and Eady 16 May 1944.

35. Ibid., Keynes memorandum 16 May 1944.
36. Ibid., Brand to Eady, Keynes and Waley 23 May 1944.
37. FO371/40588, Opie to Ronald 9 May 1944.
38. FO371/40588, Opie to Foreign Office 24 May 1944.
39. T247/28, Keynes to Waley and Eady 30 May 1944.
40. Diary 736, p. 106.
41. T160/1270/F18373, 12 June 1944.

Chapter 15
1. Fed. Res.
2. Fed. Res., Bourneuf to Burke, 20 June 1944.
3. Diary, 746, pp. 133–9.
4. Ibid., pp. 139B–C.
5. FO371/40917, Keynes, International Monetary Fund, 21 June 1944.
6. FO371/40948, Keynes to Hopkins 25 June 1944.
7. NA.RG59.800.515–BWA/6–2444.
8. FO371/40948, Keynes to Hopkins 25 June 1944.
9. Diary, 747, pp. 60A–C.
10. NA.RG59.800.515–BWA/6–2444, Collado notes.
11. FO371/40589, Keynes to Foreign Office 28 June 1944.
12. NA.RG59.800.515/6–2844.
13. Fed. Res., American meeting 26 June 1944.
14. Fed. Res., and NA.RG59.800.515–BWA/6–2444.
15. Fed. Res.
16. FO371/40589, 28 June 1944.
17. Ibid., 26 June 1944.

Chapter 16
1. *Christian Science Monitor*, 5 July 1944.
2. FO371/40918, Miles memorandum 8 July 1944.
3. J. M. Blum, *From the Morgenthau Diaries* (Boston: Houghton Mifflin, 1967) vol. III, p. 251.
4. Diary 749, pp. 1–53 and pp. 143–72.
5. Diary 748, p. 228.
6. *Proceedings*, pp. 79–83.
7. Goldenweiser Papers, Bretton Woods Conference, Box 4.
8. FO371/40918, Miles memorandum

8 July 1944.
9. Goldenweiser Papers, Bretton Woods Conference, Box 4.
10. Diary, 749, pp. 210–11.
11. *Proceedings*, p. 1136.
12. Ibid., pp. 109–11.
13. Diary, 749, pp. 224–87.
14. Diary, 753, pp. 77–91.
15. *Commercial and Financial Chronicle*, 20 July 1944.
16. FO371/40919, memorandum on Conference, p. 40.
17. *Proceedings*, pp. 331 and 730.
18. FO371/40916, Bretton Woods delegation to Foreign Office 6 July 1944.
19. *Proceedings*, p. 144.
20. Diary, 752, pp. 40–86.
21. Diary, 750, pp. 77–125.
22. Diary, 751, pp. 250–310.
23. Diary, 752, p. 48.
24. Diary, 754, pp. 22–30.
25. Diary, 749, pp. 143–72.
26. *Chicago Daily News*, 7 July 1944.
27. *Commercial and Financial Chronicle*, 21 Sep 1944.
28. *New York Herald-Tribune,* 13 July 1944.
29. *Christian Science Monitor*, 12 Aug 1944.
30. Cited in *Financial News*, 26 July 1944.
31. *Deutsche allgemeine Zeitung*, 8 July 1944.
32. Diary, 754, pp. 154–62.
33. Ibid., pp. 164–79.
34. Diary, 750, pp. 77–125.
35. Ibid., pp. 269–70.
36. Diary, 752, pp. 202–16, and 754, pp. 14–20.
37. Diary, 754, pp. 115–39.
38. FO371/40916, Keynes to Hopkins 8 July 1944.
39. Diary, 753, pp. 133–64.
40. White, 'Postwar Currency Stabilization', *American Economic Review*, XXXIII, no. 1, part 2, supplement, p. 387.
41. White Papers, Box 8, item 24a, p. 124.
42. *New York Times*, 9 June 1944.
43. Fed. Res., Bourneuf notes, p. 4.
44. FO371/40916, British delegation to Foreign Office 12 July 1944.
45. Diary, 753, pp. 77–116.
46. Fed. Res., Bourneuf notes.

47. Diary, 753, p. 133.
48. Diary, 753, pp. 135–6.
49. Diary, 754, p. 3.
50. *Daily Telegraph*, 29 July 1944.
51. *Proceedings*, p. 330.
52. Diary, 755, pp. 161–96.
53. *Proceedings*, p. 920.
54. Diary, 756, p. 70.
55. Ibid., pp. 53–64.
56. Ibid., p. 121.
57. Ibid., pp. 137–69.
58. *Proceedings*, p. 51.
59. FO371/40917, Foreign Office to British delegation 9 July 1944.
60. Diary, 752, pp. 33–36.
61. FO371/40916, Keynes to Foreign Office 10 July 1944.
62. FO371/40916, Foreign Office to Keynes 11 July 1944.
63. Diary, 753, pp. 122–32.
64. Ibid.
65. Diary, 753, pp. 77–116.
66. FO371/40918, Keynes to Chancellor 14 July 1944.
67. Diary, 755, pp. 199–200.
68. Diary, 754, pp. 3–13.
69. Ibid., pp. 140–53.
70. Ibid., p. 252.
71. Diary, 755, pp. 199–200.
72. Diary, 753, pp. 133–64.
73. Ibid., p. 162.
74. *Financial News*, 17 July 1944.
75. Diary, 755, pp. 69–93.
76. FO371/40918, Keynes to Chancellor 17 July 1944.
77. Ibid.
78. Diary, 756, pp. 46–52.
79. T160/1375/F17942/010/2, Keynes to Anderson 21 July 1944.
80. Diary, 756, pp. 251–7.
81. Ibid., pp. 258–60.
82. Diary, 757, pp. 13A–B.
83. FO371/40918, Keynes to Foreign Office 21 July 1944.
84. *Proceedings*, pp. 1197–1206.
85. Diary, 757, pp. 1–13.
86. Bareau Lectures.
87. *Proceedings*, pp. 1240–2.
88. Ibid., pp. 1244–5.
89. Ibid., pp. 1237–8.
90. Ibid., pp. 1235–7.
91. Ibid., pp. 1224–8.

Chapter 17
1. *The Times*, 21, 22 and 23 Aug 1944.

2. Ibid., 24 Aug 1944.
3. Ibid., 29 Aug 1944.
4. Ibid.
5. Ibid., 28 Aug 1944.
6. Ibid., 30 Aug 1944.
7. Ibid., 5 Sep 1944.
8. *Daily Express*, 10 Aug 1944.
9. *Financial News*, 23 Aug and 15 Nov 1944.
10. FO371/45662, Keynes memorandum 17 Sep 1944.
11. Ibid.
12. FO371/45662, Keynes to White 6 Oct 1944.
13. FO371/45662, Keynes memorandum 29 Dec 1944.
14. Ibid.
15. Ibid.
16. FO371/45662, undated draft from Keynes to Morgenthau.
17. FO371/45663, Brand to Keynes 23 Feb 1945.
18. FO371/45664, Brand memorandum 1 Mar 1945. Opie memorandum, undated.
19. FO371/45663, Keynes to Brand 4 Apr 1945.
20. FO371/45663, Keynes to Brand 8 Mar 1945.
21. FO371/45664, Keynes to Brand 5 Apr 1945.
22. FO371/45664, Halifax to Foreign Office 21 Apr 1945.
23. House Hearings, p. 128.
24. FO371/45664, Foreign Office to Halifax, 3 May 1945.
25. Ibid.

Chapter 18
1. *New York Herald-Tribune,* 23 July 1944.
2. *Commercial and Financial Chronicle*, 14 Sep 1944, repr. from National Economic Council.
3. Ibid., 31 Aug 1944.
4. Diary, 752, p. 279.
5. Diary, 657, p. 6.
6. Ibid., pp. 20–2.
7. Diary, 766, pp. 20–31.
8. Diary, 763, pp. 219–20.
9. Diary, 808, pp. 62–63.
10. *New York Times*, 15 Oct 1944.
11. *Commercial and Financial Chronicle*, 16 Nov 1944.
12. Diary, 793, pp. 86–7.
13. Diary, 825, pp. 216–21.

14. *Wall St Journal*, 13 Apr 1945.
15. Ibid., 16 Apr 1945.
16. *New York Times*, 17 Apr 1945, and *New York Herald-Tribune*, 23 Feb 1945.
17. *Christian Science Monitor*, 26 Mar 1945.
18. *New York Times*, 4 Mar 1945.
19. *New York Herald-Tribune*, 23 Feb 1945.
20. FO371/45663, Campbell memorandum 16 Feb 1945.
21. *Christian Science Monitor*, 8 and 27 Feb 1945.
22. FO371/45662, Opie to Keynes 18 Jan 1945.
23. Diary, 807, pp. 151—6.
24. Practical International Financial Organization Through Amendments To Bretton Woods Proposals. American Bankers Association, Feb. 1945.
25. *New York Times*, 5 Feb 1945.
26. Diary, 816, pp. 108—18.

Chapter 19
1. Diary, 805, p. 163.
2. Diary, 825, pp. 120—2.
3. House Hearings, pp. 4—57.
4. Ibid., pp. 66—74.
5. Ibid., pp. 94—108.
6. Ibid., p. 144.
7. Ibid., pp. 145—58.
8. Ibid., pp. 159—85.
9. Ibid., pp. 345—67.
10. Ibid., pp. 405—73.
11. Ibid., pp. 543—89.
12. *New York Times*, 25 May 1945.
13. Senate Hearings, pp. 6—88.
14. Ibid., pp. 241—51.
15. Ibid., pp. 301—17.
16. Ibid., pp. 318—49.
17. Ibid., p. 527.
18. *Congressional Record — House*, 5 June 1945, pp. 5540—66.
19. Ibid., pp. 5567—70.
20. Ibid., pp. 5573—7.
21. Ibid., pp. 5577—82.
22. Ibid., p. 5584.
23. Ibid., pp. 5589—90.
24. *Congressional Record — House*, 6 June 1945, pp. 5640—6.
25. Ibid., pp. 5667—73.
26. Ibid., pp. 5675—77.
27. *New York Times*, 8 June 1945.
28. *Congressional Record — Senate*, 16 July 1945, pp. 7556—72.
29. Ibid., pp. 7572—3.
30. Ibid., p. 7573.
31. Ibid., pp. 7575—6.

Chapter 20
1. *The Times*, 21 July 1945.
2. *Financial News*, 3 Oct 1945.
3. T160/1375/F17942/01015, Keynes memorandum 28 Sep 1944.
4. Cab. 66/60, report by Lord Keynes 12 Dec 1944.
5. FO371/45662, report Dec 1944.
6. Diary, 815, pp. 53—4.
7. FO371/45664, Keynes memorandum 14 June 1945.
8. *The Economist*, 21 July 1945.
9. *Financial News*, 6 Feb 1945.
10. *Daily Telegraph*, 5 July 1945.
11. *The Economist*, 21 July 1945. .
12. *New York Times*, 22 Aug 1945.
13. 410 HC Deb. 955—8, 29 Aug 1945.
14. Havlik Papers, Box 6.
15. Bareau Lectures.
16. Ibid.
17. FO371/45703, Keynes to Chancellor 9 Oct 1945.
18. Gardner, *Sterling—Dollar Diplomacy*, p. 201.
19. FO371/45711 Eady to Keynes 27 Nov 1945.
20. Ibid., Keynes to Eady 27 Nov 1945.
21. Bareau Lectures.
22. Havlik Papers, Box 5, US/FIN minutes meeting 13 Nov 1945.
23. FO371/45711, Cabinet Offices to Halifax 30 Nov 1945.
24. FO371/45664, Keynes to Chancellor 11 Nov 1945.
25. FO371/45664, Chancellor to Keynes 14 Nov 1945.
26. FO371/45713, Halifax to Churchill and Eden 5 Dec 1945.
27. *The Economist*, 15 Dec 1945.
28. 416 HC Deb 2671—4, 6 Dec 1945.
29. 417 HC Deb. 421—557, 12 Dec 1945.
30. 417 HC Deb. 628—36, 13 Dec 1945.
31. Ibid., 642—6.
32. Ibid., 649—50.
33. Ibid., 652—64.
34. Ibid., 665—82.
35. Ibid., 682—5.
36. Ibid., 714—36.
37. Ibid., 739—45.
38. 138 HL Deb. 677—99, 17 Dec 1945.

39. Ibid., 699—709.
40. Ibid., 725—72.
41. 138 HL Deb. 777—94 18 Dec 1945.
42. Ibid., 816.

Chapter 21
1. *New York Herald-Tribune,* 29 Nov 1945.
2. *New York Times* and *New York Herald-Tribune,* 28 Dec 1945.
3. *The Times,* 6 Mar 1946.
4. White Papers, Box 7, item 23d.
5. Rees, *Harry Dexter White,* pp. 379—80.
6. Ibid., pp. 380—90.
7. White Papers, Box 11, item 27c.
8. World and Fund Bank. Inaugural Meeting. Minutes of the Opening Joint Session of the Boards of Governors of the International Monetary Fund and the International Bank for Reconstruction and Development. Savannah, Georgia, March 9, 1946. pp. 1—2.
9. Gardner, *Sterling—Dollar Diplomacy,* p. 266.
10. *New York Herald-Tribune,* 14 Mar 1946.
11. *Selected Documents, Board of Governors Inaugural Meeting* (Washington: International Monetary Fund, 1946) p. 30.
12. Harrod, *Life of Keynes,* p. 630.
13. Fed. Res.
14. Ibid.
15. Bareau Lectures.
16. Inaugural Meeting — Summary of 12 March Meeting.
17. Document 27.
18. Ibid.
19. Bareau Lectures
20. *New York Times,* 7 May 1946.

Epilogue
1. 140 HL Deb. 912—16, 30 Apr 1946.
2. *Economic Journal,* June 1946.
3. *The Collected Writings of John Maynard Keynes,* vol. IX (1972) p. 329.
4. Committee on the Judiciary, United States Senate, *Morgenthau Diary (Germany),* 2 vol (Washington DC: US Government Printing Office, 1967); and Rees, *Harry Dexter White,* ch. 15.

5. House Committee on Un-American Activities, *Communist Espionage in the United States Government,* Hearings, 80th Congress, 2nd Session, 1948, p. 878. See also *Life,* 23 Nov 1953.
6. Rees, *Harry Dexter White,* ch. 25.

Index

Taft, Robert, 209, 252, 256–8, 262–4
Thompson-McCausland, L. P., 15, 38, 99
Times, The, 95–6, 224, 226, 266, 281
Tobey, Charles, 169, 175, 184, 209, 219, 264
Truman, Harry S., 259, 262, 271, 287–8, 306

US Chamber of Commerce, 245

Varvaressos, Kyriakos, 143, 178, 201
Viner, Jacob, 41–2
Vinson, Fred, M., 169, 176, 179–83, 187–8, 193, 200, 206, 209, 212, 216, 218, 254, 273–5, 287–90, 292–3, 295, 302

Wagner, Robert F., 167, 207, 209, 243, 263
Waley, Sir David, 38, 67, 70, 99, 116, 130–1, 152
Wall Street Journal, 93, 244–5

White, Harry Dexter, 19, 20, 65, 71, 73–4, 305–7; at Atlantic City conference, 156–8, 161–7; at Bretton Woods conference, 169–73, 175–86, 188, 191–4, 196–212, 214, 220, 231–8; at Congressional hearings, 251–8; meets Keynes in London, 62–3; planning monetary conference, 81–92, 96–8, 109–25, 139–43, 151–4; at Savannah conference, 287–8, 297, 299–302; and Stabilisation Fund, 42–7, 49, 51–2, 58; and State Department, 52–5, 59–60; and Treasury campaign, 240–4, 248–9; and Washington conversations, 99–107; youth and academic career, 40–1
White Plan, *see* Stabilisation Fund
Williams, John H., 97, 257
Winant, John G., 17, 49–50, 62, 83, 91, 117, 142, 151, 269
Wolcott, Jesse P., 169, 182–4, 193, 207, 243, 259
Wood, Sir Kingsley, 70, 72, 74, 83, 92

DISCARD

BETHANY
COLLEGE
LIBRARY